The Emperor's Mirror

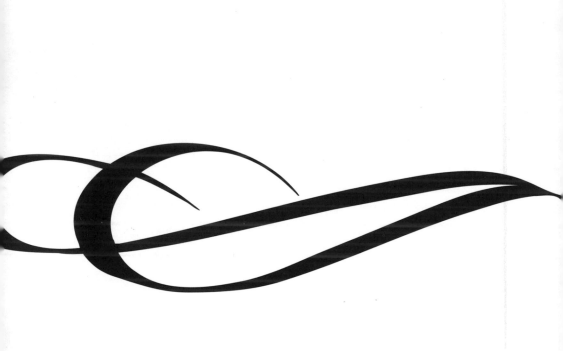

The Emperor's Mirror

Understanding Cultures through Primary Sources

Russell J. Barber and Frances F. Berdan

The University of Arizona Press

Tucson

The University of Arizona Press
© 1998 The Arizona Board of Regents
First Printing

♻ This book is printed on acid-free, archival-quality paper.
Manufactured in the United States of America

03 02 01 00 99 98   6 5 4 3 2 1

Library of Congress Cataloging-in-Publication Data
Barber, Russell J.
The emperor's mirror : understanding cultures through primary
sources / Russell J. Barber and Frances F. Berdan.
p. cm.
Includes bibliographical references and index.
ISBN 0-8165-1847-5 (alk. paper)
ISBN 0-8165-1848-3 (pbk. : alk. paper)
1. Ethnohistory — Methodology. 2. Ethnohistory — Research.
I. Berdan, Frances F. II. Title.
GN345.2.B37   1998
306 — ddc21
97-45412
CIP

British Library Cataloguing-in-Publication Data
A catalogue record for this book is available from the British Library.

Publication of this book is made possible in part by the proceeds of a
permanent endowment created with the assistance of a Challenge Grant
from the National Endowment for the Humanities, a federal agency.

Figure 11 is reproduced from Edward S. Rogers and Mary Black
Rogers, Method for reconstructing patterns of change, *Ethnohistory* 25
(4) (Winter 1978), fig. 2, p. 325. Copyright 1978, Society for
Ethnohistory. Reprinted by permission of Duke University Press.

Contents

Figures

Tables

Prologue

In the third century, Qin Shi Huangdi successfully united China for the first time, founding the short-lived Qin empire. According to legend, the emperor had a mirror with extraordinary qualities. A person looking into this mirror would see not only the true reflection of his or her face, but also the innermost characteristics of will, experience, and personality.

This mirror is much like any document or most other evidence used to reconstruct the past. A document reflects reality in some sense, but also the author's will, experience, and personality. One job of the historian — or any other researcher studying the past — is to sift through these jumbled elements and winnow accurate description from the rest. With ethnohistory, where documents written by a member of one society often describe events in another society, the problem of segregating accurate reporting from distortion is especially difficult. One theme that runs throughout this book is how these distortions come about and how to recognize and interpret them.

This book is also an introduction to the practice of ethnohistory, one of the fields of study that examines and aims to foster understanding of the human past. It is designed to lead the reader through the distinctive concepts and methods of ethnohistory and to provide insight into the conduct of ethnohistoric research. Along the way, it discusses ethics, the virtues of using complementary sources of information, the importance of planning, and the relationships among concepts, methods, and strategies.

Part 1 is devoted to concepts in ethnohistory and presents the reality-mediation model, our way of conceptualizing both the accurate and the distorted description that makes its way into ethnohistoric evidence. The concepts that underlie this model are used throughout the book. Much of what sets ethnohistory apart from related ways of studying the past is its methodology, so it is appropriate that part 2, which is devoted to methods, be the longest part of the book. Part 3 discusses strategies: ways to make the practice of ethnohistoric research more effective and efficient.

An epilogue ties up the threads that have been introduced throughout the book, and appendices provide bibliographies and a proposed outline for ethical standards in ethnohistory.

A word of explanation is in order regarding some of our choices of terminology. We have tried to define any ambiguous or contentious technical terms, and we have avoided certain terms that we believe have acquired an entrenched but unfortunate meaning in the field. A variety of common terms, however, are more difficult to deal with, terms that have connotations that can be both passionately held and passing. The descendants of the original colonizers of the Americas, for example, have been called variously "Native Americans," "American Indians," and "Amerindians." Over the last few decades, each of these has enjoyed some level of currency for a while among scholars, the public, and the people described, as indicated by the variety of terminology incorporated into the titles of activist organizations. None of these names, unfortunately, is fully satisfactory. "Native American" commemorates Amerigo Vespucci, a European scholar; even more damaging, it is easily misunderstood. This is reflected in a recent questionnaire at the authors' university, where hundreds of students of European ancestry declared themselves "Native Americans" because they were born in the United States. "American Indian" not only commemorates a European, but it also perpetuates a misunderstanding that linked the inhabitants of the Americas to India. "Amerindian" is an awkward neologism incorporating all the weaknesses of "American Indian." The native inhabitants of the Americas had no term that encompassed all the tribes of which they were composed. In short, there is no choice that is culturally sensitive, historically accurate, well turned, and unambiguous.

Accordingly, we have opted to use terms that communicate well, so long as they are not overtly pejorative, recognizing the shortcomings of those terms. We have used "American Indian" in most cases, though synonyms have been used occasionally. When a specific tribe is designated, we have tried to use that tribe's self-designation, providing it will be intelligible to the reader and cannot be confused with the identical self-designation of a different group. (Both the Apache and the Navajo, for example, use the same native term for themselves.)

We have followed the same reasoning in our choices of other terms. We have eschewed "c.e." (Common Era) and "b.c.e." (Before the Common Era) as calendric designators; they are identical to the more well-known "a.d." and "b.c." and carry whatever Eurocentric implications are embodied in these latter terms—they simply don't communicate so well to most readers. Finally, we have used "Old World" and "New World" to designate Europe-Africa-Asia and the Americas, respectively. We often have used "the Americas" as a synonym for "New World," but there is no equivalent and simple expedient to replace "Old World"; at least there is some historical basis for these designations, since archaeological evidence indicates that human beings entered the New World at a much later date than their evolution in the Old World.

Acknowledgments

This book had its genesis in a special topics class in ethnohistory at California State University, San Bernardino (CSUSB) during the spring of 1995. There being no available text that we felt met the needs of that course, we drafted one and offered it as the primary text. We subsequently expanded and revised that text into the present one, geared toward a broader audience.

We would like to express our special appreciation to the students in the ethnohistory class for their willingness in serving as "guinea pigs" and their forthrightness in providing critical assessments of an early draft. The final version was read by Edward Stark and Sharon Yellowfly; their comments and suggestions were instrumental in fine-tuning this book.

We would like to express our thanks to John Chance and Frederic W. Gleach, who provided us with useful and timely information on the American Society for Ethnohistory. We are also grateful to Linda Stockham of the CSUSB Anthropology Department for her diligent search for various calendric conversion programs, and to Lynn Beck of the Media Services Department at CSUSB for her careful rendering of the Tlaxcalan map in chapter 6. CSUSB provided funds to facilitate sundry details of manuscript preparation. We are most appreciative of all this assistance and support, but hold only ourselves responsible for the content of this book.

Concepts

Introduction

Many ethnohistorians would argue that their field of study is defined more by subject matter or methods than by concepts and theory. Nonetheless, every ethnohistorian uses certain assumptions, ideas, and principles to interpret evidence, and there is a high degree to which these are shared by the community of ethnohistorians. Building on that shared corpus, part 1 introduces the field of ethnohistory and some of its concepts.

Our goals are modest: We have not attempted to catalogue or synthesize all the various concepts or theories that are in current use in ethnohistory. Instead, we have restricted our efforts to more humble ends. In chapter 1 we discuss the scope of ethnohistory, tracing its formal definitions, its development in practice, and some of its more important concepts. Chapter 2 presents the reality-mediation model, a way to alert ethnohistorians to the potential for being misled by their information, especially documents, visual evidence, and oral accounts. Such a model, focusing as it does on the relationship between evidence and interpretation, is a particularly apt conceptual device for ethnohistory, where methodology arguably forms the backbone of the field. This chapter is a grounding for those that follow, providing ideas that recur in the more detailed methodological chapters of part 2.

CHAPTER 1

The Scope of Ethnohistory

Over the relatively few decades that ethnohistory has existed as a recognized field, ethnohistorians have devoted a good deal of time and ink to defining themselves. This chapter will present some definitions of ethnohistory, discuss them, and offer a version that we will use throughout this book. In addition, it will discuss the basic concepts that underpin ethnohistory, the history of the development of the field, and the documents that are so crucial to it.

Curiously, the major professional society for ethnohistorians was founded before there was a consensus definition of ethnohistory itself. In fact, it could be argued that there still is no consensus among ethnohistorians about what makes their field unique. Despite this situation, ethnohistorians seem quite able to identify with the field and to recognize a piece of scholarship as essentially ethnohistoric. This seeming contradiction suggests that there is a common ground of ethnohistory, but that the definitions serve a different purpose than merely identifying it. Probably the activities of ethnohistorians best define what ethnohistory *is,* while the formal statements indicate what one or another definer thinks ethnohistory *should be.*

Ethnohistory Defined by Words

Ethnohistory has been defined over and again in the latter half of the twentieth century. In the course of reviewing these definitions, we discovered more than a dozen that were substantially different and almost fifty different wordings. (See Carmack 1972 for a review of many of the definitions of ethnohistory up to the time of his writing.) The field of study has been defined by historians, anthropologists, folklorists, geographers, philosophers, art historians, and scholars of literature. Most of the definers have been ethnohistorians, but some have been outsiders looking at an unfamiliar field, and a few have even been antagonistic to the endeavor. But the best place to start is with the only definitions of ethnohistory that carry a quasi-official stamp.

Definitions from the Professional Society

The first issue of *Ethnohistory* appeared in 1955. Significantly, this scholarly journal was the first to be dedicated exclusively to the publication of ethnohistoric research; today it remains the principal ethnohistoric journal. It also is significant that *Ethnohistory* was sponsored by the precursor of the American Society for Ethnohistory (ASE), the first professional organization devoted exclusively to the advancement of the field. From its inception until the present, *Ethnohistory* has carried a brief statement of the journal's purpose on the inside cover or title page. These statements have changed over time and provide an entry point into the controversies that surround the definition of ethnohistory.

Up until 1966, the statement read:

> *Ethnohistory* is a quarterly journal devoted to original research in the documentary history of the culture and movements of primitive peoples, and related problems of broader scope.

The definition of ethnohistory included in this statement includes three important elements. First, documents are put forward as the sole source of evidence for ethnohistory; second, the subject matter of ethnohistory is "primitive" people; and third, attention is focused on these peoples' cultures and movements. This definition reflects many old-fashioned elements less popular today, but it is a good place to begin.

In 1966, the statement was amended to a form that was maintained through 1970:

> *Ethnohistory* is a quarterly journal of articles, original documents and reviews relating to general culture history and process, and to the specific history of peoples on all levels of sociocultural organization, emphasizing that of primitives and peasantries, in all world areas.

Here, the movements of peoples — an interest of nineteenth-century anthropology that had carried over into the early twentieth century but was no longer a major interest by the 1960s — was gone, replaced by a more neutral but anthropological phrase: "general culture history and process." The interest was broadened from just primitive peoples to include everyone, though interest still focused on primitives and their new bedfellows, peasantries. In this period, anthropology was ridding itself of the out-moded concept of primitiveness (and its attendant connotations of in-feriority and simplicity), and this statement can be seen as a compromise between the older ideas and the newer ones. In addition, the earlier state-ment regarding the documentary basis of ethnohistory was excised. This is a very anthropological definition with only two clues — the phrases "origi-nal documents" and "specific history" — that this might not be a general anthropology journal.

In 1971, the statement changed again:

> *Ethnohistory* is a quarterly journal of articles, original documents and reviews relating to general culture history and process, and to the specific history of peoples on all levels of sociocultural organization, emphasizing that of non-industrial peoples, in all world areas.

The only change here was to remove the peasantries and offending "primi-tives" and replace them with a more neutral and modern phrase that meant much the same thing. This statement was retained until 1981.

In 1982, the statement was simplified to:

> *Ethnohistory* is a quarterly journal relating to the culture history of ethnic peoples throughout the world.

This skeletal statement removed nearly all the defining characteristics of the earlier statements. The term "ethnic peoples" is an interesting one, reflecting the usage current in ethnic studies and some other fields: non-White or non-Anglo. In anthropological terms, of course, everyone has an ethnicity, so the phrase could be construed to mean all societies.

In 1984, only two years later, the former definition was replaced with a new one:

> *Ethnohistory* is a quarterly journal relating to the past of cultures and societies in all areas of the world, emphasizing the use of documentary and field materials and historiographic and anthropological ap-proaches.

The definition had expanded again, removing the suggestion that some peoples were excluded from ethnohistoric interest. The materials that sup-port ethnohistory once again were delineated, this time including docu-ments and enigmatic "field materials" (which could mean many things). Finally, this statement for the first time explicitly noted that ethnohistory was interdisciplinary, drawing on the concepts of both history and anthro-pology.

This statement fared little better than its predecessor, and it was amended after its second year. The statement adopted in 1986 and still printed in the journal is

Ethnohistory is the journal of the American Society for Ethnohistory.

After three decades of experimenting with definitions of ethnohistory, the journal's editors settled on the most minimal definition possible. This failure to settle on a common and detailed definition reflects differences in opinion on the nature of ethnohistory that characterized the field in these years and, to some extent, persist today.

Elements Toward a Definition of Ethnohistory

We located and analyzed dozens of definitions of ethnohistory from the literature in an attempt to ascertain their common ground. While that common ground was small, there were only eight assertions about the field that were incorporated into the various definitions, a surprisingly small number. No one definition contained them all, of course, and some pairs of assertions cannot logically coexist with one another. We present and evaluate these assertions in this section, and we will use many of them in the following section, where we assemble what we believe is an appropriate definition of ethnohistory.

Assertion 1. Ethnohistory studies past human behavior. In most cases, that behavior is many years in the past, a fact reflected in the universal presence of this assertion in the definitions. Although none of these published definitions explicitly mention this point, some recent ethnohistoric studies deal with "current" issues and events; these can be conceived as dealing with very recently past human behavior.

Assertion 2. Ethnohistory studies the small-scale, non-Western peoples of the world. These are the "primitives and peasantries" of an earlier ASE definition, "the kinds of cultures and societies that social anthropologists study in their field work" (Hudson 1966), and "the ethnic groups ordinarily relegated to the shadows of the White man's view of history" (Dorson 1961:16). During the middle part of the twentieth century, such an assertion might have made sense, since historians (at least in the American sense of the word) usually restricted their research to Western civilizations, and anthropologists normally covered the rest of the world. This division increasingly broke down in the later years of the century, however, and historians today routinely study West African kingdoms or American Indian societies; conversely, anthropologists are fully at home studying day-care centers in Seattle and the meat diet of modern Irish, as well as their traditional studies in corners of the world remote from Western cities. Incorporating this assertion in a definition of ethnohistory would mean embracing the unacceptable notion that non-Western and Western peoples are somehow fundamentally different — that there is real history for Westerners, and ethnohistory for all the rest. Eric Wolf (1982: 19) and others have leveled persuasive criticism against precisely that notion. No definitions since 1970 have included this assertion.

Assertion 3. Ethnohistory is a method or an approach, not a theory or a philosophy. This common assertion appears in most definitions, as in that of Phelan (1959:viii–ix), who defines ethnohistory as "the effort to combine sound historical practices with some anthropological techniques." Accepting this viewpoint means that ethnohistory is characterized by the way it derives its conclusions, not necessarily by the nature of those conclusions, the way they are fit into larger syntheses of knowledge, or the underlying ideas about behavior that scholars bring to their research. We concur that methods are one of the major factors that unify ethnohistory, while it is very difficult to find a theory or philosophy that is unique to the field. We also recognize that the intricate interweavings of method and theory sometimes make it difficult to separate these two elements.

Assertion 4. Ethnohistory is based primarily on documentary evidence. Some definers have claimed documents as the sole basis for ethnohistoric research, but most have followed the more reasonable path of making them the most important basis for the field. Documents preserve testimony from the past in a way unlike almost any other medium, and it is with justification that historians and ethnohistorians usually make them central in their research. Individual ethnohistoric researchers or research projects, of course, sometimes rely entirely on nondocumentary evidence, though the field as a whole remains largely reliant on documents. Most ethnohistorians sensibly use any data source that is reasonable and available, whether it be documents, archaeology, or oral history; the utility of documents, however, means that they usually will be the primary data source.

Assertion 5. Ethnohistory is based primarily on oral accounts composed by the non-Western, indigenous people under study. This viewpoint is espoused primarily by specialists in Africa (e.g., Fagan 1985:585), no doubt under the influence of the strong contributions that oral accounts have made to ethnohistory for that continent. Nonetheless, we maintain that in most places, including many parts of Africa, ethnohistory relies as much — and often more — on documents as it does on oral history. We do recognize, however, the importance of incorporating oral evidence whenever it is available, and chapter 11 discusses this source of information more fully.

Assertion 6. Ethnohistory is based on a partnership of disciplines. Most definitions incorporate some version of this assertion, although there is considerable disagreement about details. A minority view favors a multidisciplinary approach in which different disciplines maintain their independent coexistence; this viewpoint is expressed by Cline (1972:15), who has argued that the component disciplines within ethnohistory are inherently different in goals and approaches and therefore will ultimately lead to several distinct ethnohistories, particularly "historical ethnohistory" and "anthropological ethnohistory." Most definitions, however, favor considering the field interdisciplinary: sharing and merging the concepts and approaches of its component disciplines. To be truly interdisciplinary, ethnohistorians will have to step outside their disciplinary training and experiment with ideas and methods more usual for other fields of study. We believe this is an appropriate and distinctive characteristic of ethnohistory.

Among those who argue that ethnohistory is essentially interdisciplinary, there is some disagreement over exactly which disciplines are involved. By far the majority of definers consider history and anthropology to be the core disciplines (e.g., Jennings 1982). Others, however, have seen history and folklore (Dorson 1961) or history and archaeology (Baerreis 1961) as the primary partners. We view history and anthropology as the primary partners by virtue of volume of contributions to date, but we also recognize that ethnohistorians are drawn (and may in the future be drawn in even greater numbers) from many other disciplines. Each partner discipline has made, and will make, its unique contribution to ethnohistory.

Assertion 7. Ethnohistory is historiographic. Historiography is the study of the practice of history, focusing primarily on methodology and philosophy. In the sense used here, the term focuses on the critical use of documents, particularly in terms of their probable authenticity and accuracy. (This subject is covered as "source analysis" in chapter 7.) Saying that ethnohistory is historiographic, as Lurie (1961:80) and others do, means that ethnohistorians do not simply accept at face value every jot of information in a document. Literature in the mid-twentieth century repeatedly criticized ethnohistorians, particularly anthropologists, for uncritical acceptance of information in documents. Those criticisms were so effective that the historiographic nature of ethnohistory today is universally accepted by its practitioners.

Assertion 8. Ethnohistory is ethically neutral and relativistic. Cultural relativism refers to a philosophy of ethical neutrality that causes a person to resist interjecting moral judgments into the analysis of events or processes. This is essentially an anthropological concept in origin, although it can be traced back to philosophers before it became a bulwark of the anthropological approach. It has been incorporated into several definitions of ethnohistory (e.g., Sturtevant 1966). In the late twentieth century, cultural relativism has become much more common among non-anthropologists — particularly historians — than it was fifty years before. Here we have the same pattern of the previous assertion but with the disciplinary roles reversed: this time the idea was common in anthropology and spread to history. Accordingly, we see this assertion as basic to the definition of ethnohistory.

Assertions 7 and 8 form an interesting interplay. Some of the definers, particularly Lurie (1961), emphasize these points, and their definitions sometimes devolve to very simplistic formulas. An anthropologist who knows how to do source analysis becomes an ethnohistorian; a historian who is a cultural relativist becomes an ethnohistorian. While these distinctions might have been useful at one time, this reasoning would mean that most anthropologists and historians are ethnohistorians, making such simple equations virtually useless.

Our Definition of Ethnohistory

As stated earlier, formal definitions of a field of study probably are most useful in delineating what an individual believes *should* be the scope of that field, and our definition is no exception. It may include some research that other definitions might exclude and vice versa. It has the virtue of defining a field that, despite overlap with other fields of study, has distinctive subject matter and methodology.

We can construct the foundation of this definition of ethnohistory from the acceptable assertions of the previous section. Accordingly, we preliminarily define ethnohistory as an interdisciplinary field that studies past human behavior and is characterized by a methodology based primarily on documents, the use of input from other data sources when available, and the incorporation of historiography and cultural relativism. This definition is fine as far as it goes, but we believe it insufficiently distinguishes ethnohistory from other fields — especially history and historical anthropology — in terms of subject matter.

Many of the distinctions that earlier definitions drew between ethnohistory and either history (as a whole) or anthropology have become blurred as historians and anthropologists have freely borrowed perspectives from one another. Historical anthropologists use documents, and historians of all sorts subscribe to cultural relativism. If ethnohistory is to have a distinctive niche of its own, it must be differentiated from the rest of history and the rest of anthropology. This brings us to some essential questions: Is ethnohistory different from other history? Is ethnohistory different from historical anthropology? Does ethnohistory actually exist as a discrete field of study, or should the term be junked?

We believe there is a difference that is rooted in the essential nature of the database for ethnohistory. Virtually all ethnohistoric research is focused on societies in contact and cultures in conflict. The interaction between two or more peoples is, therefore, a significant characteristic of ethnohistory. This interaction is reflected in the topics chosen (which often capitalize on the attendant conflicts between societies), the sources used (which most often are written by a member of one society about members of another), and by the relativist stance (which avoids taking sides in the conflicts). Accordingly, we incorporate this interaction criterion into our definition of ethnohistory. (The importance of this assertion was anticipated by Washburn: "I suspect that it will be precisely in the field of the relationship between European and non-European societies that the greatest utility of the ethnohistorical approach will be found" [1961:42]. Eric Wolf [1982:19] echoed this sentiment in his classic study integrating the histories of Europe and colonial lands.)

Taking all of this into consideration, we arrive at our definition of ethnohistory:

> Ethnohistory is an interdisciplinary field that studies past human behavior and is characterized by a primary reliance on documents, the use of input from other sources when available, a methodology that incorporates historiography and cultural relativism, and a focus on cultural interaction.

This definition doubtless declares some research ethnohistoric when its authors would have thought otherwise, and it probably excludes some research that normally would be considered ethnohistoric. Whatever shortcomings it may have, this definition avoids what we see as a greater fault: drawing an arbitrary division between ethnohistoric studies directed to non-Western societies and studies similar in nature but dealing with Western society. Whether the subject is Yankee gold miners in the multi-ethnic gold camps of California, or Chinese merchants in Indonesia, or Tupinamba encountering Europeans in sixteenth-century Brazil — any of these is fair game to ethnohistory as we define it. Similarly, a study of the functioning of Veddan society based entirely on Indian sources is no more ethnohistoric than a study of the Magna Carta based solely on English sources. To some extent, of course, good research is good research, and it matters little how we classify it; a field of study, however, profits from having well-defined subject matter.

Ethnohistory Defined by Actions

Formal definitions aside, ethnohistory is what ethnohistorians do. Looking at ethnohistorians, their research, and their scholarly output can provide an idea of how ethnohistory is defined in practice.

Training and Backgrounds

Most ethnohistorians have been trained in either anthropology or history, with slightly more probably coming from an anthropology background. A smaller number of ethnohistorians received their training in geography, art history, linguistics, comparative literature, and other fields. More and more ethnohistorians are earning graduate degrees from interdisciplinary programs that draw their faculty from the history and anthropology departments and sometimes from other departments as well.

Ethnohistorians with different kinds of training often conduct subtly dissimilar kinds of research. Historians, for example, traditionally have focused their attention on certain aspects of human behavior such as politics, law, military affairs, and economics. These topics provide familiar terrain, and many historians will find them rewarding places to conduct research. Social historians in the last three decades or so have extended the breadth of historical study, but the greatest historical efforts remain in the more traditional arenas. Anthropologists, too, have their typical topics of traditional anthropological interest, such as contact between societies, religion, kinship and family organization, and subsistence. Geographers tend to direct their focus more toward issues related to land use, resources, and the use of space; folklorists usually focus on oral accounts; and ethnohistorians from other fields also bring ideas of fruitful topics with them. As is befitting an interdisciplinary field, however, there is considerable overlap in the sorts of research conducted by ethnohistorians trained in different disciplines.

Topics of Research

A quantitative study of the contents of the journal *Ethnohistory* reveals interesting patterns in the kind of research conducted by ethnohistorians (Barber and Berdan n.d.). The entire run of this journal was examined, and its articles were sorted into different categories such as topic and approach. (This method is called "content analysis" and is discussed at some length in chapter 8.)

In the early years of the journal, virtually all of its contributions focused on American Indians of North America. Over time, however, the geographical coverage broadened, and articles appeared on peoples in the Swiss Alps, sub-Saharan Africa, the Marquesas Islands, and Peru. Today, there is still more research on native North American groups than on any others, but the geographical distribution of research is increasingly global.

Studies of the human past can be either synchronic (focusing on a single period and the unity within it) or diachronic (focusing on the change that takes place over time). Both history and anthropology are equally interested in the two kinds of studies, so it is not surprising that their offspring, ethnohistory, has always welcomed both as well.

The topics addressed by ethnohistorians run the gamut. A few titles of articles in *Ethnohistory* from the first half of the 1990s give a flavor of the range:

— "Maori Prisoners and Slaves in the Nineteenth Century"
— "Land Litigations in an Andean Ayllu from 1592 until 1972"
— "Shamanism and Christianity: Modern-day Tlingit Elders Look at the Past"
— "Contesting Authenticity: Battles over the Representations of History in Morelos, Mexico"
— "Images of Society in Klondike Gold Rush Narratives: Skookum Jim and the Discovery of Gold"
— "Continuity under Colonial Rule: The Alcalde System and the Garifuna in Belize, 1858–1969"

— "The Warrior and the Lineage: Jesuit Use of Iroquoian Images to Communicate Christianity"
— "Stages in the Historical Process of Ethnicity: The Japanese in Brazil, 1908–1988"
— "Voices of Disaster: Smallpox around the Strait of Georgia in 1782"
— "Shields and Lodges, Warriors and Chiefs: Kiowa Drawings as Historical Records."

These titles give a small indication of the broad range of possible topics addressed through ethnohistory. There are, however, subjects of enduring interest that continue to attract a large share of interest among ethnohistorians.

Acculturation, the taking on of the way of life of an alien society, is a common focus, probably because cultural contact and conflict are themes inherent in ethnohistory. Within the general field of acculturation, religious conversion and shifting economic patterns are particularly popular. Demography, especially population collapse in the face of introduced diseases, also attracts scholars. The interrelations of war, diplomacy, and law are the subject of many studies, as are the maintenance of ethnic identity and tradition in the face of changing circumstances. There are many such areas of ethnohistoric concern, but these are exemplary in that they are based on the interaction of peoples highlighted in our definition of ethnohistory.

Concepts

The primary goal of all ethnohistorians is to illuminate the past. Information about earlier human activities is hidden away in documents and elsewhere, and part of the ethnohistorian's task is to ferret it out, collect it, and make it available. The next step is to take that information and interpret it, trying to construct notions of how different factors interacted and brought about certain events or conditions. Ethnohistorical facts do not speak for themselves; rather, they have to be put together in plausible ways to try to explain something about human activity in the past: how something happened, and why it happened.

The tools for putting together facts in plausible ways are concepts. Of course, the variety of concepts used by ethnohistorians is enormous and ever-expanding, as each discipline and practitioner brings more to the collection; each piece of research draws on some subset of those concepts, many of which are in broad use in other fields, especially the social sciences.

Conceptual Building Blocks

Though the diversity of concepts used by ethnohistorians is great, certain basic and central concepts are so widely used in ethnohistory that they warrant special attention here. They can be divided into two sets: approaches and assumptions.

Approaches. When conducting research, a scholar makes decisions about how to conceive the problem and go about solving it. The researcher consciously makes most of those decisions while pondering the options, but some may be made less consciously, conditioned by the researcher's habits, training, experience, and culture. These choices constitute the scholar's approaches to that piece of work. It is critical to remember that these are choices between acceptable alternatives, selected in an attempt to optimize the likelihood of deriving interpretations that further knowledge.

One useful way to organize these approaches is into dichotomies: polar opposites that represent the end points of a continuum. These dichotomous pairs are presented here as mutually exclusive opposites, but a scholar often can choose an intermediate position between the extremes. One such dichotomous pair of approaches is synchronic-diachronic. Synchronic refers to a focus on conditions at a single point in time; diachronic refers to a focus on change over time. For example, a synchronic study of Jesuit proselytizing among the Iroquois might focus on efforts at the early missions in the 1660s, while a diachronic study might contrast early efforts in the 1660s with later efforts in the 1710s. As with all of these dichotomous pairs, each approach is perfectly valid, and an ethnohistorian's choice is purely a matter of opting for the one that appears most likely to be productive and that fits the researcher's personal preference.

Another dichotomous pair is emic-etic. These terms are derived from the linguistic terminology of "phonemic" and "phonetic," and they parallel them in meaning. Emic refers to a way of looking at the world based on the conceptions, perceptions, and beliefs of the people being studied. Etic, in contrast, refers to a way of looking at the world that is based on the analytic conceptions of the ethnohistorian; these sometimes are characterized as "objective," but (as discussed at length in chapter 2) such objectivity is impossible, or at least unconfirmable. A study of why the Tupinamba periodically relocated their villages could be either emically based or etically based; the former would focus on the reasons the Tupinamba gave and presumably believed, while the latter would focus on "deeper" reasons that the ethnohistorian believed were "really" at the root of the

Tupinamba decisions. While most scholarship aims ultimately to come to some etic understanding of events and processes, the etic approach can be criticized as placing the researcher in an unduly privileged position as the arbiter of conceptual correctness.

A piece of research can also follow either the particularist or the nomothetic approach. The particularist approach involves studying a single case intensively, going into idiosyncrasies and specifics in great detail, and producing an interpretation of that single case. In contrast, the nomothetic approach (sometimes called the scientific approach) involves studying many cases to find their commonalities and draw a general conclusion that will apply to many (ideally, all) cases. An ethnohistoric study of seventeenth-century English courts in eastern Connecticut to assess and interpret discrimination against Native Americans is particularist; a nomothetic study might examine colonial courts in eastern Connecticut, Peru, Goa, the Dutch East Indies, Nigeria, and other places to assess and interpret patterns of discrimination against native peoples in colonial courts, producing a general statement.

Still another pair of approaches focuses on the importance of personal influence versus social forces. Research on personal influence (formerly known as "great-man interpretations") emphasizes how individuals, their personal qualities, and their decisions shaped events. Research that centers on social forces, on the other hand, draws attention to the ongoing processes in society that shape an individual's actions. A study that focuses on tactical decisions made by the leaders at the Battle of the Little Big Horn is following the personal-influence approach, while a study emphasizing armaments, supply lines, and attitudes regarding warfare takes the social forces approach. Much ethnohistory that follows the biographical approach (e.g., Wilson 1983; Gough 1982) singles out an influential individual, examines that person's life, and interprets how personal decisions and actions shaped broader events. This is a classic application of the personal-influence approach; however, other ethnohistoric studies using the biographical approach (e.g., Boyer and Gayton 1992; Namias 1993) focus on "typical" individuals or even groups of individuals, following much more of the social-forces approach.

Some studies focus on a single factor in explaining a process or event, while others investigate a broader set of considerations. A single-factor interpretation has the advantage of theoretical elegance and simplicity of understanding; critics who find a single-factor interpretation to be oversimplified can incorporate other factors and develop a multiple-factor interpretation. A study that might examine the role of economics in Mormon conversions among the Blackfoot would be single-factor research, while examining the roles of economics, social status, and factionalism in conversion would use a multiple-factor approach. Some scholars argue that almost no sociocultural phenomena relate to only a single factor and therefore multiple-factor studies are always preferable. Single-factor research, however, does not require accepting that only one factor is of importance. Rather, one could follow this approach to bring attention to a previously neglected factor or as part of research leading to a simplified model (discussed further in this chapter).

The final dichotomous pair to be considered is quantitative versus qualitative approaches. Some research is quantitative, concentrating on the measurement of factors and effects under consideration; other research is qualitative, using characteristics or properties without reference to measurement. A study of women's participation in Sioux politics is quantitative if it uses numbers to measure how many women have been involved or how strong their involvement has been; it is qualitative if it relies entirely on narrative or anecdotal information that does not include measurement. Much ethnohistoric work is qualitative, sometimes because the evidence makes it difficult to do quantitative research, sometimes because of the preferences of the ethnohistorians, and sometimes because of the nature of the problem being studied. Quantitative research is the ideal of the sciences since it provides more powerful modes of analysis than qualitative research, and many researchers studying sociocultural phenomena follow the lead of the natural sciences and apply the quantitative approach.

Every piece of ethnohistoric research is shaped by the researcher's choices in terms of these approaches. The researcher may choose an approach that lies at either end of the continuum represented by the pair, but intermediate positions that may better suit the researcher are possible in most cases. Nevertheless, it is difficult to conceive of a study that does not require making some sort of choice in each of the six pairs discussed above.

Assumptions. The paired dichotomous approaches discussed above represent strategic options available to a researcher in ethnohistory. In other words, a researcher typically considers which options — all of them reasonable and acceptable — will be *most* useful for the research at hand. The next set of concepts to be discussed differs in that a researcher may reject some alternatives as simply inappropriate for *all* research.

Assumptions are conceptualizations of how the world operates. All interpretations in ethnohistory (or any other field) are based on a scholar's assumptions about what things are important and how they interrelate. These assumptions shape interpretations profoundly as one or another factor is discarded or showcased and potential connections are drawn or erased. In the next paragraphs we discuss a few assumptions that are important in ethnohistory, again using the format of dichotomous pairs.

One important pair contrasts ideationalist and materialist assumptions. The ideationalist assumption maintains that human behavior is primarily shaped by ideas, ideologies, and values. The materialist assumption, in contrast, maintains that human behavior is molded primarily by the need to assist survival, whether the human actors realize this or not. The taboo on the eating of pork among Jews and Muslims, for example, can be explained using either assumption. An ideationalist might say that pigs are considered unclean because they fall between traditional Middle Eastern categories of animals, having a cloven hoof yet not chewing the cud; the idea system (the categories produced by language and culture), therefore, is at the root of declaring the pig odd, dangerous, and taboo. In contrast, a materialist might say that eating pigs in the Middle East is basically inefficient anyway, since pigs compete with people for similar food; by this interpretation, the pork taboo is an effective means of protecting people from unwise behavior, though the people involved may not recognize this effect. Clearly, choosing the ideationalist or materialist assumption often shows an individual scholar's outlook on the world and reflects that person's conclusion regarding its dominant processes. Sometimes, however, an individual might find a materialist interpretation compelling in one case and an ideational interpretation persuasive in another.

The second set of assumptions to be considered here is conflict versus consensus. A scholar subscribing to the conflict assumption believes that individuals or groups working for their self-interest will struggle with one another, forming the driving force for human behavior. Scholars accepting the consensus assumption, on the other hand, believe that people usually cooperate, focusing on common interests and submerging their self-interests to bring about actions that promote the common good. For example, through the eyes of the conflict assumption, the establishment of prices in the California gold rush was the result of selfish merchants maximizing their profits in a condition of scarce goods, while the consensus assumption would see this as a good-faith attempt to provide goods in a time of need, despite the problems of supply and consequent high prices. As with ideationalist and materialist assumptions, a scholar may adopt an across-the-board acceptance of either conflict or consensus as dominant in the world or select different assumptions for different cases.

Finally, the determinist assumption maintains that the same factors produce the same results every time; the stochastic assumption maintains that chance plays a role, permitting the same conditions to produce potentially different results. The determinist assumption has produced spectacular results in many of the physical sciences, as with Newtonian physics. In the study of human activities, however, it has a less successful history. Environmental determinists of the first half of the twentieth century, such as Ellsworth Huntington (e.g., 1915, 1945), exemplified some of the shortcomings of interpreting human behavior utilizing this assumption, particularly the poor fit between predicted and observed occurrence of sociocultural forms in specific environmental zones. In contrast, the stochastic assumption is in keeping with various conceptions of human free will and chaos theory. It does not assume, however, that there is no patterning in events or behavior whatsoever, since the chance factor usually is considered relatively small, permitting general (though imperfect) patterning to be recognized.

Many more assumptions underlie interpretation in ethnohistory and related fields, but these suffice as examples of choices each researcher makes to guide interpretation — choices that can profoundly affect interpretation.

Interpretive Frameworks

Interpretive frameworks are conceptual structures designed to help scholars interpret evidence, and approaches and assumptions are the building blocks of these frameworks. Sometimes these interpretive frameworks are formalized: written down and published. Sometimes they are informal and implicit, perhaps not entirely consciously worked out. Sometimes they lie between these extremes. In any case, every interpreter of ethnohistoric evidence has some kind of interpretive framework that directs the process. Although of different kinds, these frameworks often are divided into paradigms, theories, and models.

A paradigm is a more or less integrated and consistent set of approaches and assumptions that forms the basis for drawing conclusions. A paradigm, in a sense, is a way of seeing things: a general system of ideas about how the world operates that colors our modes of interpretation. Different paradigms, of course, produce very different interpretations of the same evidence. Partially because ethnohistory draws its practitioners from such diverse backgrounds, there are many paradigms in use at once. This is a source of strength for the field, but ethnohistorians subscribing to different paradigms may have difficulty appreciating one another's work if they are separated by too wide a divergence of assumptions and approaches.

An example of one of the many paradigms of ethnohistory is the evolutionary paradigm, which seeks to recognize regular patterns of change over time, often defining stages that occur in sequence. This paradigm can be applied to a great diversity of topics, including artistic expression, politics, settlement, acculturation, and many others. The evolutionary paradigm is assembled from the following approaches and assumptions: diachronic, etic, and nomothetic. Stated differently, ethnohistorians who follow the evolutionary paradigm are interested in change over time, creating and using their own analytic categories to compare different cases, and searching for general patterns that characterize a range of cases. An example of the evolutionary paradigm used in ethnohistory is Christopher Reichl's (1995) study of the Japanese of Brazil, in which he discusses stages in the evolution of ethnic identity; Reichl argues that these stages are similar to ones through which immigrants and their descendants elsewhere pass.

A theory is a more specific system of approaches and assumptions linked together by a logical argument and framing the way evidence is interpreted. Theories may be relatively broad, covering a wide range of topics, or quite specific, focusing on a single topic.

One of the broad theories that serves as an example of its class is functionalism, which argues that many or most behaviors prescribed by value systems serve some useful purpose ("function") for the society. While those behaviors may not have originally arisen to meet the needs of society, they serve in that manner. Some versions of functionalism argue that the success of the community that adopts a functional behavior ensures that the behavior will survive, a process analogous to natural selection in biological evolution. Most modern theories of functionalism recognize that not every behavior has a function, and that some behaviors are neutral or counterproductive. Another important facet of functionalism is that the function of a behavior may not be recognized by the people who practice it. Functionalism, then, draws on the following approaches and assumptions: synchronic, etic, particularistic, and consensus. In other words, it examines a process at a single point in time, uses analytical categories, discusses particular cases, and assumes that society works for the overall benefit of its members.

Functionalism has been criticized on a variety of grounds. First, it produces what many believe to be a false impression of causation: that societal need automatically produces the behavior to meet that need. Second, it has been denounced as the intellectual equivalent of the mother who says, "Everything always works out for the best"; in other words, functionalism relies heavily on the consensual assumption, which some scholars reject. Third, it focuses attention on a static view of a society, diverting attention from diachronic and other issues that some scholars find more significant or interesting.

Despite these criticisms, functionalism remains a vital part of the theoretical arsenal of the social sciences and is widely used in ethnohistory. Donald Messerschmidt's study of the Thakali of Nepal (1982), for example, discusses religious and ideological orientation in the twentieth century as ways to cope with broader social problems, particularly political ones. In another example, William Starna, George Hamell, and William Butts (1984) conducted a study analyzing reasons why the Iroquois shifted the locations of their villages regularly. They looked at soil depletion, diminution of firewood supplies, and insect infestations of fields and concluded that these ecological factors acted in concert to encourage regular village removal.

Another class of interpretive frameworks is the model: a picture, in words or visual images, of how or why a process operates. The model should provide a simplification that permits us to better understand how the process might work, drawing our eyes to relationships that are critical and central, omitting whatever appears to be mere detail or masks essential patterns. In selecting what to include in the model, the creator risks two errors: a model overburdened with detail becomes cumbersome, obscuring more than it reveals; on the other hand, a model that is oversimplified may leave out significant elements and relationships. In a sense, every model is oversimplified, since it *must* leave out elements that have a bearing on the overall process. A successful model strikes a productive balance between these two pitfalls.

Models can serve different purposes. Those that focus on how a process operates are descriptive models, while those that concentrate on motivations or underlying causes are explanatory models. The links between a model's elements cannot be observed and often cannot be verified in any way, so it is a mistake to attribute more significance to a model than it warrants. A model is not a presentation of reality or anything like it; rather, it is a scholar's construction of how or why a process might occur. As such, it is an interpretation, not a fact. Consequently, the way to judge a model is by its utility: how well it helps us conceive of something and examine it. A good model will suggest connections that might not otherwise be obvious, draw attention to central factors, and strip away camouflaging detail. Sometimes a flawed model will draw attention to new relationships that had been previously overlooked, leading to its refinement.

Models are common in ethnohistory. David Jenkins (1995), for example, provides an intricate, formal, and self-identified model that suggests that Andean status systems were structurally parallel to the Inca myths that legitimized them. As another example, David Meyer and Paul Thistle (1995) discuss the locations of seasonal congregation centers of the Cree along the Saskatchewan River, relating subsistence, band structure, and the spacing of these congregation centers in what is a model, despite the fact that they do not label it as such. (Indeed, models often are not identified explicitly by their creators.) Chapter 2 of this book also presents a model of ethnohistoric description.

There is a vast literature on concepts and interpretive frameworks in the social sciences, and the interdisciplinary nature of ethnohistory ensures that most of these have made or will make their way into ethnohistoric research. This section certainly has made no attempt to describe all of them; rather, it has presented a discussion of a few basic conceptual elements and how they combine to produce interpretive frameworks.

A Brief History of Ethnohistory

No one yet has written a thorough history of ethnohistory, and this brief treatment will not remedy that situation. It will, however, provide a concise synopsis of several trends, processes, and events of significance to the development of modern ethnohistory. It draws heavily on various articles from *Ethnohistory* (especially articles from the Symposium on the Concept of Ethnohistory, published in 1961) and general reviews of ethnohistory published about once per decade in the *Annual Review of Anthropology* (Carmack 1972; Spores 1980; Krech 1991). These latter articles are particularly rich in bibliographies of ethnohistoric research.

To trace the history of ethnohistory, it first is necessary to define terms. On the one hand, this can be the history of the word itself, in which case the history will be relatively brief but straightforward. Alternatively, it can be the history of the concept as defined here, in which case the history will dip back millennia and be quite varied. Finally, it can be the history of the modern, self-identified field of study, in which case the history will extend back only about half a century.

The Word

The word "ethnohistory," or a variant of it, apparently was first used in 1909 by Clark Wissler (1909:xiii). At that time it was used as a two-word phrase, "ethno historical," and it described documents that dealt with American Indian history. For the next three decades, the term appeared sporadically, always referring to the evidence, not to a specialized field studying the evidence. By the 1940s, "ethno-history" was used widely to describe both the act of interpreting the evidence and the resulting interpretations. Finally, by around 1950, "ethnohistory" began to be used as a nonhyphenated term with its modern meaning.

The Concept

The concept of ethnohistory, divorced from the term, has a much greater time depth. Given the definition of ethnohistory adopted in this chapter, Herodotus, Ibn Battuta, Xenophon, and many other scholars of antiquity were ethnohistorians: they used documents and other sources with at least some historiography and relativism to understand past cultural interactions. In their times, however, they viewed themselves simply as historians or, even more basically, as scholars. The idea of segmenting scholarship into distinct fields was ill-formed in their times. Indeed, setting ethnohistory off from the rest of history is parallel to the racial and ethnic segregation of the formative era of the field. It is just possible that prejudice was one factor in the development of ethnohistory as a distinct and named field.

There were, however, historians as early as the eighteenth century who devoted themselves particularly to the histories of interaction between Euro-Americans and American Indians. In the mid-eighteenth century, for example, Cadwallader Colden wrote a history of the Iroquois of northeastern North America (Colden 1747). Its table of contents reads like that of any other history of the era: wars, treaties, and negotiations. Admittedly, the well-developed diplomatic system of the Iroquois might have encouraged this approach, but Colden focused on the same issues that contemporary histories of France, Russia, or Italy emphasized.

The birth of anthropology in the mid-nineteenth century siphoned off a great deal of potential interest in American Indians that otherwise would have been directed to history. Scholars who might have become historians of American Indians chose instead to be anthropologists and devoted major attention to material culture, kinship, and other traditional concerns of anthropology. As a result, Indian history largely languished, with the exception of a small contingent of historians, most of whom dealt with issues of local historical interest only.

Finally, in the second quarter of the twentieth century, interest in American Indian history reawakened in North America. The prominence of anthropology in the study of American Indian societies encouraged historians to turn to anthropological literature for assistance, bringing ideas — especially cultural relativism — into American Indian history and sparking the movement toward the modern field of ethnohistory. As anthropologists began reading the output of these historians, the potential of documentary evidence as a source for anthropological studies became clear. At this point, a cadre of dedicated scholars from both anthropology and history began welding together the modern field of ethnohistory.

The chronology in Latin America was similar. Following a period of initial interest shortly after the Spanish conquest, historical research into native societies and their history dwindled until the mid-twentieth century (Spores 1980:577–578). While ethnohistorians have been active in all Latin American countries, Mexico and Peru have received the most attention.

As did the Americas, Africa got off to an excellent start in history (ethnohistory, by the definition of this book), then languished. The Muslim world contributed such great scholars as Ibn Khaldun in the fourteenth century (Niane 1984:7 ff.), but these efforts mostly died out by the sixteenth or seventeenth century. The slackening of interest in African history lasted until the revival of the 1920s, from which time interest has continued into the present (Kense 1990:140–141). African ethnohistory in the sense of relativistic interpretation, however, developed largely in the second half of the twentieth century.

Ethnohistory in other parts of the world developed even more slowly than in North America, Latin America, and Africa. Intensive ethnohistoric research in Oceania began in the 1970s, largely as an attempt to supplement ethnological and archaeological information (Spores 1980: 578), and most ethnohistoric research in Oceania to this day has been conducted by ethnographers. In Asia, as well, modern ethnohistoric research largely postdates 1970 (Barber and Berdan n.d.). Today, however, ethnohistorians study the inhabitants of all the continents, both native and immigrant, in all historic periods.

While the roots of the modern concept and practice of ethnohistory can be traced further back in time, ethnohistory clearly is a child of the mid-twentieth century. Arising almost simultaneously in Africa, North America, and Latin America and a bit later elsewhere, it was part of the expansion of scholarship that followed the end of World War II. The 1950s were a time of considerable experimentation in the crossing of traditional disciplinary boundaries, and ethnohistory grew out of the resulting hybridization. The historical climate of that period, too, encouraged study of non-Western subjects, as the Western world became more aware of and linked to the non-Western world.

The Field of Study

The development of a body of scholars who identified themselves with this new, hybrid field marks the beginning of ethnohistory in the third sense: a self-conscious field of study with adherents, formal organizations, journals, and conferences. By 1950 the planning that would lead to the founding of the American Society for Ethnohistory was well underway.

The forerunner of the American Society for Ethnohistory was the Ohio Valley Historic Indian Conference, founded in 1954. Its name was changed first to the American Indian Ethno-Historic Conference and then, in 1966, to the American Society for Ethnohistory. Under its various names, this organization published the journal *Ethnohistory* and sponsored an annual conference at which research papers were presented. The journal's early issues resonate with the enthusiasm that many of the founding members of the society brought to the infant organization.

Much of this mid-century North American interest in ethnohistory seems to have been linked to archaeology, which already was an established, semiautonomous field within anthropology. Because of archaeology's ambiguous position—within anthropology yet somehow set apart —graduate students were expected to specialize in archaeology yet pass general examinations that included the rest of anthropology. As a result, archaeologists became familiar with historic and other sources of information and frequently looked to historical records to help them flesh out their reconstructions of prehistoric societies.

An important development in this era was William Duncan Strong's (1935, 1940) direct historical method: a means of linking up historic peoples with prehistoric archaeological sites and cultures. Working in the North American Plains, Strong reasoned that the Late Prehistoric tribes there must have become the historically known ones. He therefore advocated locating sites historically identified with known tribes, excavating the sites and characterizing the material culture of that tribe, and then working backward from historic sites to prehistoric ones. As progressively earlier sites were excavated and linked to one or another tribal sequence, Strong and his followers were able to trace ethnic/tribal sequences back in time.

This method was very well received in archaeology, since it provided archaeologists with a way to flesh out the skeletal reconstructions of pre-history by borrowing information known about historic descendants. This stimulated research into both historic archaeology and ethnohistory, but it is important to note that the intrinsic interest was in prehistoric archaeology; these other specialties were seen primarily as supporters of that main enterprise. In this sense, much of archaeologists' initial interest in ethnohistory as a field was derivative.

This archaeological legacy is evident in the contents of *Ethnohistory* during its first several years. Many articles were concerned with defining the nascent field; some pursued topics that fit squarely into today's vision of the field, but many were really archaeological in nature. In addition to articles applying the direct historical method, many articles were devoted to ethnoarchaeology, the use of historic and ethnographic information to aid interpretation of archaeological remains. (Ethnoarchaeology is a form of analogy, discussed in chapter 13.) Articles on ethnoarchaeology are scattered through *Ethnohistory* in its early years, and as late as 1973 an entire issue was devoted to a symposium on ethnoarchaeology (Adams 1973). In retrospect, these efforts appear somewhat out of place in an ethnohistory journal, since modern scholars more typically view ethno-archaeology as a part of archaeology, with goals of improving and expand-ing archaeological interpretation, not primarily assisting in ethnohistoric understanding. Nonetheless, the presence of these articles helped establish a strong base of support for the society, its journal, and the new field of ethnohistory. Indeed, many of the founding members of the Ohio Valley Historic Indian Conference were better known for their archaeological research than for their ethnohistoric contributions.

Another factor encouraging the growth of ethnohistory was the wan-ing of an antihistorical tradition that had developed in anthropology. Under the influence of certain functionalists, particularly A. R. Radcliffe-Brown and Bronislaw Malinowski, the discipline of anthropology had moved away from historical studies, instead focusing more on synchronic studies. The well-known biases of these individuals had a powerful effect in stultifying diachronic studies and those based on historical evidence. By the mid-twentieth century, functionalism was becoming less dominant in anthropology, and more historically minded practitioners were taking the places of Radcliffe-Brown and Malinowski. Anthropology then began opening up toward more historical studies, stimulating the growth of ethnohistory.

Still another source of interest in ethnohistory was the rise of Indian land claims (Spores 1980:577). Following World War II, there were hundreds of Indian legal claims for the restitution of, or compensation for, lost land. The U.S. Indian Claims Commission held hearings at which anthropologists and historians figured prominently as expert witnesses. The immersion in historic documents required for this testimony promoted ethnohistoric research in general and was the foundation of some ethnohistorians' expertise. Various articles in *Ethnohistory* were based on research stimulated by land-claim testimony, and all the articles in one early issue (Ray 1955) were from a symposium on ethnohistory and Indian claims litigation.

By the late 1960s, much of the preliminary defining work for the field had been accomplished, and ethnohistory was established firmly enough to be able to devote itself to the business of conducting ethnohistoric research. Most articles treated some issue of American Indian ethnohistory, often descriptions of cultural characteristics or analyses of acculturation.

In the 1970s, several shifts are obvious in the articles in *Ethnohistory*. First, the geographical distribution of articles was becoming more global. True to its initial goals, *Ethnohistory* and its sponsoring organization were originally devoted primarily to North American Indian topics. By the 1970s, the North American emphasis of earlier years was giving way to a broader spectrum of regional coverage, still largely devoted to North America but increasingly including articles discussing Latin America, Africa, and the rest of the world. Second, the number of authors was increasing. In the early years, much of the burden of writing articles was carried by relatively few authors; by the 1970s, the field had grown to the point that the task of conducting research and writing articles was shared more broadly. Third, the early focus on articles dealing with definitions of ethnohistory and its relationships to other fields was passing. As the field matured, such self-examination occupied a smaller portion of attention, and most articles reported substantive ethnohistoric research.

Through the 1980s and into the mid-1990s, ethnohistory has continued to grow, both in the numbers of practitioners and the breadth of their interests. The fusion of its component fields, especially anthropology and history, has progressed far enough that Krech (1991:349) has written of the "interpenetration" of ideas from these fields. By this he means that concepts and perspectives from both history and anthropology are so widely known by practitioners in both fields that they can draw on them freely, regardless of which discipline they originated in. Clearly, since most ethnohistorians were trained in either history or anthropology, this means that their shared body of concepts is considerable.

While most ethnohistorians believe that significant disciplinary characteristics persist, it is becoming increasingly difficult to identify an author's "home discipline" on the basis of the ideas, methods, or knowledge that went into a piece of research. Difficulty in identifying "home disciplines" is a characteristic of a mature interdisciplinary field whose members are fully familiar with the ideas and practices of the component disciplines that have forged it. We hope and expect that this trend will intensify in the future.

Documents

Because ethnohistory is so dependent on documents, it is wise to discuss them a bit and establish a terminology. Documents consist of any materials that include a written message or depiction on them. This very broad definition includes handwritten or printed written texts, scrawled notes, drawn maps or pictures, paintings, photographs, and anything else designed to communicate a message visually. Most documents are on paper, parchment, or some similar substance, but others are engravings on rock, photographs on film or glass, inscriptions on coins, and a pledge of undying love scratched into a fence post.

A few specialized words denote certain forms of documents. *Manuscripts* are hand-written documents, often unpublished. A *codex* (plural *codices*) is a special kind of manuscript, often incorporating both words and pictures and sometimes folded accordion-fashion or in some other manner; the term is used almost exclusively for Mexican and medieval European documents. A *book* is usually a manuscript that has been reproduced by printing or hand-copying and has been bound into a volume. *Inscriptions* are writing or pictures in relief, such as the words and images cast or stamped onto a coin, an engraving cut into a rock face, or a message scratched into the plaster of a wall. *Graffiti* are word messages painted or drawn onto either walls or small pieces of broken pottery. Originally defined for ancient Italy, graffiti occur in some form over most of the world. *Illumination* refers to the carefully drawn graphics, particularly ornamental letters, that adorn some manuscripts designed for the elite. The term is used primarily in reference to Islamic and medieval European examples.

Documents, regardless of their form, are divided into two major types. Primary documents are ones composed by a person who was present at the time and place being described or discussed. A letter written home by a Chilean miner discussing the rigors of nitrate mining is a primary document, as is Sir Richard Burton's description of the plants he encountered on his explorations of East Africa. Secondary documents, on the other hand, are documents composed by a person who is collecting or commenting on the original information provided by primary documents. A scholarly book that uses the Chilean miner's letter as part of its sources and discusses life in nitrate mining camps is a secondary document; a newspaper account based on an interview with Sir Richard Burton is a secondary account of his explorations in Africa. (Of course, the newspaper account could include primary information, too, such as what Burton wore during the interview, his mannerisms, and the timbre of his voice. These primary data, however, relate to the interview, not Burton's travels.) Secondary documents often, but by no means always, were written long after the events or conditions being discussed had occurred; primary documents often, though not always, were composed shortly after the events transpired.

Many documents include both primary and secondary sections. A traveler's account of Japan in the late nineteenth century, for example, might include primary information about the celebrations that the traveler observed, but it also might include secondary information about what the rituals represented, information gleaned from a guidebook or from discussion with a local missionary. As will be discussed at length in chapter 7, earlier authors did not always feel compelled to reveal which portions of their accounts were primary and which were secondary.

The distinction between primary and secondary sources is traditional in history and ethnohistory, and we will use it throughout. Nonetheless, some critics prefer not to make the distinction, believing that it obscures more than it illuminates. As they see it, the authors of ethnohistoric documents were rarely fully aware of where ideas and information came from and almost never were interested in trying to separate the two. Documents, therefore, are an inextricable tangle of primary and secondary elements. By trying to project our ideal dichotomy onto a real document, we force that document into one or the other camp; once it is labeled, we have expectations of a document and are less likely to be wary of its snares and shortcomings. To be sure, the distinction between primary and secondary documents is analytic, not inherent, and it is unwise to place too much significance on the designation of a document as one or the other. Rather than discard the concept completely, however, we prefer to use it with caution and recognize its limitations.

Both primary and secondary sources are important to the ethnohistorian. The value of the primary sources lies largely in their potential to provide factual (though, perforce, incomplete and selective) information on the past. They are usually the best sources for collecting descriptions of events, conditions, and activities. While they often include the authors' opinions about why things happened as they did, these may be wildly unlikely. For example, Louis Hennepin (1698) attributed what he saw as the Indian inclination to violence to the fact that they ate a great deal of meat. Although this explanation made good sense to a seventeenth-century Frenchman coming out of the medieval European medical tradition, it makes little sense in light of modern nutrition and medicine. Thus Hennepin's explanation casts considerable light on historic French attitudes regarding humoral medicine, but does little to illuminate the relationship between Indian diet and personality.

Secondary sources, in contrast, are strongest at providing interpretations. Interpreting the example above, a modern scholar might attribute violence to the effects of European liquor, the competitive demands of the fur trade, or some other factor deemed more plausible in modern thinking. These explanations benefit ethnohistorians by giving them ideas to criticize or refine, often in light of how well an interpretation accords with their own data sets. While a well-researched secondary source will report facts (derived from primary sources) accurately, there always is a possibility that facts will become distorted in the retelling. Even if the facts are represented perfectly, the writer of a secondary source has selected facts that serve his or her needs, and some of the facts not included might be the ones that would be of greatest use to the reader. Consequently, there is no substitute for consulting primary sources to collect facts.

Because of these relative strengths and weaknesses of primary and secondary sources, ethnohistorians must use both. It usually is considered sensible to read a variety of secondary scholarly sources early in a research project to get a general idea of what is known about the subject and what interpretations ethnohistorians have offered to date. Scholars then usually turn to the primary sources, checking the facts on which others have based their interpretations, looking for other facts whose significance might not yet have been recognized, and digging into the limits of extant information. After gathering the data or while poring through them, ethnohistorians may come up with novel interpretations, permitting them to write documents (books or articles) that extend the fund of secondary sources in ethnohistory.

Of course, the diversity of documents used by ethnohistorians is tremendous. While no list can be complete, ethnohistorians commonly use the following types of documents:

— Journals and diaries
— Letters
— Accounts by travelers (both foreign and domestic)
— Published books of the period in question
— Government reports
— Censuses (both published reports and raw data)
— Court records
— Wills and probate documents
— Laws, regulations, and executive orders
— Military records
— Religious records (including baptismal, marriage, and death records)
— Newspapers
— Native chronicles
— Maps, plans, floorplans, and elevations
— Visual images (including drawings, paintings, engravings, and photographs)
— Scholarly books and articles

Most of these sources usually would be considered primary sources or would include sections that could be considered primary sources. The scholarly books and articles are, of course, secondary sources that might include excerpts or translations of primary source materials.

While ethnohistory, by our definition, always involves interaction between societies, it is common for the documentary evidence to be unequally divided between those societies. Ethnohistorians working in North America, for example, often find that most of their documentary sources were written by Europeans and reflect European cultural viewpoints. DeMallie (1993) shows that Native American accounts provide a valuable counterpoint and often are more numerous than researchers assume.

As ethnohistorians conduct their research, they often find it desirable to tap other sources of information. These may include oral accounts, folklore, historical archaeology, experimentation, and whatever else might shed light on the issues they are exploring. So long as an ethnohistorian can make an argument for why information is relevant, it is fair game to use.

CHAPTER 2

The Reality-Mediation Model

This chapter presents a model to describe how an author processes information to produce a document or oral account. Like any model, it is an ideal picture of how its creators conceptualize something, not truth incarnate. The utility of a model is not measured in terms of how close it is to truth, since that can never be known; rather, its value lies in how useful it is in assisting people to understand a process and look analytically at its components. The components of this model all have been presented by others before, but this chapter brings them together in a systematic, integrated way.

The reality-mediation model, as we have named it, offers a vision of the act of description, which it depicts as a complex interplay between the author and reality, not as the simple, almost mechanical, recording process it is sometimes assumed to be. In this sense, the documents of ethnohistory are akin to the images in Qin Shi Huangdi's mirror, described in the prologue: they are reflections shaped by the authors' experiences, convictions, and desires.

The value of the reality-mediation model, as we see it, is to structure our conception of historical description. By delineating the various forces that can mold a historical description, it focuses our attention on those forces, permitting us to better recognize their effects. It directs our skepticism regarding the accuracy of historical evidence.

Description, Interpretation, Facts, and Etiologues

In the normal course of writing an account, most authors make use of two processes: description and interpretation. These processes are closely interrelated but conceptually distinct in significant ways.

On the one hand, most accounts use description: the process by which events, actions, and conditions are perceived by sensory means and recorded. It is description, for example, when Henry Stanley (1982) observed in his correspondence to the *New York Herald* that a nineteenth-century Cheyenne village he visited was horribly smelly and could be detected downwind for miles. Similarly, it is description when Ezana (in Davidson 1964:55–56), the fourth-century king of the Ethiopian Axumites, told of a battle where his troops destroyed the grain and cotton of his enemies and drove them into the Seda River. Each of these accounts presents information that could have been collected by an observer using the input from vision, hearing, and the other senses.

On the other hand, written accounts typically also include interpretation: the drawing of conclusions on the basis of information obtained from description. For example, Stanley did not stop at a description of the smells of the Cheyenne village; he went on to conclude that the foul smells were the natural outgrowth of what he believed to be the Indians' slovenly character. Ezana also incorporated interpretation into his account when he wrote that the reason his enemy was driven into the river was their terror at his awe-inspiring Axumites. Whenever an author draws conclusions — particularly ones related to causation, motivation, or intention — that writer is using interpretation.

Although description and interpretation are conceptually distinct in the ideal, they are intermeshed, and sometimes almost indistinguishable, in real thought and writing. In his account of the battle at the Seda River, Ezana did some interpretation. His senses told him that grain and cotton were destroyed, but only through interpretation could he attribute ownership to his enemies.

The situation is complicated by writings that are ambiguous in terms of what is being presented. Consider, for example, the following quotation from Bayard Taylor, a journalist during California's gold rush in 1849, discussing restaurants there: "The latter [Chinese restaurants] are much frequented by Americans [Anglo-Americans], on account of their excellent cookery" (1850:89). Taylor clearly ate at the restaurants, so we can assume that he could observe how many Anglo-Americans dined there, but the reason for their dining there is a bit more obscure. He may have asked several of them why they chose that spot, and they may have said that they liked the food; in that case, his presentation of the reason for their patronage is really a veiled description of their statements. Alternatively, he may have liked the food himself and assumed that others shared his opinion and ate there for that reason; in that scenario, the second part of his statement is clearly an interpretation.

Another description of Chinese restaurants in the gold rush exemplifies a related difficulty of differentiating description from interpretation. William Kelly, an Irish writer who spent about a year in California, wrote in 1852 that "amidst the host of competitors, the Celestials carry off the palm for superior excellence in every particular. They serve everything promptly, cleanly, hot, and well cooked" (1852:151). Here, objective observation and judgment are merged, particularly in the criteria for excellence. Whereas Kelly's nineteenth-century Irish palate may have judged a meal to be cooked appropriately, an Italian patron (or a modern American) might have judged the meal an overcooked mess. Similarly, promptness, cleanliness, and heat all must be judged relative to one's experience and standards. Thus simple description often is blended with interpretation of various sorts, but despite the occasional difficulty of deciding whether an assertion is a description or an interpretation, there are very good reasons for making the distinction.

Description, as we conceive of it, is rooted in reality. By this statement we mean that the phenomenon being described actually exists (or existed) in some sense, and that it really has (or had) certain characteristics that could be perceived by human sensory apparatus. Clearly, Cheyenne villages had some olfactory characteristics, as do all human communities, and Stanley's nose presumably would have been capable of discerning them. Ezana had enemies that he met in battle, and his eyes could see the outcome.

This point may seem basic, but not all scholars agree that reality is a crucial factor in description or even that it exists. Michel Foucault (1970), for example, maintains that "truth" is constituted solely by those beliefs that attain a high level of acceptance by a society and are confirmed by their cultural system; resemblance to reality is not even entertained as a reasonable criterion. From Foucault's point of view, reality is somewhere between irrelevant and imaginary. Most scholars, however, agree that there is some set of events that really transpired. Many scholars maintain that it may not be easy or even possible to describe them in a satisfactory manner (e.g., Collingwood 1946, 1965), but they accept that the events themselves had some kind of reality.

Philosophers frequently identify three major schools of conceiving reality: idealism, phenomenalism, and realism (Blackburn 1994). Idealism focuses on the construction of reality through our mental processes, the ways in which human cognition places its stamp on the way it perceives the universe; phenomenalism emphasizes how human sensation experiences the world; and realism argues that there is some sort of external reality that human beings perceive with greater or lesser degrees of imperfection. The important point here is that very few scholars actually deny the existence of reality, though they may deny our ability to perceive it. More frequently, idealists and phenomenalists simply find it more interesting or fruitful to focus on their chosen emphases, but this does not necessarily mean denial of all reality. There is, after all, a substantial logical difficulty of denying the existence of an external reality: the persons doing the denying find themselves existing in the very world whose existence they deny. Consequently, although the concept of reality cannot be simply assumed innocently, we believe it does (and should) underlie the historical enterprise.

Once we accept the notion of reality, we can conceive of it as an ideal about which we can never attain full or completely accurate knowledge. But we can try to construct a reasonable picture of reality through descriptions, each of which provides an approximation of that reality. The descriptions probably differ greatly in how closely they resemble reality, but there often will be some level of agreement. When scholars agree that certain descriptions are probably accurate renderings of reality, they are called facts. Facts, of course, can be found to be wrong and can be revised, but — at least for the period of their currency — they are considered to be accurate.

Interpretation, on the other hand, lies in very different philosophical terrain. It is unclear that causation, motivation, and intention have anything akin to the reality-grounding of description. Sensory input is the basis for the observation that underlies description, but the reasoning that underlies interpretation is far more dependent on the assumptions, mental processes, and experience of the interpreter. For example, ten observers from radically different personal and cultural backgrounds could be asked to observe a volcanic eruption and produce reports of what they sensed. Despite the differences among their reports, we could expect a certain core of similarity in description: the air was hot and sulfurous, there were winds blowing up the cone, red-hot molten material was flowing down the slope, birds were soaring overhead. Interpretations by the same observers, however, would be likely to vary tremendously, ranging from plate tectonic to mythological paradigms.

It is always tempting for scholars to assume a privileged position, presuming that their own paradigm is more rational or useful or modern or correct than those of others, but there is no justifiable basis for this presumption. We may be wedded to the notion of tectonic movements and the inexorable forces of physics, but another observer may be equally committed to Pele and the caprices of that Hawaiian volcano goddess. Without any clear objective reality to anchor interpretation, its nature is necessarily more variable than description. Therefore it is unreasonable to discuss the results of interpretation as facts; rather, we will call them *etiologues,* suggested causes believed to produce phenomena. While interpretation is a process, an etiologue is the result of that process; the relationship between description and fact is parallel to that between interpretation and etiologue.

Plato's famous allusion of the shadows in the cave may assist in grasping this. For Plato, reality was like something inside a cave, beyond the observer's view. There were, however, shadows cast on the irregular sides of the cave, flickering as a fire flared and subsided. These shadows, while not reality themselves, were reflections of reality, though the reality itself could not be seen: these shadows are the facts produced by the act of description. This conception is similar to ours, with a true reality extant but inaccessible, able to be sensed only indirectly. Foucault, in contrast, might say either that there was nothing casting the shadows or that he did not care what it was. In contrast, those who believe that a complete knowledge of objective reality is attainable would argue that the shadows bear no distortions and are perfect images of the object that casts them. Should the shadows stimulate a viewer to guess why the something in the cave behaved as its shadows suggested, these guesses would be etiologues produced through the process of interpretation.

To sum up, then, description is the process of trying to characterize reality as perceived through the human senses. Successful descriptions, or the distilled commonalities of several descriptions, are widely accepted and considered facts, at least until further information dislodges them in favor of new or different facts. Interpretation, on the other hand, is the process of assigning causation and understanding relationships through the drawing of conclusions based on facts; these conclusions, of course, are shaped in part by the background of the interpreter. Since it is unclear that there is any objective basis for interpretation, causal explanations vary more greatly than facts and are given a distinct name: etiologues. We may feel very comfortable with a particular etiologue and be convinced of its truth, but an equally rational person may reject it because of the premises that underlie the conclusion. Facts may be so well agreed upon that there is very little likelihood that they will be overturned, but there always is a greater level of uncertainty with etiologues. This is in keeping with our view that facts are discovered (though perhaps in distorted forms) and etiologues are constructed.

Reality Mediation

Our primary concern in formulating the reality-mediation model is to produce a picture of how a description comes to differ from the reality it supposedly portrays. The set of processes by which an author converts information into a description (which necessarily differs from reality) is called *reality mediation*.

As we conceive this process, an observer receives sensory stimuli in enormous numbers. Some are ignored, while others are taken into the observer's mind. The observer then processes the stimuli in his or her mind, rejecting some as insignificant, making others central in significance, and placing others somewhere in between. The stimuli are integrated into meaningful patterns, and these are then examined in relation to what the observer already knows or believes to be true.

As an example, our observers at the volcanic eruption would be assaulted by sensory stimuli including heat, light, movement, air pressure, sound, smells, and perhaps pain. Out of this jumble of sensory stimuli, each observer would start assembling a picture that was coherent in terms of the observer's own view of how the world operates. While each observer would receive more or less the same sensory stimuli, how they interpreted those stimuli could vary tremendously. A geologist, for example, would be likely to see an intimate physical-chemical relationship, so that the smell of sulfur, the presence of lava, and the feeling of heat all would be part of the same phenomenon; birds soaring near the eruption would be seen as taking advantage of convection currents to make their flight effortless. The geologist's perception of this phenomenon would be colored by the simultaneous interpretation of an eruption based on the current paradigm in the geological sciences and more broadly in physics. The Pele worshiper, however, would sense about the same stimuli but might reject the presence of birds as unimportant, while focusing on the shaking and rumbling that Pele's adherents interpret as the result of her movements.

What are the differences between a description and the reality on which it is based? They vary tremendously, of course, from case to case, and our inability to ever really know reality prevents us from being able to answer this question satisfactorily. We can, however, list four ways that mediation affects the content of a description during reality mediation: selection, emphasis, transformation, and fabrication.

Selection refers to the process by which certain portions of reality are excluded from a description. In some places, soaring birds use rising air currents over a hot lava flow to keep them aloft, but our observers of the volcanic eruption might not have included the behavior of birds in their descriptions. Reasons could be various: one observer might be near-sighted and not see the birds, another might be enthralled with the drama of the eruption itself and not even notice the birds, and still another might see and notice the birds but decide they were not part of the event and therefore not relevant to the description.

Related to selection is *emphasis,* the placing of greater importance on some elements of a description than on others. While selection deals with the presence or absence of something in a description, emphasis deals with the degree and ways in which the thing is treated. One observer might simply note that soaring birds took advantage of the updrafts, while another might go into detail on the species, behavior, and numbers of the birds. Once again, sensory ability to observe, the focus of the observer's attention, the assignment of significance relative to the central issues of the description, and other factors could affect how much emphasis an element receives in a description. In a sense, selection could be considered the ultimate in emphasis, whereas other elements are deemphasized to the point that they disappear from the description altogether.

In *transformation,* an element of reality is included in a description but is modified in some way. One observer of the eruption might be a member of Bat Conservation International, and wishful thinking might incline this individual to interpret the birds as bats. Another observer might misjudge and misreport the birds' number or color because of faulty vision. Still another might be so impressed by the temperature of the eruption to consider that no creature could seek that heat, therefore leading the observer to believe that the birds really were farther away from the volcano. Special interests, divergent goals, and different experience can cause observers to report an event very differently. The modes of transforming information in a description are very diverse and can be insidious in their subtlety.

Finally, *fabrication* is the making up of information to include in a description. Purposeful lying is one process through which fabrication can distort a description, and self-delusion is another. One observer of the volcanic eruption entertaining ideas of selling an account to a tabloid newspaper might consciously invent sordid details to make the story more marketable; a Pele worshiper might see Pele herself walking through the molten lava, presumably a result of self-delusion.

Fabrication is naturally of great importance to ethnohistorians, since recognizing it is crucial to their research, and examples of fabrication are many. Samuel de Champlain, for example, wandered away from his party and was lost north of Lake Ontario for four days in 1615. In explaining how this occurred, he wrote: "I lost my way in the woods, having followed a certain bird that seemed to me peculiar. It had a beak like a parrot, and was of the size of a hen. It was entirely yellow, except the head which was red, and the wings which were blue, and it flew by intervals like a partridge. The desire to kill it [to examine it more closely] led me to pursue it from tree to tree for a very long time, until it flew away" (Champlain 1907:299). No bird of this description exists today in the region, and it is doubtful that any ever did, but Champlain probably felt the need to produce such a lure to explain how a seasoned explorer became so thoroughly lost.

An author can also fabricate within a description without any conscious intent to delude the reader. When André Thevet, a sixteenth-century French geographer, described the death and mutilation of Jean Ribaud, a French captain, at the hands of the Spanish, he wrote that "his face with his beard, which was very long, his eyes, nose, and ears they cut off when he was dead and sent them all to the Isles of Peru to exhibit them" (1986:152). Thevet almost certainly was wrong about the Spaniards mutilating Ribaud's body (Lowery 1911:425–429; Thevet 1986:152 n. 55), but he probably believed this was true, since it fit a common French stereotype of Spanish military behavior. Even with no evidence to support a belief, an author who is convinced that something is true may include it in a description; the author may not see this as lying, but merely as filling in a gap in the evidence.

Selection, emphasis, transformation, and fabrication modify the information presented in a description, further distancing it from reality. The factors that can produce this modification are many, and some have been introduced in the examples above. Taken as a category, those characteristics that reside in the describer's mind and affect description we define as a *mind-set,* and they include the following:

— Knowledge of language and nonverbal communication systems to permit the understanding of communication
— Linguistic categories and structures that encourage certain modes of thought, which in turn condition the way an event is perceived

—Cultural knowledge that permits the understanding of persons' actions and their significance in cultural context

—Expectations and prejudices conditioned by culture, experience, and personality, including stereotypes

—Vested interests that may promote prevarication

—An author's ability to express a description in written form

These factors span the entire process of perceiving an event, conceptualizing it, and creating its description. Mind-set bears some similarity to worldview, a long-established term, but differs in a crucial sense: "worldview" often is used to refer to a view of the world that is more or less shared by the members of a community or society, whereas "mind-set" is designed to refer to an individual's personal set of characteristics. The relationship between mind-set and worldview, therefore, is analogous to the relationship between personality and culture.

In addition, failures of the senses—conditions making it impossible for the observer to properly receive stimuli—can further distort the picture produced in a description. A near-sighted or blind person cannot be expected to see distant scenes well, and even a person's stature can affect ability to see events if there are intervening obstacles.

A classic example of the effect of mind-set on description comes from the reports of anatomically fantastic people in the early years of Europe's exploration in sub-Saharan Africa, the lands bordering the Indian Ocean, and the Americas. In the fifteenth and early sixteenth centuries, European travelers reported seeing or hearing of various bizarre forms of humanity, including dog-faced people, people whose heads were below their shoulders (with facial features in their chests), and the sciopods ("umbrella-footed people"), a race with a single spatulate foot that was held over one's head when seated, as a parasol. In 1499, for example, Sir John Mandeville (1964:105) described several of these human forms, including the sciopods, whom he located in Ethiopia and—on the basis of his wording —whom he may have observed for himself. The most interesting feature of these reports is not that they are so odd, but rather that they mirror descriptions of fantastic races discussed by Herodotus in the fifth century B.C., revived by Pliny in the second century A.D., and preserved by a variety of medieval European writers. Sciopods and other monstrous races were a part of the European worldview at the time of the voyages of exploration, and they became part of individuals' mind-sets, resulting in their inclusion in accounts of those voyages: what was expected was realized. Grafton (1992) explores in depth the impact of European worldview (and, by extension, mind-set) on their perceptions of new lands and peoples encountered during these voyages.

While the effects of reality mediation may be quite visible and recognizable in a document, we doubt that it is possible to determine whether the distortion was purposeful or inadvertent. As we see it, the characteristics of mediation, regardless of whether the author was consciously trying to deceive or was deceived by his or her own mind-set, will be similar. For those who wish to indict authors they believe have been deceitful, we suggest that convincing arguments will be rare.

The core of the reality-mediation model, in summary, is that various personal and cultural factors make it impossible for any observer to perfectly capture reality in a description. Every description, rather, is the result of the interaction between reality and the author's mind-set.

One way to visualize the effects of reality mediation is through various physical metaphors. We can think of an object (reality) being rendered as a photograph (description), with a filter (mind-set) between the object and the photographic film selectively screening out some of the light that otherwise would register on the film; this metaphor emphasizes the exclusionary function of the mind-set, pointing out the effects of selection and emphasis in mediation. We also can think of a buffet (reality) from which the author chooses items to fill a tray (description) based on the author's diet, hunger, preferences, and values (mind-set); this metaphor also highlights the selection and emphasis effects. Alternatively, we can conceive of an object (reality) producing a reflection (description) in a mirror with imperfections (mind-set); this metaphor emphasizes the transformation effect that can creep into description without the knowledge or will of the author. Finally, we can envision an artist who paints a convincing foreign landscape (description) from imagination (mind-set) while seeing only local urban squalor (reality) from the studio window; this metaphor emphasizes the fabricative effect of mediation. None of these metaphors conveys the totality of the reality-mediation model, but each communicates a portion of our vision of it.

Goals and Deconstruction

The reality-mediation model suggests the inadequacy of the ingenuous assumption that documents simply report the truth and can be straightforwardly mined for facts. Rather, it presents an image of documents as stews in which reality, authorial mind-sets, and audiences' expectations swirl about, intimately mixed and blended with one another. This section discusses how to separate these different components.

Content-Oriented and Source-Oriented Goals of Analysis

In a sense, we can see a document as a stretch of sand, its surface blown smooth by the wind. On this sand are the traces of two who have passed by: reality and the author's mind-set. The clumsy tracker might confuse the two or think that all the tracks were from a single creature. The skilled tracker, however, can analyze the tracks, factoring out those from each source.

Similarly, the ethnohistorian can look at a document in two profoundly different ways. In one case, the ethnohistorian is seeking to understand something more about reality and is trying to focus on evidence relevant to this goal; we call this the *content-oriented goal*. This is contrasted with the *source-oriented goal*, where the ethnohistorian is primarily interested in understanding more about the author and the author's mind-set.

Consider, for example, the following quotation from an oral account given in the 1930s by Arnold Gragson, a freed American slave, recalling slavery days: "I was born on a plantation that b'longed to Mr. Jack Tabb, in Mason County, just across the river, in Kentucky. Mr. Tabb was a pretty good man. He used to beat us, sure, but not nearly so much as the others did, some of his own kin people, even" (quoted in Mellon 1988:263). Ostensibly this account is telling us about Jack Tabb, and it certainly does so. We learn that Tabb owned a plantation and slaves, and we learn that he beat his slaves less than most owners. But it also tells us a great deal about Arnold Gragson. The fact of placing "Mr." before Tabb's name (when no one else in Gragson's account warrants a title), the acceptance of beating as a background phenomenon to be expected even of "a pretty good man," the studied avoidance of using any term that might legitimize the claim of ownership by the slave masters — these points paint a vivid picture of the author and his mind-set.

Just as the Gragson account can be studied with either the content-oriented goal or the source-oriented goal in mind, so can any document. Both goals are time-honored and valuable purposes of ethnohistory, and this text will discuss them throughout.

Deconstruction

The first step in pursuing the source-oriented goal of analyzing a document is recognizing that an author's mind-set can produce significant effects in that document. Used in its broadest sense, *deconstruction* refers to the process of identifying the conscious choices and unconscious consequences of the author's mind-set that help shape a document or other account. Unfortunately, the euphonious sound of this term has inspired scholars of various persuasions to define "deconstruction" in widely divergent ways and to quarrel vociferously with one another over which definition is proper. Following the broad sense used here, deconstruction has been a part of scholarly activity for centuries, although its formal definition and detailed examination began in the mid-twentieth century.

For some scholars, deconstruction is an end in itself. By their reasoning, the effects of mind-set are so overwhelming that there is no reality reflected in a passage; consequently, readers can assign any number of meanings to it. According to Leitch, "most texts can be made to generate an almost infinite set of refined statements about meaning . . . meaning is belated production" (1983:58). From this viewpoint, the author takes on an almost passive role, while the reader is the active agent creating meaning in a passage. If a text can be read so many ways by different readers, its reflection of reality becomes (at best) suspect, and a sensible scholar will shift attention to the more dominant — and presumably more important — enterprise of disentangling the intentions of the author and the unintended consequences of the author's mental state. To these scholars, deconstruction thus becomes the only reasonable purpose for examining a passage.

Other deconstructionists, however, have a less pessimistic view of how much reality is reflected in a passage. For them, the effects of mind-set are significant but not necessarily overwhelming. Consequently, they advocate using deconstruction for mixed purposes — sometimes as an end in itself, and sometimes as a means to factor out authorial effects, leaving a residue of description that has some basis in reality. It is to this latter tradition that we align ourselves.

Deconstruction, then, can become a powerful tool in evaluating descriptions presented in documents. By working backward simultaneously from the document and from what is known of its author, the deconstructionist can draw tentative conclusions about the author's viewpoints, biases, knowledge, and motives: these often are known as *subtexts*. Thoughtfully carried out, deconstruction can provide a portrait of an author to guide the evaluation of a description he or she has provided.

As with most powerful tools, however, there is potential for abuse. Used less carefully, deconstruction can be little more than an excuse to impugn an author, attributing any manner of nasty motives or attitudes with little or no justification. A self-indulgent deconstructionist can carry out character assassination in the name of "reading the text." Self-restraint and scrupulous attention to a balanced and fair reading of the evidence are the protections against such abuses.

The Intellectual Heritage of the Reality-Mediation Model

The previous discussion has gone into considerable detail to paint a picture of how we believe documents and oral accounts are shaped. These categories constitute the majority of historical evidence in most scholarship, and we believe that their importance justifies the detail of the discussion. We have endeavored to produce a consistent and systematic model, devising several terms in the process. The danger in all this is that we might (falsely) convey the impression that we have invented these ideas or written about them for the first time.

Let us be very clear: the reality-mediation model does not comprise new concepts in ethnohistory. Some substantive studies, such as those by Neumann (1991) and Trouillot (1996), are based on implicit assumptions that are quite similar to those of the reality-mediation model. The ideas and relationships in the reality-mediation model are mostly ones that are current in history, ethnohistory, and the various historical disciplines. We have merely systematized these ideas (elaborating on them a bit), presented them in an integrated manner, and drawn attention to their consequences.

Historians and ethnohistorians have not been very forthcoming in constructing models of their disciplines, evidence, and activities. We have found no other model that covers the ground of the reality-mediation model, although the treatments by C. Behan McCullagh (1984), Michael Stanford (1986), and Patricia Galloway (1991) deserve mention.

McCullagh, a philosopher of history, is concerned with how historians can hope to construct rationally justified interpretations of history, recognizing the inherent flaws in the factual data on which those interpretations are based. He founds his discussion on empiricist assumptions similar to ours: there is a reality, and there are methods that can produce reasonable probabilities of recognizing it. From there, he expands on modes of inference regarding the truth of a historical description. He directs some discussion to the roles of bias and an author's linguistic usages, but the main thrust is toward a philosophical understanding of the logical strategies that historians use in their research. In this sense, McCullagh's work covers some of the same ground as the reality-mediation model, but from the opposite direction. McCullagh's discussion focuses on historians and their activities as the central issue, with the authors of primary sources only of secondary interest. The reality-mediation model, in contrast, focuses on the authors of primary sources and the process of description, relegating scholars to a secondary position.

Stanford, also a philosopher of history, sketches out what he considers the "structures" of historical activity. These structures are relationships between elements that have effects on the structure of the whole. In history they include structures that characterize the events that took place in the past, as well as the processes whereby those events are translated into historical evidence and the evidence is subsequently interpreted by the historian. In a sense, the reality-mediation model is a depiction of the structure of the translation between events and evidence. Stanford aimed to present the broad view of history in abstract, leaving it to others to explore narrower issues in greater detail (1986:190).

Galloway couches her conception of the relationship between ethnohistoric data and reality in terms of "text formation processes." These comprise all the processes that shape ethnohistoric data and are analogous to the "site formation processes" that Michael Schiffer (1987) defined and discussed for the formation of the archaeological record. Galloway (1991: 457–467) carries the analogy further and refers to "excavating" a text by inferring the formation processes that have shaped it. Her basic conception is very similar to the reality-mediation model, but it has not been elaborated in such detail.

Our version of the reality-mediation model has taken advantage of various writings that have come before it. It has been shaped in particular by various streams of contemporary thought, some in history and some outside. The basic conceptualization of the process that produces a document as a form of communication comes from information theory, where such a process often is modeled as a channel along which information travels. As the information moves along, some is lost, noise is introduced, and other modifications in the information take place. The critical theorists of the Frankfurt School, the hermeneuticists (Heidegger 1977), and the deconstructionists (e.g., Foucault 1970; White 1978) also have made an impact with their insistence that all historical evidence is distorted communication, though we have rejected the conclusion that logically follows their reasoning: that all interpretations of a communication are potentially equally valid. Finally, we have incorporated ideas from critical historiography (e.g., Clark 1967), the branch of historical study that evaluates documents for shortcomings and misleading information. Critical historiography has come of age in the twentieth century and now is a part of virtually every historical endeavor. All of these streams of thought have come together in the reality-mediation model.

Methods

Introduction

Much of what sets ethnohistory apart from related fields is its methodology. It is therefore not surprising that part 2, which is devoted to methods, constitutes the bulk of this book. The methods discussed in this section cover a variety of topics that provide the ethnohistorian with necessary tools and approaches directed toward achieving interesting and reliable research results.

Chapter 3 discusses paleography, the decipherment of the various types of writing in documents. Decoding a document's written forms constitutes the most basic process in ethnohistoric research. Chapter 4 follows with a discussion of calendars, dates, and ways to convert from one calendric system to another. In chapter 5, the focus shifts to linguistic issues involved in reading and interpreting documents; especially important are matters of identifying changes in linguistic forms over time. Chapter 6 covers related issues in the interpretation of place-names and personal names. Ways of assessing the authenticity and credibility of documents are the subject of chapter 7 on source analysis. Since many ethnohistoric data are amenable to quantitative analysis, and statistical tools can reveal interesting ethnohistoric patterns, chapter 8 is devoted to various ways of quantifying information from documents. Chapters 9 and 10 treat the related issues of interpreting visual images and maps. Chapter 11 introduces and discusses the value of complementing documentary evidence with additional sources of information, especially oral accounts and archaeology. Each chapter in this section includes one or more substantive case studies. These studies, ranging from a source analysis of Tupinamba cannibalism to a linguistic analysis of Martin Frobisher's accounts, are designed to exemplify the generalizations that form the core ideas of each methodology chapter.

CHAPTER 3

Paleography

Webster's Third New International Dictionary defines *paleography* as ancient manners of writing and the identification and decipherment of ancient writings. Paleographic work, according to this definition, broadly encompasses the decipherment of all manner of writing systems that have been devised in human history. These include an enormous variety of expressive forms, from glyphic renderings of Egyptians and Mayans, to cuneiform tablets of Assyrians and Sumerians, word and syllabic writings of Chinese and Japanese, and an array of alphabetic systems of Phoenicians, Greeks, Romans, and many others. It also includes more recent printed and written documentation. As the printing press was busily turning out typeset books as early as the late fifteenth century in Europe (and movable type was in use earlier in Korea and China), handwriting continued everywhere to also produce a vast amount of documentation, from public records to private correspondence, from travelers' journals to epic poetry.

This chapter inquires into the nature of writing and how its various forms condition the information being related in a document or text. While reams could be (and have been) written on this topic, the overview presented here emphasizes writing conventions in general and covers relevant areas of technology, numbers, abbreviations, punctuation and spelling, standardization and variation in styles, and considerations in identifying an unknown author using paleographic clues. The chapter concludes with a case study of English paleography in India.

Writing, to varying degrees of accuracy and efficiency, may be called "visual language." There is considerable debate and disagreement among scholars on what might be truly considered "writing" or a "written system." Some (e.g., Gelb 1963) prefer to restrict "writing" to alphabetic systems alone, while others (e.g., Boone 1994; Hanks 1989) advocate a broader definition that would include pictorial imagery as well. We favor a broadly based notion of writing, since linguistic communication can be achieved via a wide range of systematically presented visual images and symbols (and their combinations). We also recognize that while alphabetic systems most closely parallel spoken language, even those systems only partially replicate the spoken word. Take, for example, the glottal-stop sound in English (as in "uh oh"), which has no specific corresponding alphabetic symbol, or homographs such as "bear" (as an animal or as an ability to withstand) or "entrance" (as an opening or as being spellbound). All writing systems leave out some linguistic information, with some just leaving out more than others. Pictographic writing, for instance, provides less linguistic information than does alphabetic writing. But the difference is more one of degree than of kind.

Several different types of writing can be usefully distinguished. Pictographic writing relies largely on understandable sequences of pictographs (alternatively called pictograms). These are images that quite directly signify the object depicted: a picture of a deer means "deer," that of the sun, "sun," that of a canoe, "canoe." This seems fairly straightforward; however, identifying pictographs typically requires considerable additional knowledge (by the contemporary reader and writer, as well as by the modern scholar). Pictographs often served as mnemonic devices, or memory joggers, which the well-informed reader could understand, and the scribe or artist was readily able to supply, but this supplementary information is usually lost to the modern researcher. Related to this, pictographs were frequently highly stylized. It might not be readily obvious that the Aztec pictograph of a cave indeed signifies a cave (fig. 1); it may help to know that caves were sacred entrances to the underworld and more than mere geologic formations, and that there was a stylistic canon for representing them (Berdan 1992). Similarly, Egyptian hieroglyphs stylized the sun as a circle-and-dot (fig. 2a) and water as a squiggle (fig. 2b) (Zauzich 1992). The style and arrangement of pictorial images typically were also subject to aesthetic considerations and constraints. Egyptian hieroglyphs saw glyphic clusters (words) as correct and proper only when neatly arranged into rectangles, even when it required a rearrangement in the order of elements within a word.

In general, pictographs are not generally linked to the linguistic form of the thing being represented: pictures represent objects in the real world, not the linguistic names given to those objects. Yet, to confuse the translation enterprise, systems that are essentially pictographic may also contain ideographic and phonetic elements, pictorially represented. Ideographs are somewhat more abstract than pictographs, using the picture to represent an associated concept or selecting a notable attribute of the object to represent the whole item. Thus an ideograph of the sun may

Figure 1. Aztec glyph of a cave, from the sixteenth-century *Codex Mendoza*. The circular object on top of the stylized cave is a ball of thread. Together the two elements yield the place-name "Oztoticpac." (Reprinted, by permission, from Berdan and Anawalt 1992, 4: folio 10v)

represent not just itself but also "heat," "light," or "day." A rabbit may denote "timidity," and a footprint "travel" or "journey." In denoting parts for the whole, boots and spurs might symbolize "cowboy," a mortar and pestle might indicate an "apothecary," and the foot of a deer might signify "fleetness." Pictorial images may also contain phonetic elements (meaningful sounds) relating specific sounds to specific symbols. These same symbols may serve as pictographs and/or ideographs, as in many Egyptian hieroglyphs. So an oval (fig. 2c) could mean mouth, speech, or the sound represented in English by the letter "r"; a "seven-shaped curve" (fig. 2d) could denote a folded cloth or /s/; and so on. Similarly, the Aztec glyph for water (*atl*) could mean the liquid itself or the sound /a/. Or a footprint could mean a foot, a journey (and its path), the direction in reading, or the sound /o/ (for *ohtli* [road]). Pictorial systems containing phonetic elements do not phonetically represent all the sounds of the language pictorially. For instance, Egyptian hieroglyphs contained phonetic signs for consonants; Aztec glyphs used pictographic symbols for a few vowels. As with pictographs and ideographs, there is considerable missing information expected to be known and supplied by the reader's cultural knowledge.

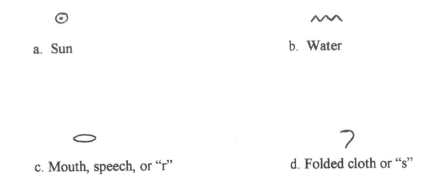

a. Sun

b. Water

c. Mouth, speech, or "r"

d. Folded cloth or "s"

Figure 2. Some Egyptian hieroglyphs.

It should be quite obvious that translating pictorial writing is not as straightforward as it might at first seem. Interpreting logographic (word-sign) writing entails somewhat different problems. In logographic writing, the linguistic name of the object or concept is more important than its pictorial representation (although things in the real world may indeed serve as these symbols). Written symbols are therefore more abstract than in pictographic writing. Chinese and Mayan are good examples of this type of writing. Word-writing systems can encompass the full expression of the concrete to the abstract, without leaving informational gaps (as with pictographic writing). However, a large number of symbols must be learned: written Chinese contains approximately 60,000 characters (Mair 1992), although a grasp of about 5,000 is sufficient for everyday literacy. As with pictographic writing, cultural assumptions are often embedded in these symbols. For instance, in Chinese the symbol for "one woman under roof" actually denotes "peace," while "two women" means "quarrel" and the symbol for "three women" indicates "adultery."

It is usual for logographic systems to also contain phonetic elements, especially in the form of syllable-signs. Syllabic writing ties the written symbols more directly to the spoken language itself. Mayan glyphs, for example, may display a logograph along with a syllabic component (such as when the glyph for hill [*wits*] appears attached to the symbol for the syllable *wi*). One additional complication in Mayan writing is the substitution of equivalent forms — any one logograph or syllable may have several forms, and these may be used in a variety of combinations (Stuart 1994).

Some writing systems rely exclusively, or nearly so, on syllable-signs. The famous Cherokee syllabary, developed by Sequoyah (George Guess) in 1821, contains 86 symbols matching the syllabic arrangements in that language. Elsewhere, in the eastern Mediterranean world, during the last couple of millennia B.C., pictorial writing developed into largely syllabic writing expressed in abstract cuneiform symbols (reducing the number of necessary signs from about 2,000 to 600). A further reduction in the number of symbols became possible with the advent of alphabetic writing, in which one symbol ideally represents one discrete sound.

Alphabetic systems probably emerged around 1000 B.C. at Phoenician Byblos (the town's name meaning "rolled book," from which come *Bible, bibliography,* and related words). The alphabetic concept spread rapidly both east through southwestern Asia and west through Europe and northern Africa. Adopted and adapted by Greeks, Romans, Arabs, and successive groups, alphabetic writing became a common medium of communication in those regions. Because studies in ethnohistory frequently rely on European sources from the fifteenth to nineteenth centuries, scholars often derive a good deal of their material from the many and diverse scripts of alphabetic writing.

A recent and particularly far-ranging summary of writing is Peter T. Daniels and William Bright's *The World's Writing Systems* (1995). Other good summaries of writing systems in general include Boone and Mignolo (1994), Gaur (1992), Jackson (1981), Jean (1987), and especially Martin (1994).

The Technology of Writing

Through history, writing has been executed on nearly every imaginable relatively flat surface. In Egypt, papyrus, cloth, stone, and wax tablets were popular media; in Mesopotamia, baked clay tablets and stone; in Greece, marble; in the Arab world, paper, parchment, and ceramic vessels; in India, birch bark, palm leaves, and copper; in Mesoamerica, tree bark, deerskin, and stone; in North America, animal skins, wood, and stone surfaces, as well as beadwork; in China and Turkey, silk; in Europe, parchment, vellum, and paper . . . the list goes on and on. Writing implements ranged from brushes of animal bristle or papyrus, reed sticks, styluses, engravers, quill pens, and so on (Jean 1987:158–159). Pens and brushes furthermore required inks of one sort or another, usually based on carbon combined with various other natural elements.

Different styles of writing were sensitive and responsive to these various combinations of media and instruments, each offering different possibilities and limitations. Papyrus, being relatively brittle, could be rolled but did not lend itself well to folding or binding; on the other hand, the more pliable parchment and vellum, made of soft animal skins, could be easily folded and arranged into bound books. Parchment surfaces, properly prepared, were smooth and even; paired with the quill pen, more refined lines could be produced than with a reed pen or brush on the rougher papyrus. As another example, the Sumerians, Babylonians, and their neighbors impressed wedge-shaped styluses into moist clay tablets to form messages in cuneiform script. The technology is of considerable significance in this case, because the narrow wedge shape of the impression is very uniform and unlikely to produce, for example, a wide range of pictographic images. These symbols therefore display a level of abstraction and conventionalization greater than that of their pictorial ancestors. Roman monuments, overwhelming their viewers with the glories of imperial achievements, frequently rose well above eye level, requiring the incision of very large and deeply cut letters into the stone. These large, square capital letters contrasted noticeably with the more cursive script used by Romans for more informal documents (such as personal correspondence) and usually executed on wax tablets.

Other factors could impinge on the use of various media. As an example, some materials, such as vellum, were so expensive in medieval Europe that they were sometimes scraped clean and reused, thus denying the modern scholar access to a good deal of written documentation. In a similar vein, economic concerns of supply and demand surrounded medieval and Renaissance papermaking in Europe. Prior to the widespread use of the printing press, paper was so expensive that, for the most part, only the best-endowed monasteries could afford it, and access to it was severely limited by its price. Later, when the popularity of the printing press created an immense demand for paper, sufficient quantities were not readily available. In England, for instance, demand for linen and cotton rags for papermaking so far outstripped supply that the 1666 Parliament decreed that only wool was to be used for burying the dead, thus saving the other materials for the printing press (Nickell 1990:75).

Seemingly subtle variations in writing instruments could yield markedly different results in individual writing efforts. For instance, goosequill pens extracted from the bird's left wing were preferred by right-handed writers, while left-handers preferred those from the right wing. The curvature of the quill was a factor in this selection; an inappropriate quill choice could result in awkward and uncomfortable writing. Quills also had to be frequently and repeatedly sharpened; consequently, the quality of the penknife and the dexterity of the knife wielder had a great deal to do with the appearance of the written word. In addition, "ragged and feeble" letters would result from a quill improperly cleaned (Nickell 1990:8). Quills also ran out of ink frequently, sometimes requiring the writer to lift the pen from the page at an inconvenient scriptorial moment. Antedating the quill pen, Greek split-reed pens had the rather annoying habit of flooding ink onto a horizontal writing surface, requiring the scribe to innovate with a tilted surface.

Similarly, different inks yielded different results. A simple carbon-and-gum ink was subject to easy erasure by rubbing or washing: an advantage if the writer was prone to mistakes, but a disadvantage if the document was intended to have a long life. Many different and creative recipes for devising inks were developed over the centuries: some penetrated deeply into paper and bled through; some required coloring agents to enhance their intensity; others oxidized over time and turned from black to an anemic brown. Medieval European and Arabic illuminated manuscripts contained a rainbow of colors to enhance the books' sometimes sacred value and visual beauty. Some of these colors were difficult to control and posed serious problems for the illuminators. Verdigris (a green color) had the tendency to corrode parchment; blue azurite was often gritty; and earth colors tended to thicken in the brush or pen.

These examples suggest that materials (whether surface, implement, or ink) applied to the enterprise of writing could at times affect the nature, form, and actual execution of written symbols. These media therefore need to be taken into consideration in the study of any primary document (see Martin 1994). Writing technology is discussed further in chapter 7 in the context of source analysis.

Some Considerations in Paleographic Interpretation

Writing styles tend to follow defined patterns through time and space, and they conform to some extent to a writer's intentions in producing a document. Many styles can be usefully characterized according to their emphasis on particular, defined forms. For instance, majuscule writing, where all letters are of similar height (all uppercase) can be distinguished from minuscule writing, corresponding to the modern use of lowercase letters. In the history of European scripts, majuscules generally preceded uncials (rounded characters), which served as the predominant book script until the ninth century A.D., when uncials were replaced by the more cursive minuscules. Cursive writing, where letters are linked (often by a rapidly moving pen), can be distinguished from more deliberately executed calligraphy. Cursive or calligraphic styles may use ligatures, which are conjoined letters, or at least adjoining letters that touch at some point. Secretarial hands differed from vernacular ones, the former being elaborate and designed for formal purposes, while the latter tended to be dashed off more hastily and intended for more informal ends; understandably, secretarial hands tend to be more standardized, and vernacular hands tend to exhibit more idiosyncratic variation.

Volumes have been written on the details of paleographic decipherment (see appendix A for a selective bibliography). Most pertain to specific languages, times, places, or orthographic styles, and no attempt is made here to go into such depth. Instead, some selected matters are highlighted that can provide a basic groundwork for paleographic undertakings. These considerations are numbers; abbreviations; spelling and punctuation; standardization and variation in expression; and the use of tables, indexes, and alphabetization. For expository purposes, the emphasis in this chapter is on texts written in English.

Designating Numbers

Documents frequently contain numbers, whether they appear in the context of dates, tax or tribute records, commercial or merchandizing accounts, duration of a journey, casualties on a battlefield, consumption at a feast, quantities of ingredients in a recipe . . . the possibilities are almost endless. Written systems typically have specialized symbols for numbers, and number symbols take many forms in the world's writing systems. Pictographic systems may employ a selection of pictorial symbols (such as a banner for "20" and a priestly bag for "8000" in Aztec), vertical lines (each meaning "1" among the North American Dakota Sioux), or the bar ("5") and dot ("1") arrangements in Mayan writing.

Tally sticks (where units were simply notched on a special piece of wood or bone) were widespread in Europe, Asia, the Pacific, and elsewhere. The concept is the same as that used by the Hollywood frontier gunslinger, tallying his victims by notching the stock of his gun. Similar to tally sticks is the widespread use of knots in numeration. Among the most notable examples are the knotted-and-fringed strands made from straw or reeds by the Ryukyu Islanders (in the northern Pacific Ocean) and the knotted cords, or *quipu,* used by the Inca of Peru. Less well known but following the same concept, German millers in the early twentieth century indicated quantities of meal or flour by the shape of the knot tying the sack.

Most ethnohistoric documentation originating in western Europe employed Roman or Arabic numerals, or combinations of the two systems. Roman numerals predominated in the centuries before A.D 1500, after which Arabic numerals came increasingly into use. The popularity of Arabic numbers was no doubt related to their greater computational ease.

Roman numerals were written as capitals (I, V, X, L, C, D, M) or in lowercase cursive form (i or j, v, x, l, c, d, m). A "j" was usually substituted for "i" when alone or at the end of a number (thus making falsification of a number rather difficult). The arrangements of digits within a number could take different forms. For instance, "4" could be written as "iv" or "iiij," "400" as "CCCC" or "CV" or "iv^c." Superscripts were popular in denoting large numbers: thus "3,000" could appear as "iii^m," and 60 (3 $\times$ 20) as "ii^{x}j^x." (The year "1998" could be written as "j^{m}ix^{c}iii^{x}j^x xviii.") The rules were flexible and much seems to have been left up to the discretion of the writer, who could choose to write "251" as either "ijClj" or "CC.i^{x}j^x.xj" (Tannenbaum 1967:154); both were acceptable and understandable.

Ordinal numbers were expressed with superscripts of "do" (for secundo), "o" (for primo, tercio), "to," "no," "th" (or its alternative "tie"), and so on. For numbers above 20, the superscript was a "th," indicating that 22, for instance, should be read as "two and twentieth" (not "twenty-twoth") (Tannenbaum 1967:154).

In the transitional European sixteenth century, a seemingly ruleless meshing of Roman and Arabic numerals was common, and the combining of both systems still occurred as recently as the nineteenth century. These combinations took a variety of forms: the number "14" could appear as "x4," "202" as "CC2," "1504" as "I.5.IIII," "1482" as "M.CCCC.8II," "1515" as "I5X5," and so on (Menninger 1992:287). Such mixes should be expected in European documents from the sixteenth to nineteenth centuries. Other arrangements also occurred: sometimes a date would be written in Arabic numerals, and its attached monetary account in Roman numbers (Menninger 1992:287).

The Arabic numerals themselves appear in several variable forms. At times a 1 was hooked (fig. 3a) so as to look disarmingly like a "2"; some writers finished off their "2" with a horizontal rather than vertical stroke (so it resembled a "1," "3," or "7"); the number "4" could be taken for a "9" (when written as in figure 3b); "5" often looked like a "9," "4," "h," or "q"; "6" resembled "G"; "7" took on the appearance of the letter "a" or the numbers "1" or "2"; "8" could be mistaken for "9" or "g"; and "9" resembled "g," "q," "y," "2," or "8" (Tannenbaum 1967:155–157). The caution conveyed here is simply that great care should be taken in transcribing and interpreting numbers, for they may not always be what they at first appear.

Abbreviations

In Europe at the end of the medieval period, writing passed out of the scholarly monasteries and fell more and more into secular hands. Beauty as a paramount goal in writing (as in calligraphy, where Greek *kallos* means "beauty") generally became replaced by the need for speed. This led to the rise of cursive and vernacular hands; it also made the abbreviation of oft-repeated letters and letter sequences a handy efficiency device.

Some abbreviations were very common and highly conventionalized across western Europe, whether executed, for instance, in Spanish, French, or English. This in many cases reflects a Latin ancestry (Martin 1949). While some abbreviations are highly idiosyncratic, most followed standardized rules and can be described by just a few categories: contraction, elision, and brevigraphs (adapted from Tannenbaum 1967).

Contraction was extremely common and involved the deletion of one or more letters in a word. Examples of contraction include "Mr." for "Master" and "Mrs." for "Mistress." Usually a period, colon, horizontal stroke above the abbreviated word, or vertical line through the final letter called attention to its contracted form. Often a word's final letter(s) were subject to deletion, as with "yond" for "yonder." Sometimes a horizontal bar or vertical tick can be confused with a writer's momentary exuberant flourish or simply an ink blot. Nasals (m and n) were frequent omissions (wherever they were found in a word) and were usually marked by a horizontal bar as in "womē" for "women" and "dañ" for "damn."

Elision involves the merging of letters of adjacent words. This often occurred with "the" when the following word began with a vowel (yielding, for instance, "thaction" for "the action" or "thandes" for "the handes" [Tannenbaum 1967:121]). At times an apostrophe would mark the elision, although the apostrophe might not always appear where expected (as in "tho'nely" for "the only"). Other letters occasionally lost were "k" ("taken" becomes "ta'en"), "v" ("over" becomes "oer"), "d" ("needle" becomes "neele"), and intervocalic "th" ("father" becomes "fa'er," and "whether" becomes "where"!) (Tannenbaum 1967:122–123). Sometimes a small word or words would be absorbed by larger preceding ones: the

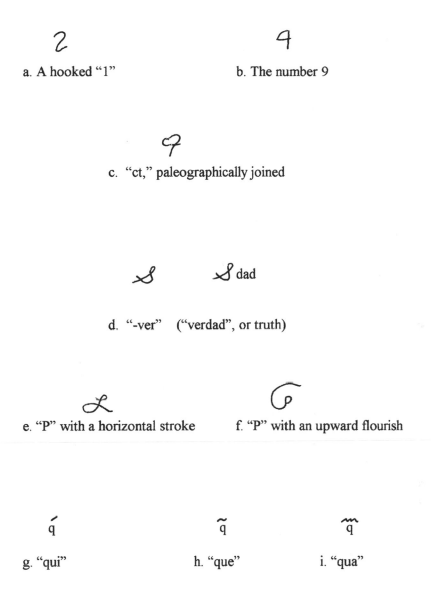

a. A hooked "1" b. The number 9

c. "ct," paleographically joined

$\mathcal{S}$ dad

d. "-ver" ("verdad", or truth)

e. "P" with a horizontal stroke f. "P" with an upward flourish

g. "qui" h. "que" i. "qua"

Figure 3. Some European paleographic conventions (a–c: English; d–i: Spanish).

transcriber must be alert that a simple word like "but" could as well mean "but it," "but to," or "but the" (Tannenbaum 1967:124). With elision, words that may appear easily recognizable may have quite different meanings.

Brevigraphs are symbols that stand for a variety of common abbreviations. In Spanish, syllables that end in -er (as in -ver, -ber, and so on) were frequently written without the -er, substituting instead a flourish around the surviving letter (see fig. 3d). Some care must be exercised in interpreting these symbols, as the same flourish could as well indicate "ar," "or," "ur," or similar syllables. This was particularly common with such syllables beginning with "p" (as in "per," "par," and "por"). Here the omitted letters were usually indicated by a horizontal stroke or upward flourish (as in figures 3e and 3f). While there were a great many brevigraphs, an especially common one involved "q." This set of brevigraphs (fig. 3g–i) is of interest because it actually distinguishes among "qui," "que," and "qua."

Other widespread conventions, while not exactly abbreviations, do offer challenges to the transcriber. For instance, a habit of joining letters with an added stroke can obscure a letter's form (making "ct" appear as in figure 3c, which also resembles an "a"). The practice of melding certain letters together (such as ae: æ) was sufficiently popular to find its way onto the printing press. While many dots, tittles, bars, and flourishes represented standardized and well-known abbreviations, some were mere marks of enthusiasm or clumsiness on the part of the writer. Most of these idiosyncracies can be recognized by closely examining patterns in the writer's personal style.

English writing over the last few centuries has embraced abbreviations with relish. Consequently, documents in English are peppered with abbreviations, particularly for first names, titles, and frequently used legal words. While there were common patterns of abbreviation, there was a great deal of individual variation. Usually an abbreviation consisted of the first two or three letters of the word and the last letter, but sometimes it would be just the first few letters of the word. Occasionally a nickname would be used as an abbreviation. While letter combinations usually were rendered as in the original, "Ch" rarely was written as "X," drawing on the Greek letter *chi*, which is pronounced like the English "ch" but resembles an "X" in form. Sometimes a horizontal bar would be drawn over the last letter or letters; sometimes the last letter of the word would appear raised above the writing line as a superscript; sometimes a period would appear after the abbreviation; and Quakers frequently used a colon after an abbreviation. Sometimes there would be no indication at all that a word was an abbreviation, and the reader would be expected to figure it out from

Table 1. Some Common English Abbreviations

Abbreviation	Meaning
Edw	Edward
Benj	Benjamin
Abra	Abraham
Eliz	Elizabeth
Jos	Joseph
Fran	Francis
Thos	Thomas
Thos	Thomas
Jas	James
Jim	James
Chas	Charles
Reb^a	Rebecca
Saml	Samuel
And^w	Andrew
dec^d	deceased
sev^t	servant
s^d	said (as in, "of the said party")
Comm^{tee}	Committee
s s	supra scriptum ("as written above")
Mr	mister
Messrs	misters
Mrs	mistress
Dr	doctor

context and experience. Examples of a few common abbreviations and their meanings are given in table 1.

Any of these abbreviations (except the superscript endings) could appear with a line over the last letter or letters, a terminal period, or a terminal colon. Alternatively, they could be rendered with the superscript ending. All of the following forms, for example, could indicate "Rebecca": Reba, Reb^a, Rebā, Reba., Reba:. To further complicate matters, the same structural variants could be made on a different set of letters, perhaps "Reb" or "Rebca."

One common English usage in both handwriting and typeset printing was the runic thorn (Norse superscript y), a letter that resembles "y" and in the fifteenth century was merged with it. Subsequent to that time "y" was used as an abbreviation for "th." In its earlier forms, the "y" was raised above the line of letters, but in later forms it was on the same line or the letters that followed it were raised instead. Consequently, all of the following forms were equivalent to "the": ye, yᵉ, and ʸe. Other words could have the Norse superscript "y" used to replace "the," as with "yese," "yose," "yem," "yee," and "yat." (The "ye" as in "Ye Olde Shoppe" is merely an orthographic variant of "the," commonly mispronounced now as "ye.") The Norse superscript "y" typically was used with simple and commonly occurring words, such as those listed above, but it rarely was used in longer words, as "yespian" for "thespian." Occasionally the Norse superscript "y" was combined with abbreviations to produce complicated renderings, as "yᵗ" for "that."

Sometimes an abbreviation familiar to modern readers carried a different meaning in earlier times, as illustrated by the following example (Palmer 1985:36). Among English speakers in nineteenth-century North America, a single set or pair of double quotation marks in a financial record usually did not indicate "the same as directly above," as it would now. Instead, this notation typically meant "nothing to record at this date"; "do" (abbreviating "ditto") was typically used to indicate a repeat of the preceding entry. Misreading quotation marks obviously could result in a major miscalculation in such a financial ledger.

Spelling and Punctuation (and Related Matters)

Until the advent of Samuel Johnson's dictionary (first published in 1755 in England) and Noah Webster's similar effort in America (his speller was published in 1783, followed by his dictionary in 1806), English spelling was, to use their term, chaotic. This "chaos" was not peculiar to English, for fluid spelling was common throughout Europe (to the horror of the French Academy, which tried, and continues to try, desperately to standardize written French).

Spelling practices were not totally unpredictable, however, and variations tended to follow some readily discernable patterns. For instance, it was common for some letters to be substituted for one another, even by the same writer, in the same text or the same word. Popular variants were "v" and "u," "i" and "y," "i" and "e," "o" and "u." In another vein, it was not uncommon for consonants to be doubled, yielding, for example, "spinnage" for "spinach." The reader of ethnohistoric documents should not be surprised to encounter these sorts of variations.

Many other reasons also account for lack of uniformity in spelling. Consider the scholars of fifteenth- and sixteenth-century England who determined to reform English spelling by relating words to their Latin or

Greek ancestors (changing "indite" to "indict," "dette to debt," and "oure" to "hour"). Consider also how variant spellings reflected social gaps: in eighteenth-century England the aristocracy was sometimes spelling "certainly" as "sartinly" and "again" as "agane" (McCrum, Cran, and MacNeil 1986:133). It is always important to consider not only the time and place of a text, but also whatever can be discovered about the writer.

With the advent of the printing press in the fifteenth century, certain selected spellings of words became the "established norm" and tended to favor some dialects of the spoken language over others. When William Caxton, a merchant-entrepreneur, brought the printing press to England around 1476 and began printing existing works, he chose London English as his standard, resulting in spellings such as "right" (reflecting its pronunciation as "richt") (McCrum, Cran, and MacNeil 1986:86). This was an individual decision; combined with other printers' individual decisions, and the fact that many early printers of English works were Dutch and understood English as a second (or third) language, it is easy to see why even the printed word is confusing in English. In the United States, Noah Webster was himself responsible for many English spelling changes (e.g., color for colour, fiber for fibre) (McCrum, Cran, and MacNeil 1986:242). Despite attempts to standardize spellings, variations continue today. The term "archaeology," for instance, also can be seen as "archeology," being spelled differently by the U.S. federal government, other public agencies, academic institutions, and the media (SAA 1995a).

Punctuation in sixteenth- to nineteenth-century manuscripts was, to use Tannenbaum's words, "lawless and haphazard" (1967:139). While many marks were available to the reader, they were frequently omitted and often used inconsistently. The end of a sentence, for example, was occasionally marked by a period, but often by a comma, a slash (/), a semicolon, or nothing at all. Colons or periods also frequently indicated abbreviations. The end of a question might be marked with a question mark, but as well by a comma, period, colon, or slash. On the other hand, question marks often indicated an exclamation. One of the best ways to deal with the haphazard use of punctuation, as with spelling, is to meticulously study a given writer's manuscripts in a hopeful (and often fruitful) search for recognizable patterns.

As with punctuation, the seemingly erratic spacing between words often poses difficulties for modern transcription. In some cases, nonspacing was the rule, as with formal capital Roman inscriptions WHICHREAD-SOMETHINGLIKETHIS. In other cases, such as Renaissance handwriting of western Europe, words may be flawlessly divided, flow eloquently into one another, or have breaks in the middle of words. Furthermore, the end of a line did not always signal the end of a word, and any word might beg in on one line and end on the next (as in the previous line).

The rather fluid nature of spelling, punctuation, and spacing in ethnohistoric documents can make the transcription enterprise more than challenging. One little trick in surmounting these difficulties is simply to read the manuscript aloud, directly hearing the words to discern word and sentence boundaries and the meanings intended. This may also help you to recognize words that are spelled unusually or idiosyncratically.

Standardization and Variation

Complications of functional equivalents, substitutions, and variations exist in pictographic, logographic, syllabic, and alphabetic systems. Consider that the Aztec sound "pan" can be represented by either a flag or a footprint depending on aesthetic arrangements. Also consider alphabetic Arabic script, where each letter has four variations depending on its location: at the beginning of a word, between letters, at the end of a word, or standing alone.

And then there are the many different, and acceptable, ways of designing individual letters in alphabetic writings throughout the world. These are not idiosyncratic variations, but alternatives built into the writing system — alternatives that need to be taken into account when reading such documents. Handwritten letters of seventeenth- and eighteenth-century English, as it was written in the Americas, are a bit difficult to decipher for those familiar only with the modern versions of handwriting (Kirkham 1965). A few of the more common confusions are found in figure 4.

Many variations have already been discussed under topics of numbers, abbreviations, and spelling/punctuation. We have stressed the conventionalized nature of such variations, as well as the possibilities for idiosyncratic input. But it is worthwhile here to also consider aesthetics. A thin line is often drawn between writing and art for nonalphabetic systems, but alphabetic writing was (and is) also frequently presented as an art form. Arabic calligraphy, for instance, represented a sacred activity, not only straightforward communication.

In the Muslim world, "the goal in writing was not only the invention of letters and dots, but fundamentals, purity and virtue" (Rubin 1994:3). Some Arabic calligraphy was indeed applied to a variety of decorative motifs (such as horses or birds drawn using calligraphic symbols) — and

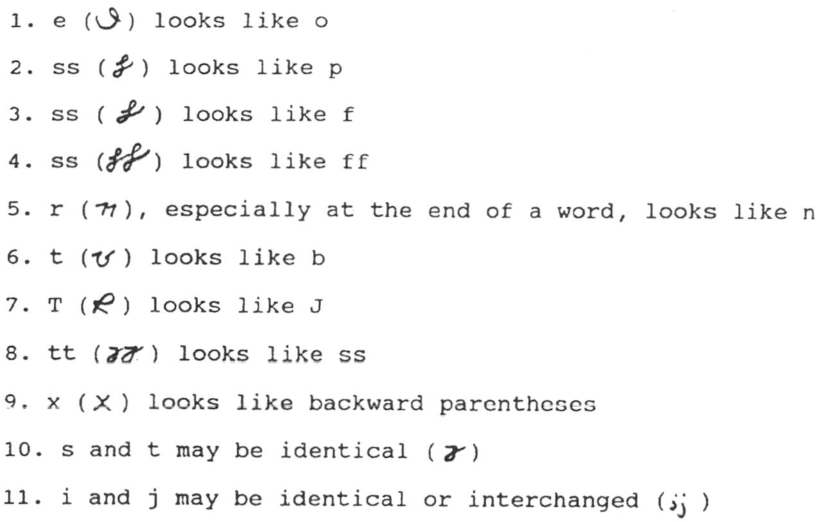

1. e (◌) looks like o

2. ss (◌) looks like p

3. ss (◌) looks like f

4. ss (◌) looks like ff

5. r (◌), especially at the end of a word, looks like n

6. t (◌) looks like b

7. T (◌) looks like J

8. tt (◌) looks like ss

9. x (X) looks like backward parentheses

10. s and t may be identical (◌)

11. i and j may be identical or interchanged (◌)

Figure 4. Some handwriting variations in seventeenth- and eighteenth-century English.

artistically enough to be almost disguised (to the uninitiated). Such disguise and unfamiliarity with Arabic were probably involved in the eighth-century King Offa of Mercia's (Britain) choice of a coin design: although stamped with his title "Offa Rex," the coin, probably selected for its attractiveness, nonetheless boldly stated in Arabic script that "Mohammed is the prophet of God" (Metcalf 1991; Dolley 1964).

Like Arabic calligraphy, European illuminated manuscripts were also considered sacred books, and great care was taken to make them as beautiful as possible. Some copyists, however, were more skilled than others, and some more dedicated. Some exhibited a sense of humor beyond that expected in the strict, regulated cloisters, as when a messy mistake was not hidden or corrected but rather highlighted with a laughing monk drawn in the margin, pointing accusingly at the error.

Regionalisms and specific linguistic interactions can yield discoverable patterns in writing. For instance, while English, French, Dutch, Spanish, and Italian all had slightly different writing systems, they were all based on Roman letters, and typeset printing in these languages was similar in eighteenth- and nineteenth-century America. German, however, at that time was rendered into Gothic letters, a variant on Roman, and the resulting handwriting differed considerably from that used in English. Many immigrants to the nineteenth-century Midwest were of German extraction and wrote German upon their arrival — and often for generations after. This experience sometimes affected their English writing, making a knowledge of German script useful in deciphering the English.

Aside from aesthetics and regional cultural patterns, many idiosyncratic factors come into play in understanding written documents. Perhaps one of the most individualized elements of handwriting is the autograph signature, which did not gain broad appeal in Europe until the fifteenth century. Prior to that time, seals (belonging not only to royalty but to commoners and corporate communities as well) served to validate and authenticate documents (Martin 1994:137–144). In the past it was expected that sophisticated men and women of the upper classes would design their signatures and practice writing them, and many people still do today. Novels depicting British public school life in the early nineteenth century abound with examples of students repeatedly writing their signatures to impress it into their motor habits. As a result, it is not uncommon for a signature on a document to differ quite markedly from the text, even though they were written by the same individual. Typically, if it differed from the text, the signature was more elaborate, stylish, and standardized. An illiterate individual might affix a sign, often a cross, as a name validation, surely indicating that another individual, as a proxy, had written the document at the signer's behest. If a *secretarial* (formal and official) signature was applied to the end of the document by the actual writer, that signature usually matches the handwriting of the document, but not other actual signatures of the named person.

Tables, Indexes, and Alphabetization

While tables and indexes are not strictly paleographic issues, they bear strongly on how an ethnohistorian can use documents. Beginning in the sixteenth century, European authors (or their publishers) began including various tabular aids to assist the reader in finding particular parts of a text. The most common forms of these aids were the table of contents and index.

The table of contents (often reduced to merely "the table") was a listing of the headings of a book, set in the sequence they followed in the text, sometimes with page numbers included. The table of contents most often was placed at the end of a book (as it is today in most of Europe), but it sometimes was placed at the beginning, especially in English-speaking countries. Chapter and other major headings would be included, but lower-level headings to sections within chapters might be excluded.

The index was a topical listing, giving pages where selected items or issues discussed within the text were mentioned. A thorough index would include topics that never appeared in the headings yet were treated in the content. Indexes came into common usage by Europeans in the seventeenth century, though most books still did not include them until well into the nineteenth century. When an index was included, it almost always was placed at the end.

While an index or table of contents sometimes can assist the ethnohistorian in finding the appropriate section of a book, they should be used with care. This is especially true when using old sources, particularly ones from before 1850. First, they typically are woefully incomplete prior to that date, often omitting major issues that consumed great portions of the writing. Even when an index is moderately complete, it might not include entries on the issues a reader is most interested in; alternatively, the entries may be there, but not in a form that the modern reader could easily recognize or might think to check. A mid-eighteenth-century cookbook, for example, might include liver and heart under the heading of "umbles." Second, using an index or table of contents can encourage the reader to examine only the pages singled out by it; simply plucking a fact from its context leaves the ethnohistorian unable to assess its probable accuracy, an issue discussed further in chapter 7.

A final point relates to indexes and any other lists that are purported to be in alphabetical order. These lists may not be in the sequence a modern user would expect. First, alphabetical conventions were slightly different in earlier times. For example, a vowel diphthong including "y" (e.g., "-oy-") in eighteenth-century English typically would be placed in its position as if it included an "i" (e.g., "-oi-"); thus "oysters" would appear in a list between "offal" and "old cheese." Also, in eighteenth-century English, "i" and "j" often were merged, so that a list might include "jam," "ice," "jelly," "jilliflower," and "isinglass" in that order. Second, not all writers had equal knowledge of the alphabetic sequence or were equally assiduous in its application. John Worlidge, for example, in his 1704 *Dictionarium Urbanicum et Rusticum* made three errors in alphabetizing eighty-four entries under "A" and five errors in eighty-seven entries under "T"; this extrapolates out to an error rate just under 5 percent. Many alphabetizers seem to have lost their way after they reached "t," especially in languages like French, where only foreign words begin with "w," and few words of any sort begin with letters after "v." In general, expect tables of contents and indexes to be imperfect aids. Use them only in recognition of their incompleteness, and be sure to check broadly for an alphabetic entry that may not be where expected. Finally, be wary of consulting a reference too narrowly, potentially losing the context in which a fact occurs.

Identifying an Unknown Author with Paleographic Clues

Just as an accent can help identify an unknown speaker, handwriting can point out characteristics of an unknown writer. Styles of writing have differed by nationality, period, education, class, and gender, and these styles are quite well known. Sometimes a distinctive style of handwriting can pinpoint characteristics of the writer of a document, suggesting one or another of the recognized candidates for authorship; even if it cannot indicate or eliminate known individuals, it often can provide information useful in evaluating the author.

The angular hand, for example, is a distinctive style of writing in use mostly between 1880 and 1920. It was taught exclusively in private girls' and women's schools and was perceived as a "feminine" script; men never were expected to learn the style, and it was never taught in public schools. Angular script was taught mostly in England and its possessions, though a few American schools also taught it (Osborn 1929). A document in angular script would identify the scribe almost certainly as a woman who was of school age between 1880 and 1920 and wealthy enough to have attended a private school, and who probably lived in Britain or its possessions (or less likely in the United States).

Forensic handwriting specialists have developed a corpus of works focusing on methods of interpreting handwriting to identify an unknown writer. Despite their primary focus on legal applications, these sources can be valuable to the ethnohistorian interested in handwriting as a clue to authorship. Though old, the classic work by Osborn (1929) is still useful; more recent works are by Smith (1984) and Hilton (1991). For comparing a sample of handwriting to the handwriting of a known writer, see Rendell (1994).

Case Study

SOME EXAMPLES OF ENGLISH
PALEOGRAPHY IN INDIA

The following pages provide three examples of seventeenth-century English handwriting in India (figs. 5, 6, and 7), along with their transcriptions into modern type and a discussion of paleographic conventions found in these examples. All are from *The Diary of William Hedges, Esq.* (Hedges 1964). Hedges was assigned as an agent of the East India Company in Bengal and entrusted with those commercial duties from his arrival in Bengal in 1682 until his departure late in 1684. His journey home to England took more than two years and extended his diary entries into 1687 (Barlow, in Hedges 1964, 1:4–5).

A number of letters related to Hedges's commission are included in the three-volume publication of his diary: three such letters constitute our examples here. Sir Thomas Grantham, central to the 1684 letters reproduced as figures 5 and 6, was a knighted admiral actively engaged in the sea commerce and conflicts of the time (Hedges 1964, 2:clx–clxxxv). The 1701 letter reproduced as figure 7 postdates Hedges's stay but documents related commercial events: it was sent from Madras by Thomas Pitt, governor of Fort St. George, to his London agent, Stephen Evance (Hedges 1964, 3:i–clxvi).

Transcription of Figure 5

Deare Sr Novemb^r 11° 1684.

I hope this will be Satisfactory to yor Honor to let you know y^t yesterday I composed the difference with those Stoute Rebells of BOM::BAY upon no: dishonourable termes I assure your Honour, last night I brought on board with me twelve bags of Gold taken out of the Returne I shall take y^e

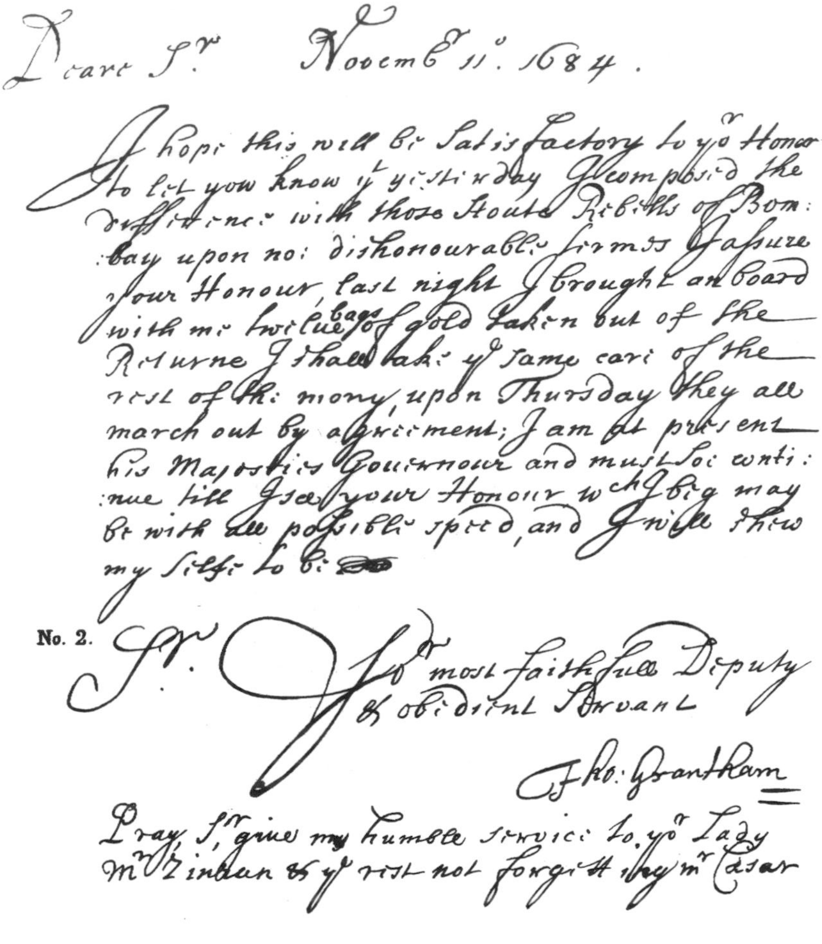

Deare Sr   Novembr 11. 1684.

I hope this will be Satisfactory to yor Honor
to let you know yt yesterday I composed the
difference with those Stoute Rebells of Bom:
bay upon no: dishonourable termes I assure
your Honour, last night I brought on Board
with me twelue bags of gold taken out of the
Returne I shall take ye same care of the
rest of the mony, upon Thursday they all
march out by agreement; I am at present
his Majesties Gouernour and must Soe conti:
nue till I see your Honour wch I beg may
be with all possible speed, and I will shew
my selfe to be

No. 2.   Sr   Yor most faithfull Deputy
                        & obedient Servant

                              Tho: Grantham

Pray Sr giue my humble service to yor Lady
Mr Zinban & ye rest not forgett my mr Casar

Figure 5. Letter from Sir Thomas Grantham to Mr. Child, November 11,
1684, a sample of seventeenth-century English paleography. (Reprinted,
by permission, from Hedges 1964: plate 9)

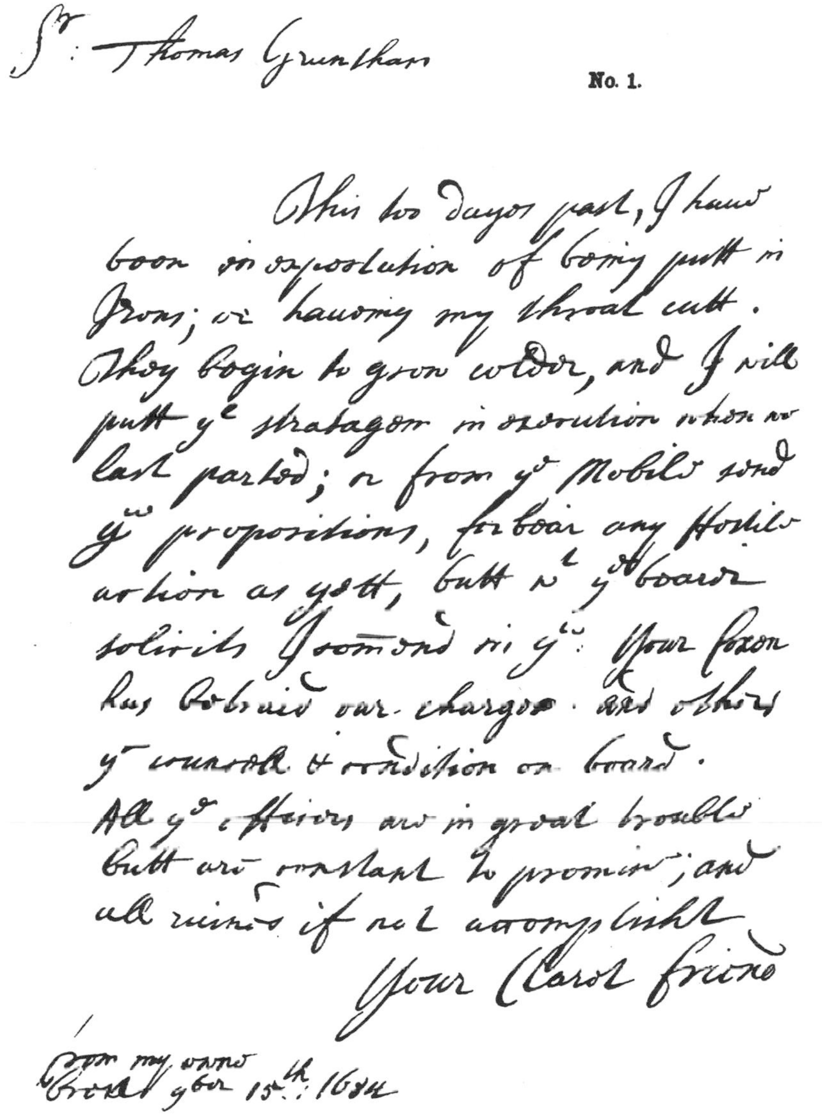

Sr Thomas Grantham

No. 1.

[handwritten letter]

This too dayes past, I have
been in expectation of being putt in
Irons; or having my throat cutt.
They begin to grow colder, and I will
putt ye stratagem in execution when we
last parted; or from ye Mobile send
ye propositions, forbear any Hostile
action as yett, butt wt ye board
solicits Groomond in ye Your prison
has Robired our charges and others
ye counsell & condition on board.
All ye officers are in great trouble
butt are constant to promise; and
all ruined if not accomplisht
Your Constl friend

From my owne
Broad ober 15th: 1684

Figure 6. Letter from Captain Keigwin to Sir Thomas Grantham, September 15, 1684. (Reprinted, by permission, from Hedges 1964: plate 9b)

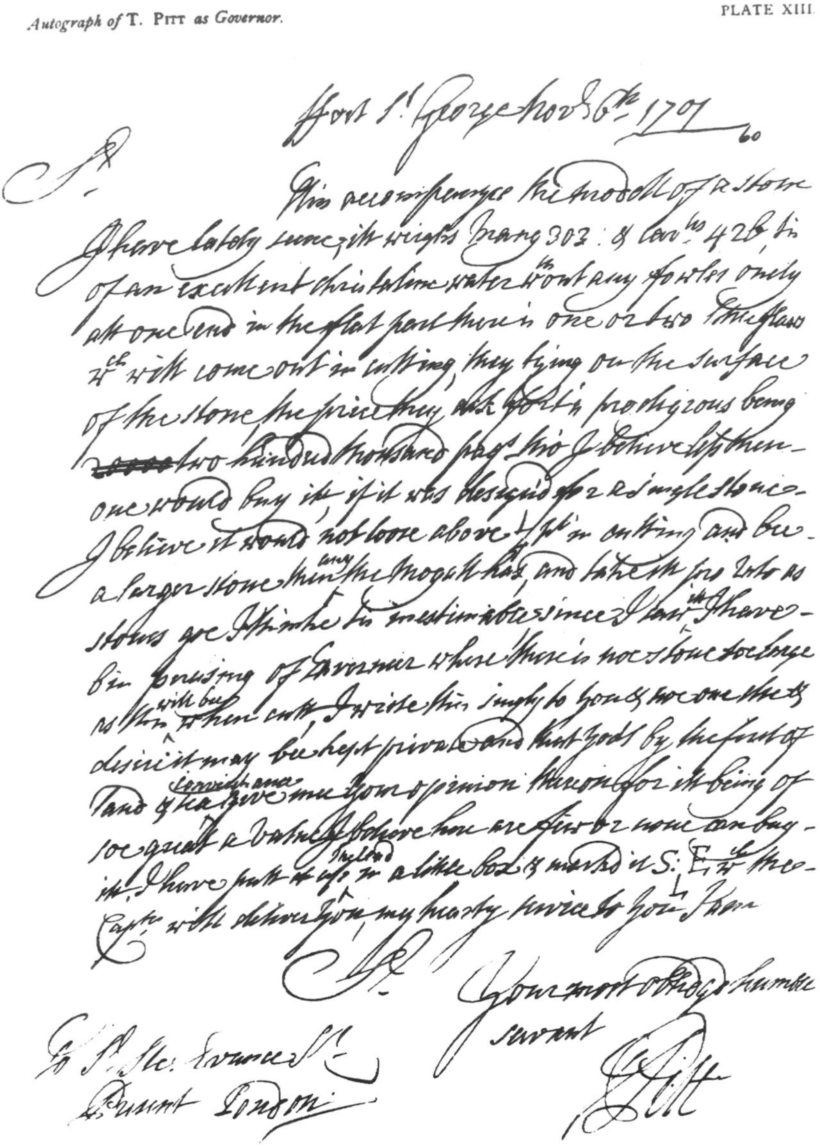

Figure 7. Letter from Thomas Pitt to Sir Stephen Evance, November 6, 1701. (Reprinted, by permission, from Hedges 1964: plate XIII)

same care of the rest of the mony, upon Thursday they all march out by
agreement; I am at present his Majesties Governour and must soe conti::nue till I see your Honour, wch I beg may be with all possible speed,
and I will shew my Selfe to be

S^r Yo^r most faithfull Deputy

& obedient Servant

Tho: Grantham

Pray, S^r, give my humble service to yor Lady Mr Zinzan & ye rest not
forgetting m^r Cæsar

Transcription of Figure 6

S^r: Thomas Grantham

This too dayes past, I have been in expectation of being putt in Irons;
or haveing my throat cutt. They begin to grow colder, and I will putt y^e
stratagem in execution when we last parted; or from ye Mobile send y^o
propositions, forbear any Hostile action as yett, butt w^t ye bearer solicits I
comend in y^o. Your Coxon has betraid our charges. and others y^r counsell
& condition on board. All ye officers are in great trouble but are constant
to promise; and all ruin'd if not accomplisht

Your Claret friend

from my owne
brest [?] 9^her 15th: 1684

Transcription of Figure 7

Fort St George Nov^br 6th 1701
S^r

This accompanyes the modell of a Stone I have lately seene; itt weighs
Mang [*mangelin,* an Indian measure used for weighing precious stones]
303: and car^tts [carets] 426 tis of an excellent christaline water w^thout any
fowles onely att one end in the flat part there is one or two little flaws w^ch
will come out in cutting, they lying on the surface of the Stone, the price
they ask for tis prodigious being two hundred thousand pag^s thô I believe
less then one would buy it, if it was design'd for a Single Stone, I believe it
would not loose above ¼ p^t [part] in cutting and bee a larger Stone then
any the Mogull has, and take it pro rata as Stones goe I thinke tis inestima-
ble Since I saw itt I have bin perusing of Tavernier where there is noe
Stone Soe large as this will bee when cutt. I write this singly to you & noe

one else & desire it may bee kept private and that you'l by the first of land & sea conveighance give mee your opinion theron for itt being of Soe great a value I believe here are few or none can buy itt. I have put it [the model] up Inclos'd in a little box & mark'd it S: E wch the Cap^tn will deliver you, my hearty service to you I am

    Sr Your most oblidged humble servant

        T Pitt

To Sr Ste. [Stephen] Evance, K^t [Knight]
Present London.

    These three examples contain a number of paleographic conventions discussed in this chapter. Numbers appear as quantities or as dates. Numbers included in figure 7 are either written out or appear as digits, including a fraction. In one case a large number (20,000) is crossed out and replaced by "two hundred thousand," correcting an error and making the amount (in this case, a price) explicitly clear. Dates are included in all three letters. In figure 5, a Latinized "11°" is written, while in the third letter the ordinal is designated as "6th." An interesting variation is found in figure 6, which indicates the month by "9^ber" (September).

    Abbreviations are rampant in all three letters. The thorn ("y") appears as "y^t" (that) in figure 5 and as "y^e" (the) in the first two letters. Other common abbreviations include "Tho:" for "Thomas," "comend" for "commend," "w^ch" for "which," "design'd" for "designed," "ruin"d" for "ruined," "tis" for "it is," "w^thout" for "without," "M^r" for "mister," "S^r" for "sir," "Capt" for "Captain," and "yor" for "your." Within each letter, such abbreviations are used liberally and fairly consistently. Variations, however, do appear. For instance, "Sir" is abbreviated as "S^r" in figure 5, as "S^r:" in figure 6, and as "S^r." in figure 7.

    Each letter exemplifies fairly consistent spelling patterns. At times the spelling follows phonetic guidelines, as with "too" for "two" and "accomplisht" for "accomplished" in figure 6. Certain spelling conventions are obvious and can be seen in the practice of doubling consonants and vowels (as with "butt," "itt," "counsell," and "bee"). An extra "e" was added to the end of some words, yielding spellings such as "thinke," "soe," "Returne," and "Selfe." While these specific usages were quite consistent, they do not seem to follow any overarching rule other than the individual writer's style; dialect usages and momentary whims may also have played a part. Similarly, while titles and dates are consistently capitalized, other words (such as "Irons," "Selfe," and "Stoute") appear to be more idiosyn-cratically capitalized.

These examples illustrate a variety of paleographic conventions and variations of the sorts ethnohistorians encounter when studying older manuscripts. They demonstrate how ethnohistorians must be alert to rec-ognize patterns yet flexible to cope with exceptions.

CHAPTER 4

Calendrics

It is difficult to conceive of ethnohistory without some means of keeping track of chronology. Indeed, the popular conception of history of all kinds is that it revolves around dates. Ethnohistory, as well as history in general, is far more than just dates, of course, but placing events and processes in temporal order and context is a critical part of the endeavor. Recognizing contemporaneous events and conditions is crucial for synchronic studies, and seeing trends and sequences is equally important for diachronic studies. Actually dealing with dates and chronology, however, is sometimes made more complicated by the fact that different peoples around the world have devised diverse ways of conceiving of and reckoning time. The general study of these different conceptions and reckoning systems is known as calendrics. This chapter discusses the principles underlying different calendric systems, the complexity of these systems, and techniques for converting dates from one system to another.

Basic Principles of Time Reckoning

While presumably all societies have recognized the concept of time, not all have conceived of it in the same manner. One classical distinction is between cyclical and linear conceptions of time. In the linear conception, time is seen as a stream flowing continuously in a single direction toward the future from a fixed starting point; there are no reversals or returns. The cyclical conception, in contrast, sees time more like a whirlpool, where the stream of time curves back on itself, returning to an earlier spot. Although this dichotomy is convenient, it is easy to make too much of it; most societies seem to have recognized both aspects in their calculation of time. In the European tradition, for instance, the cyclical nature of the year is emphasized by the progression and repetition of the days of the week and the months of the year, while the linear aspect is reflected in the steady succession of numbered years.

The Astronomical Basis: Days, Months, and Years

Virtually every known system of keeping track of time is based ultimately on astronomical phenomena. The most important and widely used cornerstones for calculating time have been the rotation of the earth to produce days, the revolution of the moon around the earth to produce lunar months, and the revolution of the earth around the sun to produce solar years.

Some small-scale societies have taken these recurrent events and used them in a loose and flexible manner. In such a society, there typically would be named seasons, as with the five seasons of the Iroquois, each defined by the typical activities of that time of year (Fenton 1951:42). Beyond this level of timekeeping, there typically would be no naming or numbering of days, weeks, months, or years; indeed, some of these might not exist as concepts. Among the Iroquois, for example, the lunar month and solar year were used (Waugh 1916), but they apparently had no concept of the week. This simple system meant that the Iroquois and other peoples like them were forced to count backward or forward from a known event to approximate a date. The seventeenth-century Iroquois might identify an event as occurring "four days ago" or "three months after the first Frenchman arrived in the village."

Other societies have used astronomical events as building blocks to create formal systems of time reckoning. Such a system produces names for day positions within the year and usually defines named units made up of groups of days; it may also provide a means of identifying a particular year. Such a system is known as a calendar, and calendars are the source of historians' dates.

The difficulty for anyone trying to construct a tidy calendar is that the astronomical units with which they must work — the day, the lunar month, and the solar year — are not simple multiples of one another. By definition, the length of a day is exactly 24 hours. The moon, however, requires 708.16 hours to complete its circuit around the earth, amounting to 29 days, 12 hours, 9 minutes, and just under 40 seconds. The solar year of 8765.812778 hours (365 days, 5 hours, 48 minutes, and 46 seconds) is not an even multiple of either a day or a lunar month. As a result, any simple system of reckoning time will inexorably produce disparities. Using a simple 365-day year produces a reasonable approximation of the solar year, but that year has 12.37 lunar months. The excess beyond 12 months amounts to a bit over 11 days per year. By this token, New Year's Day would fall about 11 days earlier per year, and over a modest 32 years this holiday would have migrated all around the year. Some groups, such as the Muslims, find this acceptable and have constructed a calendric system accordingly, but most prefer their holidays to fall at the same season each year.

To solve this problem, some calendars have months of different lengths, as in the modern calendar in use in most of the world today. Alternatively, it is possible to keep the months the same length but add an extra set of days to take up the slack, an approach used by the ancient Mesoamerican solar calendar. (Such additions to keep a calendar more or less in order are called *intercalary*.) A final option, adopted in the Muslim calendar, is to simply ignore the problem and let dates migrate around the seasons.

No matter how months are reconciled (or not) to the year, another calendric problem is inherited from astronomy. Since the solar year is not evenly divisible by the length of the day, over time New Year's Day will fall earlier and earlier. Clever manipulation of the months can keep that day at the same date within a month, but it will fall about one day earlier in the seasonal cycle every four years; after a few hundred years, it will fall in an inappropriate season. Many calendars add intercalary days at fixed intervals to avoid this problem, but this poses more problems, since the shift of New Year's Day is not exactly one day every four years. If its users want to keep a calendar consistent over a long span, they must employ a complicated set of intercalary days.

Of course, at one time no one realized that intercalary days would be necessary, and even after their necessity was understood, the lengths of the lunar and solar cycles were not measured with sufficient accuracy to permit working out an optimal plan for calendars and intercalations. As a result, at various times in history adjustments have been made to calendars, sometimes skipping days altogether or adding them wholesale. When France instituted a calendric reform in 1582, ten days had to be dropped, and December 9 (in the old system) was followed directly by December 20; consequently, December 10 through 19, 1582, never officially occurred in Paris.

The Cultural Basis: Multiyear Spans, Weeks, and Hours

While astronomical cycles underlie calendric systems, purely cultural concepts also have played a role. The concepts of decade, century, and millennium have been very important in European timekeeping, as evidenced by historical nicknames such as "the Gay '90s" and "the Splendid Century," and by numerous millennial cults appearing near A.D. 1000 and 2000.

Their importance lies not in their astronomical significance, but in the numerological significance of numbers ending in zeroes. European culture conceptualizes such numbers as the end of a sequence, preparing people to anticipate either the end of the world or some other major change. In other societies with other concepts, similar anticipation follows at the end of other cycles. (The example of the ancient Mexican calendar round is discussed later in this chapter.)

Smaller units of time also may spring from astronomically arbitrary — but culturally significant — sources. The ten-day week of the Egyptians and the seven-day week of the Middle East and Europe are based on no astronomical cycle, although those using the seven-day week often have considered it one-quarter of the lunar month, though this is an inexact fraction. The week probably originated as an easy way to keep track of periodic markets and similar events, imposing a system that would make them fall on the same day of the week. Only some calendric systems incorporate weeks and named weekdays.

Even the definition of when a particular day begins and ends differs from system to system. In the Islamic and Hebrew calendars, the date changes at sundown; in traditional medieval Europe, the date changed at dawn. The modern Western practice of using midnight as the dividing point between dates would have been impractical and cumbersome, of course, before the invention and widespread use of clocks. This detail of when a date changes is mostly important for dealing with events that took place during the dark hours, such as El Noche Triste of the Aztec conquest.

It is also possible to create subdivisions of the day, though relatively few societies around the world have done so. Except for dawn, midday, and sunset, there are no astronomical bases behind these units of time. The Western system of hours, minutes, and seconds developed out of the base-sixty Sumerian numeric system. The eleventh-century system of China, equally arbitrary, divided the day into 96 equal but tiny parts (Needham, Ling, and de Solla Price 1986).

All of these complications, born of the messiness of earthly astronomical cycles and the arbitrariness of human culture, have led to a bewildering array of calendars around the world. A comprehensive work on calendrics (Parise 1982) provides conversion information on forty-five calendars, of which over half are still in use. Several societies have simultaneously used solar and lunar calendars, sometimes producing a single composite date, sometimes two separate dates. Religious reckoning often has followed a calendar different from that for secular timekeeping in both ancient and modern societies. Some societies have used calendars to produce a date designating a position within the year but have had no sequence of numbered years, referring the date to a position within a ruler's reign. (The ancient Hebrews used this system, as recorded in the New Testament of the Bible, as when Luke 3:1–6 describes John the Baptist's preaching as beginning "in the fifteenth year of Tiberius Caesar.") Given this complexity, it can be a major task for an ethnohistorian to convert dates from one system to another and place them in relation to one another.

The Mechanics of Converting Dates

Fortunately, ethnohistorians rarely have to work with more than two or three of the various calendars at a time. Converting from one system to another is fussy work that easily can produce errors, but the principles are simple enough: find a time when dates in both systems are known, then work forward or backward in both systems simultaneously until the desired date is reached.

The Gregorian and Julian Calendars

The calendar most broadly used today is the Gregorian calendar, named for Pope Gregory XIII, who commissioned its creation and ordered its implementation in 1582. His calendar has the familiar months (with slightly different names in various languages), numbers of days per months, and a system of intercalary days at leap years. This system also differentiates years before and after the nominal birth of Jesus of Nazareth (actually probably in error by about four years). Dates before this nominal event are designated in English as "B.C." (before Christ); dates after are designated "A.D." (Anno Domini [in the year of our Lord]). In recent years, some scholars have renamed these epochs "B.C.E." ("before the Common Era") and "C.E." ("Common Era") in an attempt to remove the Eurocentric and Christian bias inherent in the other terms. These designations have not caught on much among scholars and are generally unknown among the public. Since the Gregorian calendar is in use virtually everywhere in the world today and is the standard for most scholarly writing, ethnohistorians usually will convert dates into this system. Dates in the Gregorian calendar are considered "New Series" and sometimes are designated by "N.S." in parentheses after the date.

The predecessor to the Gregorian calendar in Europe was the Julian calendar, named for Julius Caesar, who implemented it in 46 B.C. It consisted of the same months as the Gregorian calendar with the same numbers of days (after the first few years of adjusting the system); the number of days per year totaled 365, and an intercalary day was added every four years. Dates in the Julian calendar are called "Old Series" and often are marked "O.S." within parentheses following the date.

Because astronomy would demand an intercalary day every 4.0338657 years rather than the four mandated by the Julian calendar, the Julian calendar gradually fell out of step with the seasons. By Pope Gregory's time, ten excess days had accumulated. The Gregorian calendar refined the intercalary system by declaring that century years (those ending in oo) are leap years only if they also are exactly divisible by 400. (This puts off the inevitable dissynchrony for a few millennia.) In order to restore the calendar, however, Gregory had to declare ten days suppressed; that is, dropped. Consequently, in areas that immediately implemented the papal decree, October 5, 1582 (O.S.) became October 15, 1582 (N.S.); October 5 through October 14 simply never occurred officially. The sequence of days of the week continued uninterrupted: October 4 was a Thursday and was followed by October 15, a Friday.

The new calendar, however, was resisted in many quarters. Part of this was because of religious politics: Catholic countries were far more willing to adopt the reform than were Protestant ones. Dropping so many days made for a very short month, creating confusion and disrupting monthly schedules of payments; changing the rules for intercalary days meant overcoming inertia. Perhaps the greatest resistance came from the fact that it was difficult for most people to see the urgency of correcting a calendar they had grown up with, especially when the system created no appreciable problems in the span of a person's lifetime.

Resistance to the new calendar in England and its colonies included a religious angle. Calvinists believed that the hour of one's death was preordained, and some other Christians had adopted this belief, notably Irish Catholics. Given this notion, there was great concern that losing ten or more days from the calendar would result in shortening persons' lives by an equivalent amount. This was the major cause underlying the Irish riots of 1752, and Benjamin Franklin considered it a sufficiently important issue to devote an article to it in his *Poor Richard's Almanack*. Franklin assured his readers that a calendric correction would not shorten their allotted spans and that it would be "an indulgence . . . to lie down in peace on the second of this month and not perhaps awake till the morning of the fourteenth" (Saunders 1752).

As a result of differing degrees of resistance, the switch from the Julian

Table 2. Dates of Conversion from the Julian Calendar to the Gregorian Calendar

Place	Julian Date	Gregorian Date
Alsace	Feb. 5, 1682	Feb. 16, 1682
Bavaria	Oct. 6, 1583	Oct. 16, 1583
Belgium	Dec. 22, 1582	Jan. 1, 1583
Bohemia	Jan. 7, 1584	Jan. 17, 1584
Denmark	Feb. 19, 1700	March 1, 1700
England, Scotland, Wales, and Ireland	Sept. 3, 1752	Sept. 14, 1752
France	Dec. 10, 1582	Dec. 20, 1582
Holland (most parts)	July 1, 1700	July 12, 1700
Italy (most parts)	Oct. 5, 1582	Oct. 15, 1582
Portugal	Oct. 5, 1582	Oct. 15, 1582
Russia	March 5, 1920	March 18, 1920
Saxony	Nov. 4, 1699	Nov. 15, 1699
Spain	Oct. 5, 1582	Oct. 15, 1582
Sweden	Oct. 5, 1582	Oct. 6, 1582

Note: Typically, colonies of a country converted at the same time as the home country. Although these dates reflect official governmental conversion, individuals and locales did not always make the conversion at the same time.

calendar to the Gregorian calendar took place at different times between 1582 and 1920 at different spots on the globe. Some of the places that switched late had to drop additional days as a result of the continued accumulation of discrepancies in the interim; England, for example, waited long enough that eleven days had to be dropped.

Table 2 presents the dates when various places converted from the Julian calendar to the Gregorian calendar. The table should be used with the caveat that there was a great deal of variability in adopting the Gregorian calendar. Sometimes adjacent communities adopted the new system on different dates, especially in Germany and other areas with a mosaic of Catholic and Protestant domination; sometimes individuals within a community changed over at different times or used both calendars simultaneously. In such cases, inevitably there is more ambiguity regarding which system is being used for a particular date. Usually a colony would follow the practices of the home country, though it can be expected that com-

Table 3. New Year's Day in Various European Countries and Regions

Place	Dates	New Year's Day
England	1339–1751	March 25
	1752–present	January 1
France	various–1363	March 25
	1363–1452	Easter
	1455	January 1
	1456–1566	Easter
	1567–present[a]	January 1
Germany	until 1508	various
	1508–present	January 1
Holland	until 1532	Easter
	1533–present	January 1
Italy	until 1745	highly variable
	1745–present	January 1
Portugal	1383–1420	March 25
	1421–1581	December 25
	1582–present	January 1
Scotland	1339–1599	March 25
	1600–present	January 1
Spain	1350 or 1383 1581	December 25
	1582–present	January 1

[a]France briefly used the French Revolutionary calendar, with its novel month names and structure, between 1793 and 1805.

munication difficulties kept reform from effectively being transmitted to some of the more isolated colonies in a timely manner.

To further complicate matters, the date that was considered the beginning of the new year changed over time as well. In the Julian calendar, the first day of the year originally was March 1, but that date had migrated to March 25 for much of Europe by the sixteenth century. Many countries converted to using January 1 as the first day of the year when they adopted the Gregorian calendar, but some adopted the calendar and the new beginning of the year independently. Scotland, for example, adopted January 1 as the first of the year in 1600, though it retained the Julian calendar for more than a century longer; England, in contrast, changed to the January new year only when it adopted the Gregorian calendar in 1752. Table 3 provides information on New Year's Day for some European countries.

The impact of these various differences between the Julian and Gregorian calendars sometimes has a major effect on the rendering of a date. George Washington's birthday, for example, is traditionally given as February 22, 1732 (N.S.). But his birth certificate (if one had been written) would have read "February 11, 1731" (O.S.). Because Virginia was an English colony, it retained the Julian calendar in the 1730s, so the eleven days had not yet been dropped; in addition, England still celebrated New Year's Day on March 25, so Washington was born near the end of 1731 (O.S.), not near the beginning of 1732 (N.S.).

Some countries followed even more bizarre paths of converting to the Gregorian calendar. Sweden decided to ease into the conversion in 1700, dropping only a single day from the year but apparently intending to drop an additional day each year until its calendar was in agreement with other national calendars. This plan misfired, however, and for eleven years Sweden stayed one day ahead of the Julian calendar and nine days behind the Gregorian calendar; only by 1853 did Sweden complete its implementation of the Gregorian calendar.

Given the complexities, quirks, and halting nature of converting from the Julian to Gregorian calendar around the Western world, how did individuals cope with the conversion? Urban English diarists in the years surrounding 1752 followed a simple expedient: they skipped from October 4 to October 15, sometimes noting that this was "the dropping." Rural colonial diarists, perhaps deprived of newspapers and other means of knowing that the adjustment date had arrived, were more likely to continue with October 6 and the following days, perhaps dropping the days later on.

A ship's log normally included a continuous sequence of dates, starting with the ship's departure date, based on the system of its country of origin, regardless of where it stopped or passed through. Chronometers, once invented and put into widespread use as aids to navigation, were maintained without resetting to adjust for time zones. (The chronometers were used in the calculation of longitude, and resetting them would destroy their usefulness in this task.) In addition, nautical practice placed the beginning of the day at noon, a throwback to the days before the widespread use of clocks, when midnight was difficult to calculate. The upshot of these practices is that a date reported in a document might be somewhat inaccurate, or at least misleading. Scott (1920:34) cites the example of James Cook's first sighting of Australia. His journals record this occurring at 6:00 A.M. on April 19, 1770. Cook had been sailing westward from

Europe through fourteen time zones without resetting his time; he had crossed the international date line; and he was considering each day to begin at noon. As a result of these combined factors, current scholarship corrects the date to April 20 (Scott 1920:34) or even April 21 (McCullagh 1984:11).

In Europe, where communities only a few miles from one another might simultaneously recognize different dates, residents must have been familiar with all local systems and able to make the necessary conversion easily. Travelers, too, might have been aware of the complexities of date-keeping; alternatively, they might blithely have maintained a journal or records using their homeland's system, even though it was at odds with the local one. All of these complexities mean that an "exact" date appearing in a document may not be as exact as it appears.

Other Calendars

For many ethnohistorians, conversion from the Julian to the Gregorian calendar is the only calendric calculation they will need to perform. In some parts of the world, however, other calendars were in use. A few of these are noted briefly here, largely to exemplify the variety of calendric systems. More details on specific calendars can be obtained by consulting various sources, especially Parise (1982), Boorstin (1983), Aveni (1989), O'Neil (1975), and MacDonald (1897).

For ethnohistorians working in the northern two-thirds of Africa, the Middle East, parts of India, and Indonesia, the Islamic calendar is often the most important. This linear calendar, the official church calendar of Islam, begins July 16, 622 (N.S.), the date Muhammad arrived at Medina at the end of the Hejira (his flight to escape persecution). Islamic dates are calculated after this date using the Islamic lunar year of 354 days. Consequently, the calculation of a Gregorian date from an Islamic date is a bit more complicated than simply adding 622 to the Islamic date, because the different lengths of year have to be taken into consideration. In English-language writing, dates in the Islamic calendar traditionally are followed by "A.H." (Anno Hejirae [in the year of the Hejira]). There are some regional and sectarian variants to the Islamic calendar.

Ethnohistorians in Mexico and adjacent regions must be able to convert dates from the native calendars. The Aztec calendar serves as a model for several related calendar systems in use there (Caso 1971). While the various central Mexican city-states all used the same calendar, it appears that the same date was not always celebrated on exactly the same day in different places, perhaps as a result of applying the intercalary days differently. The Mexican calendar had two simultaneous cycles. The first (the *xihuitl*) had 18 months of 20 days each with 5 annual intercalary days, resulting in a 365-day solar year. Each month had a name, as did each name-number combination within a month. The other cycle (the astrological *tonalpohualli*) had 20 day signs and 13 numbers that rotated simultaneously, creating 260 unique sign-number combinations.

Any particular date in the xihuitl or tonalpohualli cycle would come around only once every 365 days or once every 260 days, depending on which cycle you looked at; the coincidence of the two dates, however, would occur only once every 52 solar years. This 52-year cycle, a calendar round, was tremendously significant because the world was vulnerable to destruction at the end of each calendar round. There is no formal way of noting which calendar round a date falls in, so any date out of context could be attributed to various Gregorian equivalents. While Gregorian time reckoning is basically linear, ancient Mexican reckoning was predominantly cyclical.

Computer Conversion Programs

Calendric conversions are a perfect chore for computers because they require performing a large number of arithmetic calculations and keeping track of one's place in the process. To date, however, no commercial program for converting dates in a wide range of calendars has emerged as the standard in the field. There are a few commercial programs for converting between the Hebrew and Gregorian calendars and for calculating Christian holidays; there also are various shareware programs of unassessed accuracy. Dates converted through the use of appropriate computer programs, once they become available, should be more reliable than those converted by hand calculation.

The Embeddedness of Time in Culture and Society

A system of time reckoning forms part of the cultural backdrop that members of a society use to structure their behavior. For them, it seems a natural way to divide time, and it is unlikely to be commented on. Careful reading of a document, however, can reveal significant aspects of behavior with respect to time, some of which the participants may not have overtly realized.

Certain activities, for example, must be attuned to nature's seasons. "It was January, so I put on my heaviest coat." This statement is obvious to the New Englander or Finn, but a Nigerian or Argentine might not understand it so automatically. The English folk song "Here We Go Gathering Nuts in May" equates craziness with collecting nuts out of season, an allusion largely lost on an increasingly urban population.

Other activities are geared to days or dates for purely cultural reasons. Seventeenth-century comments about eating fish on Friday would have inspired no surprise in Catholic France; a statement that food always tastes better during Ramadan would make sense to a fasting Muslim; a modern American, regardless of religion, would know that it is too late to do Christmas shopping on December 28.

The author of a document usually is writing for an audience that shares a common cultural conception of time and will assume that a reader can recognize the significance of time references. The ethnohistorian, therefore, must always be alert to the cultural meanings of dates and other time references in reading a document; however, allusions of the sort discussed in the previous two paragraphs can be understood fully only with the benefit of a fairly detailed knowledge of the author's culture.

Astrology is a particularly important cultural aspect of dates. Most societies that use calendric systems attach particular significance to certain dates. Birthdates, for example, have been widely believed to shape person alitics. Among the Aztec, a person born on the day Two Rabbit was fated to be a drunk; in China, anyone born in a year dedicated to the rabbit is likely to be clever; and in the European tradition, those born under the constellation of Leo are expected to be outgoing and aggressive. Equally important in many astrological systems are appropriate days for beginning activities. The declaration of India's independence was arranged to occur at an astrologically propitious time (Collins and La Pierre 1975:181, 196, 228, 334); Aztec trading parties avoided departing on unlucky days like 1 Serpent, 1 Crocodile, 1 Monkey, or 7 Serpent (Sahagún 1950–82: bk. 9, chap. 3); and the number of conferences held in the United States always drops off when a Friday falls on the thirteenth of a month, considered a very unlucky combination.

Contact and conflict between different time-reckoning systems can result in interesting accommodations. The traditional Aztec week had five days, but the Spanish introduced the seven-day European week, which posed a problem with the periodic market system geared to a market rotation among five towns, one for each day of the week. In adopting the seven-day week, the Indians retained the five-market structure but assigned the two largest markets a second day each in the rotation.

A Few Conventions in Calendric Notation

Dates are extremely common in many classes of ethnohistoric documents, and their very frequency inclined writers to develop abbreviations to make their notation quicker or easier. The following comments refer primarily to dates in documents written in western European languages.

The usual sequence of presenting calendric information follows national and linguistic patterns. Dates in English traditionally have been presented as month-day-year, often with various punctuation separating the day and year, such as "January 23, 1923." Beginning in the twentieth century, however, British writers increasingly have presented the day first, as with "23 January 1923"; this pattern has become popular in English-language scientific publications everywhere. In other European languages the more common pattern is day-month-year, sometimes with prepositions separating the elements, as in "23 de janvier de 1923" or "23 janvier 1923."

From the late eighteenth century onward, dates sometimes have been abbreviated as numbers divided by slashes or dashes, as with "3/6/1792" or "3-6-1792." Such designations could be read as either the third day of the sixth month (June 3) or the sixth day of the third month (March 6) in 1792. Usually Anglo-American sources presented month before day, while all others (including British sources) presented day before month. To be sure, it usually is wise to try to find an unequivocal date to ensure that you know the pattern the writer was following, since there were personal idiosyncrasies. The notation "17/2/1812," for example, makes it clear that the writer was placing day before month, since there is no seventeenth month.

Sometimes, particularly in the seventeenth and early eighteenth centuries, English writers would abbreviate a month by combining a numeral and letters. The ninth month, for example, could be abbreviated as "9ber," combining its place in the annual sequence and its last few letters. During this era of differing starting months of the year, this designation could be read as either September (for someone using January as the first month) or December (for someone using March as the first month). Consequently, it is wise to find an unequivocal designation to be sure that you are reading such abbreviations as the writer intended. Abbreviations of this form usually were restricted to months ending in "-ary" or "-ber."

If months were written out in letters, they often were abbreviated. The most common abbreviations were simply shortened versions of the month names, such as "Inv" ("invierno," Spanish for "January") or "Jany:" ("January" in English). Occasionally, writers — particularly the more literate ones — abbreviated Latin versions of month names.

The century or so before 1752 was particularly confusing, calendrically speaking, because England was becoming increasingly out of step with the rest of Europe. By 1600, virtually all the rest of Europe had adopted the Gregorian calendar and the January 1 beginning of the year. To remove some ambiguity in dates during the disputed January-February-March period, some English writers in the century before 1752 included both versions of the year in their dates. This usually was accomplished by presenting the Julian year over the Gregorian year, separated by a horizontal line: "February 25, $\frac{1699}{1700}$" was the year 1699 for the English (who would not move into the new year for another month) and simultaneously 1700 for the French, Scottish, and others (who had moved into their new year almost two months before). Writers made no effort to include both Julian and Gregorian versions of the day of the month, only calling attention to year differences.

The abbreviation "inst." holds a special place in European time notation. It came into use around 1500 and was enormously popular in dates from the seventeenth century well into the nineteenth, yet it is not even mentioned in most historical dictionaries, including the massive *Oxford English Dictionary* (discussed further in chapters 5 and 7). "Inst." was the abbreviation for the Latin "instantem" or its French and English equivalent "instant"; in either case, the word meant "current" and referred to the last calendric occurrence of a particular date. For example, "December 23 inst." referred to the last time that December 23 had occurred before the time of writing. "March inst.," on the other hand, could refer either to the current month (if the document was written during March) or to the most recent March (if written in any other month). The usage of "inst." would make no sense in undated documents, and it occurs most frequently in letters and journal entries, where its meaning usually is obvious.

Case Study

PLACING TWO EAST AFRICAN
VISITORS IN SEQUENCE

The Swahili culture of East Africa spanned the tenth through sixteenth centuries, extending along the coast of what today is southern Somalia through Mozambique. Affluent local traders brokered resources from Africa to Arab and other traders, and this region thrived. There is a variety of descriptions of some of the major ports, but two are particularly prominent and important because their descriptions differ in some significant respects in terms of architecture and other features in the city of Malindi, a major commercial center in East Africa. One was written by Ibn Battuta, an Arab scholar who visited the area in 732 A.H. (No more specific date is available.) The other description is an extract from the logbook of Vasco da Gama, the Portuguese explorer, on Easter Sunday, April 15, 1498 (O.S.). To evaluate the significance of the differences in their descriptions, it is necessary to determine the chronological relationship of their observations, an operation that illustrates the complexity of — and potential for arithmetic or logical errors in — calendric conversion.

The first decision is to convert all dates to the Gregorian calendar. Any single calendar would be fine, but this is the one most frequently used by scholars. Ibn Battuta's date can be converted by the following steps:

1. Calculate the number of years between 732 A.H. and the founding of the Islamic calendar. Since there is no year 0 in the Islamic or any other calendar, this is calculated by subtracting 1 from 732: $732 - 1 = 731$.
2. Calculate how many days are in 731 Islamic lunar years of 354 days apiece: $731 \times 354 = 258{,}774$ days since the Hejira.
3. Divide that number of days into Gregorian years of 365.2425 days apiece: $258{,}774 \div 365.2425 = 708.5$ Gregorian years.

4. Convert the starting date for A.H. dates (July 16, 622 A.D.) from a Julian date to a Gregorian date, following these steps:

— For the period between the beginning of the Islamic calendar (July 16, 622) and the implementation of the Gregorian calendar (October 5, 1582 [O.S.]), calculate how many leap years with intercalary days were implemented under the Julian calendar but would have been skipped under the Gregorian calendar; these are any century years evenly divisible by 400. In this case there would be two: for A.D. 800 and 1200.

— Subtract these two days (which would not have been added in the Gregorian system) from July 16, 622 (O.S.): July 16, 622 A.D. (O.S.) − 2 days = July 14, 622 (N.S.) This is the Gregorian equivalent date.

5. Add the number of Gregorian years since the Hejira (708.5) to the Gregorian version of the starting date for A.H. dates (July 14, 622: somewhere in 1331.

This date of A.D. 1331 (N.S.) is an approximation of Ibn Battuta's description. If it were critical to specify the earliest and latest possible dates for his account, it would be necessary to calculate the Gregorian equivalents to the first and last days of 731 A.H.

Next, convert Vasco da Gama's date of Easter Sunday, April 15, 1498 (O.S.) into a New Series date. This is accomplished through the following steps:

1. For the period between the date in question (April 15, 1498 [O.S.]) and the implementation of the Gregorian calendar (October 5, 1582 [O.S.]), calculate how many leap years with intercalary days were implemented under the Julian calendar but would have been skipped under the Gregorian calendar. These are any century years evenly divisible by 400. There were no such years, so the answer is 0.

2. Subtract one day for each of those years (since the Gregorian calculation would not have added them at all): April 15, 1498 − 0 days = April 15, 1498.

3. Add the ten days that had accumulated as a discrepancy between the Julian and Gregorian calendars by October 5, 1582: April 15, 1498 + 10 days = April 25, 1498 (N.S.).

4. Finally, calculate whether April 25 would be a different year under the Gregorian calendar than under the system used by the Portuguese at that period: December 25 was New Year's Day for them at that time, so the year number remains the same.

The Gregorian equivalent for this date, then, is April 25, 1498 (N.S.).

Comparing the Gregorian dates for the descriptions of Ibn Battuta (A.D. 1331) and Vasco da Gama (A.D. 1498), it is clear that Ibn Battuta was describing Malindi over a century and a half before Vasco da Gama, plenty of reason in itself for their descriptions to differ significantly.

As this case study demonstrates, the arithmetic of converting dates is tedious and sufficiently convoluted to permit plenty of opportunity for errors. Computer calendric-conversion programs, when available and reliable, will remove the possibility of arithmetic mistakes, and they will certainly remove a tedious task for the ethnohistorian. When only a few dates must be converted, however, it may be less bother to simply perform the conversions by hand than to locate a conversion program and learn how to use it.

CHAPTER 5

Linguistic Analysis

While nearly all the chapters in this book touch on some aspect of language in ethnohistoric documents, this chapter focuses more specifically on the sort of information revealed by particular linguistic forms. Indeed, the mind-set of an author is often laid bare by linguistic clues embedded in a manuscript. This chapter covers processes and consequences of linguistic (especially semantic) change, the use of linguistic clues to identify an anonymous writer, problems encountered in document translation, and the use of major language references, notably the *Oxford English Dictionary* (*OED*). To simplify discussion, most of the examples will be drawn from varieties of the English language. The chapter concludes with a case study of language use in Martin Frobisher's sixteenth-century accounts of encounters with the Inuit.

Processes and Consequences of Language Change: Words as Artifacts

Language, like all aspects of culture, has considerable potential for change and variation. All of language is susceptible to change: the sound system, lexicon (vocabulary), and syntax or grammatical structure. Evidence for changes in all these arenas can be discovered in ethnohistoric documents, but the most obvious changes and variations are typically in the realm of semantics, reflecting a language's lexicon or "dictionary."

Numerous types of forces drive language change. Three such factors are adaptive radiation, selective borrowing, and cultural emphasis. All of these processes can be discerned in documentary sources and can aid us in refining our ethnohistoric analyses.

Language is learned, and that process of learning is not identical from person to person or from generation to generation. Everyone has a limited and unique group of "teachers" and a unique learning situation, leading to small variations in individual language use. This fact sets the stage for a force in language change called *adaptive radiation*. Given even minute variations from individual to individual, and from group to group, when individuals or groups separate from one another, their languages tend to slowly drift apart. For instance, British settlers in North America encountered new landscapes and adapted existing words such as "gap" and "clearing" to the novel setting, giving them slightly different meanings. Strange flora and fauna (such as hickory, squash, and groundhog) were given innovative names or names borrowed from indigenous peoples (such as *coyote,* which traveled through Spanish from central Mexican Nahuatl [*coyotl*]). New ways of life and technology necessitated new verbal labels, and so emerged words such as "backwoodsman" and "bobsled." Some words with a long history in British English took on variant meanings in the North American colonies: "corn," for instance, changed from labeling a generic cereal crop to specifically designating maize (McCrum, Cran, and MacNeil 1986:121–122). Clearly, vocabulary (as well as phonetics and grammar) was subject to forces of diversification as people became separated across the span of the Atlantic Ocean.

On the other hand, people come into contact with one another, and *selective borrowing* of linguistic forms frequently occurs (sometimes by choice, sometimes not). The Norman Conquest of Britain in 1066 introduced a plethora of French-derived terms on a Germanic (Anglo-Saxon) base. These words were not randomly scattered throughout the language assemblage but conformed to the social and political realities of the time: the Normans were the conquerors, the Anglo-Saxons the conquered. Thus terms for meat on the plate (the aristocrat's plate), such as beef, veal, mutton, and pork, all derive from Norman French. The animals on the hoof, tended by the conquered villagers, retained their Anglo-Saxon names: cow, calf, sheep, and pig. Thus, a dual linguistic arrangement for domesticated animals emerged in Norman Britain. One general exception is the use of chicken in both contexts: chicken more often landed on the table of a peasant and did not readily acquire the more exalted term "poultry."

Languages also diversify as the assemblage of words in a language follows a culture's or group's special interests or emphases. This *cultural emphasis* is reflected in the repletion of words for tropical birds among the South American Tupinamba, the voluminous vocabulary describing cattle among the pastoral east African Nuer, or the linguistic emphasis on armament and battlefield strategy by Hernán Cortés's Spanish conquistadors in Mexico. Such emphases provide clues to the writer's individual interests and cultural biases.

These (and other) pressures for linguistic diversity have combined over time to yield distinctive languages and dialects. The English language, for instance, resulted from successive contact among Celtic, Roman, Germanic, Viking, and French peoples, all of whom contributed important linguistic elements to the British English potpourri. From the sixteenth century on, English spread about the globe. As English-speaking groups became separated from one another, the language radiated into new forms, yielding dialects and subdialects of American English, Australian English, Indian English, and so on, each designed to communicate its own particularities and emphases.

Of all aspects of language, the lexicon tends to be the most sensitive and responsive to the forces of change. A glimpse into the world of etymology (the origins and shifting meanings of words) yields a wealth of historical information and a sense of caution in translation and interpretation. As will become obvious, many well-known words carry distinctly different meanings today than they did in prior centuries. In delving into etymologies, it is useful to systematize the sorts of changes words undergo, so as to be able to anticipate a word's meaning as it appears in its historical context. These changes are consequences of the above linguistic processes; the most important ones for readers of ethnohistoric documents include extension and specialization, shifting and fading, and amelioration and perjuration.

Some words, initially denoting something quite particular, become extended over time. Classic examples are "Kleenex" expanding to mean all tissue, "xeroxing" to mean all photocopying, and "Coke" to mean any soft drink. Perhaps less well known is the British practice of "hoovering," or vacuum cleaning, after the Hoover vacuum cleaner. These may be somewhat predictable extensions. But what about the word "thing" (as general a word as can be imagined), which simply meant "assembly of people" in Old English/Norse (Heller, Humez, and Dror 1983:203)? Or, ironically, would it be anticipated that our word "dunce" could have derived from the name of a respected medieval scholar, John Duns Scotus (Heller, Humez, and Dror 1983:59–60)? With specialization, in contrast, a word's meaning becomes more narrow over time. For example, the verbs "manufacture" (to produce by hand) and "manure" (to work by hand) have the same basic French derivation, but both have developed into specialized forms of "work" or "produce," the first commonly in an industrial context, the second associated directly with fertilizer.

Many instances of extension derive from the contact between languages: the North American moose was typically referred to as "cow" by early English writers, maize was called *blé d'inde* (Indian wheat) by the French, and sheep were termed *ichcatl* (cotton) by the Mexican Nahua (Aztecs). The examples of both extension and specialization are legion, and the possibility that a word has undergone such change should always be considered by the ethnohistorian. Furthermore, a given word may waffle from specific to general to specific meanings (or vice versa): the word "salary," for example, in Roman times referred specifically to "salt money," later acquiring the generalized meaning "regular payment for services" or "wages," and still later becoming again specialized to contrast with "wages" and refer to "regular payments made for professional or white-collar services" (Heller, Humez, and Dror 1983:164–165).

Words frequently shift or transfer meaning; for example, colors whose names come from specific foods and drinks: orange from the orange, plum from the plum, chartreuse from a liqueur (the liqueur itself taking its name from a French town), and burgundy from a deep red wine (which in turn took its name from a region in France). The word "groom" has undergone a number of curious shifts over the centuries: from "male person," especially "male servant," the word came to mean "an officer in a royal or noble household," from thence to a "male servant in charge of the horses" (so one can, for instance, groom a horse today, and not just horses, but oneself, and a person for an office as well) (Heller, Humez, and Dror 1983:81–82). And consider "dirt" (unclean matter), "earth" (ground), and "soil" (from "nightsoil"), all having shifted today into rough equivalents.

Very often a word continues in use with its earlier meaning lost to common knowledge. The word "jungle," deriving from a Sanskrit word referring to dry desert lands, came to mean uncultivable or uninhabitable lands, and then dense, verdant rain forests. For most of us the original meaning of the word is quite lost. And how many of us recall that a gymnasium (related to "gymnosperm") was a site for naked exercise, or an arena or a sandy place for competitive events (cf. Spanish *arena:* "sand")? Although you might readily recognize each of these words in historical documents, you must consider that they may carry meanings quite lost to contemporary common usage. Word meanings can also fade from existence, with the words becoming obsolete; how many people today recognize the word "firken" as a pail-like butter tub?

Some words experience changes in values attached to them. With amelioration, some words with initial negative meanings gradually acquire more positive (or at least, non-negative) connotations. Such is the case with current usage of "bad," which in some contexts means "good." "Nice" has had a checkered history. In the thirteenth century, it meant stupid or ignorant; in the fourteenth, silly; in the fifteenth, coy and shy; in the sixteenth, subtle and fastidious; from the eighteenth century to the present, agreeable and good (Heller, Humez, and Dror 1983:131) — from "stupid" to "agreeable" in five centuries.

Perjuration is the opposite process, where meaning shifts from positive (or neutral) to negative. The example of "dunce" applies here, as does that of "junk," deriving from reed, rush, and rope. The word "villain" used to simply denote a person attached to a country house. Again, the caution to the modern reader is simply that the connotations of words, as well as other aspects of their meanings, can change, and these possibilities need to be taken into account in understanding documentary sources.

In addition to these types of changes, others take place when people speaking different languages come into contact with one another. A new language is rarely (if ever) adopted wholesale by speakers of another; it is far more typical that selected aspects of a language are incorporated into the existing tongue, often with discoverable and patterned modifications. Over the course of some eight centuries that the Moors spent in the Iberian Peninsula, a great many Arabic words entered Spanish. Many of these, such as *algodon* (cotton), *alfombra* (carpet), and *alcalde* (an official) were formed in Arabic of "al-" (the) and a noun. The Spaniards always heard the "al" with the rest of the word and interpreted it as one word, adding their own article and yielding, for instance, "el alcalde". In a further elaboration, when the Spaniards conquered the Aztecs and established their government across the Atlantic in New Spain, the Nahua (Aztecs) tended to hear *los alcaldes* as a plural (there were typically four such officials on a town council), and added their own plural, "-meh." From Arabic to Spanish to Nahuatl (Aztec), the word became reinterpreted as *los alcaldesmeh:* the-the-official-s-s. The key in interpretation is to be aware of such processes of transformation and to expect them.

Using Linguistic Clues to Identify an Anonymous Writer

Ethnohistorians often deal with documents written by unknown authors, and it frequently is useful to know something about the author to be able to better evaluate the document. Language usage can provide valuable clues to the personal identity of the writer, or at least to some of the writer's characteristics.

If you are examining an anonymous description of a gold-mining operation, for example, and the document refers to adits, slurry ponds, and cyanide sludge, you might reasonably conclude that the writer had some formal training in mining engineering, since these terms are used in textbooks and professional literature. If a second document referred to a belly gulch, a three-ounce trench, and a China rocker, the author was more likely a miner who learned the trade in the field, since these are folk mining terms. A third document using many of the same terms as the second but also including jenny rocker, an Australian term, might indicate the national origin of the miner. Finally, consider a fourth document that speaks of a broad-bladed pick and the deep trench at the end of the place where the waterwheel turns; the author of this document probably is just a visitor inexperienced in mining, since there is no evidence of knowing the technical terms for even the most simple equipment. Each of these documents could be expected to provide very different types of information, all potentially useful.

Aside from actual terminology, the way information is presented can offer insights into a writer's background, experience, and mind-set. For instance, the wife of a doctor in a gold-mining camp, who had little direct contact with mining operations, wrote home that "In many places the surface soil, or in mining-phrase, the 'top dirt,' 'pays' when worked in a 'Long Tom.' This machine, (I have never been able to discover the derivation of its name,) is a trough, generally about twenty feet in length, and eight inches in depth, formed of wood, with the exception of six feet at one end, called the 'riddle,' (query, why riddle?)" (Clappe 1992:119–120). Although this description is quite detailed, the writer is clearly not directly involved in mining activities and even tends to distance herself from it ("in mining-phrase"). She tends to lack the terminological confidence displayed in an account of an actual miner: "We carried our dirt in hand barrows some fifty to seventy-five yards to the creek where we had two sluice boxes and a long Tom to wash the gold" (Reinhart 1962:33). This miner's practicalities contrast, in turn, with the more formal prose of a Geological Survey professional who wrote that "The quartz is mined, the same way as any other mineral, then crushed to a very fine powder by mills. This powder then runs in water in shallow troughs, over quicksilver, which takes up the gold" (Brewer 1974:454). Some of the same terminologies overlap in these documents, but variations in context and tone can provide the ethnohistorian with important clues about the authors.

Language can be used to infer a wide variety of an author's characteristics: education, ethnic or national background, native language, regional background, political or social views, age, and economic status all are reflected in language usage. (See Dalzell 1996; Canfield 1992; Anderson, Berdan, and Lockhart 1976.) Clues to look for include

— Degree of formality and properness in usage
— Size and specialization of vocabulary
— Use of structure or words from another language
— Regional or ethnic terms, especially slang
— Value judgments projected onto political views, social groups, and the like
— References to experiences available only to those of a particular social or economic group (e.g., attendance at an inaugural ball for a president)
— Knowledge (or lack thereof) of topics typically learned through formal education (e.g., the Latin language or Greek philosophy)

Occasionally the author of a document is unknown but could only be one of a limited and known set of possibilities, and the ethnohistorian sometimes can use language to identify the writer or at least to narrow the field. *The Diary of a Forty-Niner* is a good example (Canfield 1992). Found in an abandoned cabin in California's Gold Country in the 1880s, this document is the diary of a miner who worked the gold fields between 1849 and 1851. Although it had no author's name on it, it was known who had been mining in this community during those years, and the number of possible authors was limited to about a dozen. The fluent use of English with no apparent influence of other languages suggested a native speaker of American English. Since the writing of the diary was flawed with numerous spelling errors and reflected a limited vocabulary in terms of fancy words, well-educated candidates were eliminated. The New England regional usages of the diary eliminated others, and recognition of intimate familiarity with the practices of farming eliminated the remainder, leaving Charles Anderson of Connecticut as the apparent author.

Some Matters of Translation

Quite obviously, understanding words is a necessary ingredient in an accurate interpretation of a document. Since words (and language sounds and syntax) change over time, it might be said that the modern reader of early historical sources is indeed translating them, whether across different languages or across time in a single language.

The Subtleties of Translation

The problems of translation are compounded if you are working in a second (or third) language. Direct translation is often complicated not only by difficulties in evaluating intended meanings, but also by problems in understanding the subtleties of differing worldviews.

Intended meanings can be evasive, and at times even a literal translation can mislead the naive reader. Take, for example, the statement by Saddam Hussein, the leader of Iraq during the Gulf War of 1991, that blood would flow in the streets and that Iraqi soldiers would suck the eyes out of American soldiers. This statement apparently was accurately reported and literally translated. Most English-speaking readers will compare it to political statements in their own experience, primarily produced in their home country. As a result, they are likely to interpret Saddam's statement as a violent, strident threat. To an Arabic speaker, however, the statement has a very different cultural context. Men in Arab culture, especially public figures, can gain considerable prestige by making exaggerated statements, particularly in situations of conflict. Arabic-speaking readers will see beyond the literal meaning of the statement, comparing it to a wide range of other statements in their experience. As a result, conventional phrases ("blood flowing in the streets") will be interpreted as such, and hyperbole ("suck out the eyes") will be recognized as rhetorical exaggeration. The result is that the cultural meaning of Saddam's statement for an Arabic speaker is far less severe and extreme than a literal translation suggests to an English speaker.

The distortion caused by a literal translation is compounded when an ethnic stereotype is reinforced by the distorted message. Many Americans have an impression of Arabs as bomb-throwing, fanatical, and violent (an image fostered by some movies). In that context, there is less inclination to question whether the ferocity of the literal translation might be overstated in the English version. The confusion that can arise from literal translation should not surprise American speakers of English. Imagine the reaction of foreign visitors to a major league baseball game. Asked what the crowd is so vehemently screaming, they might be told, "Kill the ump!" Coupled with the reputation of American baseball players for bench-clearing brawls and the stereotype of violent Americans, the visitors might receive a very wrong impression of the message intended by the crowd and the intensity of its emotion.

Every writer of a primary document has a particular mind-set, and those conceptualizations often creep into the written documents. The presence of these ideas and attitudes is often subtle. For instance, one of the most important documents on Aztec culture was produced by a Franciscan friar, Bernardino de Sahagún, in the latter half of the sixteenth century. Preserved today as the *Florentine Codex,* this massive collection of cultural material was verbally elicited by Sahagún from elderly Aztec informants in their native language of Nahuatl. On the surface, it would seem that this information is an inviolable reflection of Aztec culture. Yet, Sahagún's medieval ecclesiastical upbringing emerges in the very structure of the document. Medieval thought, especially as applied by a man of the cloth, reveled in "a place for everything, and everything in its place." Linguistically, it pursued a universal, divine origin for all linguistic forms. In tune with these beliefs, Sahagún sought organization (and not just simple organization, but *completeness* of organization) and one-on-one correspondences between Nahuatl and Spanish linguistic forms. However, his concept of organization did not exist in Aztec thought, and the semantic parallels he sought likewise were unrealistic. Reflecting his times and his background, Sahagún's philosophy and beliefs crept into a document that appears, on the surface, to be quite thoroughly Aztec. The impact of his mind-set on the writing of this native-language document is subtle but, of course, must be taken into consideration.

Euphemism and Dysphemism

Skilled writers often aim to manipulate the sentiments of their readers through their careful choice of words. To contemporary readers from the same culture as the writer, the detailed connotations of each word are usually known, and the meaning comes through clearly. Over the gap of time or cultural difference, however, that meaning may be obscured to the ethnohistoric reader. Two classes of such words that can be particularly difficult for such a reader are euphemism and dysphemism.

A euphemism is an everyday and acceptable word or phrase used as a replacement for one that is less acceptable. Euphemisms in English largely relate to bodily functions, death, and unpleasant political realities. The Victorian "necessary," for example, merely denoted a bathroom (in itself a euphemism, since baths are not the most common function performed there); "nightsoil" is hardly soil in the modern sense, but a more direct designation would have offended many eighteenth- and nineteenth-century English speakers; a dead person in modern North America is often referred to as having "passed away"; and men's trousers and undergarments were called "inexpressibles" in eighteenth- and nineteenth-century England. Euphemisms are not limited to English, of course. German, for example, has provided the world with one of its most powerful euphemisms: the "concentration camp." In modern China, complaints over advertisements for dog meat led to the development of the current euphemism of "fragrant meat." Euphemisms serve as a shield to protect the reader from the shock of reality stated baldly.

In contrast, dysphemism is used in a deliberate attempt to insult, shock, or outrage the reader. Here, an everyday word is replaced with one that has strong emotional value, often because it touches a nerve of truth that everyday usage avoids. During the Vietnam War, for example, soldiers from the United States sometimes were jeered by antiwar activists and called "killers," an accurate enough designation of the ultimate purpose of soldiers, but one that stepped enough outside the realm of common usage to be considered dysphemism. During the McCarthy era of the 1950s, communists were searched out with incredible zeal by Americans ready to label anyone with vague leftist tendencies as a "pinko," another example of dysphemism. Many insulting terms, ranging from "queer" to "pizzaface," are dysphemisms. If a euphemism is a shield to protect our sensibilities, a dysphemism is a sword to wound them.

Of course, whether a word is a euphemism or a dysphemism depends in part on one's view of reality. Ho Chi Minh, for example, was the leader of North Vietnam in the Vietnam War and before that in colonial Vietnam's fight for independence from France. Was he a "freedom fighter" or a "commie overlord"? In a sense, both are true, but the decision of which is the more accurate descriptor is a matter of point of view and political judgment; whichever term is left over becomes either a euphemism or a dysphemism.

Recognizing euphemism and dysphemism is important in interpreting an ethnohistoric document. A writer may consistently use terms with negative connotations in a dysphemic attempt to denigrate a person or society; euphemisms can be used equally well to serve the opposite end. In addition, a writer may use euphemisms out of habit or respect for the sensitivities of readers, even if the overall aim of the writing is to produce a negative image of the people described. In a sense, interpreting euphemisms and dysphemisms is the same as reading any other words: the goal is to fathom their true meaning; however, as with hyperbole, expressions of modesty, and the like, euphemisms and dysphemisms have another layer of meaning that can obscure the author's intended meaning. Rawson (1981) provides a dictionary of euphemisms in English, though it is far from complete and is weakest in historical usage; Allan and Burridge (1991) provide a more general treatment of the principles underlying euphemism and dysphemism.

Formulaic Writing

The translation of documentary texts can be made easier if the writer used recognizable formulas to construct the document. For instance, wills from sixteenth-century Mexico written in Nahuatl followed a highly conventionalized order. They began by invoking the deity, declared the testator to be physically ill but mentally sound, and offered his or her soul to God. This was followed by an itemized listing of willed items: the first generally referred to expenses for burial and Masses, followed by real estate and movable goods. If any debts had to be settled, they were then mentioned, followed by an indication of the executors (Anderson, Berdan, and Lockhart 1976:23–27). Translation of many documents (from wills to land-dispute documents to tax records) can be greatly facilitated by recognizing their predictable sequences, and an understanding of those patterns is a useful tool in deciphering ethnohistoric materials.

Although formulaic writing makes translation easier, it poses all sorts of problems in terms of accuracy. Certain formulaic phrases often were included, even when patently untrue; for example, an official document ending with the phrase "signed in my presence" should not be taken as proof that the signer actually was in the presence of the official who prepared the document. In some cases it is equally possible that the document was sent back and forth by mail for convenience.

Even greater errors could be promulgated by the slavish acceptance of the truth value of formulaic writing. Explorers and traders from Elizabethan England, for instance, typically carried with them a set of royal greetings and decrees addressed to a variety of countries and rulers. Some of these places and people were real, others were vaguely reputed, and still others were purely legendary or mythical; some of these documents had blanks left at critical places, allowing names of kingdoms and kings to be filled in on the spot (Locke 1930:31–34, 159). Clearly, it would be unwise to interpret such a document as proof of the reality of a particular kingdom or monarch.

The Oxford English Dictionary (OED) *and Other Language References*

In the mid-nineteenth century, a plan unfolded to develop a comprehensive dictionary of the English language. This dictionary, the *Oxford English Dictionary* (*OED*), was originally bound in ten volumes and took more than half a century to complete, its various segments being published between 1884 and 1928 (Green 1996). Since that time it has been reprinted into twelve (and more recently twenty) volumes (and a compact two-volume set and CD-ROM) and augmented by *OED Additions.*

The *OED* is considered the ultimate authority on all matters relating to the history of words in the English language. Its second edition (published in 1995 in twenty volumes) defines more than 500,000 words, including their pronunciation, variable forms, and etymology. This compendium is particularly valuable for the ethnohistorian working in English, for it includes some 2,400,000 quotations, putting each defined word into the context of documents written at various times in the history of the word's usage.

The *OED Additions* take into account recent changes in the English language (since the third *OED* edition is not due until around 2010). Each of its two volumes contains some three thousand "new" English words from all over the English-speaking world, as well as commonly used loan words from other languages (such as *norteamericano* from Spanish). Like its parent volumes, it contains a generous supply of contextual quotations.

The emphasis of the *OED* is on etymologies. Changes in meanings are meticulously traced through long periods of time so that the evolution of each word is documented and available. It is an invaluable resource for the ethnohistorian who wishes to glean specific word meanings and nuances. It should be consulted with shameless frequency.

Excellent as they are, the *OED* and *OED Additions* are not the only useful sources on etymologies. Samuel Johnson's *A Dictionary of the English Language* (1755) provides an excellent idea of eighteenth-century usages (where he tells us, among other things, that a lexicographer is "a writer of dictionaries; a harmless drudge"). Noah Webster's *American Dictionary of the English Language* (1828) provides a nineteenth-century view of American English. The compendious *Dictionary of American Regional English* (Cassidy 1985–; in three volumes so far, covering terms A–O) includes some two and a half million folk expressions with etymologies styled after the *OED.* The regional Americanisms contained in this massive and extremely useful dictionary were derived from both interviews and publications, the latter including sources such as small-town newspapers and regionally based novels. Similar sources, although somewhat less expansive, are *A Dictionary of Slang and Unconventional English* (Partridge 1984) and *A Concise Dictionary of Slang and Unconventional English* (Beale 1989). A further helpful source is *The Oxford Companion to the English Language* (McArthur 1992). This thick volume provides complementary information to the various dictionaries, treating the many aspects of linguistics (anything from jargon to motto to toponym) in a context of language change and variation. Together, these many sources, along with others discussed in chapter 7, provide a sound, basic set of tools for translating and interpreting ethnohistoric documents. Other specialized reference materials should also be consulted when needed, as well as similar references in languages other than English.

Case Study

MARTIN FROBISHER'S ACCOUNTS

Between 1576 and 1578, Sir Martin Frobisher conducted three expeditions in search of the Northwest Passage, a route to Asia through extreme northern North America. Although Frobisher was unsuccessful in finding such a route, he wrote a compelling account of his voyages and the people he encountered (Frobisher 1867; originally published in 1578). Frobisher dubbed the place he explored "Meta Incognita," and today it can be identified with the area around Baffin Island, in northeastern Canada. The people he described apparently were the Inuit.

The following excerpts are taken from Frobisher's descriptions of his second and third voyages (Frobisher 1867:137–138, 285) and illustrate how language of earlier centuries can be difficult to interpret appropriately. Frobisher describes some of the activities of the people he met in Meta Incognita:

> Upon the maine lande over against the Countesse's Iland, we discovered and behelde to our great marvell, the poor caves and houses

of those countrie people which serve them (as it shoulde seem) for their winter dwellings, and are made two fadome under grounde, in compasse rounde, like to an oven, being joyned fast one by another, having holes like to a fox or conny berrie, to keepe and come togither. They under-trench these places with gutters, so that the water falling from the hills above them, may slide away without their anoiance, and are seated commonly in the foote of a hil, to shielde them better from the colde winds, having their dore and entrance ever open towards the south. From the ground upward they builde with whales bones, for lacke of timber, whiche, bending one over another, are hand-somely compacted in the toppe togither and are covered over with seales' skinnes, whiche instead of tiles, fenceth them from the rayne. In eache house they have only one roome, having the one halfe of the floure raysed with broad stones a foote higher than ye other, whereon strawing mosse, they make their nests to sleepe in. They defile these dennes most filthylie with their beastly feeding, and dwell so long in a place (as we thinke), untill their owne sluttishness lothyng them, they are forced to seeke a sweeter ayre and a new seate, and are (no doubt) a dispersed and wandring nation, as the Tartarians, and live in hords and troupes, withoute anye certayn abode. . . .

And they kindle their fyre with continuall rubbing and fretting one sticke againste another, as we do with flints. They drawe with dogges in sleads upon the ise, and remove their tents therwithal, wherin they dwel in sommer, when they goe a hunting for their praye and provision againste winter. They doe sometime parboyle their meate a little and seeth the same in kettles made of beasts skins: they have also pannes cutte and made of stone very artificially: they use preaty ginnes wherewith they take foule.

These passages include words spelled quite differently than modern spell-ings; indeed, Frobisher often spells the same word several ways at dif-ferent spots in his account. Once the variant spellings are taken into con-sideration, much of the writing remains easily intelligible to the reader of English more than four centuries later.

There remains, however, a series of words that are likely to be un-familiar to modern English readers, or that are used in very different ways. Several of these are listed here and explained:

Fadome: Little used today and typically spelled "fathom," this word expressed a measurement embracing both outstretched arms, or about six feet.

Conny: This word, meaning "rabbit," has passed largely into colloquial usage in modern times.

Berrie: Obsolete by the seventeenth century, "berrie" meant "burrow."

Keep: This word means "to protect," coming from the same derivation as the "castle keep."

Come: The *OED* lists nine pages of meanings for this word, but Frobisher's meaning was "to enter."

Compacted: Frobisher uses this word in its earliest known sense, referring to something tightly joined together.

Fenceth: This word, coming from a common root with "defense," means "protect."

Floure: Only the similarity of this spelling to the modern "flour" makes this word difficult; it would have been pronounced to rhyme with "poor" and refers to a floor.

Strawing: This word, obsolete in modern English, means "scattering" and comes from a common root with "strewing," which carries a similar meaning.

Nests: In Frobisher's time, "nest" referred to either the place where a bird laid its eggs (the more common meaning) or a snug retreat for a person; it is unclear whether the connotation of this phrase was intended to convey brutishness on the part of the Inuit (see "dennes" below).

Dennes: In Frobisher's time, as today, the primary meaning of "den" was the abode of an animal, not of a person; his use of this term may connote bestiality on the part of the Inuit; alternatively, however, the word may be interpreted in a less common meaning in use since the fourteenth century, that of a place hollowed out from the ground.

Sluttishness: "Sluttish" and its derivatives originally referred to dirtiness, as it was used by Frobisher here; the modern extension of reference to prostitutes is only from the sixteenth or seventeenth centuries onward.

Lothyng: Today "loathe" means "hate" or "have extreme aversion," but in Frobisher's time it was more likely to mean "disgust."

Seate: A seat was a place of residence, an obsolete usage that is maintained today only in terms like "county seat."

Fretting: This word referred originally to "eroding or wearing away" and was extended to include "rubbing."

Therwithal: This word, which has faded to obsolescence, means "besides."

Seeth: Now used almost exclusively as an intransitive verb, "seethe" was used as a transitive verb meaning "to boil (something)" well into the nineteenth century.

Artificially: From the fourteenth century onward, "artificial" and its derivative words referred to things made in imitation of nature or made with especial skill; Frobisher used the word in the second meaning, one that had become obsolete by the end of the eighteenth century, as the word became more specialized in meaning.

Preaty: The oldest known meaning of this word is "cunning, clever, artful," the meaning Frobisher used here; the modern meaning of "beautiful" was created by extension only in the fifteenth century.

Ginnes: Since Chaucer's time, a "ginne" was a device or machine, coming from the same root as "engine"; this meaning was beginning to fade by the late seventeenth century, although it has occasionally been used as a deliberate archaic form by poets since then; the context here suggests it refers to a trap.

All of these meanings are taken from the *Oxford English Dictionary*.

With modernized spellings, punctuation, and usage, the Frobisher passages could be rendered as follows:

Upon the mainland over against Countesse's Island, we discovered and beheld to our great marvel the poor caves and houses of those country people which serve them (as it seems) for their winter dwellings and are made two fathoms [12 feet] underground, in compass [shape] round like an oven, being joined solidly one to another, having holes like a fox or rabbit burrow to protect and enter through. They under-trench these places with gutters, so that the water falling from the hills above them may slide away without their annoyance and are seated commonly in the foot of a hill to shield them better from the cold winds, having their door and entrance always open toward the south. From the ground upward they build with whale bones (because they lack timber), which, bent one over another, are well joined together at the top, and are covered over with seal skins, which instead of tiles protect them from the rain. In each house they have only one room, having one half of the floor raised with broad stones a foot higher than the other, whereon scattering moss, they make their beds to sleep in. They defile these dens [or underground dwellings] most filthily with their beastly feeding [eating raw meat], and dwell so long in a place (as we see it), until their own filth disgusts them and they are forced to seek sweeter air and a new residence, and are (no doubt) a dispersed and wandering nation, as the Tartars, and live in hordes and troupes, without any certain abode. . . .

And they kindle their fire with continual rubbing of one stick against another, as we do with flints. They draw sleds with dogs upon the ice, and remove their tents besides, wherein they dwell in summer, when they go hunting for their prey and provisions against winter. They do sometimes parboil their meat a little and boil the same in kettles made of animal skins; they also have pans [bowls] cut and made from stone very artfully; they use clever devices to take fowl.

The usage of the word "horde" in the first passage is especially noteworthy because it is an example of an assumption on the part of the writer. Prior to the early to middle seventeenth century, the word referred quite specifically to the nomadic tribes of the Tartars of central Asia. In using the term, Frobisher was assuming that the Inuit in some way resembled the Tartars with which he and his readers were familiar. Of course, the movements and social organization of the Inuit were quite different from those of the Tartars, and the extension of "horde" to them was imprecise and misleading. This use of a familiar term for something newly encountered is the same phenomenon as the English calling the North American porcupine "a hedgehog," and the Spanish terming the Central American jaguar "*el tigre.*"

CHAPTER 6

Interpretation of Names

It would be a rare ethnohistoric document indeed that lacked names of people and places. In some cases a person or locale may serve as the focal point of a document. Alternatively, individuals, groups, settlements, or geographical features may provide essential and intriguing backdrops for a document's primary thrust. Whatever role they play in a document, personal and place-names provide important clues to past activities and relationships. This chapter explores toponyms (place-names) in terms of the processes involved in naming places, the types of names applied to the cultural and geographic landscape, the interpretation of place-names, and the importance of studying toponyms.

Personal names (all linguistic elements identifying an individual) are scrutinized in terms of patterns in the processes of naming people, and problems and potentials in interpreting personal names. A brief discussion of tribal names outlines a few of the problems that can arise when trying to recognize tribal synonyms. Case studies on toponymic patterns in Tlaxcala, Mexico, and personal names in the early Jewish community of New York round out this chapter. In focusing on toponyms and personal names, it should be kept in mind that these are but two aspects of onomastics, the general study of names and naming.

Toponyms

Processes Involved in Naming Places

Names endow places with identity and specificity. They conveniently distinguish one place from another and at the same time highlight particular meanings attached to each locale. For instance, a murky water hole called "Badwater" expressly warns visitors of that spot's qualities as opposed to "Clearwater" farther along the trail.

Each culture devises names for relevant features and habitations in its landscape (Stewart 1975:13). Such relevance may derive from the need to provide guideposts for traveling in a landscape, the desire to lay political or cultural claim to an area, or the need to express a feature's peculiar or perhaps dangerous attribute (such as "the Slot" along a raging river or "Dead Man's Curve" along a serpentine road). Geographical features such as mountains, rivers, and forests are likely candidates for naming — although a mountain's name may pertain to one peak or an entire range, a river's name may change along its course, and various parts of a forest may be differently named. The boundaries of a geographical feature may also be viewed differently from culture to culture (and even person to person), the name of the feature also being applied differently.

Similarly, names pertaining to human occupation may cause some ambiguity or confusion. A town's name may refer physically to its corporate boundaries or demographically to its inhabitants, and it may include only the settled area or encompass the surrounding countryside as well, where each individual field may also carry its special name. These habitation names may be more or less closely tied to the physical attributes of the surrounding landscape. For example, the general term for a named city-state in Aztec Mexico was *altepetl,* literally "water-hill." While these physical attributes were considered basic to a viable human settlement, they were not always obviously present (as with a settlement in a wide open valley). Yet each such political entity was labeled "altepetl" and often written with the polity's name on or inside the glyph of a hill; the designation carried a heavy load of proprietary symbolism along with geographic bounding. And, of course, there is sometimes coincidence between the name of a geographical feature and that of a nearby habitation, such as Round Butte, Montana, named for a nearby rotund natural feature, or Zigzag, Oregon, named for the twisty Zigzag River (Wolk 1977:163, 165).

Ethnohistorians using names as clues to past behavior can assume that, in most cases, place-names were not randomly assigned. Rather, they conformed to cultural premises and goals and followed linguistic conventions and creativity. These regularities in naming patterns, then, should reflect to some degree the cultural and social realities of past times when places were named. This, in turn, is directly related to who was empowered to do the actual naming. English colonists in North America, for example, often replaced native place-names with English ones, whereas Spanish and Portuguese settlers in Latin America generally did so at a substantially lower rate. This can be related to quite different colonial goals: the English tended to replace native populations on the land, while the Spanish and Portuguese emphasized wealth extraction using native labor. Consequently, the English linguistic imprint on the land tended to be more pervasive than that of the Spanish or Portuguese, who were more content to adopt and adapt native-language place-names, and who were more prone in general to cultural blending than were the English (Roberts 1993).

At a political level, naming a place had the effect of claiming it. With this in mind, the sixteenth-century French cosmographer André Thevet in effect confiscated two islands (one of them mythical anyway) by baptizing them with his own name; he thereby "exercised a symbolic and purely theoretical empire over territories that in fact escaped the control of both the king and his geographer" (Lestringant 1994:120). At an even more idiosyncratic level, patterns for naming may not be easily discerned — or even exist. Lewis and Clark consciously applied all thirty-three expedition members' names to natural features on their 1804–6 journey to the Pacific, but while some of these names were tied to specific events (such as Floyd's River, where Sgt. Charles Floyd died), most appear to have been chosen randomly and without particular heed to rank or other discernable criteria (Large 1995). Similarly, Christopher Columbus occasionally went into a "veritable naming frenzy" during his voyages to the West Indies, sometimes naming a single place twice (Todorov 1984:27–28). Another example is the naming in California of Mojave Desert communities along the railroad. Most such settlements were named for stations and sidings and postdate construction of the railroads. The names of transfer stations were assigned alphabetically from the Colorado River westward by Lewis Kingman in 1895, and ranged from Amboy to Goffs. In 1905 the sidings between these stations were also given names, this time by an anonymous namer who derived the names from classical mythology; alphabetically ordered, they extend from Argos to Hector (Gudde 1969:9, 13, 137; USGS topographic maps).

Some toponyms were bestowed with the sarcasm and sardonic humor often associated with frontiers; Forest Grove and Cold Springs, both in the arid Great Basin of eastern Oregon, are treeless, dry, and hot much of the year. Thus, while we may assume that the process of naming largely conforms to cultural patterns, an eye should also be kept open to the possibility of personal whimsy.

A Toponymic Typology

A common and convenient way to deal with the vast multitude of place-names is by grouping them into eight categories based on their genesis. These categories (derived from the extensive toponymic research of

George Stewart [1958, 1975]) highlight the motivations, circumstances, and cultural premises involved in the naming process. Names in any of the categories often consist of generic and specific components. The generic denotes the general class of name, such as "river," "city," "ford," "wood," or "-ton" (for town). The specific element modifies or elaborates on that general class, as with the "Big" in Big Wood, the "Charles" in Charleston, or the "Lonely" in Lonely Gulch. Although this arrangement is extremely common, it is not absolutely necessary in understanding the name of a place. In particular, well-established generics may be omitted or dropped over time, as with the Mississippi (River), the Rockies (Mountains), and New York (City). Of course, some names, such as Chicago and York, never had a generic element at all.

Descriptive Names. These names simply describe the observed qualities of a place. Obviously, standards, experience, and criteria for naming will differ from namer to namer: what is "Little Mountain" to one individual may be "Big Hill" to another. One's background also influences a descriptive name: it seems likely, for example, that the namer of "Rabbit Ear's Pass," with jutting peaks resembling rabbit ears, had some familiarity with rabbits and those animals' signal qualities. The names may be quite literal, as with "Red River" or "Desolation Wilderness," or they may be more general and metaphorical, as with "Mil Cumbres" (Thousand Peaks).

Associative Names. These names identify a place in terms of some distinguishing cultural characteristic. Examples include "Mill Creek," "Electric City," and "Frenchman's Cay." Associative names provide clues to notable historic activities in a locale, such as the establishment of a mill at Mill Creek, Electric City's relationship to Grand Coulee Dam, or the settlement of Frenchmen on a small spit of Caribbean land.

Incident Names. These names refer to a specific event, whether real or fictional, associated with a location. "Burnt Cabin Point" is a reminder of a specific incendiary disaster, while "Massacre Rock" suggests one type of social interaction, and "Council Bluffs" quite another.

Possessive Names. A possessive name denotes an individual who was closely tied to the location and its history. In many cases these names indicate ownership or control over the settlement or area. Names such as "Cooperstown" (named by James Fenimore Cooper's father), "Pocahontas" (in Virginia), and "Juneau" (named for local prospector Joseph Juneau) all conform to this very common pattern. Some possessive names are bestowed with the intent to honor an individual or conserve a person's memory. Examples of such commemorative names include Bolivia (for Simón Bolívar), Virginia (for the unmarried Queen Elizabeth I), and Washington (in numerous places). Saints' names are commonly attached to parishes or churches, and the name then becomes associated with the more-encompassing surrounding settlement; these may be considered commemorative and include places such as San Antonio, San Bernardino, and Santa Monica.

Commendatory Names. Places named in a commendatory fashion attempt to characterize a place as especially positive, lucky, inspiring, or hopeful. Names so bestowed would include "Inspiration" (in Arizona), "New Era" (in Michigan), and "Excel" (in Alabama) (Wolk 1977:160–161). The reverse, however, also happens, as with negative or derogatory names such as "Devil's Hole," "Disaster Inlet," and "Seldom Seen" (Stewart 1975:129–130). In some cases, negative names have been consciously altered to carry more positive meanings: "Poverty Ridge" was transformed into "Prosperity," "Poorman's Bottom" into "Sunshine Valley," "Crazy Hollow" into "Pleasant Valley," "Fighting Corners" into "Friendship," and "Cape of Storms" into "Cape of Good Hope" (Stewart 1975: 128, 131; Wolk 1977:180).

Manufactured Names. The hallmark of manufactured names is creativity: they are consciously coined and call attention to the namer's originality. Thus "Tesnus" is "sunset" spelled backwards; "Texarkana" combines overlapping elements of "Texas," "Arkansas," and "Louisiana"; "Azusa" derives from "A to Z in the USA"; and "Zzyzx" was contrived to secure a lasting place in a gazetteer.

Mistake Names. Sometimes the name of a place is misunderstood, misinterpreted, or mistranscribed; when the error becomes embedded into the name, we have mistake names. One of the best examples is Nome, Alaska, whose original designation as "No Name" was miscopied and cartographically solidified. Place-names may often be spelled differently by different writers, but until recently, spelling conventions were quite fluid, so these cannot really be considered mistakes. Shifts in spelling are also frequently associated with shifts in pronunciation, especially across languages: "Caresso Creek" derives from Spanish *carrizo* (reed) and "Oregon" from French *ouragan* (hurricane). In an attempt to mold an existing name into their own language, individuals may wildly reinterpret names: "Kaap

Hoorn" (for the Dutch city of Hoorn) slid into English as "Cape Horn" and was subsequently adopted into Spanish as "Cabo Hornos" (Cape Ovens), a far cry from the name's original intent (Stewart 1975:153).

Shift Names. These names have been transferred from one area to another and typically indicate the origin of immigrants to the new site or settlement: "New Jersey" was named after the Channel Island of Jersey; "Holland" (Michigan) harks back to the Netherlands; and "Germantown Flats" (New York) signals a Teutonic background for its settlers. Although such names may appear obvious, they can also be somewhat deceptive. For instance, "Norway" (Michigan) was named for large stands of Norway pines in the region; the local population claims very few Norwegians (Wolk 1977:118).

This typology—although neither perfect nor fully comprehensive—serves as a helpful entree into understanding the genesis of individual place-names. Like any typology, it should be used as a guide, keeping in mind that several categories may pertain to a single name: an incident name may as well be a possessive name, or an associative name could also be classed as a commendatory one. It should also be remembered that Stewart based this typology primarily on Western premises and examples; it is as yet undetermined how applicable the typology is to naming patterns in non-Western cultures.

Afable and Beeler (1996:189–190) suggest a different typology for American Indian place names including (1) descriptive names, (2) locational names, (3) names referring to human activities associated with a site, and (4) names referring to history, mythology, or folklore. In addition to some variation in categories, these typologies also differ in emphasis and nuances. North American Indians rarely named places after persons, but it has been a common practice among Euro-Americans; American Indians also used locational designations such as "upriver" and "downriver" or "offshore" and "inshore" in contrast to the Euro-American custom of modifying location with cardinal directions (Afable and Beeler 1996:189–190).

The Interpretation of Place-Names

The ethnohistorian wishing to gain the greatest mileage from toponymic study—and likewise desiring to avoid the trickiest pitfalls—can make five initial assumptions about naming patterns:

— A place is named with some purpose in mind.
— Every place-name has (or had) a meaning.
— The meaning relates (or related) to something distinctive about the place.
— Once established, a name tends to endure.
— Once established, however, linguistic changes in a name will follow changes in the language generally, particularly phonetic changes.

There are, of course, notable exceptions to these broad statements. In particular, many names may become completely lost when the local inhabitants leave or are displaced; name replacement through military conquest has been quite common around the globe. Similarly, place-names are at times victims of changing political conditions and undergo purposeful name changes in response to those conditions. Nonetheless, it is well worth the ethnohistorian's energy to test each name against these standards.

Assume, then, that every place has been named with a particular purpose in mind. Since some types of names tend to suit some purposes better than others, the names themselves are left behind as vestiges of those purposes. For instance, descriptive names such as "Broken Top Mountain," "Chimney Rock," and "Cave Rock" are all attached to distinctive landscape features that could have served adequately as orientation guideposts and travel landmarks, particularly to the initiated traveler. Names based on incidents or personal associations would serve less well to guide travelers. On the other hand, places endowed with personal names often suggest that the namer was intent on claiming (or at least being identified with) the site or area. And names of the incident genre tend to memorialize an event and tell the ethnohistorian what was considered a notable event at that particular time and place. Of course, caution must be exercised to avoid overinterpreting intents, for alternative explanations are often possible: a personal name may be given because an individual died — rather than lived — there, or the diagnostic shape of a natural feature may be obvious to one observer but less obvious to another.

If a place-name is meaningful and that meaning relates to some special quality or event, the ethnohistorian's task is to ferret out the place-name's distinctive meaning and thereby gain some insight into the characteristics of the place. Incident names provide insight into geographically localized events, associative names highlight significant cultural characteristics, possessive names identify prominent individuals, descriptive names indicate significant (and thereby named) features of the landscape, and so on. In ancient Mexico, "Ytzucan" (Place of Obsidian), "Yztapan" (Place of Salt), and "Teocuitlatlan" (Place of Much Gold) all suggest settlements associated with those valued resources. "Tenayucan" (Place Full of Walls) suggests a cultural feature; "Teziutlan" (Place of Hail) highlights an unusual climatic event; and the name "Tezcatepec" (Hill of Mirror) identifies the historical figure Tezcatzin (Revered Mirror) with that town's founding (Paso y Troncoso 1905, 6:31). It is a safe assumption that these names were not doled out randomly or capriciously, although at times alternate interpretations of their etymologies are possible and reasonable.

It can also be assumed that place-names tend to be persistent and enduring, though not immutable, so it is worthwhile seeking naming patterns deep into history. For instance, the Roman term *castra* (camp) survives in English place-names such as Lancaster, Rochester, and Chesterfield (Stewart 1975:225–226), although these sites were most likely given these names by the early English rather than the Romans. Linguistic changes (particularly phonetic ones) tend to obscure some original names and their intended meanings: "Nottingham" was derived from a man named Snot (the "s" being fortuitously dropped), and Netherfield may well derive from *naeddre,* an early form of "adder" (Stewart 1975:264–265).

There are further complicating factors in the interpretation of place-names. First, a place may have different names for different segments of society, and second, a name may be changed to reflect a society's shifting political and moral thrusts. Both of these considerations can be illuminated with a single example. In California's gold rush country, more than a dozen communities (mostly camps) made it onto Anglo maps and into Anglo literature as "Greasertown," so named because of their predominantly Mexican populace. The locals, however, had other names for these same places; for example, "Oro Grande," "Santa Maria," and "Paradiso." Nowadays, politics and mores make "Greasertown" unacceptable, but the other names have been forgotten with the abandonment of the communities.

The interpretation of place-names becomes a bit tricky when names have been transferred from one language to another. Such transfer occurs generally in three different ways: phonetic transfer, translation, and visual transfer (Stewart 1975:54). In phonetic transfer the basic linguistic form of the name is adapted to the phonetic repertoire of an intrusive language, such as the variant Spanish and English pronunciations of Los Angeles or Rio Grande. Sometimes such transfers result in a fairly dramatic shift in meaning: in Australia, for instance, the aboriginal place-name "Dilliget" became, by phonetic analogy, "Delegate," much as "Cambowea" became "Gunblower" (Stewart 1975:134). Translation of a name from one language to another involves some degree of bilingualism and also suggests a certain amount of linguistic imperialism: so "Cabo de Boa Esperanca" in Portuguese became known as "Cabo de Buena Esperanza" in Spanish and "Cape of Good Hope" in English. Understanding a place's name from visual imagery or the written word can also involve transformations across languages: for example, the accent in "Florida" migrated from the Spanish penultimate syllable to the English initial syllable, most assuredly through such visual transfer.

In any of these instances, the opportunities for misunderstandings and mistranslations loom quite large. Among these are beheadings, tele-scopings, recastings, and downright translation blunders that significantly transform original meanings. Examples of all of these can be found in the modern state of Wisconsin: the native name "Ozaukee" was beheaded by the French to "Sac" (thence to "Sauk" by the English, as in Saukville); "Marie-Antoinette" was telescoped to "Marinette" (as county and city); "La Montagne" (the Mountain) was recast to "Lamon Tangue" (a creek); and "the Dalles" (flat stones) slid phonetically into English as "Dells," suggesting a completely different physiographic feature (Cassidy 1985).

Phonetic similarities across languages provide especially fertile ground for the reinterpretation of place-name meanings and the consequent loss of original meanings. The Celtic word *mawr* (big), for instance, often came into English as "moor" (referring to open, rolling, infertile land), a word that also competed with "mor," referring to murders and hence special incidents. Thus, a name such as "Morpeth" could mean "Big Path," "Moor Path," or "Murder Path," each possibility evoking a quite different history or character of the place (Stewart 1975:259, 267). Alternative interpreta-tions can also be attributed to the development of varying folk etymologies over time. The name of "Searchlight" (Nevada) for example, has been variously attributed to the need for a searchlight to find gold in a local mine, the inspiration that two brothers received from striking a match, and the name of mining developer Floyd Searchlight (Wolk 1977:176; Alotta 1994:477). In general, it is a useful strategy to consider the possible trans-formations that place-names have experienced over time, as well as the potential for alternative explanations for their derivations and meanings.

The Value of Place-Name Study

Understanding something of place-names and being able to correlate them with places on the ground is of obvious importance to ethnohistory, but the value of studying place-names goes beyond this. The ethnohistorian can often glean considerable information from a careful study of the place-names contained in a document. Toponyms can aid in the interpretation of past geographical conditions; cultural values, ethnicity, and geographical origins of the namers; and sociopolitical conditions and historical relations in the past.

Toponyms are frequently suggestive of past geographical conditions, whether part of the physical or cultural landscape. Perceived attributes of physical features often can be surmised from their names: "Black Mountain," "Red Butte," "Sawtooth Mountains," and "Salton Sea" are all descriptive names that highlight observable qualities of notable spots on the physical landscape. Even if those qualities change over time, the name tends to survive as evidence of a prior state. For instance, "La Cienega" (the Swamp) is now integrated into the Los Angeles metropolitan area, its street name the only reminder of the land's earlier condition. On the cultural side, a generic element such as "landing," frequently found in New Jersey place-names, indicates the establishment of settlements along waterways suitable for transport (Zinkin 1980:62–63). Upgrading "Salem Landing" to "Salem Wharf" suggests the increased importance of the settlement (or at least increased traffic through it) (Zinkin 1980:64).

Similarly, the application of the generic "cartroad" or "cartway" provides glimpses into the types of conveyances used at the time of naming, as well as the nature of the road so named. It is also possible to gain a perspective on everyday activities: "Potters Alley," "the Brew House," "the Brick Kills," and "the Tanyard" all suggest the distribution of specialized economic activities (barring, of course, the unlikely possibility that these places have been named after people called Potter, Brew, Brick, and Tan). "The Fishing Place," "the Market Place," and "the Old Burying Ground" likewise denote places of special activities (Zinkin 1980:66, 69–72). Some such places have long since disappeared or been substantially transformed under subsequent historic developments; for example, the urban cover of Danbury, Connecticut, conceals earlier native settlements of Pahquiote ("Cleared Land," as for planting), Tankiteke ("Forest Dwellers"), and Unkawa ("Beyond the Fishing Place") (Huden 1962:163, 246, 260). In such cases the place-names offer mute testimony to activities and conditions of the past.

Place-names are also often indicative of the cultural values of the namers and serve as clues to their geographical origins, ethnicity, experience, and mind-set. The geographical origins of namers are most readily discerned in shift names such as "New Sweden" (Maine), "New Braunfels" (Texas), "New Germany" (Minnesota), and "Belgium" (Wisconsin); the examples are legion. Similarly, the ethnicity of the namers or settlers is suggested by place-names: "Iowa" and "Tuolumne" are among the many examples of names identifying occupants according to ethnic criteria. Often such names are the work of outsiders, resulting in generalized names such as "Indian Wells" and "Chinatown."

The mind-set, experience, and established linguistic categories of namers are frequently revealed by looking at how they named specific features of the landscape. For instance, many English names in eastern Massachusetts reflect the southeastern England topographic experience of the namers. These settlers had at their disposal only a limited range of topographic designations (such as hill, river, brook, and swamp) to transfer from their homeland to the far more varied landscape in Massachusetts. In order to adjust to that greater geographic variety and scale, they found it necessary (or at least convenient) to apply those few names to a broader variety of landforms than they would have in England. Thus the vast wetlands of Great Swamp and the diminutive bogs of Lamb's Swamp are both nonetheless labeled "swamp" (see Krim 1980).

Place-names also can serve as guides to past historical conditions and relations. In particular, political affiliations and social relations can become manifest as names on the land. The state of Washington was named "New Georgia" after King George III of England in 1792; when the United States acquired the area from England in 1846, the territory's name was changed first to "Columbia" and then shortly thereafter to "Washington" after the first president of the United States (Wolk 1977: 56). Such meanderings of names based on political control are not unusual, and they can be helpful in discerning political relations as well as in dating documents. It is also important to be aware of such variations so that the same place can be identified when it appears under different names.

Name changes can also be generated in response to changes in the political and social climate. The "Flower Pot" pub in England, for instance, was originally called "the Madonna," with its early sign featuring the Virgin and Child and a humble, unremarkable flower pot. When religious images became unfashionable (and downright unsafe) under Cromwell, the innkeeper prudently changed the pub's name and visual emphasis to the very neutral "Flower Pot" (Ashley 1980:47). Wars frequently sparked name changes. For example, "Haviland's Privilege" in Vermont was renamed "Sage City" during the American Revolution: Haviland was a Tory, Sage was a local revolutionary. Similarly, the occasion of World War I prompted some American towns with German names to change them during the war: Germantown, California, changed its name to Artois; Potsdam, Missouri, was renamed Pershing in honor of the World War I American general; and Brandenburg, Texas, became Old Glory. New Germany, Minnesota, was called "Motordale" only during the war, returning to New Germany at war's end (Wolk 1977:112). In this latter case, historic loyalties bent only temporarily to political expediencies.

Dictionaries and analyses of place-name derivations abound. These range from local to regional to national to global studies. The work of George Stewart (1958, 1970, 1975) is particularly useful for its broad scope and thoughtful analyses. The journal *Names* can also be mined for insightful studies and extensive bibliographies.

Personal Names

Ethnohistorians can glean a good amount of information from studying the names of individuals mentioned in historical documents. Far from being arbitrary symbols, names are indicative of genealogical and interpersonal relationships, ethnicity, geographical origins, gender, and social status and therefore have considerable value in ethnohistoric interpretations. Here we will explore the general principles underlying personal-naming conventions, as well as potentials and pitfalls in interpreting personal names. Given the great variation in personal naming patterns, we are using the term "personal name" to refer to all elements of a person's name, however constructed.

From the point of view of most ethnohistoric research, names are used primarily to identify someone. A great deal of other information is derivable from scrutinizing personal names, but most research will not call for such detailed examinations. A number of issues pertaining to the use of names to identify individuals include:

— Multiple names for the same individual
— Identical names for many individuals
— Linguistic corruption of names by outsiders unfamiliar with the language
— Confusion of a general title with a specific name
— Change in a person's name, for either idiosyncratic or predictable cultural reasons
— Use of parallel systems of names for different social contexts

These matters are discussed throughout the following sections on naming processes and interpretation.

Processes Involved in Naming Persons

The purpose of a personal name is to affix a distinctive, definable label on an individual, and the world's cultures have devised a diversity of ways to do this. The Nuer men of Sudan are given birth-names but take their most popular names from the characteristics of their favorite oxen (such as "Rolnyang" [Striped Shoulders]); Nuer women similarly derive personal names from oxen and cows (Evans-Pritchard 1965:18). Aztec names were often based on calendrics, with a person carrying the name and fate of his or her birthdate (such as "Four Rabbit" or "One Flower") in an astrological-style ritual calendar. Spanish personal names given at birth consist of a given name and two surnames, the father's preceding the mother's (such as "Maria García Lopez"). The Welsh derive their surnames from a very limited pool (such as "Evans" and "Jones") and therefore replace a particular individual's surname with some occupational or idiosyncratic characteristic (such as "David Death" for an undertaker). Clearly the structure and content of naming conventions vary considerably and reflect matters of importance in a culture, ranging from cattle among the Nuer to fate among the Aztecs and bilateral kinship among the Spaniards.

Because languages vary in the grammatical devices used to design personal names, it would be a mistake to assume that personal names necessarily consist of a sequence of given name and surname as was, and is, common in most northern European traditions. Examples of grammatical variations between and within cultures are legion. Vietnamese and Korean names place the family (or clan) name first, followed by middle and given names. Names of male citizens in imperial Rome typically contained three elements: a forename, a surname, and an idiosyncratic name. The last of these three names might indicate something peculiar to the individual, designate kinship relations, or commemorate some outstanding achievement. A Roman citizen's name, then, might be "Marcus Tullius Cicero" (Salway 1981:740). In actual practice, however, the forename might be abbreviated (as in "M. Tullius Cicero"), forename and surname might be reversed in order (as in "Tullius Marcus"), or a full three-part name might be reduced to the surname alone (as in "Tullius"). This last option was common with Roman women, who were frequently not given forenames. Grammatical variations in the construction of Roman names, along with the use of a surname alone by all females of a household, can create tricky problems of personal identification for the ethnohistorian (Salway 1981: 740–741).

Grammatical diversity also appears in the way descent affiliations are embedded in personal names. The northern European designation "son of" can appear as "David Richardson" in English, "David ap Richard" or "David Richards" in Welsh, and "James MacGee" or "Richard MacClure" in Irish. English borrowed the Norman "Fitz-" ("son of" and sometimes "illegitimate child of") as a prefix, resulting in surnames such as "Fitzgerald" and "Fitzpatrick" (Hook 1982:105). The Irish "O'" (as in "O'Leary" or "O'Brien") means "grandson of," and its popularity speaks to the importance of recognizing alternating generations among the Irish. Still other types of grammatical variations occur. Some names apparently composed of two elements were conceived by their bearers as only one; an example is Aztec calendar names such as "One Rain," which should be viewed as a single unit, not two separate elements.

Cultures, like languages, use a variety of devices and bases for creating personal designations, including genealogy, titles, calendrics, places, personal attributes, and situational context. Commonly, more than one of these means is used in a single culture (see figure 8).

Perhaps the most usual cultural information embedded in personal names is genealogical: names frequently designate specific lines of descent and other kin relationships. The application of a father's or paternal ancestor's name (patronym) or mother's or maternal ancestor's name (matronym) is common and signals the individual's membership and place in a particular kinship group. A functional equivalent to these devices is the practice of teknonymy, whereby a parent is named according to his or her offspring (e.g., "Father of John," "Mother of John"). A parent's personal name is thereby often displaced by this new name and may (or may not) change again and again with the birth of each successive child (Alford 1988:91). The system of teknonymy is not restricted to parents; grandparents may also acquire such new designations (e.g., "grandparent of John," where they are probably already known as "parent of John's father or mother"). Reverse teknonymy, where a child may be referred to as "son or daughter of Henry," is also known. Additionally, personal names can indicate lineage or clan affiliation, place in an age-grade system, and birth order (Alford 1988). Whatever specific form they take, such personal names provide clues to actual social relationships as well as to organizational principles meaningful in a society.

Social principles reflecting asymmetrical relations are sometimes embedded in titles used as personal names or as parts of personal names. The use of titles often signals special status in a society (usually rather elevated). Some of the titles — such as "Duke of York," "Archbishop of Canterbury," or "King of Ghana" — are generalized titles held by successive

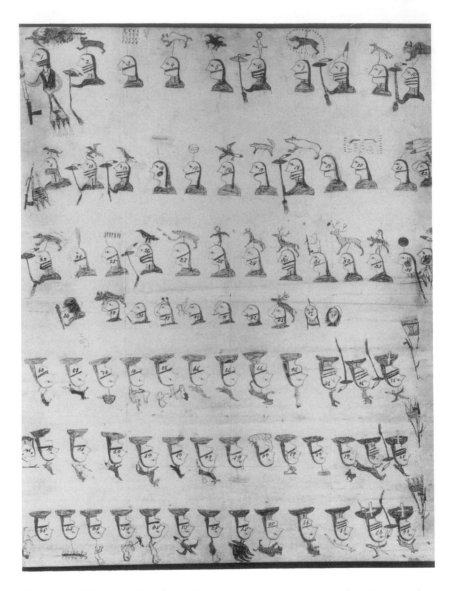

Figure 8. Pictographs of Oglala Sioux personal names. The pictographs are attached to each individual's head and predominantly denote animals (some of which also had mythological significance) or events in the person's life. (Reprinted, by permission, from *Handbook of North American Indians* 17:207, fig. 2)

individuals. When these titles are used in the absence of other names, it is obviously necessary to know the relevant time period in order to attach a specific individual to the title. Other titles, such as the Aztec "Tlacochcalcatl" (Keeper of the House of Darts), were carried by several eminent persons in the society at the same time; again, additional information is necessary to identify specific individuals. Distinguishing titles from names becomes an especially acute problem when cultures are in contact. Seventeenth-century New Englanders seemed to think that "Squaw Satchem" was a single individual, not a generic name for any female leader. Some such terms — called "non-kin-role terms" by Alford (1988:161) — tend to focus on "the role-governed nature of the relationship, the authority of the superior, and the social distance required of the individuals." These include titles such as "sergeant," "judge," "senator," "reverend," "doctor," and "professor," and often precede a surname. Still other titles, such as "Mr." or "Ms.," are broadly applied and typically attached to a surname. Their use suggests some formality and social distance, and can occasionally provide general guidelines for dating a document or event; "Ms.," for instance, while appearing as early as the 1920s, only came into general use in the latter half of the twentieth century.

Sometimes there is a fine line between a title and other personal-name designations. Among the historic Iroquois, personal names were considered the property of a particular clan. Upon birth, a child was awarded one of those names that was not in use; later, an individual might be granted a more prestigious name by the mature women of the clan, an event celebrated with a feast. Since some names were associated with certain positions and levels of prestige, the granting of a new name often was a formal recognition of the elevation of an individual through personal successes. Assuming a chief's name frequently led to assuming that chief's official position (Tooker 1978:424–426). With no method for creating larger numbers of names, it is unclear how this naming system operated in the face of increasing populations.

While titles typically convey a sense of politeness, propriety, or recognized power, epithets serve as name substitutes and terms of address. These may carry meanings ranging from intimacy ("Sweetheart") to respect ("Ace") to insults ("Dumbo"). Their use in ethnohistoric documents can reveal much about personal characteristics and relationships (see Dunkling 1990). An individual's personal attributes often become highlighted as epithets in the common practice of bestowing nicknames (originally "ekenames," "eke" meaning to "add on"). These additional names are bestowed on individuals as they develop unique characteristics or roles and usually do a better job of distinguishing persons from one another than do given names (Alford 1988:82–85).

There are four general arenas where nicknames appear. First, nicknames may highlight individuals' notable physical features in order to distinguish them from others with the same birth-names. In English, relative age, size, or exaggerated features resulted in nicknames and subsequent surnames such as "Young," "Whitehead," or "Short" (Matthews 1967:138–147). Second, behavioral characteristics often emerge in nicknames: a cheerful person might be nicknamed "Blythe" (or its variant "Bligh"), a strong and severe one "Stark," or a quick one "Sharp" — English examples of the positive side of this process. Examples such as "Robert Nagod" (No Good) and "Hugh the Ass" illustrate the derogative side of such nicknaming (Alford 1988:149–153). Third, nicknames may describe occupations: English surnames such as "Butcher," "Baker," and "Fisher" most likely derived from nicknames (Alford 1988:112–113). And fourth, nicknames may focus on place of origin, a matter discussed below. Some individuals may become known by several nicknames; John Adams was variously called "His Rotundity," "Atlas of Independence," "Duke of Braintree," and "Colossus of American Independence" (Dickson 1986:166). Although the above examples are drawn from English, the act of bestowing nicknames is extremely common, though not terribly well documented, in the world's cultures (see Alford 1988:82–85). One issue of the journal *Names* (Skipper and Leslie 1990) is devoted to the practice of nicknaming.

Calendrics serve as another basis for endowing personal names. For example, it was common for Aztec infants to be given calendric names based on date of birth. If, however, a child was born on an unlucky day — such as Nine Jaguar, consigning the person to a life of misery — he or she could be named for any of four successive days; Ten Eagle and Eleven Vulture, for instance, were far more favorable. Consequently, a person's calendar name may not precisely coincide with the date of birth.

Named days of the week also served as a basis for a great variety of personal names in many African societies; the general pattern of these names is presented in table 4 (Dillard 1971, 1976:91). During the American slave era, names underwent predictable linguistic transformations. In some cases, direct translations were made into English, so names such as "Tuesday" or "Friday" emerged. This occasionally became extended to other temporal designations, yielding names such as "March" or "Christmas" (Dillard 1976:19). Other changes were more subtle and derived from phonetic similarities between the African languages and English,

Table 4. Representative African Day Names

Day	Male Name	Female Name
Sunday	Quashee	Quasheba
Monday	Cudjo	Juba
Tuesday	Cubbenah	Beneba
Wednesday	Kwaco, Quaco	Cuba
Thursday	Quao	Abba
Friday	Cuffee, Cuffy	Pheba, Phibbi
Saturday	Quame, Kwame	Mimba

Source: Dillard 1976:91.

turning "Quaco" (Wednesday) into "Quack," "Quashee" (Sunday) into "Squash," and "Phibbi" (Friday) into "Phoebe." These anglicized names thus came to lose their day-name meanings as they entered English parlance, acquiring new meanings in the process (Dillard 1976:19–20). With only seven weekdays, many individuals shared the same name. There are also cases of multiple surname adoption in the United States: the prominence of certain surnames among American Blacks (e.g., Barfield, Peyton, and Robinson) resulted from their slave ancestors' being assigned their owner's surname, although this practice was less pervasive and more variable than often thought (Genovese 1976). A similar pattern sometimes developed on Indian reservations; for instance, a Lakota Sioux (Al Sarnovsky, pers. comm.) reports that an Indian agent named Sarnovsky gave his surname to many Sioux.

Personal names also frequently derive from an individual's place of birth or residence, as is the case for Bernardino de Sahagún, who hailed from the Spanish community of Sahagún, and Aubry de Coucy, lord of Coucy in northern France (Tuchman 1978). In Europe, such place attributions frequently became embedded or interpreted as surnames over time, yielding names such as Guildford, Lublin, and Rodham. Surnames were also often derived from natural features in the landscape. "Woods, stones, fields, plains, swamps, enclosures, or fenced-in places and trees are natural objects in all the Old World countries and have served to name the people living on, or near them" (Smith 1973:xvi). Surnames such as "Hill," "Brooks," "Ford," and "Pines" all suggest residence close to such features.

A person may also be named in accordance with a particular notable situation, although the situation may have little to do with the person named. Young Pawnees, for instance, were given birth names by mid-wives, and second names by their fathers upon their return from war parties. This second name was used by the individual until marriage, when another name was apparently bestowed (Alford 1988:38). Life-cycle and "event" information are therefore embedded in such names, although deciphering an individual's multiple names can become complicated.

Naming techniques relying on approaches such as divination and dreams can result in names that appear to carry more social meaning than they really do. For instance, the Lozi of Africa call out the names of ancestors in front of an unnamed child, waiting for that child to cry at the mention of one of them; this determines the name (and signals the return of the ancestor) (Alford 1988:40). Other names may be bestowed in recognition of a notable event closely coinciding with the person's birth; the Tiv of Africa may name a person "Akpetso" (he just died) or "Iyor-kosu" (people were arguing) (Alford 1988:43).

Any individual may (and often does) carry more than one name at a time, drawing on these various naming processes. Some are quite ob-vious, such as a combination of kin name, title, and nickname. In situa-tions of culture contact, other naming patterns emerge. This includes the use of parallel systems of names for different social contexts, as among many American Jews who have a "Jewish" name used in ritual contexts and an "American" name for everyday use. These often are viewed as close correspondences to one another, such as "Richard" and "Rabin." Sim-ilarly, Hong Kong Chinese often have both a Chinese and an English "first" name, and these, too, are often seen as linked. Such dual names are associated with an individual's assumption of multiple roles within a com-plex, plural society.

In interpreting names bestowed according to these processes, the overarching question deals with the extent to which such names corre-spond to social realities, reflect social roles, and/or reveal patterns of social interaction.

The Interpretation of Personal Names

As a general rule names simultaneously perform the dual functions of categorizing and differentiating individuals within a society or group. Since each culture has discoverable personal naming conventions, names that appear in ethnohistoric documents can frequently be attributed ex-tended meanings that help identify a person's place in the social scheme.

Therefore, whatever naming design is used, certain questions about personal names can be usefully asked:

— What kinds of clues are revealed about genealogical or other interpersonal relations?
— What kinds of information about a person's ethnicity, gender, occupation, or social status are contained in a name?
— Does the name reveal anything about the person's geographical origins?
— Has the name been coined or bestowed recently enough to convey information about the individual, or is it a relic of ancestral conditions?
— Is the name the result of linguistic or cultural changes over time?

Genealogically, names reveal details of vertical kinship relationships in a majority of the world's cultures. The researcher should beware, however, of some pitfalls in interpreting names as genealogical guides. In the first place, a kin name may be bestowed with more ceremony than kinship in mind; the naming of Lozi children mentioned above is one such example. Also, some practices have the consequence of changing an individual's personal name, often making precise identification of an individual difficult. This is especially true with teknonymy, when a parent changes his or her name upon the birth of successive children. The same individual could be referenced in several documents over a period of time, each time under a different name.

Name changes are not restricted to teknonymy but occur frequently and for a variety of reasons. These include name change at puberty, at marriage, at parenthood, at the death of a relative, during illness, or after a significant accomplishment (Alford 1988:85–90). In general, these name changes correlate with stages in the life cycle (as at puberty), a change in status other than life cycle (as with an outstanding accomplishment), or an association with a status considered dangerous (as during illness or at the death of a relative). Thus a change in name according to these rules signals changes in a person's identity and in his or her position in the overall social network. This often results in a quagmire of names, requiring considerable sorting skills on the part of the researcher, but such names can provide key information for the ethnohistorian.

Less-formalized devices for name-changing involve the use of nicknames. Referring to a person by a positive or negative nickname obviously affords clues to the relationships between persons, or at least an attitude of one toward another; Abraham Lincoln was "Honest Abe" to some, but "the Illinois Baboon" to others. Another particularly good indicator of personal relations is the form of address; consider, for example, "Dearest Winnie" versus "Sir Winston."

Whether applied to genealogical or other cultural realms, different naming patterns may emphasize some cultural and social aspects over others. Alford (1988:31–34) suggests that the use of patronymic and matronymic devices is more significant in complex and unilineal societies where inheritance of property and titles as well as membership in a corporate kin group are focal social dimensions. Important clues to a society's social arrangements can be gleaned from studying collections of personal names: especially revealing in terms of genealogy are the relative importance of collective kin groups, paternal and maternal lines of descent, the arrangements surrounding extended generations (such as grandparents), and birth order. Furthermore, names can embed diverse cultural information. North American Indian names, for example, can also allude to place of origin or birth; astronomical or climatic phenomena; and animals, plants, or other natural objects (French and French 1996:214).

Ethnicity, gender, occupation, and social status can all become part of an individual's personal name. Since personal names are manifested in language, they obviously reflect the particular linguistic patterns of particular societies; names are therefore often a handy device for identifying a person's ethnicity. Similarly, some cultures maintain gender-specific naming patterns. Nicknames frequently follow gender and occupational lines, and titles can usefully reveal a person's special status.

To the extent that languages and ethnicities coincide (or at least overlap), an individual's cultural affiliation or background can be generally inferred from his or her name. Both the phonetic content of a name (e.g., "Guiseppe" versus "Joseph") and its structure (e.g., "John Smith" versus "Mary O'Leary") can offer clues to a person's ethnicity. Types of names, as well as actual names, also appear with greater or lesser frequencies in certain cultures: names based on occupation are far more common in German than in other European languages, "Kim" is the most common Korean name, "Murphy" and "Kelly" rank high among the Irish, and "Stoltzfus" is characteristically Amish (Hook 1982:106, 120, 316, 333).

It should be cautioned that these are but tendencies requiring corroborative support, and the ethnohistorian should take care to not overinterpret names. A French woman may marry a Spanish man and carry the name of "Hernandez" throughout her married life, thus confounding the ethnohistorian's designation of ethnicity. Other problems arise from sheer coincidence, as with "Lee," a common name in both Chinese and English, and the Japanese name "Ohara," which may be confused with the Irish "O'Hara." The name "Jonas" may be Hebrew, Welsh, or English (Hook 1982:243, 307). In addition, the same name, even deriving from the same source, may transcend groups that consider themselves ethnically or nationally different from one another. "Jones," a signal Welsh name, is also common in England, but the use of this same surname in no way implies that the Welsh and English consider themselves unified. Similarly, names in world languages such as English, Spanish, and French have been adopted by (or applied to) a great many diverse ethnic groups in the course of colonialism. Again, this does not mean (say, on a national scale) that Mexicans consider themselves ethnically unified with Spaniards or Peruvians, or that smaller cultural groups within a country such as Mexico do not recognize and hold to finer distinctions of ethnic identity. Where a pool of names is shared by a wide range of people spanning a variety of ethnic groups, the ethnohistorian must be keenly aware that names do not necessarily imply unity but could also reflect historic connection, overlap, or coincidence.

In addition to these considerations, a name often undergoes changes that mask a person's ethnic affiliation. Sometimes this is a conscious acculturation decision, sometimes an error on the part of an immigration official. Changes can also occur through spelling shifts or translations; in a sample of Detroit Arabs, sometimes "Suleiman" was changed to its phonetic neighbor "Solomon," "Najib" became "James," and "Boutros" was transformed to "Peter" (Hook 1982:275). Examples of name changes through translations or partial translations are legion, as when German "Schneider" became English "Taylor" or Polish "Kolat" (Christmas tree) became German "Tannenbaum" (Hook 1982:326, 336). Sometimes a name viewed as complex by a dominant culture can lead to name assimilation and loss of the name's ethnic specificity; thus in the United States, "Li-Tu Yutang" may become "Jimmy Lee," and a man named "Szefczyk" might change his name to, say, "Sheppard" (Hook 1982:322). Jewish names are especially interesting and difficult to interpret because Jews so frequently "assimilated their Jewish names with non-Jewish names current in the countries where they lived" (Smith 1973:xxv). Yet these changes generally followed predictable linguistic patterns: "Rabin" became "Robin," "Babowitz" became "Barber," and "Moskowitz" was shortened to "Moss."

Caveats also apply to the identification of individual gender, occupation, and social status from personal names. Some cultures use the same pool of names for both genders, and even where gender-specific names occur, there is occasional overlap; consider the names "Chris" and "Leslie" in English. Many occupation-related English names that began as nick-names and became entrenched as surnames came to be attached to persons with entirely different occupations: the grandson of Robert the Butcher was no butcher at all, and the Barber of this book is neither a hair-trimmer nor a bloodletter. Nicknames based on personal attributes or achievements likewise pertained to the original name-bearer but not necessarily to his or her descendants carrying the name as a surname.

Also posing problems are the meanings of titles and honorifics, which may vary across groups as well as change over time and space. Although the sixteenth-century Spanish prestigious title "Don" applied to Spaniards of the very highest rank and was assigned primarily by birthright, the Spaniards in colonial Mexico extended the title to the native (Nahua or Aztec) nobility as well. It was, however, somewhat reinterpreted in this latter context to apply to both birthright and personal accomplishments, and the title could therefore be attained within one's own lifetime (Lock-hart 1992:125–126). The point is that the criteria for use of the same title, "Don," varied from Spanish to Nahua, indicating somewhat different meanings. Application of the title "Don" also changed over the centuries in Mexico in a general sense, becoming more and more broadly applied until, in the eighteenth century, one had only to be "respectable and solvent" to carry this previously exclusive honorific (Lockhart 1992:126).

Personal-naming patterns also develop as a part of geographic region-alisms. Names accompany the geographic arrangements of language and dialect variation. For instance, in the nineteenth century, differences in name emphasis developed between the United States and England, with the Americans favoring the first name over the middle, whereas the reverse was true for the British. Consequently, in America the middle name was often omitted or reduced to an initial, while in England the first name became so abbreviated (Stewart 1979:29). A good example of regional variation within the United States is the customary use of both first and middle names (sometimes in nicknamed form) in the southern and south-central part of the country, yielding names such as "Shirley Jean" and "Bobby Don." Among Arabic speakers, "specific names are favourites in certain countries" (Schimmel 1989:75). The rendering of Arabic names also varies grammatically, so names ending in "-un" are popular in North Africa and medieval Spain, while names in Yemen more popularly end with an "-an" (Schimmel 1989). Discovery of such names in a document thus allows the ethnohistorian to posit geographic origin.

Name types and patterns change over time, with and without culture contact. The transformation of nicknames and place-names into surnames throughout Europe is one such process. Linguistic dynamics are at work on names as they are in all parts of language (see chapter 5). So, for instance, early Welsh names designated "son of" with "ap," as in "David ap Richard" (David, son of Richard), but over time the "a" was dropped, and the "p" assimilated with the following name, yielding surnames such as "Pri[t]chard," "Powell" (from "ap Howell"), and "Pugh" (from "ap Hugh") (Hook 1982:81). Although slightly disguised, these names still contain genealogical information.

Personal names also undergo transformations in situations of culture contact. As mentioned previously, Aztec calendar names consisted of two words (a number and an element) perceived as a single unit. Spaniards who encountered these names in sixteenth-century Mexico applied their own mind-set in integrating Aztec names into their own familiar system, which explains why the name "Pedro Tochtli" (Peter Rabbit) appears in a sixteenth-century colonial Mexican document, combining the Spanish given (baptismal) name "Pedro" with the latter half of a native calendrical name. The Spaniards apparently interpreted the number part of the calendrical name as a given name (replacing it with "Pedro") and the element part of the name ("Tochtli") as a surname, which was retained (Berdan 1982:85).

Another example of name change and adaptation in the context of culture contact comes from Indian names. In India, it is customary for persons to be called and known by their last names; some Indians living in the United States succeed in maintaining this simply by reversing their first and last names, thus adapting to the common American practice of calling a person by their first name. This results, however, in a common interpretation of the Indian's "real" first name as the last, and vice versa. Names may also be intentionally changed by an individual in an attempt to more readily realize personal goals; Aurore Dudevant became "George Sand" to avoid the stigma of being a female author, and Elijah Poole became "Elijah Muhammed" to express a particular religious-political conviction. These and other types of personal-name transformations can be viewed as windows into the nature of relationships among members of merging cultures.

We would like to stress a final caveat regarding the interpretation of personal names as they appear in ethnohistorical sources. In short, names may not be as they appear, or mean what they seem to mean. Writing conventions can confound interpretation, especially where one language is written in another. A tonal language such as Vietnamese, for instance, may be rendered ambiguously in a historical document written by, say, a

French or English author. If the necessary diacritical marks are not included in the document, names may appear that have more than one meaning: "Ba" can mean "three," "grandmother," "poison," or "residue"; "Tho" can mean "poem," "fiber," "to breathe," and "workman" (Hook 1982:309). Gleaning a particular meaning from such ambiguities requires further stealth on the part of the ethnohistorian. In the realm of spelling (also discussed in chapter 3), variations are considerable, and a single person's name might take wildly different forms: the German name "Schultz" in Pennsylvania records appears as "Shilt," "Shiltz," "Sholes," "Sholts," "Sholtz," "Shoults," "Shoultz," "Shults," "Shulz," and eleven additional variants (Hook 1982:121). Beyond spelling, there is often more than one possibility for a name's meaning, even when the spelling is consistent. Take, for instance, a person named "Crook," who may not have been a criminal at all but rather a person living at a turn in a stream or road, a person who carried a shepherd's crook, or a resident of the town of Crook (of which there were several in England and Scotland) (Hook 1982:72). Such possibilities alert us to seek, wherever possible, supportive information in drawing interpretive conclusions.

Bibliographies of personal-name studies are a handy place to begin research on this topic. Especially comprehensive are *Names and Naming* (1987) and *More Names and Naming* (1995), both by Edwin D. Lawson. Dictionaries of personal names, usually focusing on name etymologies, abound. Notable among these are works by Hanks and Hodges (1988, 1990), Stewart (1979), and Smith (1952, 1973). These sources focus primarily on European and European-derived names; name studies for other places and peoples are scattered and sparse, but a good synopsis for North American Indians is presented by French and French (1996).

Tribal Names

Ethnohistorians sometimes are confronted with a bewildering array of tribal names in their sources. Although not always obvious, many of these names really are synonyms. For the Abnaki of northeastern North America, for example, all of the following are recognized synonyms: "Wabunaki," "Tarratines," "Owenunga," "Openango," "Moassons," "Wabanoaks," "Whippanaps," and others (White 1913:1–5). Even though ethnohistorians and other scholars have expended far less energy on this aspect of naming than on personal and place naming, its importance warrants a brief discussion here.

The multiplicity of names referring to the same ethnic group can derive from a number of sources. Sometimes a tribal name used in a document is the name that the members of the society call themselves, such as "Dene." More frequently, explorers and other travelers heard a new tribe described by their neighbors before actually encountering them, hearing first the neighbor's name for the tribe, such as "Apache" (which in Zuni means "enemy"). Other examples of the first-encountered term actually being a pejorative include the Cree's description of the Inuit as "Eskimo" (eaters of rotten meat) and the Algonquin's characterization of the Mohawks as "Iroquois" (real adders). Europeans with limited linguistic knowledge sometimes misunderstood or garbled native words, producing such corruptions as "Nunsey" for "Minasinink" (White 1913: 316–317). Some tribes were given European names as descriptions or translations of their own names for themselves, as with "Blackfoot" (a literal translation of "Siksika") or "Flatheads" (describing the result of the cultural practice of cranial deformation). Finally, some new names reflected the disruption of tribal entities by European intrusion, as with California mission names; for example, the various Indians around Mission San Gabriel became known as "Gabrieleños."

These and other factors mean that ethnohistorians may have to unravel a complicated skein of tribal names to identify which group is being discussed. The complexity is illustrated in J. N. B. Hewitt's description (in White 1913:415) of the etymology of "Seneca": " 'place of the stone,' Anglicized form of the Dutch enunciation of the Mohegan rendering of the Iroquoian ethnic appelative *Oneida.* " This an understudied topic, and there is a great deal of research yet to be done on the processes involved in the creation of tribal names.

Case Study

PLACE-NAMES OF TLAXCALA, MEXICO

Toponyms found in the modern state of Tlaxcala, Mexico, exemplify many of the processes involved in interpreting place-names. Tlaxcala, in central Mexico, has an ancient indigenous heritage, but the early peoples inhabiting the region (such as the Mixteca-Puebla and Olmeca-Xicalanca) have left little or no toponymic imprint on the land. Later arrivals such as the Tolteca-Chichimeca and the Tlaxcallans spoke versions of the Nahuatl language, and Nahuatl place-names are pervasive throughout Tlaxcala, undoubtedly reflecting (1) the military and political dominance enjoyed by Nahua groups and (2) the presence of Nahua in the region at the time of the Spanish conquest. Spanish place-names are also common, likewise reflecting the ascendancy of Spanish control in colonial New Spain.

Place-names in Tlaxcala display a wide range of types (see figure 9). Descriptive names are found much more commonly in Nahuatl than in Spanish and include names such as "Tetlatlauhca" (On the Red Stones), "Xalostoc" (On the Cave of Sand), and "Cuautla" (Forest). Associative names, denoting specific cultural characteristics, are also common in Nahuatl; e.g., "Cuexcontzi" (Small Place of Food Bins), "Mitepec" (On the Hill of Arrows), and "Hueyotlipan" (On the Big Road). Incident names are a bit more difficult to ascertain but might include names such as "Tlacualoya" (Place of Eating), "Tetzoyo" (Debt Obligation), and "El Milagro" (the Miracle). Possessive place-names are rare for communities in Tlaxcala, but a few Spanish ones appear as hybrids with Nahuatl, including "Melendeztla" (Place of Melendez) and "Muñoztla" (Place of Muñoz). Possessive names are applied more frequently to small plots of land in this region. Similar hybrid names are common for haciendas in nearby Cholula (Dykerhoff 1984:240).

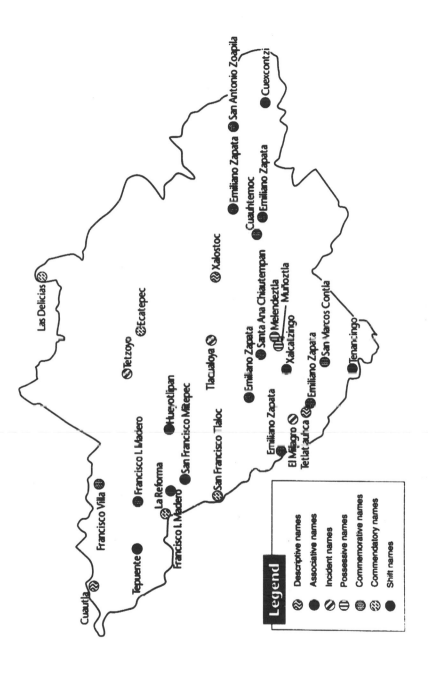

Figure 9. Place-names in the state of Tlaxcala, Mexico.

Some Spanish commemorative names such as "Emiliano Zapata," "Francisco Villa," and "Francisco I. Madero" appear as fairly recent additions to the landscape. The place-name "Emiliano Zapata" occurs no fewer than four times in the state of Tlaxcala, and "Francisco I. Madero" appears twice. The repetitive use of names such as these can make identification of a particular locale problematical. Native commemorative names are applied less frequently than Spanish ones, but "Cuauhtemoc" is a notable example in Tlaxcala and was certainly named following the Spanish conquest. A prominent commemorative characteristic of Spanish place-names is the use of saints' names, often in combination with an existing Nahuatl name, producing "Santa Ana Chiautempan," "San Marcos Contla," "San Antonio Zoapila," and so on. Nahuatl possessive names are far more likely to denote entire ethnic groups rather than individuals, suggesting a difference in cultural emphasis between Spaniards and Nahuas. Commendatory names occur only occasionally. Names denoting Nahua deities include "Ecatepec" (On the Hill of Ehecatl [the god of wind]) and "San Francisco Tlaloc" (Tlaloc being the god of rain). Some Spanish names, such as "La Reforma" and "Las Delicias," seemingly were chosen to inspire. Shift names are also found in Tlaxcala, but the ethnohistorian would want to confirm their presence with corroborative evidence. In Nahuatl, the addition of the suffix "-tzin" (little), as in "Xalcatzingo," suggests the transfer of people from one town to another: nearby Tulantzinco was reputedly settled by people from Tula, much as Tlaxcallantzinco was founded by immigrants from Tlaxcalla (Dykerhoff 1984:239).

This case study also illustrates changes in naming patterns, especially in the context of linguistic and cultural contact. As Spanish came to prevail as the lingua franca of the land, notable linguistic transformations took place in the existing Nahuatl place-names. Expected phonetic substitutions (such as "s" for "x") occurred, but seemingly with less frequency than in other areas of Mexico. The common locative suffix "-tlan" typically became reduced to "-tla," but if "-tlan" was retained, a Spanish accent was added. An especially interesting adjustment was the spelling change from Nahuatl "-ll-" (pronounced as a long /l/) to Spanish "-l-," as in "Tlaxcalla" to "Tlaxcala." This actually did much to conserve sounds relatively close to the native pronunciation, since the Nahuatl "-ll-" would have been read in Spanish as, roughly, "-y-." Spanish and Nahuatl generics and specifics sometimes melded grammatically, as "in Cortesco, Rosastitla" (Among the Roses) and "Tepuente" (Stone Bridge) (Anaya Monroy 1965).

What do the Nahuatl, Spanish, and Nahuatl-Spanish hybrid place-names reveal about cultural conditions and historical changes in this region? As far as the indigenous names are concerned, it is of interest that the Nahuatl names so thoroughly replaced the earlier names that previous inhabitants must have imposed on the land. This suggests either a dislocation or absorption of the earlier populations by the Nahuatl-speaking migrants, strong administrative control by the Nahua overlords, or both. Conquest of the region by the Spaniards, however, did not result in the same degree of name-changing. This linguistic conservatism may be linked to the role the Tlaxcalans played in the Spanish conquest as allies of Cortés, and the relative favor and autonomy they enjoyed for some years following the conquest, which included the restriction of Spanish settlers in the Tlaxcalan region. Phonetic adjustments conforming to the Spanish language reflect the preeminence of the Spaniards as new lords of the land, but little in the way of translation or visual transfer seems to have taken place. The Spaniards appear to have been satisfied to adopt existing names whose sounds, in any event, did not deviate greatly from those in Spanish.

The most common Spanish names relate to patron saints and are usually paired with existing Nahuatl names. This pattern reflects the pervasiveness of the spiritual side of the Spanish conquest and its symbolic manifestations in names on the land. While Spanish and Nahuatl names are often paired and even hybridized (as in "Rosastitla"), the Nahuatl elements have been broadly retained over the entire region, even though Nahuatl is no longer spoken so extensively (an observation also made by Dykerhoff [1984:235]). The names have become fossilized and persist regardless of the language spoken by the present-day inhabitants.

Case Study

PERSONAL NAMES IN THE EARLY
JEWISH COMMUNITY OF NEW YORK

There is no roster of Jews in early New York City, but the graves still extant in the Chatham Square Cemetery provide a partial list. The earliest grave records the death of Benjamin Bueno de Mesquita on October 21, 1683, followed by about four deaths per decade for the next few decades. Table 5 presents the first twenty names recorded for individuals buried in the Chatham Square Cemetery. All information on these individuals comes from the detailed work of de Sola Pool (1951).

The general pattern for naming in Jewish Europe followed a different pattern than in Christian Europe. In Europe, Jews had maintained for centuries a ritual surname, often based on tribe or parentage, and most Jews used only a first name in most transactions. Shylock in Shakespeare's *Merchant of Venice,* for example, would have had a Jewish surname, but he would have used only his given name in transactions outside the Jewish community. Not until the sixteenth and seventeenth centuries did most European Jews take on surnames for public use, an adoption fostered by governments in the hope that fixed surnames would make tax collection and military conscription easier. In some areas, names were assigned, and only the payment of bribes or bonuses would fend off embarrassing or unpleasant names. Consequently, especially in Germany, Jews sometimes found themselves with surnames like "Schmalz" and "Eselkopf," meaning respectively "chicken fat" and "ass's head" (Hook 1982:261–271; Kaganoff 1977).

In some areas, particularly Iberia and the Netherlands, Jews were allowed more freedom in choosing their own surnames for public, general use. In those areas, Jewish surnames often were indistinguishable from

Table 5. Names of the First Twenty Persons Buried in New York City's Chatham Square Cemetery

Benjamin Bueno de Mesquita	Sarah Bueno de Mesquita
Moredecai Abendana	Isaac Pinheiro
Joseph Pardo	Samuel Levy
Bianca Henriques Granada	Moses Cohen Peixotto
Sarah Pardo	Abraham Haim de Lucena
Bilhah Gabay Faro	Sarah Rodriguez de Rivera
Rebecca Marques	Moses Levy
Elijah Ilhoa	Jacob Louzada
Joseph Tores Nunes	Rebecca Gomez
Sarah Henriques Granada	Rachel Rodriguez Rivera

Source: de Sola Pool 1951.

those in use by Gentiles, incorporating occupations, geography, personal attributes, and the other characteristics discussed earlier in this chapter.

The names of the first twenty Jews known to be buried in Chatham Square Cemetery provide a good deal of information about the Jewish community in New York in the seventeenth and early eighteenth centuries. In particular, they furnish insights into ethnicity, pseudonyms and nicknames, surname origins, name changes, and kinship.

Eighteen of the twenty individuals under consideration had surnames that originated with the Sephardic Jews of Iberia. Seven are unequivocally Portuguese, six are unequivocally Spanish, and five could be either; the remaining two surnames (both "Levy") are Ashkenazy names, from Germany. The preponderance of Sephardic names relates particularly to the Spanish Inquisition. Its inception in Iberia led to thousands of Jews leaving for places where persecution was less severe; many chose Brazil, but the Inquisition followed them. Many then fled to Barbados, the nearest English colony, a Protestant holding where the Inquisition could not follow. From there, some went to Nevis and Jamaica, and some left all these places for the burgeoning commercial center of New York. The preponderance of Sephardim over Ashkenazim in New York merely mirrored a typical pattern throughout the Americas.

The majority of the Jewish surnames in this group are indistinguishable from Gentile names, though some are more common as Jewish than as Christian names. The given names in the group, however, are predominately Old Testament names favored among European Jews, and although few of these names are unequivocally Jewish, several (such as "Mordecai" and "Isaac") are ones that a contemporary commentator would have recognized as "probably Jewish."

The primary exceptions here are three names that contain unambiguous Jewish elements. "Levy" is an exclusively Jewish name that designates a descendent of the Levi tribe. "Cohen Peixotto" is a compound surname composed of a standard Portuguese second element and a distinctive Jewish first element. Cohens, along with Kaplans, Kahns, and other families whose names derive from the same Hebrew word, are members of the priestly clan and traditionally have certain ritual restrictions placed on them. In addition, the name confers a certain prestige, reflecting ancient status. We know that within the Jewish community, Moses Cohen Peixotto sometimes presented himself merely as "Moses Cohen," although he seems to have used the full surname outside the Jewish community. Abraham Haim de Lucena was the other individual whose name welded a Jewish element ("Haim," meaning "life") with a geographical element in the European tradition ("de Lucena").

Samuel Levy was more frequently known as "Samuel Zanvill," his Jewish familiar name. His gravestone inscription includes a double acrostic that spells out "Samuel Zanvill" — not "Samuel Levy." The flexibility of the application of these familiar names is made clear by the fact that Samuel's brother, Moses, was never known by this familiar surname. Similarly, Joseph Pardo was known familiarly as "Joseph Brown" and "Saul Brown."

The Rodriguez Rivera family, represented in our list by Rachel, exemplifies another form of pseudonym usage, as well as name change. In Spain, the family had used this surname (suitably ambiguous, since it was in use by both Jews and Christians), and as Marranos (crypto-Jews posing as Christians) they had used the names of Christian saints for their given names. Upon arrival in New York, however, they forsook these names, adopting the Old Testament names of Sarah, Abraham, Rachel, Isaac, Jacob, and Rebecca. The switch to these names was so complete that their earlier names have been lost to history.

Other names indicate the Iberian custom of merging father's and mother's names into a compound surname. These include "Tores Nunes," "Rodriguez de Rivera," and "Lopez de Ponseca." In all cases, the merger of the names had been completed prior to the seventeenth century, and the current generation had inherited the name intact from a parent of the same name.

These names also indicate certain principles of kinship reckoning current at the time in New York's Jewish community. A wife adopted her husband's surname (as with Benjamin and Sarah Bueno de Mesquita), and a child was given the surname of his or her father (as Rachel — with minor modification — with her mother Sarah and father Abraham de Rivera). The fact that individuals of the same surname rarely or never married could be used to infer that an exogamy rule was in place, but these rules are, of course, well acknowledged in other sources of information.

Finally, various surnames listed in table 5 indicate something about the recent ancestors of the persons represented, particularly their city or region of origin. The families of Bueno de Mesquita, Henriques Granada, Gabay Faro, and Haim de Lucena all incorporate a geographical element into their names. These elements become even more significant when it is remembered that these families took on formal surnames only in the three or four generations preceding immigration to America.

CHAPTER 7

Source Analysis

Scholars always have to consider ways that their data can mislead them, and this is particularly true for ethnohistorians. The documents that form the basis for most ethnohistorical research can provide valuable, accurate information, but — as the reality-mediation model suggests — they also can provide distorted or false information based on mistakes, misunderstanding, confusion, ignorance, or deceit.

The general study of documents in terms of how much of their information should be believed is called source analysis. Traditionally, source analysis is divided into two types. External analysis (also known as external criticism and, in the field of museum studies, authentication) aims at determining whether a document is authentic, that is, whether it was written by the person claimed and at the date claimed. Internal analysis (also known as internal criticism) tries to decide how credible a document may be; that is, how accurately its contents represent the facts of what really happened.

Historians have developed a series of approaches to source analysis, and these are widely used by ethnohistorians. In fact, it is critical that ethnohistorians submit every document (and other similar evidence) they use to source analysis. Of course, some documents are well known and have been studied a great deal by other scholars, and many of their strengths and weaknesses are already known, but even these documents must be assessed in terms of their appropriateness for each piece of research to which they are potentially applicable. Relaxing one's vigilance can mean uncritically accepting inaccurate information as true and laying one's research open to criticism.

Considering source analysis's importance and near-universal application in historical research, surprisingly little published material discusses it in general. Langlois and Seignobos (1898) provided the initial statement of the modern principles of source analysis, introducing most of the terms and concepts used today. Gottschalk (1958), Clark (1967), and Shafer

(1980) present useful treatments of the subject, and most historiography texts contain one or more chapters on it. Wood (1990) has provided a review of source analysis and associated issues as they relate to ethnohistory.

External Analysis

Submitting a document to external analysis asks the question "Was this document written at the date and by the author claimed?" At its simplest, external analysis is intended to detect fakes, forgeries, and other purposeful attempts to mislead; it also aims to recognize misidentifications, misdatings, and false attributions of documents by scholars. Sometimes, however, the issue is more complicated, as when a manuscript has been copied several times by hand (each with minor differences from the original) over a century or more. In this case, you may be trying to establish which is the original document from which the others were derived. Nevertheless, in every case the goal is to determine the date and authorship of a document.

Historical Continuity

One useful measure of a document's authenticity is historical continuity: whether the document can be traced in a more or less unbroken chain from the time of writing (or at least the distant past) to the present. The papers of Richard Nixon, former United States president, for example, are almost certainly authentic because they were transmitted directly from the White House to Nixon's home office to the Nixon Library. (They may not be complete, of course, but they probably are authentic.) In contrast, the Vinland map purchased by Yale University purportedly was drawn in the fifteenth century or earlier, yet there was no clear record of its whereabouts until it surfaced around 1957 (Skelton, Marston, and Painter 1965; Washburn 1971, especially Parker 1971). Consequently, the Vinland map should command a higher level of concern over authenticity. Of course, lack of historical continuity does not definitively indicate that a document is false, but it is a flag to the researcher that this possibility needs assessing. Documents that show historical continuity, on the other hand, are likely to be genuine unless very unusual circumstances indicate otherwise.

Historical continuity sometimes can be more difficult to assess than the preceding paragraph may suggest. A document can take on great importance within a family or community, and sometimes its actual history can be obscured as a consequence. Errors in communicating information about the document, small elaborations that accumulate over time, outright falsehoods that are accepted by the next generation — these and a host of other factors can produce a distorted account of the document's history that may create a false impression regarding its historical continuity, often with no complicity or prevarication on the part of the current owners.

Physical Examination

Many techniques of external analysis focus on scientific scrutiny of the document itself: its ink, paper, and so forth. Such investigation of a document is known as physical examination. This scientific detective work is not what most ethnohistorians have been trained for, and the actual tests usually are run by specialists from museums, large research libraries, and forensic criminology laboratories. Sometimes archaeologists, chemists, physicists, and other specialists may be called in for highly specialized aspects of the examination. The ethnohistorian, however, should have some idea of the sorts of questions that physical examination can answer in order to direct specialists' efforts to the areas of greatest concern. Reviews of methods of physical examination as they relate to documents include those by Harrison (1963, 1981), Haselden (1935), Hilton (1982), Nickell (1990), and Verzosa (1960).

Some aspects of writing have been discussed along with paleography in chapter 3, but other aspects have to be considered before discussing physical examination more fully. The essentials for producing a document are a flat surface (e.g., paper) and a liquid or solid writing medium (e.g., ink); an applicator (e.g., pen) is also required if the writing medium is liquid. The technology available has changed over time for each of these essentials, and various technologies have come into and gone out of style over time in different places. Consequently, knowing in detail the kind of writing materials used to produce a document can help ascertain when and where it was written. A host of techniques of physical examination have been developed to identify writing materials, often with startling accuracy. These techniques of physical examination obviously demand that the original document be available, and some of them require the sacrifice of some portion of the document (often a tiny fragment) to destructive tests. Such testing naturally requires full consent of the parties in whose care the document has been entrusted.

Literate societies usually find it convenient to be able to roll, fold, or stack documents for easy transportation and storage, so flexible materials such as parchment and paper have been the most common materials for recording the written word. Parchment (synonymous with vellum) is a very thin, supple, fine-grained animal skin, specially prepared to serve as a writing surface. It has been used in various places around the world, particularly in Europe prior to about the thirteenth century, in India at least from the third century B.C., and in Mesoamerica before the sixteenth-century introduction of Spanish paper. Paper is a synthetic material, made by soaking vegetable fibers in water, then pounding or rolling them out to form a thin sheet. Paper in the form of papyrus was first developed in Egypt by 2500 B.C. The Chinese originated paper independently around the second century A.D., and their form of paper spread around the world. It reached Egypt by the eighth century, Spain by the twelfth century, the rest of Europe in the succeeding centuries, and all of the world through the agency of European colonialism. There also were indigenous papers in use in Mesoamerica, Polynesia, and Indonesia, but these were later replaced largely by European-style paper.

Each piece of parchment tends to be individualistic, and it is difficult to conclude its place or date of manufacture. There are, however, details of manufacture that sometimes permit an analyst to assign a date or place of origin. The type of animal skin used may suggest one or another era or place, since cow, goat, sheep, and antelope skin all have been used for parchment. The washing, stretching, scraping, and abrading to smoothness are common to all parchments, but the final step of preparation — dressing the surface with chalk, alum, or some other fine material to make it more readily accept ink — varies in terms of the powder used, sometimes permitting an identification of the place and period of manufacture. The type of skin and type of dressing powder used can often be determined by an expert's microscopic examination of the parchment. Reed (1976) provides great detail on the manufacture and identification of parchments.

Papers are characterized by their composition and structure. The composition of most papers in the Chinese-European tradition prior to the nineteenth century was linen rags or something similar; during the nineteenth century, processes for using wood pulp were devised, and less expensive papers were increasingly made of this substance. The rag papers continued to be produced, however, because of their superior quality and ability to resist yellowing and cracking with time, problems that plague wood papers. Various additives ("sizing") have been added to papers in different times and places to give them better writing surfaces.

The structure of paper includes such qualities as thickness, coarseness of fibers, roughness of surface, and orientation of fibers. These qualities all are easily discernable, usually under a microscope. Papers in the European tradition often bear watermarks, makers' insignias that are visible when light passes through the paper. (The watermark is caused by a wire design placed in the mold during the rolling out and pressing of the paper.) These watermarks originated in the fifteenth century, and there are quite good records of watermarks of all the major and many of the minor papermakers. Watermarks are an excellent way to identify the place of origin and range of dates for paper and have been collected by Briquet (1968) and Heawood (1950). The range of conclusions that can be drawn on the basis of the physical examination of paper is discussed by Stevenson (1962).

Ink, at its simplest, is a dark powder suspended in water. Over millennia, this was refined to a mixture of black pigment (usually "lampblack," a form of finely powdered carbon), gelatine or glue, and water. The resulting India ink was the most common ink around most of the world for the three millennia prior to the end of the nineteenth century. At that point, the chemical industries of the world began devising new compositions with different virtues. From the point of view of ethnohistory, most documents are early enough so that they would be expected to be written with India ink, and a later ink is usually a clear indication of a recent document or a fraud. Mitchell (1937) provides data on historic inks that can help identify them. Cahill, Kusko, and Schwab (1981) have pioneered the use of proton-induced X-ray emission (PIXE) techniques to analyze the trace elements in inks, leading to the nondestructive identification of their composition and origins.

The most common alternative to ink in premodern documents was pencil. Pencils originally were simply tapered pieces of lead, clay, or other natural materials soft enough to leave a line. Sixteenth-century Europe developed the graphite pencil, composed of a thin cylinder of graphite in a holder. The expense of procuring such pieces of graphite led to the development of a graphite-clay mixture, pressed into sticks from powder, held in a holder. From the nineteenth century onward, the mixture of materials in pencil lead has become more complex. Physical examination permits the discrimination of early-, middle-, and late-period pencils, helping to date documents.

Finally, pens, the most common delivery system for ink, have gone through a tremendous evolution. Medieval European pens were cut bird quills; by the beginning of the nineteenth century, metal versions in the same form were available; by the mid-nineteenth century, there was a profusion of patent pens, including the fountain pen that survives (though precariously) into the present. While all of these pen tips have similar shapes, their flexibility differs, and that characteristic is reflected in how abruptly a stroke ends. Physical examination can identify different pen types, easily differentiating pre-1800 pens from post-1800 pens.

A final note about physical examination is in order. Physical examination can tell whether a document was produced by appropriate technology, but it cannot tell whether it is authentic. The techniques of physical examination are easily learned by consulting a library, and anyone forging a document could use materials that would appear authentic, even under rigorous testing. Finding an old sheet of paper in a sheaf of old documents in an antique shop, making one's own India ink from lampblack and gelatine and water, cutting one's own pen from a chicken feather—these are the only steps needed to fool most physical examinations. The work of a determined and knowledgeable forger can be almost impossible to detect by physical testing.

Penmanship

Another category of evidence for external analysis comes from the penmanship of handwritten documents. It usually is very difficult for a forger to imitate a handwriting style or the handwriting of a particular individual because the mental and physical habits of one's own handwriting interfere. As a result, many forgers "draw" the writing, taking far more time than someone usually would when writing naturally. This results in a series of telltale signs, including:

— Shaky strokes
— Blunt beginnings and ends of strokes (where the writing implement was consciously placed on and lifted from the paper, rather than the "flying stroke," where the implement was gradually lifted from the paper as the stroke was being completed)
— Retouching (where a portion of a letter is returned to and refined, producing a double line)
— Greater amounts of ink in a line than otherwise might be deposited, due to slow movement of a pen

Any or all of these signs might be present with a forgery. The best forgers, of course, will leave few or none of these behind.

If a document is believed to be legitimate but the authorship or period is in question, penmanship can aid the external analysis. Since styles of penmanship have varied with the nationality, education, class, and gender of the writer, the style can be used to deduce a writer's probable characteristics. An example of this is discussed in chapter 3 along with some sources that discuss the techniques of handwriting analysis.

Rarely, a document produced by an alternative technology can be analyzed by methods and techniques analogous to those used in analyzing penmanship. An embroidered sampler in the collections of the Victoria and Albert Museum (fig. 10) provides an example (King 1960: plate 31). The top line reads, "Eleanor Speed began this Sampler De^{br} 12 1783"; the bottom line reads, "Eleanor Speed finished this May the 6 1784"; various text and pictures appear between these two lines. Careful examination of the first and last lines, however, reveals that the spacing and precision of execution for "Eleanor" in both places differs from that of the rest of the embroidered text; further, additional thread has been cross-stitched on the third digit of the year, converting "1733" and "1734" to "1783" and "1784," respectively. The intervening material remains apparently unaltered. Clearly the name of the maker and dates of production are partially forged, though the rest of the sampler appears original. Similar analysis can be applied to carved inscriptions and other kinds of non-handwritten script.

Anachronisms

Anachronisms are words, usages, items, or concepts that appear in a document supposedly written at a time when they either did not exist or were out of fashion. William Shakespeare's *A Midsummer Night's Dream* is set in the Athens of ancient Greece, yet in act 3, Puck speaks of "the gun's report." Needless to say, guns were not around in ancient Athens, and any reader foolish enough to think that the play was written in that period would find this anachronism disquieting.

Anachronisms are of two types. An *anticipatory anachronism* is one that refers to something that has not yet been created. A purportedly first-century Dead Sea Scroll that discusses a helicopter attack contains an anticipatory anachronism, as does a supposed fifteenth-century document that describes a "rusty pen tip." The other type, a *retrospective anachronism,* refers to something that existed at an earlier time but has passed out of currency. Abraham Lincoln saying, "Oh, drug!" as an expression of dismay is an example because this expression was in vogue two centuries before and had been out of fashion since then. Calling an electric refrigerator an "ice box" is another example of a retrospective anachronism.

It is important to distinguish between these types of anachronisms

Figure 10. The Eleanor Speed sampler, showing reworking. (Photograph courtesy of the Victoria and Albert Picture Library, Victoria and Albert Museum)

because they carry different degrees of force in external analysis. An anticipatory anachronism normally is damning to a document's authenticity and carries tremendous weight in declaring a document counterfeit. Retrospective anachronisms, on the other hand, are less powerful; for example, Abraham Lincoln might have read *Robinson Crusoe* (which contains "Oh, drug!") and lots of older people in the late twentieth century continue to call refrigerators "ice boxes." Retrospective anachronisms can provide a case for fraud, but they have to occur in numbers or patterns that are unlikely in an authentic document.

Not all anachronisms are as clear-cut as the examples discussed above, and recognizing them can require considerable knowledge of how language has changed. Consider the following contrived sentence, which follows the structure and contains some words and phrases common to late-eighteenth-century writing, but which is peppered with anachronisms: "Recently returned from an isolated existence and desiring fancy sustenance, I purchased a plate of sherbet and a mug of tredure, for which I tossed the attendant a farthing."

> *isolated:* Even though "isolation" had been in use for more than a century, the first recorded use of "isolated" in English was in the 1820s, and even then it was considered an affected mode of speech; the usual late-eighteenth-century forms were "isoled" or the French "isolé."
>
> *sherbet:* This word today refers to a frozen dessert, but before 1840 it designated a liquid fruit drink that never could have been placed successfully on a plate.
>
> *tredure:* This word refers to a bread soup but was current in English only till the 1500s and doubtless would have been meaningless to an eighteenth-century reader.
>
> *tossed:* The verb "to toss" has been used in English since 1634 to refer to the up-and-down action of the sea; the usage as "throwing" comes from the game of cricket and was first recorded in 1833.

The score is two definite (and one possible) anticipatory anachronisms and one retrospective anachronism—a very poor showing for a single sentence.

To find possible anachronistic words in a document, make a list of the candidates, remembering that some words that "sound right" may actually be anachronisms. Then search out large dictionaries and other sources that list dated occurrences of the word. For English, the most important source is the *Oxford English Dictionary* (*OED*), discussed in chapter 5. But the *OED* rarely will be sufficient to do a thorough job. Specialized dictionaries tracing the origin and uses of phrases (e.g., J. W. Bartlett 1968; Partridge 1986) sometimes permit the recognition of an anachronistic expression or cliché. Dictionaries of slang and colloquialisms (e.g., Farmer and Henley 1970; Partridge 1950, 1961; Lighter 1994–; Grose 1963; Weseen 1934; Wentworth and Flexner 1975) are especially important because many words and phrases were in use as slang before they made it into the literature that most lexicographers examine. (For example, while "smog" is dated in standard dictionaries only from the 1950s onward, it appeared in pulp novels of the 1930s and reportedly was in street use in Seattle as early as the 1920s.) Some words might be regionalisms, so dictionaries of dialects and regional language are useful (e.g., Wentworth 1940; Thornton 1962; Major 1994; Bartlett 1989; Cassidy 1985–). Finally there are various historical dictionaries (e.g., Mackay 1987), some of which provide information on specialized topics such as rural industries, trades, navigation, and so forth (e.g., Guillet de St. Georges 1970; Worlidge 1970). Most European languages have some sources that are useful for dating usage, although few are so thorough as the *OED* and the other resources for English. For non-European languages, the sources are highly variable. Once you have exhausted the relevant sources, you can be moderately confident about which words might be anachronisms.

Words are not the only possibilities for anachronisms. Typical spellings change over time, as witnessed by the American dropping of "u" for most English words ending in "-our" (e.g., "rancour" and "rancor"). Sentence structure, though a difficult aspect to analyze, is subject to fashions and has changed over the years. Polite forms also have their eras of popularity, and George Washington never closed a letter with "Yours truly," even though a letter with his forged signature did so (Rendell 1994:20). Concepts also have their spans of currency, and a can opener (by any name) should never appear in a document of the American Civil War because this specialized implement had not yet been invented. (Knives and other handy implements were used to open tin cans in this period.)

Some care has to be exercised in the use of word anachronisms in external analysis. To decide that a document is a fake on the basis of a single anachronism may not be justified: it depends on the anachronism. Anticipatory anachronisms certainly carry more weight than retrospective anachronisms, but even they can be misleading. The word "isolated" in the fictitious passage analyzed earlier certainly was not standard usage in the late eighteenth century, but it is conceivable that a writer might have created it using the normal rules of English. Many people today use words like "computate" and "orientate" as back-formations from accepted words like "computation" and "orientation," and words such as "administrate" have made it into formal, proper English through this route; someone might have taken "isolation" (a word in existence in this period) and formed "isolated" from it at a date before it was formally acceptable. Sometimes one word of a logical pair comes into common usage before the other, as with "easternmost" and "westernmost"; even though the first usage of "easternmost" is recorded fully a century after the first usage of its partner, it is reasonable that a writer using one might use the other.

Conceptual anachronisms are anachronisms that place an idea — rather than a word — in an inappropriate time. They demand as much caution as any other anachronism in their interpretation. Some of the easiest conceptual anachronisms to recognize are related to technology because inventions often have been cataloged and their dating is often fairly easy. At the other end of the spectrum are philosophical concepts, which are easy to reinvent independently and consequently very difficult to date. Would a letter from a seventeenth-century explorer necessarily be unauthentic if it referred to the way that some kinds of animals survived better than others because of their physical characteristics, weeding out those with the least desirable characteristics? This certainly is Charles Darwin's concept of survival of the fittest, but the idea could have been thought up independently by the earlier explorer. Such anachronisms are inconclusive alone and can only be used as part of an argument.

In using anticipatory anachronisms for external analysis, be alert to ways that a writer might have anticipated a later usage. If you cannot find any way that a writer could have come up with a word or concept at a certain date — yet that word or concept is used in a document — you have a strong argument for its being unauthentic.

"Anachronisms are the rock on which counterfeit works almost always run most risk of shipwreck" (Farrer 1907:2). The difficulty of projecting oneself back in time linguistically, culturally, and conceptually is so great that few forgers are able to craft convincing texts that will survive the test for anachronisms.

Consistency with Well-Established Sources

Certainly it is unreasonable to expect every authentic document to be in total agreement with all previously acknowledged sources. The reality-mediation model argues that different authors will present different versions of any event or circumstance, and common sense and experience are in accord. Nonetheless, it is clear that a faked document well might disagree with a preponderance of recognized sources. This might simply result from the forger's limited knowledge of the literature or from an attempt to amplify the document's importance, placing it central to a major rewriting of history. Inconsistency with existing sources should usually not be used as the sole reason to doubt authenticity, but it definitely can be one of several reasons in an argument for counterfeit status.

The Final Decision

The vast majority of documents encountered by ethnohistorians are authentic, but it is wise to carry a germ of suspicion about every document. Sometimes you hear that a forger would not bother producing a fake unless there is financial profit to be gained, but this clearly is not true. Forgers' motivations vary tremendously. Some are trying to sell their work, but others are just trying to fool the experts. Still others are trying to make their ancestors appear favorably in history. Many are searching for fame, and a few are trying to document some pet theory. Most forgeries are amateurish and easy to detect, but the most competent forgers will avoid all the easy errors, making detection very difficult.

A final point about external analysis deals with the unit that is analyzed. We tend to think of a bound volume as the basic unit of a document because that is how most modern documents are produced. Remember, however, that old documents may have gone through several bindings and rebindings, were sometimes broken into sections and bound separately, and were sometimes bound together with unrelated works. Bundled manuscripts, therefore, may include a mix of authentic and forged materials. The basic unit of external analysis often has to be the work (e.g., a letter or essay) or even the page. The best physical examination of one page does not necessarily support a conclusion about a different page.

Here is a checklist of factors to consider in external analysis:

— Can historical continuity for the document be traced?
— Are the physical aspects of the document appropriate? The paper? The ink? The pencil? The pen?
— Is the handwriting appropriate in terms of date, style, and characteristics fitting for the purported author?
— Are there anachronisms in words, phrases, spellings, polite usages, structures, or concepts?

—Is the document adequately consistent with the corpus of well-established sources?

Internal Analysis

Once you have decided that you understand who wrote a document and when, internal analysis allows you to assess how much faith you should have in the accuracy of the document. You may decide that the document probably is very reliable in terms of some things and less so in terms of others. A document written by a botanist, for example, could be expected to be very accurate and perceptive in terms of plant life of a region, yet the same writer might have little interest in or knowledge of local religion. Internal analysis cannot provide absolute and uncontestable assessments of a document, but it can help to evaluate where you can place greater or lesser faith.

Internal analysis is simply the opposite side of the reality-mediation coin. While the reality-mediation model focuses on those factors that can cause a document to reflect something other than objective reality, internal analysis attempts to examine how those same factors might have affected the particular document in question. It is an attempt to pursue the content-oriented goal, sifting out accurate description for use.

The Author in Space and Time

The most basic question one should ask of an author is whether he or she was physically in a position to know the things reported in a document. André Thevet, for example, was a French cosmographer who wrote extensively on Canada in the mid-sixteenth century. Major parts of four of his books (Thevet 1986) were devoted to Canadian topics, but his qualifications were largely that he had passed "very close to Canada" (Thevet 1986:xx) on his return trip from Brazil. In truth, Thevet also claimed to have discussed Canada at length with Jacques Cartier and others who had explored there, but his personal experience did not coincide with the detail that he sometimes included in his works.

Authors who have not visited a place but write about it have several options. It was not uncommon for authors to question travelers and incorporate their answers into later accounts, often without notes or references. Sometimes an author would simply extend information known from one group to another, working on the assumption that different tribes or ethnic groups in an area were pretty similar. Occasionally authors just invented stories. In the opinion of Robert Schlesinger and Arthur Stabler, the modern editors of Thevet's Canadian work, Thevet used all of these techniques. One lengthy postmodernist analysis of Thevet's work (Lestringant 1994) uses the word "invent" to refer to the process whereby Thevet wove together personal experience, information borrowed from others, assumption, and fabrication.

The time elapsed between the observation and the reporting of events also can affect the detail and accuracy of an account. If an observer sees something, goes back to a tent, and writes an account immediately, it is unlikely to be distorted by faulty memory. On the other hand, an account written many years later may incorporate all sorts of errors, wishful thinking, and rethinking in light of later experiences. Joseph Long, for example, was an English fur trader who spent the years between 1768 and 1787 in upper Canada (encompassing modern Ontario). Eventually he found himself wanting to return to England but destitute, so he borrowed money from a friend and then contracted with a London publisher to write an account of his years "among the savages" in order to pay the debt. His account (Long 1791) was based on recollections of many events that had taken place as much as twenty years before; so far as we know, Long had never expected to write a book and had kept no notes. Even discounting any obvious vested interest in producing a book that would sell well, Long's account may have been distorted by the elapsed time between the events and the writing. The longer the interval, the potentially more serious the distortions.

The Author's Knowledge and Cultural Status

Presence in the right place at the right time is a prerequisite of knowledge, but it is not enough. The author also has to have the information, attitudes, and experience to be able to appreciate, understand, absorb, and accurately report the events transpiring. In the terminology of the reality-mediation model, the author's mind-set has a profound effect on the document produced.

Take, for example, a traveler who witnessed a series of events that seemed to represent a ritual. If that traveler did not understand the language of the people, it might be impossible to do more than guess what the ritual was about. Commonly, however, travelers assume that a ritual they see is a version of the rituals familiar from their own culture. Consequently, their accounts often are couched in phrases borrowed from the vocabulary of their own rituals, subtly distorting the content of their description. A good example of this is Juan Nentvig's conclusion that among the Seri and Apache, "the only homage noticed is to the devil, and that is based on fear and stupidity rather than inclination" (1980:58). Nentvig really had witnessed socially acceptable religious practice directed toward the spirit world, but in his own culture and mind, any worship that did not involve the Christian god was devil worship, so he used those words, complete with their European connotation of deviance. The modern reader, however, should read a very different meaning into them.

All historians have to be attentive to how well an author's cultural background permits understanding of the events transpiring, but this is especially true of ethnohistorians. Since ethnohistorical documents so often are written by an author of one culture observing people of another, this problem is acute. The most reliable authors usually are ones who understand the language and have had sufficient experience with the people in question to be able to interact fairly well.

In general, the more a writer knows about a subject, the more accurate that person's account is likely to be. Joseph Long, after his years of residence with the Ojibway discussed earlier, was likely to understand when someone from that culture was angry, but less-experienced observers might have misinterpreted outward expressions. Sailors usually are good observers of weather and water; botanists usually are good observers of plants; tax collectors usually are good observers of buildings and property. Some issues are more likely to be observed well by women than by men, or vice versa, depending on traditional gender roles. Male writers from Europe, for example, have been notoriously bad at describing many of the foods they ate, typically making little effort to discuss the mode of preparation; their female counterparts, on the other hand, frequently avoided discussing politics, agriculture, or other fields outside their real or expected expertise. Knowledge and familiarity, of course, do not always beget accuracy; prejudices and familiar modes of conception sometimes can survive a flood of experience and evidence that might seem to contradict them or at least demand some revision. Nonetheless, the chances of accurate reporting are generally higher among knowledgeable reporters than among the ignorant.

Sometimes outsiders bring a fresh insight to observation. New England and adjacent regions, for example, have hundreds of semisubterranean stone buildings that are known archaeologically. (Some amateur interpreters claim these to be Phoenician or Druidic structures, but all that have been investigated produce late-eighteenth- and early-nineteenth-century Euro-American pottery.) Curiously, virtually no contemporary accounts mention these buildings, and it was left to foreign visitors such as de Crèvecoeur (1957) to inform us that these were root cellars used to store turnips for the winter feeding of sheep. It is noteworthy that the local accounts also failed to mention outdoor toilets, although these clearly existed, too. Sometimes a thing is too familiar to bother writing about or is a slightly improper subject that would lower the image of the writer if mentioned.

Even if the observer is in a physical and cultural position to understand what is going on, there is no guarantee that the person will perceive or report events accurately. Bias, a predilection toward one or another interpretation, can intrude on one's judgment, sometimes without the observer being aware of it. Sporting events bring out the bias in most observers, as when a close play at the plate divides the supporters of two baseball teams. It is inconceivable that every Red Sox supporter had a clear view and every Yankees fan was obscured, nor is it likely that all the fans in the stadium are lying about what they saw. Rather, it is most likely that their expectations and wishes colored what they saw and interpreted, producing diametrically opposed reports, although in some cases the reports may be intentional misrepresentation. Bias can affect anyone's judgment, especially that of an observer who is unwary and not guarding against it, and all ethnohistoric accounts have been filtered to some degree through the biases of their authors.

Not all authors, however, are equally biased. At one end of the continuum, a missionary's account of cannibalism among the Iroquois may reflect the revulsion and condemnation felt by the author, resulting in an account that magnifies the frequency of cannibalism and relates the practice to devil worship and other concepts that would have made no sense to the Iroquois. At the other end of the continuum, an account may suffer from subtle bias, as when an observer versed in Christianity sees a ceremony of the modern Iroquois Longhouse religion; familiarity can foster greater recognition of the Christian elements, leading to an account that overemphasizes the Christian elements and underemphasizes the native elements.

Ethnohistorians usually become familiar with the biases of the authors who produced the major documents in their region of interest. Some authors are notorious for unfettered bias, while others are revered for their discipline in controlling their biases. Some authors may have been highly biased on certain issues, such as religion or race or economics, yet quite dispassionate on others. Sometimes authors with contrary biases have written accounts that present the same event or circumstance from widely divergent perspectives, and these can be highly illuminating. Knowing an author's bias often can help assign a high level of reliability to some aspect of that writer's account. For example, when Nentvig (1980: 58) grudgingly admits that the Apache and Seri were not idolaters (despite the common European expectation that devil worshipers would be idolaters, too), this conclusion runs against the probable bias of the author and should be taken very seriously.

Related to bias is vested interest, the recognition that one's self-interest is served better by communicating one message than another. Most documents are written for a particular purpose that is quite different from an ethnohistorian's. William Wood, for example, was commissioned to present in 1634 a report for the English Puritans on the land and potentials of New England (Wood 1898:ii). It is little wonder, then, that he characterized the Aberginians to the north as "but the scumme of the country," that the "savage Mowhackies" to the west are described as "cruell bloody people . . . yea very Caniballs," and that the Indians of the Puritan colonies are described as "wise, lofty-spirited, constant in friendship . . . iust and equall in their dealings; not treacherous either to their Country-men, or English" (Wood 1898:60, 64). While there may or may not be some truth in Wood's characterizations, a publicist writing to potential immigrants would have a strong incentive to favorably present the colony that hired him.

Of course, vested interest does not mean that an account automatically will be distorted, but it should alert the ethnohistorian to the possibility. As with bias, when an author reports something that runs counter to his or her vested interest, this is strong support for its reliability.

In the past, many historians and ethnohistorians have been quick to accuse writers of primary sources of lying—purposefully deluding their readers. One well-known work lumps together as "lying" the various effects we call emphasis, selection, and distortion (as well as some others), emphasizing that position with the provocative title of *Travelers and Travel Liars, 1660–1800* (Adams 1962). Internal analysis often leads a scholar to suspect an author of being less than scrupulous with the truth, but we believe that these suspicions usually are best left as such and not turned into accusations. The diverse factors that shape an account are sufficiently complicated that self-delusion, error, or any of several other factors may have produced most inaccuracies. Attacking the morality of long-dead authors may be emotionally satisfying, but it rarely is either productive or unequivocally supported by evidence.

The Genre of the Account

Social experience leads an individual to recognize various recurrent modes of presenting information. These modes—or at least the digested classification of them—are really categories that serve to structure an audience's expectations; recognizing an account as falling into a certain category leads an audience to expect characteristic elements. As defined by Elizabeth Tonkin (1992:2, 50–65), each of these categories is a *genre,* a conventional form of discourse. Although her focus was on oral genres, Tonkin acknowledged that written genres also exist, and we use the term to refer to conventional forms in all modes of conveying information.

A genre is related to, but significantly different from, formulaic writing. In contrast to formulaic writing, which is defined by a recurrent pattern of identical words or phrases (see chapter 5), a genre is defined by a recurrent pattern of content within an account. For example, a northern European fairy tale might begin with the phrase "once upon a time" and end with "they all lived happily ever after"—both examples of formulaic writing—and it might have an evil monster, a misbehaving but repentant child, and a rescue of the child by a hero—examples of elements that characterize the fairy-tale genre.

Some literary critics and folklorists have tried to produce universal classifications of world literature, assuming that there must be some underlying commonality in the ways that the world's societies have conceived of proper storytelling. These attempts are courageous but almost certainly doomed to failure; the diversity of world cultures is probably too great to permit the collapsing of literary genres into universal types. Instead, each society defines its own genres, establishing which elements are always present, sometimes present, or never present. To understand a genre, it is necessary to examine examples from the society in question. Even genres that appear superficially to resemble one another greatly have distinctive features that differentiate them.

In some societies, genres are given names and are referred to as conscious categories. The romantic novel, epic poem, and political broadside of the Western literary tradition are well-known examples. In other societies, genres may be recognized by their characteristics but left unnamed and implicit. It is perfectly possible, of course, that a society may recognize some genres with names and leave others to a less-formal recognition; in fact, this probably is the most common case.

Occasionally, an individual invents a new genre, and literary history devotes considerable effort to identifying and analyzing such innovations. The vast majority of accounts, however, are more conventional, following preexisting conventions rather than establishing new ones. Preexisting genres lead both the creator and the consumers of an account toward certain expectations in terms of content, tone, style, sequence, format, length, and other characteristics.

Tonkin (1992:44–48, 55–62) presents a contrast that drives home the significance of genre in the information presented in two accounts. She discusses an oral autobiographical account of Blamo Kofa, a member of the Liberian community of Jlao, in which the author freely praised himself as a warrior, using such phrases as "I am leopard firm!" and "I'm very brave!" Kofa was presenting an account in the socially recognized genre of heroic boasting, and his statements about himself were expected to be extravagant and universally praising; listeners hearing anything less would be disappointed and might read any number of unflattering subtexts into Kofa's performance.

In contrast, modern academic scholarship in the Western tradition is a genre that creates an expectation of (false?) modesty on the part of an author. Prefaces a few decades ago were strewn with obviously formulaic and insincere sentiments of the author's lowly and insignificant contributions contrasted to the purportedly massive contributions of reviewers and editors. Every field has an example of the rogue scholar who defied convention and touted his or her own contributions in a preface, violating expectations and appearing to many readers as a self-centered ingrate. Once again, the expectation created by the genre conditions the content and tone of the presentation.

Another example of the effect of genre on an account comes from Clyde Milner's (1987) comparison of diaries and reminiscences written by Euro-American pioneers in Montana. Several individuals kept diaries, written when entering Montana, and then published reminiscences that were written later but were based on those diaries. Milner noted systematic differences between the two kinds of writing. The diaries included few perilous incidents, and Indians appeared only very rarely, usually assisting the pioneers when lost or low on food. In contrast, the reminiscences inflated the number of dangerous situations and elevated the Indians to a constant and menacing presence, either in person or in threat. Milner interprets this as a means of building a "shared memory" in order to establish a historical identity as Montanans, but it also can be seen as an effect of genre: reminiscences should include drama and dangerous Indians, so an author will place them there.

A good ethnohistorian must learn the conventions of a genre and keep them in mind when assessing an account's reliability. Clearly, it is impossible to read a single account within a genre and assess it well. Only after reading several accounts will it be possible to begin picking out which elements are conventional within a genre and which are unique to an account. The conventional elements must be considered simply that: elements that may or may not be accurate in a literal sense but are included because they are expected. However, the unique elements — those that diverge or go beyond the conventional expectations — may provide information about the particular case and be meaningful for interpretation. Only by considering each case in relation to its genre can these potentially useful points be extracted from the account.

Inherent Plausibility

The final factor in internal analysis is probably the hardest to consider: the plausibility of an author's account. Although ethnohistorians have to be alert to recognize a radically new fact in an account — perhaps one that could revise current interpretations of major issues — some facts simply do not make sense in light of the larger corpus of ethnohistoric sources.

Thevet (1986:20–21), for example, described numerous earthquakes to which Canada was subject, explaining that the inhabitants took themselves and their domestic animals inside when this occurred and prayed to a female idol with long hair. Although eastern Canada occasionally experiences a seismic tremor, neither historical records nor geological studies suggest that this has ever been frequent or profound; the only domestic animal known in pre-Columbian eastern Canada was the dog; and this mysterious long-haired idol does not appear to fit anything known in Algonquian or Iroquois culture. Thevet may have placed his report in the wrong part of the world, confused himself, or fabricated the entire discussion. When dealing with less clear-cut cases, of course, assessment is harder. In general, the more evidence (and the more *kinds* of evidence) that contradict a document, the more difficult it will be to accept the information in that document as accurate.

The Final Decision

The final decision of internal analysis has to be based on all the factors discussed above. Here is a checklist of factors to consider in internal analysis:

—Was the author in a physical position to report events or conditions?

—How much time elapsed between the events discussed and the writing of the account?

—Did the author have the cultural background, including language proficiency, to understand what he or she observed?

—What were the author's biases, and how might they have affected reporting?

—What was the author's vested interest, and how might it have affected reporting?

—What elements of the account are formulaic or expected within this genre, and which are unique and potentially meaningful?

—Is the report inherently plausible?

—How well does the report fit in with other evidence on the same issue?

Plagiarism and the Ethics of Writing

Modern law and ethics recognize and condemn plagiarism, the written use of another author's words without proper citation or acknowledgment. Most modern authors are very careful about plagiarism, and there are daunting legal and professional sanctions against it. As a result, significant modern plagiarism probably is quite rare. In fact, many modern authors gravitate to the other end of the spectrum, piling up bibliographic references and accumulating authorities that support their ideas.

The concept of plagiarism, however, has not existed in all places and times. Early scholars in the Western tradition and scholars in many non-Western societies believed it appropriate (or at least acceptable) to extract portions from other persons' texts and incorporate them into their own, filling in gaps in their own knowledge or appropriating especially well-turned phrases. Rarely did they see any need to note the original author.

This kind of copying produces a serious problem for ethnohistorians. For example, Joseph Lafitau (1724) wrote a book describing the Indians of northeastern North America. It included an engraving purporting to show Huron women preparing fields with triangular hoes, a form of implement otherwise unknown in aboriginal northeastern North America (see figure 14). As it turns out, however, the illustration was lifted from an earlier work (de Bry 1591) dealing with Florida and the Gulf Coast, specifically the Timucua (Sturtevant 1968). Needless to say, the illustration bore little relation to the Huron and their cultivation practices. Lafitau (or his editor) surely felt that the illustration helped bring his book to life for the reader, but the information presented was inaccurate. (The case study in chapter 9 discusses this example more fully.)

André Thevet is a wellspring of copied material for ethnohistorians to ferret out. His *Singularitez* of 1557 presents a variety of words in Canadian languages, all of which appear in Cartier's *Brief Récit* of 1545 (Cartier 1924) and all of which are in the Italianized forms presented in Ramusio's translation of 1556 (Thevet 1986:3, 28, 28 n. 3). Although Thevet does not mention this source, he clearly consulted it and took advantage of its contents.

Sometimes an entire book was republished without the permission or knowledge of the author or publisher. In fact, the first cookbook copyrighted in the United States (Rundell 1807) was an unauthorized republication of a London cookbook. The only change was the insertion of a phrase on the title page: "by an experienced American housekeeper." In this case, the republisher probably did mean to mislead the reader, building sales by billing the book as an American product. The unwary ethnohistorian might take this book as a model of American foodways during this period, marveling at how close they remained to contemporary British foodways. Although finding the same information in two sources, providing they are independent, helps corroborate the sources and support the accuracy of their information, copied passages or recycled information mean that the sources are not independent and that the information shared by them is supported no more strongly than by a single source.

Much copying and interpolation was the result of a special kind of bias: the stereotype. A stereotype is an ideal picture of something that reduces all the members of a category to sameness, inhibiting ability to recognize variation within the category. An important stereotype among Europeans in the colonial period was "the savage" or *l'homme sauvage* (Dickason 1977). The savage was seen as a more or less consistent type no matter what society or continent: brutish, violent, childlike, and simple. The significance of this stereotype to ethnohistorians is that it encouraged European writers and editors to fill in narrative gaps with suppositions of what savages *should* have been like. If writers did not know whether the Opatas practiced infanticide, they could look to the better-known Seri or Timucua or Tupinamba, since one "savage" was expected to be much like another. The impact of this stereotype is broadly evident in many ethnohistoric documents.

What all this means is that ethnohistorians must be on the lookout for passages and images embedded in one person's work that really come from different authors. Even reliable and forthright authors were prone to copying, and since it was not considered wrong or unethical, the works of authors with unimpeachable reputations were not immune to copying. A major task of scholars who edit republications or translations of ethnohistoric primary documents is the tracing of sections that might have been copied, paraphrased, or otherwise borrowed from elsewhere.

There are many clues that help scholars to recognize copied passages. Rarely, they were set in different type or enclosed in quotation marks. More often, the only indications are sudden shifts of style, word usage, or verb tense. Occasionally there will be references to an illustration or some earlier discussion that does not appear in the document you are reading. More often, however, the copiers made subtle changes in the original text to make it fit into their work better, leaving you with little opportunity to recognize it as copied unless you remember having read it elsewhere.

Case Study
in External Analysis

THE HORN PAPERS

In 1932, W. F. Horn contacted two newspapers in western Pennsylvania, informing them that he possessed copies of eighteenth-century documents that had belonged to his ancestors, Jacob Horn and his son Christopher. These documents, which came to be known as the Horn papers, promised to rewrite the history of western Pennsylvania, but shortly after their publication (Horn, Moredock, and Fulton 1945), scholars began questioning their authenticity. A commission was appointed to examine the papers, and the process by which conclusions were drawn provides an excellent example of how external analysis works. The information in this section is drawn from the commission's published report (Middleton and Adair 1947).

The Horn papers consisted of diaries of Jacob and Christopher Horn spanning the period from 1735 to 1795, a docket purportedly from a western Pennsylvania court in session between 1770 and 1790, two maps, and other miscellaneous documents. The maps and docket were presented as original, while the diaries were said to have been copied by W. F. Horn in 1891 from crumbling originals, which since had been lost. In addition to these documents, there were a variety of artifacts, including coins, a wooden potato masher, and the like, all of which were mentioned in the diaries. W. F. Horn contributed these materials to the Greene County Historical Society and became quite a celebrity as a local lecturer.

The Horn papers were significant in several ways. They established the operation of the first English court that far west, gave locations of several lost English settlements, discussed Indian-white relations, and clarified various issues that had stymied local historians. In general, they presented levels of detail on dozens of subjects that were unavailable in any other sources. They were truly the answer to the dreams of historians of western Pennsylvania.

In fact, they were such good answers to their dreams that some historians were skeptical. Too many statements in the Horn papers contradicted other sources; other bits of information, while not at odds with established sources, were so sensational that it seemed strange that no other author had mentioned them. For example, although the Horn papers asserted that twelve thousand Indians were massacred in the Battle of Flint Top in 1748, no other sources mentioned this battle, despite an alleged magnitude greater than any other incident of Indian-white conflict in the region.

The committee that examined the Horn papers was composed of historians and an archaeologist, who also called on the services of technical specialists. Their external analysis covered all the aspects discussed in this chapter.

Historical Continuity

According to W. F. Horn, the papers and other materials had been in his family continuously since the eighteenth century. There was no means of documenting this, of course, nor would anyone expect there to be. The diaries, however, were copies, and discrepancies, inconsistencies, and errors could partly be ascribed to sloppy or inept copying.

Physical Examination

The committee commissioned Arthur E. Kimberly from the staff of the National Archives to examine the court docket and maps, which were purported to be original. He found that the paper of the docket was linen rag paper whose composition was consistent with the claimed date. It exhibited watermarks of "Henry & Co." and "Lacourade," however, and neither of these was produced until the nineteenth century. The ink used was a nonferrous blue-black ink first made in Germany in 1836; it was applied with a metal pen tip of the sort first marketed in England in 1803. The ink was somewhat smudged in some places, a pattern that characterizes this ink when it comes in contact with strong chemical bases. This was significant because the paper appeared to have been sponged lightly with household ammonia, a strong chemical base. This trick was well known to produce the appearance of aged paper, and the artificial aging of the court docket became obvious when it was noticed that some pages had edges that had not been fully treated and retained a modern appearance.

The maps produced as many physical problems. They were made on paper that was first produced in 1860; they had been washed with a mixture of brown ink and water, apparently to make them appear old and discolored; and the ink was the same as that from the docket. The maps also had some pencil markings, and these were of a graphite composition used only in the twentieth century.

On the basis of the physical examination, Kimberly concluded that the docket and maps definitely were not produced in the eighteenth century, as claimed. The earliest they possibly could date was to the latter half of the nineteenth century, although Kimberly thought they probably had been produced after 1930. Further, the evidence of faked aging indicated that they were purposeful frauds, not innocent fictions whose meaning had been lost over the years.

Handwriting

The docket and maps were supposedly the work of at least two and possibly three writers. Nonetheless, all three works showed telltale characteristics of being from the same hand. Some of those characteristics were also manifested in the diaries, even though they were claimed to be later copies. Patterns of similarity among the various documents also were found in spelling, usage, style, and vocabulary. The handwriting was not analyzed under magnification.

Anachronisms

Word anachronisms, mostly of the damning anticipatory type, were scattered throughout the Horn papers. A reproduced page of one of the diaries showed five anachronisms, and this was suggested to be typical. Examples included "trail" in 1735 (in use at this time but not used in the sense of a path until 1807) and "stow[a]way" in 1738 (coined only in 1854). "Teepee," "braves" (as Indian warriors), "ranch," and dozens of other terms appeared in the Horn papers, supposedly at dates that were decades — sometimes more than a century — before their first known English usage.

The papers also contained conceptual anachronisms. Most notable of these was the failure to note the change from the Julian to Gregorian calendar. The starting date of the diaries should have been under the Julian system, and the ending date under the Gregorian system, but neither diarist mentioned "the dropping" or made any adjustment in his dates. In fact, there were no indications that the writer was aware of the existence of the Julian calendar.

Fit with Other Sources

The failure to fit well with established historical sources is what brought the Horn papers into question in the first place. The number of anomalies was extremely high, but the nature of them also was troubling.

Christopher Gist, for example, figured prominently in the diaries and was known from other sources. The diaries contain frequent references to him until 1869, at which time he is said to have died from eating too many wild grapes and plums. The real Christopher Gist is reliably known to have died in 1859 from smallpox, yet the Horn diaries continued to mention him dozens of times after that date. The entries were not reminiscences of a long-dead friend but were notes of activities he purportedly was participating in at the time. Since a diary is written daily, or at least quite close to the time of the entry date, innocent error of this sort is inconceivable.

Many critics noted how so many of the events in the Horn papers were not mentioned elsewhere, and W. F. Horn responded by producing sources that supported the Horn papers. At least he named sources, such as "Andrea's History of Northwest Virginia." Unfortunately, there is no evidence that this and other corroborative sources named by W. F. Horn ever existed. They were in no known library, archive, collection, or bibliography; they were familiar to no scholar, librarian, or rare book dealer consulted.

The Verdict on the Horn Papers

The committee decided that the overwhelming evidence condemned the Horn papers as recent frauds. While they accused no party of the forgery, they clearly indicated that W. F. Horn was the logical culprit. He reportedly was suffering from ill health and was unable to reply to the committee's conclusions. The Horn papers now stand as an example of how a thorough external analysis can permit history to purge itself of counterfeits.

Case Study in Internal Analysis

HANS STADEN AND TUPINAMBA CANNIBALISM

In 1554, a young German seaman, Hans Staden, was captured by the Tupinamba Indians of Brazil. He lived with the Tupinamba for almost a year before escaping and making his way back to Europe, where in 1557 he published an account of his captivity and captors. In that account (reprinted in 1928), he described the Tupinamba practice of cannibalism.

According to Staden's book, the Tupinamba offered a male captive from another tribe the sensual pleasures of a woman before he was eaten. If the woman became pregnant, the child might be permitted to grow up, but at some point it, too, might be eaten.

This account generally has been accepted as factually accurate, but William Arens (1979) has criticized it, arguing that it is fundamentally flawed. Using the Tupinamba case as part of a larger study of cannibalism, Arens argues that reports of cannibalism typically (perhaps always) were bad publicity, disinformation promulgated by members of one society against members of another to dehumanize them. According to Arens, Staden was simply using cannibalism as a fabricated indication of the depravity and primitiveness of the Tupinamba. Donald Forsyth (1985) criticizes Arens's argument, and it is from the works of Arens and Forsyth that the following summary is drawn.

Space and Time

Was Hans Staden actually among the Tupinamba? All parties agree that he was, but Arens argues that his tenure there was too brief for him to have been able to see the events he described. Staden writes that he lived there nine and a half months, and Arens notes that this is scarcely long enough for gestation to have provided a baby, certainly not long enough for it to have matured to the point of being eaten as an adult.

Forsyth counters that Arens's argument would invalidate all life-cycle studies, since an ethnographer would have to live with a society for fifty or more years to see a complete cycle. He suggests that Staden may have done what modern ethnographers do: observed different people at different points in the process and asked questions of informants, forming a synthesis from information relating to several individuals.

Arens also states that Staden's book was produced nine years after the events he describes, suggesting that his memory might have been faulty. It is difficult to imagine so jaded a memory that such cannibalistic practices would become blurry in a few years, but this is unnecessary, since Arens erred in chronology: Staden's book clearly was completed by 1556, only a bit over a year after his escape.

The Author's Knowledge and Cultural Status

Staden's cultural background obviously was very different from that of the Tupinamba, and Arens argues that he was unable to fully understand what was going on around him. He further argues that Staden had little or no knowledge of the Tupi language and that asking questions of his captors would have been impossible. Forsyth counters this charge by citing quotations from Staden where he recounts conversations between himself and his captors. These statements, coupled with the detail Staden includes in his descriptions and the Tupi terms he sprinkles throughout his book, mount a strong argument that he could speak their language tolerably well.

Arens also questions whether Staden actually wrote the book that was published under his name. He posits that a simple seaman would not be able to write such a book, and that Professor Dryander, the author of the introduction, might have written the book and created the story. Forsyth counters this argument by noting that Staden's father had been a student of Dryander (itself a hint that the Staden family may have received some education) and citing various occasions when Staden mentions himself reading. He also notes that the style of Dryander's introduction and Staden's text are radically different.

While neither Arens nor Forsyth goes into bias or vested interest in depth, it is easy to see how they could fit into the analysis. Arens's general thesis is that Staden and other "describers" of cannibalism were trying to dehumanize a society, so his bias would have been against the savage Tupinamba. This notion is challenged, however, by Staden's many instances of praise and respect for the Tupinamba, not at all in keeping with this purported bias. Staden's vested interest presumably would have been to tell a good story that would sell his book, and this certainly would have given him a motive to create a pretty tale.

Genre and Expectations

This factor is difficult to assess with Hans Staden's report because it set many of the standards in defining the captivity account. To be sure, travelers had written of incidents on their journeys, and their descriptions often had included fabulous peoples and practices, so in this sense, Staden could have been including the exotic and fabulous out of the expectation of his genre. On the other hand, most scholars see Staden as the innovator of a new genre: the account of captivity among savage Indians. It is only after the appearance of Staden's book that routine, almost off-handed descriptions of Native American cannibalism began to appear. In this sense, Staden was the leader in content for this genre, not the follower of preexisting expectations.

Inherent Plausibility

This criterion is difficult to assess, of course, because Arens and Forsyth have different ideas of what constitutes "plausibility." If one accepts at least some of the hundreds of accounts of cannibalism around the world (as Forsyth does), then Tupinamba cannibalism seems reasonable; if one rejects them (as Arens does), then it does not.

One can turn to other sources on the Tupinamba, however, and see if they depict the Tupinamba as having cannibalism of the sort Staden describes. Forsyth does this and finds six primary sources describing Tupinamba cannibalism essentially the same way as Staden did. Some of these descriptions may be only veiled copies of Staden's account, but at least one goes into the Tupinamba rationale underlying cannibalism, noting that women are seen as passive carriers of children, so the child of a male captive is a member of his tribe and not a Tupinamba — fair game as a captive and candidate for cannibalism. Such additional information makes it likely that at least this account is an independent verification of Staden's account.

The Verdict on Tupinamba Cannibalism

The jury is still out on whether the Tupinamba practiced cannibalism of the sort described by Staden. Certainly the vast majority of ethnohistorians familiar with Brazil find Staden's account basically credible, but there are some adherents to Arens's broader argument that cannibalism was rare or nonexistent around the world. Using the rules of internal criticism discussed in this chapter, however, it is difficult to see why we should harbor substantial doubts about Staden's account.

CHAPTER 8

Quantitative Analysis

There are many times when an ethnohistorian might want to quantify data from documents. Perhaps a study is examining the role of tribute in Aztec society; clearly it would be advantageous to estimate how much tribute is coming from each subject community, or how community obligations compare with one another. Maybe another piece of research is interested in how fairly the California justice system treated miners of Chilean, Chinese, Mexican, and Anglo extraction, and court records could provide a means of comparison. Still another example might involve the study of social interactions of missionaries in Nigeria. Any of these examples — and thousands more — are amenable to *quantitative analysis,* a general term including any method or operation that allows a researcher to extract and interpret quantified information from documents, oral accounts, or other data sources.

Quantitative studies have become prominent only relatively recently in the disciplines that contribute most to ethnohistory. Prior to World War II, most cultural anthropologists were content to use little or no quantitative information, and quantification was largely restricted to economic studies. Since the 1950s, however, cultural anthropologists have become more likely to use mathematics to model acquaintance networks, assess relationships between different factors, and examine cross-cultural commonalities. Historians came to quantitative studies even later, mostly after the 1960s. Quantitative history was spurred forward largely by economic and demographic studies, but historians have spread their net wider in recent years, and such disparate subjects as artistic production, gender relations and power, and legal discrimination have been studied with quantitative methods. Still, quantitative analysis is not a prominent or universal feature of either discipline.

Whether treating quantitative anthropology or history, major methodological reviews fall into two classes. First, there are works that treat statistics and statistical methods, incorporating examples drawn from one or the other discipline (e.g., Floud 1979; Thomas 1976). Such works have a certain value, but they typically fail to give adequate treatment to the issues involved in conceiving and executing real quantitative research. More useful are the works that focus on how to conceptualize a problem and use quantitative data to solve it (e.g., Aydelotte 1971; Beringer 1978; Darcy and Rohrs 1995; Johnson 1978). These works typically do not explain statistical methods, assuming that the reader already has a grounding in this topic or will get one elsewhere. Katzer, Cook, and Crouch (1991) present a unique and useful overview of how quantitative methods are conceived and used in the social sciences, aimed at the reader — not the writer — of social science research.

The Virtues of Quantitative Methods

There are four major reasons why quantified data can be useful to ethnohistorians. First, they permit the ethnohistorian to present data to support a conclusion that otherwise might appear to be a subjective opinion. There is a long tradition of subjective interpretation in history and, to a lesser extent, in the social sciences generally, and it can produce excellent results in the hands of a knowledgeable expert; however, subjective interpretation provides no simple means of refutation. The scholar who has translated and read the fourteenth-century records from the Muslim courts of Mali might assert that most of the cases were civil, dealing with some aspect of trade. If this scholar's assertion is based on an impression, a critic reasonably could wonder if someone else's impression might have been different. A simple quantified table of civil, criminal, and other cases could place the conclusion beyond question.

Second, quantified conclusions frequently carry more information than other kinds of conclusions. For example, the famed colonial historian Samuel Eliot Morison (1965:177) suggested that seaport towns had considerable inequality of wealth in eighteenth-century New England, while contemporary inland towns were relatively egalitarian. As an impression, this seemed reasonable, and few would doubt Morison's qualifications to draw such a conclusion. Still, Elizabeth Little's (1980) comparison of Nantucket and Lincoln, Massachusetts, provides support for Morison's conclusion and much more. By going through probate inventories, legally mandated listings of a person's property and debts at the time of death, she was able to collect detailed quantitative data. Her analysis showed that the differences between wealthy and poor did not encompass all categories of goods, but lay mostly with land and farm animals, commodities that were held extensively only by the rich. These findings, valuable in themselves, provide the basis for more refined studies.

Third, quantification facilitates comparison. It can be difficult to achieve a balanced comparison when examining documents based on opinions. Timothy Dwight (1969) and other eighteenth-century travelers in New England frequently noted that Indian communities were universally impoverished, while their descriptions of English communities suggest that the poor were better off financially. This conclusion accords with standard conceptions of this period, but the same probate study by Little (1980) documents that poor Englishmen and poor Indians were more or less comparable in their net worth at death. Presumably contemporary impressions were colored by prejudice on the part of the observer or by differences in the external appearances of domiciles.

Fourth, quantification opens up the realm of statistical interpretation, permitting a scholar to decide whether an apparent pattern is likely to be meaningful or accidental, a virtue of quantification discussed below in greater detail.

It should be noted that there are some less laudable motives for using quantitative methods. Some scholars may mistakenly believe that an obvious pattern is more powerful if described or verified quantitatively. Others may wish to convey a false sense of concreteness and objectivity by using numbers and statistics. Still others may use quantification as a smoke screen to hide feeble thinking or flimsy evidence. These uses of quantification, although occurring from time to time, are unfortunate abuses that should not discourage scholars from the appropriate use of quantitative methods in ethnohistory.

The virtues of quantitative analysis have led many ethnohistorians to incorporate it into their research. Such analysis takes many forms, but it is useful to distinguish between two kinds of quantitative study: numerical analysis (in which quantified information placed in a document is extracted) and content analysis (in which narrative or similar information is converted into quantitative information).

Numerical Analysis: Extracting Quantitative Data from Quantitative Records

Many records to which an ethnohistorian turns are designed to provide quantitative information, and these are the data sources to which numerical analysis can be applied. The Aztecs, for example, kept tribute records: accounting sheets that listed the quantities of various commodities rendered as tribute. The study of Aztec tribute mentioned at the beginning of this chapter could take advantage of these tribute records in a relatively direct manner. As another example, California courts kept records of offenses, individuals involved as victims and perpetrators, and verdicts, and the ethnohistorian interested in the fairness of justice could go to those records, find comparable cases with persons of different ethnic backgrounds, and collect data for the study.

Various authors have examined the procedures for and values of numerical analysis as applied to different topics. Palmer (1985) discusses how personal financial records can be mined for information on individuals' economic, political, and social lives; Brown (1988) and Benes (1990) suggest how probate inventories can support quantitative discussions of economics; Mageean (1984) addresses immigration records and their use in immigration history; Ginsberg (1977) examines how documents can be used for quantifying voting history; and Johnson (1988) discusses how baptismal records from missions can be used for demographic and social analysis. Other examples abound.

In principle, numerical analysis is painfully simple. The researcher goes to the records, collects the data required, and analyzes them, either using statistics or not. Unfortunately, there are pitfalls that an ethnohistorian should keep in mind, even with straightforward studies. A few of the more common dangers are discussed briefly here.

First, the data presented in the document simply may be faulty, perhaps because the methods of collecting data were so outlandish that it may be wise to discount them altogether. Consider, for example, one member of the U.S. Congress who in the 1994 election sent out a questionnaire asking opinions on his views regarding immigration. The fine print said that all questionnaires not returned would be assumed to support this member's views, but since the questionnaires included neither envelopes nor stamps, the majority probably were thrown away. Not surprisingly, his subsequent campaign advertising trumpeted that nearly 90 percent of the electorate favored his viewpoints. As another example, it would not be sensible to compare the number of brutality complaints for different years at an Indian boarding school in hopes of documenting trends in harsh treatment. The effort might be valiant, but faith in this measure would be foolhardy because one could argue that complaints are most likely when brutality is least prevalent. In times of harsh treatment, children might fear being beaten for complaining, a strong incentive to reduce complaints.

Consequently, such a measure would be of questionable value in comparing conditions over time at a school.

Sometimes a data source might be generally accurate, but flawed for a particular subgroup. Studying income through tax returns, for example, will produce lower figures for those employed in occupations that rely heavily on tips, which usually go unreported for taxes; similarly, groups who participate a great deal in day-hire work typically will report lower incomes than they really receive. Census figures are particularly apt to be distorted by differential accuracy: itinerants typically have been mostly omitted, and illegal aliens often have tried to avoid being counted, fearing that it might result in their deportation.

Second, records sometimes report with false precision, a degree of preciseness unwarranted by the means of collecting the information. Military records of battles are prime examples of this at all periods, since there is a tendency to inflate enemy casualties, deflate one's own losses, and try to get away from the scene of the battle as quickly as possible. Casualty figures in the Vietnam War became the butt of jokes when a glance from an airplane at two thousand feet might result in a body count of 127 enemy and 12 friendly troops. When Joseph Long described "no less than thirty-five different roads" (1791:51) leading from the Ojibway settlement of "Lac la Mort [*sic*]" to the lakeside, he almost certainly was estimating rather than providing an accurate count.

Third, documents may report quantitative data in units that are difficult to interpret. During the seventeenth century, for example, the Spanish colonists in the Americas received African slaves from foreign slave traders who operated under royal licenses (*asientos*). The asientos specified how many slaves could be imported, but they did so in a curious unit usually called *pieza de India* (piece of great wealth) or *peca de India* (fleck of great wealth). The pieza was a measure of value whose definition varied over time: around 1650, a healthy male slave of prime age (fifteen to twenty-five years old) was valued at one pieza, while a healthy male slave aged eight to fifteen years was worth two-thirds of a pieza, as was a sickly male slave of prime age (Boxer 1952:231). Since no category of slave was evaluated at over one pieza per person, the number of piezas in an asiento always was lower than the number of slaves that could be imported by its authority. It is impossible, however, to estimate how much the pieza figure might differ from a head count, since that would depend on the details of age, sex, and health of the slaves imported. The issue is compounded by other considerations such as smuggling of slaves and the possibility of not importing the full complement of slaves permitted by an asiento, making the pieza figures only an inexact reflection of the numbers of slaves imported into Spanish America.

Fourth, documents sometimes systematically exclude some categories of people from their calculations. During various periods and in certain places some ethnic groups were considered legally inferior and did not appear in official records. For certain kinds of records, Jews in medieval Europe and Nazi Germany, blacks in the American South, American Indians in various places, and Chinese in California were completely excluded. Using these documents to compare populations, incomes, property holding, and the like accordingly could produce severely distorted results.

Fifth, there may be gaps in records that result from poor archival management or chance. There may have been censuses taken at five-year intervals, for example, but only the 1745 and 1910 results are still extant. With this ludicrous example, it is easy to see that using such data to recognize any idea of change over time would be silly. But what if censuses existed for 1745, 1870, and 1910? For 1745, 1825, 1870, and 1910? For 1745, 1780, 1825, 1870, and 1910? There is no rule about how complete a series of data has to be before you can make meaningful comparisons and seek trends, but you have to be able to satisfy yourself and your potential critics that the series is full enough to permit you to avoid seeing false trends.

Sixth, problems can arise when you attempt to bridge gaps in a series of data by using data from different sources. Edward Rogers and Mary Rogers (1978) encountered this difficulty when studying Weagamow Ojibway surnames using historic documents. By combining Hudson's Bay Company, Anglican Church, and Canadian government records, they were able to piece together an unbroken span of surnames for the community between 1870 and 1950. Some periods, however, were covered by only one of the sources, and the sources were not equal in depth or accuracy of coverage (see figure 11). The Hudson's Bay Company records were confused, probably because the authors were not familiar with the language of native names; the Anglican Church records, in contrast, were excellently rendered and quite complete, probably because their chief compilers were Indians who had interest and skills in rendering native names. As a result, the 1870s (when only Hudson's Bay records were available) were considerably less well known than the mid-1920s (when only Anglican Church records were available).

Seventh, sometimes documents exist in different versions. This is particularly true for early periods, when most documents were handwrit-

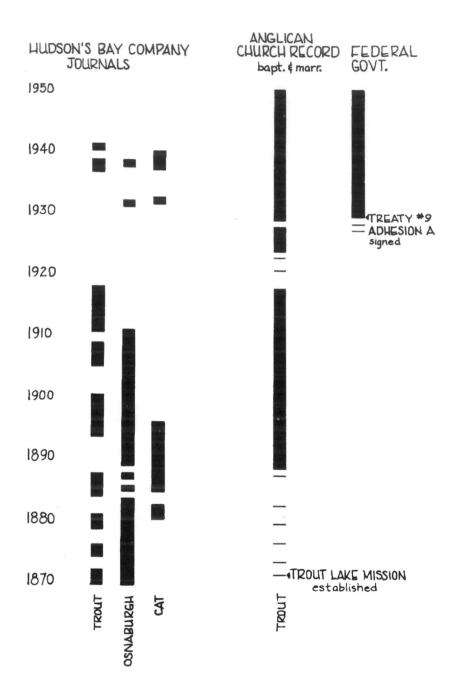

Figure 11. Strengths of various documentary sources on Weagamow Ojibway surname adoption. (Reprinted, by permission, from Rogers and Rogers 1978:325, fig. 2.)

ten. In later periods, there may be preliminary and final versions of censuses, election results, and other documents, and researchers have to be careful to use the version most appropriate for their purposes. Sometimes similar documents may contain conflicting information, as in the case of two Aztec tribute tallies that exist in pictorial form: the *Matrícula de tributos* (1980) and the *Codex Mendoza* (Berdan and Anawalt 1992). The pictorial images provide information on the specific items and quantities paid in tribute, but with one exception they do not contain details on frequency of tribute collection. Later Nahuatl (Aztec) and Spanish glosses to both documents, written separately and at different times, state that some goods were paid either four times annually (*Matrícula*) or twice annually (*Mendoza*). Using one or the other figure could have a considerable effect on the calculation of the annual tribute flowing into the Aztec imperial coffers. To further complicate the interpretation, clothing tribute in one document is glossed as individual pieces and in the other as bundles (each containing twenty items). Combined, these differences in figures result in a possible range of annual tribute in capes alone ranging from 128,000 to 5,120,000!

Eighth, the jurisdictions for record keeping may change over time. Assume a researcher is interested in examining the ethnic mix in California's Gold Country in the latter half of the nineteenth century. The gold region consisted of seven counties in 1850, but they had been divided and subdivided into twelve counties by 1870. Comparing information obtained from the court records of El Dorado County in 1850 and in 1870 could be highly misleading because areas that had been part of El Dorado County in 1850 had been split off to form new counties: Nevada, Placer, Amador, and Alpine Counties. The distribution of ethnic groups was uneven, and some of these new counties had particularly high numbers of Chinese or Chileans. Consequently, simply tracking conditions on the basis of El Dorado County's records could provide skewed and unrepresentative data.

Ninth, data may be grouped in such a way that they are difficult to use. In the previous example, a researcher might have difficulty estimating the population of Chileans in El Dorado County. Most nineteenth-century records there grouped immigrants from Chile, Mexico, Spain, and perhaps elsewhere together as "Spanish," and there is no straightforward way to determine what percentage of the "Spanish" were Chileans. The situation may become even more murky over time because the ethnic groups labeled as "Spanish" have changed over the years.

There are many more pitfalls in the use of numerical records in ethnohistory, and every study has its own dangers. The general rule is to be alert to problems, to search them out, and to expect some level of distortion in quantitative data, despite the greatest diligence on the part of the researcher.

Content Analysis: Extracting Quantitative Data from Nonquantitative Records

Numerical analysis is essentially straightforward, using existing quantitative data; content analysis, in contrast, is basically indirect, converting a narrative (that probably was never intended to provide complete or representative information) into quantitative data. Consequently, there is more room in content analysis for distortions created by the researcher's assumptions and techniques. Weber (1990) provides a rigorous introduction to content analysis, focusing largely on mathematical aspects; the work of Holsti (1969), though older, provides insights that remain useful.

Content analysis, in terms of the reality-mediation model presented in chapter 2, can be applied to either a content-oriented or a source-oriented goal. Consider, for example, the letters of Franklin Buck (White 1930), written between 1849 and 1852. These letters provide a wealth of information on the miners in the California gold rush, including the Chinese, many of whom were customers of Buck's grocery business. On one hand, a content analysis could focus on what Buck said about the Chinese and their activities, such as what they purchased at his store: the content-oriented goal. On the other hand, it could focus on how Buck perceived the Chinese — whether they were portrayed as honest and hardworking or sinister and cowardly: the source-oriented goal. Both are proper and potentially valuable uses of content analysis.

Content analysis demands some rigor in its methods lest the data generated not accurately reflect the content of the document analyzed. Nevertheless, it is also a flexible set of methods that can be tailored to the needs of a particular application. Ethnohistorians can use two major types of content analysis to tease quantitative data out of narratives: incident analysis and interval analysis.

Incident Analysis

The form of content analysis most often used to wring quantitative data from narrative documents is incident analysis (also known as *frequency count*): the calculation of the number of times an issue or viewpoint is mentioned in a work. To conduct an incident analysis, it is necessary to perform the following steps:

1. Determine the question to be asked.
2. Define what categories are relevant to the analysis, defining each one as fully and carefully as possible.
3. Read through the document, placing a tally in a category when an appropriate example is encountered.
4. Tabulate the results.

A hypothetical example will clarify how these steps work.

Assume that an ethnohistorian is interested in examining the social interactions of European missionaries in late-nineteenth-century Nigeria. A diary from a German missionary in 1880 records that individual's activities daily for that year, and the ethnohistorian decides to conduct an incident analysis on that document. The question to be asked is refined as follows: What were the relative frequencies of missionary social interactions in terms of ethnicity? The next step, defining relevant categories, is the most important one — or at least the one where the greatest errors can be made. The first definition has to be what constitutes a social interaction: Is incidental proximity enough? Must words be exchanged? Is there a criterion of duration or importance that must be met? The definition must address these and other questions so that the next steps are relatively mechanical, ideally with all decisions made ahead of time. Other definitions include what ethnic categories are relevant and how to deal with in-between cases. In this example, the researcher might define Africans, Germans, other Europeans, and others as the relevant categories; individuals of mixed ancestry and individuals whose ethnicity is not revealed must also be taken into consideration. If the definitions have been carefully made, the reading and tabulation of results should be straightforward and relatively simple, although unanticipated problems are more the rule than the exception.

It would be possible to take this incident analysis and change its focus from the content-oriented to the source-oriented goal. If the researcher were interested in assessing the author's attitudes toward these ethnic groups, it might be desirable to add another variable: whether the report of the interaction is favorable or not. The steps of the analysis would be precisely the same, except that each ethnic category would have two (or possibly three) options: favorable, unfavorable, and possibly neutral. Of course, there would have to be rigorous definitions of how to make the judgments regarding favorability. The analysis of the patterning of the missionary's responses toward members of different ethnic groups could reveal attitudes that an ethnohistorian otherwise might not recognize.

When pursuing the content-oriented goal in a content analysis, there is an implicit assumption that the document's author presented a representative sampling of interactions rather than selecting certain ones to write down. Of course, this assumption is false to some degree, since authors often eschew a representative sampling of events, instead emphasizing the unusual, exceptional, pleasant, seemingly significant, and bizarre. Selection, emphasis, and fabrication will affect the resulting document, but there is a hope that these factors of reality mediation will be minor enough for the result of a content analysis to be meaningful.

When pursuing the source-oriented goal in a content analysis, the problem caused by reality mediation becomes a virtue. Every way an author has shaped the information in a document is a reflection of that person's attitudes, and these distortions provide exactly the kind of data that are useful in examining that author's attitudes.

Regardless of whether an ethnohistorian pursues a content- or source-oriented goal, it is desirable to refine the incident analysis a bit. In the missionary example, it would be advisable to assess how likely it is that the actions and attitudes of this individual reflect those of the broader class of missionaries that are the focus of the research, and whether it might be necessary to obtain a broader sample of diaries.

An excellent example of incident analysis in ethnohistory comes from Julio Tato y Guillén's analysis (1951) of Christopher Columbus's use of nautical terminology in the log of his voyage of 1492–93. Tato y Guillén documents how the early part of the log contains relatively few of the Arabo-Portuguese nautical terms in use by Spanish sailors, instead using Italo-Mediterranean terms predominantly. As the voyage progressed, however, Columbus began incorporating more Arabo-Portuguese terms into his entries, presumably reflecting his increasing familiarity with them. Tato y Guillén also documents how, in the Caribbean after landfall, local Taino terms gradually began to replace European terms in Columbus's descriptions of native craft. The picture of Columbus that emerges from this analysis is that of a flexible individual who made efforts to learn local terminologies and who had sufficient interaction with his crew and the Taino Indians to be able to pick up and apply this terminology.

Interval Analysis

Some researchers find a difficulty in incident analysis, noting that two events may each be mentioned once, although one may be discussed for twenty pages and the other may receive just a few words. Although incident analysis counts each of these mentions as a single incident, one logically could argue that they are not of equal significance. Accordingly, some researchers conducting content analysis turn to interval analysis.

Interval analysis is the form of content analysis that measures the amount of space ("interval") devoted to a topic in a document. A good interval analysis is constructed according to the steps for incident analysis but adds one additional step: determining how to quantify the length of a passage. The usual mode is to count words, although it would be possible to use numbers of lines, column inches, line lengths, or any number of other approaches.

Interval analysis avoids the difficulty of giving equal weight to unequal treatments of events, as in incident analysis, but it presents problems of its own. First, it requires definition of the beginning and end of passages, and this often is difficult in practice, especially if the author is a disorganized writer. Second, descriptions that include a number of names tend to become inflated, with the listing of even a few names adding several words and making the event take on greater importance in the analysis. And third — perhaps the most significant in practice — the reading and tabulating of results become very time-consuming, turning the reading of even a relatively short passage into a major investment of time and effort. For these reasons, interval analysis is rarely attempted.

Regardless of what procedures an ethnohistorian follows in a content analysis, it is critical that they be described in the report of the research. The definitions of categories are particularly crucial in terms of the outcome, and it is perfectly possible that two competent researchers could perform reasonable content analyses on the same document using different categories and come to radically different conclusions. The only way to choose between these two interpretations — indeed, the only way to evaluate the quality of any content analysis — is to assess its underlying assumptions. As a result, every report of content analysis should contain explicit definitions of assumptions and terms.

Frequently ethnohistorians choose not to use content analysis or any other quantified technique, instead simply reading through the narratives and trying to draw conclusions informally. There is nothing wrong with this, but scholars have to be very careful that they are not selecting certain incidents to remember and emphasize, just as an author may have done.

Indexes

Whether using incident analysis or any other mode of quantification, it may be difficult to measure something directly. For example, an ethnohistorian may be interested in assessing the socioeconomic status of the heads of household for a community, but there is no direct way to measure this factor because it is an abstraction created by social scientists and not a tangible object. An index can get around this problem.

An *index* is a measurement of an easily measured factor used to obtain an approximation of another factor that is theoretically interesting but difficult to measure. The factor of real interest is sometimes called the *theoretical factor.* For example, a researcher might actually be interested in acculturation, the adoption of foreign aspects of lifestyle. (Although some scholars find acculturation an overly broad concept, it is widely used in ethnohistorical research.) But acculturation exists only in the conceptual arsenal of the scholar; there is no way to directly observe acculturation in a document or in behavior. Therefore, to get some quantified estimate of acculturation to Euro-American ways among Native Hawaiians, a researcher might decide to use clothing as an index, examining photographs and calculating what percentage of the individuals at different dates are wearing items of European-style clothing. Another index might be personal names appearing in documents; another might be membership in clubs or other organizations associated with Euro-American culture; still another might be the percentage of European items reflected in probate inventories. Each of these indexes has certain limitations: more acculturated Hawaiians might appear more frequently in photographs, documents might reflect "formal" names that were rarely used in everyday interaction, some clubs excluded Native Hawaiians from their membership until recently, and the officials recording probate lists might not recognize or choose to include items in the native tradition. In response to these individual problems, it would be possible to produce an index that incorporated all of these factors and others, hoping that broadening the net would increase the likelihood of producing a reasonable index of acculturation.

In order to construct a good index, it is important to make an argument that connects the index to the theoretical factor. In the examples above, the connections are quite straightforward, since acculturation is defined by the degree to which foreign ways are adopted. Other cases can be a bit less obvious. Traditional Mormon houses, for instance, were required to have at least one door per wife residing in the household, even if some of the doors were nonfunctional. (It is not uncommon in old houses to see a door leading out of an upper story and into thin air!) One way — though almost certainly neither the simplest nor the best — to assess the incidence of polygamy in a historic Mormon community would be to examine dated photographs of houses, using the number of doors as an index of the number of wives per household.

Although an index permits the researcher to quantify some variable that otherwise might be impossible to quantify, there is a price: No index can perfectly reflect the theoretical factor it is designed to measure. A Hawaiian family may present a very acculturated face in public while maintaining a far less acculturated stance in private; the same family might be highly acculturated in terms of technology but little acculturated in terms of diet. A monogamous Mormon family might have had three doors in their house simply because they wanted three routes of entry. An index never will be wholly accurate and precise, so researchers are well advised to exercise care in conceiving it — and humility in interpreting it.

Using Quantitative Data: Statistics

Once a set of quantified data is collected, patterns may or may not be readily obvious. Consider hypothetical data on convictions for horse stealing in El Dorado County, California, in 1858. Court records reveal that the numbers of persons who received different sentences for stealing a single horse were as shown in table 6. Under these circumstances, there is no reason whatsoever to resort to statistics either to present your data or to draw a conclusion. Data can be presented in a table like this one, and the conclusion is obvious: Euro-Americans received substantially lighter sentences than others.

In other cases the presentation and conclusion may be less clear. The same study might produce the data presented in table 7. Here there is no obvious pattern, and it is not intuitively obvious what to make of the data. Certainly, there is a hint that Afro-Americans are getting harsher treatment and that Euro-Americans are getting off easier, but their numbers are quite small. Are the differences great enough to be meaningful? Here is where statistics can be useful.

Table 6. Hypothetical Data on California Gold Rush Justice

| | Offender's Punishment | | |
Ethnicity of Offender	Death	Jail	Fine
Chinese	4	0	0
Chileans	3	0	0
Afro-Americans	3	0	0
Euro-Americans	0	7	12

Note: These data are so straightforward that statistical analysis is unnecessary to draw a conclusion.

Table 7. Additional Hypothetical Data on California Gold Rush Justice

| | Offender's Punishment | | |
Ethnicity of Offender	Death	Jail	Fine
Chinese	1	2	1
Chileans	1	1	1
Afro-Americans	2	1	0
Euro-Americans	4	7	8

Note: These data are much less clear, and statistical analysis probably is the only way to decide what conclusion should be drawn.

There are two branches of statistics. Descriptive statistics provides techniques for summarizing masses of numbers to make them easier to understand and compare. Inductive statistics takes the same masses of numbers and evaluates how likely it is that the observed patterning would occur by chance. If chance is unlikely to be an important factor, then other factors, perhaps including those the researcher is interested in studying, presumably are the causes of the patterning.

The statistical techniques used in ethnohistory are the same as those used in psychology, entomology, and opinion polling, and discussions of them can be found in scores of standard textbooks on statistics. Be wary of the brief introduction, which often achieves its brevity by minimizing discussion of how and why a technique works. With the easy availability of computer programs to calculate statistics, there is little need for an ethnohistorian to know how to calculate a least-squares regression line.

But there is tremendous importance for the ethnohistorian to be able to know whether calculating a least-squares regression line is justified by the data and whether such a line is even useful. In the computer era, calculations are best left to the machines; however, decisions regarding which calculations to make must be made by informed researchers who understand the problem at hand and the virtues and limitations of the techniques available.

Demography

The study of all aspects of population is known as demography. The size of a population, its structure (the relative numbers of different components of the population, such as age groups, sexes, and classes), and changes in population size and structure over time are all part of demography. It is an eminently quantifiable field of study, and ethnohistorians have devoted a great deal of research to it.

Various ethnohistoric studies have estimated the population size of particular communities (Trigger 1972), tribes (Glassner 1974), regions (Snow and Lanphear 1988), and continents as a whole (Thornton 1987). Other studies have investigated how population size has been affected by disease (Smith 1980; Herring 1994), warfare (Cook 1973b), the fur trade (Kay 1984), insects (Posey 1976), soil erosion (Cook 1949), migration (Thornton 1984), new foods (McNeill 1991), and human sacrifice (Cook 1946). Still further studies have examined how population structure has been affected by inheritance (Wiegandt 1977) and by land-use patterns (Ackerman 1976). Others have looked diachronically at population movements (Rubenstein 1977), rates of depopulation (Meister 1976), changes in racial composition (Wood 1989), frequencies of racial admixture (Jaenen 1983), and stability of household composition (Offner 1984). Some studies — such as that by Thornton, Miller, and Warren (1991) — are computer simulations: what-if projections of the implications of a particular model of population change. All of these studies are demographic in nature.

The collection of data to support demographic studies is in essence the same as collecting quantitative data for any other purpose. Drake (1972) has defined two approaches to collecting data in historical demographic studies. The first, the aggregative approach, consists of using statistics produced during the historic period under study. Censuses, military reports, and other government records that typically include demographic data are available for various periods around the world, and these can be analyzed by the methods of numerical analysis.

The second of Drake's approaches, the nominative approach, demands tracing the life histories of individuals, accumulating a data set, and calculating one's own statistics; the nominative approach, in essence, is content analysis, building a data set through the investigation of a series of individual cases. A traveler, for example, might note the household composition of families who provided lodgings, furnishing fodder for a content analysis to give some idea of what the size and structure of a typical household might have been. Alternatively, an ethnohistorian might locate a listing of all residents of a village at a particular date, find which household each one was living in at that date, and thus accumulate figures on the size of each household in the village; this nominative approach would provide data that could be summarized by statistics and used as a basis for analysis. Drake (1972:61) argues that nominative demographic studies, while requiring more effort on the part of the ethnohistorian than aggregative studies, would prove more successful, and since his prediction, the nominative approach has been quite successful, especially in ethnohistoric cases where few or no aggregative statistics are available.

A third approach to historical demography must be added to the two defined by Drake: the indicial approach, where population levels are approximated by an index. The population of a community, for example, could be estimated through the size of the settlement, measured in any of several ways. Well-documented relationships between population and the floor area of houses (Narroll 1962; Le Blanc 1971) or the overall area of a settlement (Cook and Heizer 1965) are available, as is a series of relationships between population and the number of houses or rooms in a settlement (Casselberry 1974). These general relationships are useful if no better information is available, but a relationship derived for a particular society and applied to that society is likely to be more reliable.

Hassan (1978) reviews a variety of population estimators for a community and discusses how they can be used. One index could be based on household size; if average household size for a society is known to have been 5.2, the population of a village of 35 houses could be estimated at 182 persons. An index based on floor space of houses would be likely to produce a somewhat different estimate. Other indexes would produce still other estimates, and some could be used for other purposes. The relative number of children in two modern North American communities, for example, could be approximated by comparing the number of toy stores or diaper services in each community. Using an index for demographic studies obviously is undesirable if more precise figures are available, but the imperfect and uneven data of ethnohistory sometimes reduce the historical demographer to this expedient.

Once demographic data have been obtained, a variety of standard procedures can be used for their analysis. These include calculating such statistics as life expectancy, infant mortality, and sex ratios. Many standard works (e.g., Hollingsworth 1969; Reher and Schofield 1993; Willigan and Lynch 1982) present the usual techniques for deriving these values, and specialized works (e.g., Swedlund and Armellagos 1976) provide alternative techniques for analyzing incomplete data. Drake (1972) provides a brief but cogent discussion of the limitations of historical data for demographic interpretation.

Over the decades, demography has been one of the most consistently popular subjects to explore quantitatively through ethnohistoric data. In part this reflects how amenable population characteristics are to quantification and statistical analysis. Perhaps even more important, however, is the crucial role of population size and structure in understanding how a society operates. The massive dislocations that accompanied the intrusion of Europeans into the Americas, for example, were largely rooted in the demographic disaster that attended the inadvertent importation of diseases for which Native Americans had limited hereditary resistance.

Case Study

CONVERSION AMONG THE MID-SEVENTEENTH-CENTURY IROQUOIS

When the French Jesuit missionaries arrived in what is now eastern Canada and adjacent portions of the United States, they viewed their primary task as the conversion of the local Indians to Christianity. They began with the Huron and Algonquians, and by the 1650s they were able to extend their efforts to the Five Nations of the Iroquois. This case study shows how content analysis, specifically incident analysis, can be used to assess which characteristics typified Iroquois converts in this period.

The documents used are annual and biennial reports prepared by the Jesuits and spanning 1653 to 1658 (le Moine 1654; le Quens 1656; le Jeune 1658; anonymous n.d.). This whole series of reports begins in the early seventeenth century and runs into the early nineteenth century and collectively is known as "the *Jesuit Relations.*" This series and various related documents have been collected, translated, and published in both the original language (usually French) and English; following the usual procedure, they here are referred to by the abbreviation "*JR,*" followed by a volume and page reference. Each *Jesuit Relation* was a mixed lot — of letters to superiors, journals, reports, and specially composed essays — that was sent back to France, where it was published and sold.

Following the procedure discussed earlier, the first step in a content analysis is to determine the question being asked. In this case, the *Jesuit Relations* give us some notions of who was converting to Christianity, though these notions are not always in agreement. A Jesuit making a circuit of Mohawk villages reported that he went there annually "to apply the blood of Jesus Christ by baptizing the children, the aged, and the dying" (*JR* 43:209–211). This suggests that those at both ends of the life cycle were the particular focus for missionaries, or that at least they were the most likely to convert. In contrast, another Jesuit among the Onondaga noted, "I daily baptize both children and adults" (*JR* 43:315), suggesting that there were no clear patterns of who converted.

Given these divergent representations of the conversion process, the question for our incident analysis is this: What demographic and other characteristics were most common among Iroquois converts to Christianity in this period? Particular elements to consider include gender, age, and nearness to death.

After the initial step of constructing the research question, step 2 in carrying out an incident analysis is defining the categories for which data on occurrence will be collected. In this case, it was decided that the only criterion for conversion would be baptism. From the Jesuit point of view, clearly baptism was the event that marked conversion, and it represented a commitment of sorts on the parts of the converts (although many of them probably conceived their conversion to Christianity as a grafting of new practices and beliefs onto their traditional religion). Statements of interest in, or devotion to, Christianity in the absence of baptism could arise from any number of motives and are not enough to indicate conversion. In essence, baptism is used as an index of conversion

An additional set of definitions is necessary to decide what information on converts will be collected. The Jesuits usually categorized converts into age categories, particularly "children," "adults," and "old people." Rarely are ages given in years, and in those cases they can be converted into these categories by using division points of fifteen and forty-five years of age. (These division points are roughly in keeping with what the Jesuits indicated in the rare times they identified a person by both age and age category.) Gender often was explicitly stated in the *Jesuit Relations,* and reference to the original French sometimes can ferret out a gender that was lost in the translation into English. Nearness to death could be from various causes, and they all need to be recorded. In any case where information is lacking, that too should be recorded, though it may be decided later that these cases should be omitted from the analysis.

The third step in the incident analysis is reading the documents and recording the relevant information. A few quotations will clarify some of the nuances involved in the reading. Some phrases, for example, actually indicate baptism in a metaphorical way: "We bear in our hands more than five hundred children, and many adults, most of whom died after baptism" (*JR* 44:155); "a little dying infant had been secretly sent to Paradise by the waters" (*JR* 42:101); "in order the better to solemnize the Christmas Festival, we gave its name ["Noël"] to a good Iroquois woman" (*JR* 42:137). All of these phrases indicate baptism, though only familiarity with Christian baptismal practices would permit the analyst to recognize it. Another entry would seem unusual if taken literally: "I baptized some little skeletons" (*JR* 41:97). In the context of a starving village, however, this metaphor can be interpreted as the baptism of emaciated children.

There is danger of confusing the act of baptism with interest on the part of the convert. The Jesuits usually tried to avoid baptizing those who had received little or no instruction in the Christian faith, and sometimes a baptism would be deferred or refused. "Many brought me their children to be baptized" (*JR* 43:309); Teotonharason, a respected and revered Onondaga woman, came to the priests, making "urgent request for Baptism for herself, her mother, and her daughter" (*JR* 42:99). These entries, with no further elaboration, indicate only a request for baptism, not the completion of the ceremony. In fact, we learn that Teotonharason and some of her relatives were baptized at different times, only after some time had elapsed since her initial request (*JR* 42:141, 145, 147); other relatives are not mentioned again and may never have been baptized.

Finally, since the analysis is restricted to Iroquois conversion, it is important to ascertain that an incident really pertains to an Iroquois convert. There were Algonquian, Huron, and other captives living in Iroquois villages, and some had been adopted and were considered Iroquois. Consequently, a gray zone encompassed both long-term foreign captives and newly naturalized Iroquois. In this case, the criterion for whether to include an incident or not is whether the author described the individual as a captive or an Iroquois. If the description did not make it unequivocally clear that an Iroquois was being described, the case was excluded.

Following the reading and recording of information, the fourth and final step is tabulating data so that a conclusion can be drawn. Table 8 presents the results of the incident analysis based on the most conservative interpretation possible. This tabulation excluded vague statements such as "several little children" (*JR* 44:33) and "some weak and emaciated children" (*JR* 41:101).

This tabulation permits several conclusions regarding converts. First, the numbers from different age categories appear moderately similar, as do the numbers from the different gender categories. Second, a large percentage (51.2 percent) of the converts were near death (or perceived themselves so) at the time of their conversion. Of the twenty-two individuals near death, fourteen were ill, six were captives about to be tortured to

Table 8. Conservative Tabulation of Results, Iroquois Conversion Case Study

	Children	Adults	Elderly	Total
Female	4	5 (2)	4 (3)	13 (5)
Male	2 (1)	12 (9)	3 (2)	17 (12)
Unknown	11 (5)	0	2	13 (5)
Total	17 (6)	17 (11)	9 (5)	43 (22)

Note: This analysis excludes imprecise references. Numbers in parentheses indicate those near death.

death, and three were leaving shortly for battle. (Some individuals fell into more than one category.) Third, the near-death converts are not equally distributed among demographic categories; almost half of the near-death converts were adult males, and 75 percent of all adult male converts were near death at the time of their conversion. This suggests that adult males were particularly resistant to conversion unless personal jeopardy led them to hedge their bets.

The chi-square statistical test is a means of assessing whether a particular frequency distribution is consistent with chance. This test was applied to the data in table 8 and shows that the distribution in age categories (assuming equal numbers of Iroquois in each category) is consistent with chance, but that the high frequency of near-death circumstances in the adult male category is likely to indicate a real difference (assuming near-death circumstances to be evenly distributed by age and gender). In other words, these data support the conclusions that no age group was more likely to convert than any other but that near-death circumstances inclined Iroquois to conversion.

When considered in light of seventeenth-century Jesuit statements about why the Iroquois resisted Christianity, the result of this content analysis leads to a further tentative conclusion. Sometimes the Iroquois thought of the Jesuits as evil, bringing disease and disruption (*JR* 43: 291). In addition, they were thought to lure converts into heaven, where they would be tortured to death (*JR* 42:151, 43:289–291), and some Iroquois believed that the Jesuits wrote down the names of baptized children to send to France, where sorcerers would cast spells and make them die (*JR* 42:135). Others were concerned that they would be separated from their ancestors in the hereafter if they went to the Christian heaven (*JR* 42:151). Women sometimes resisted Christianity because it forbade

Table 9. More Speculative Tabulation of Results, Iroquois Conversion Case Study

	Children	Adults	Elderly	Total
Female	4	5 (2)	4 (3)	13 (5)
Male	2 (1)	12 (9)	3 (2)	17 (12)
Unknown	31 (5)	0	2	33 (5)
Total	37 (6)	17 (11)	9 (5)	63 (22)

Note: This analysis includes imprecise references, using five as an estimate for "several." Numbers in parentheses indicate those near death.

plural marriage (*JR* 42:147), and the wars of the seventeenth century had depleted the marriageable male population to the point where some women would be unable to find a marriage partner if they restricted themselves to men without another wife. The ban on plural marriage also affected men, of course, but the Jesuits emphasized how men would always be able to find one wife, making this factor more important for women. For men, Christianity threatened the traditional Iroquois belief that dreams were premonitions that had to be fulfilled, and that failure to do so jeopardized one's health (*JR* 42:127, 135). The Jesuits preached that dreams were messages from the devil and should not be heeded, denying Christian Iroquois men an avenue that probably provided access to improved political status. Greater conversion among women, providing this pattern is accurately reflected in the documents, might suggest that political mobility was more important to men than marriage was to women.

Table 9 presents an alternative, more speculative version of the tabulation. In this version, the four imprecise references to "some" or "several" children being baptized are included, assuming each reference to refer to five children. This assumption is little more than guesswork, but it permits those imprecise—but numerically potentially significant—references to be included. One rationale for including these references is that they are all within the child category and excluding them might underestimate that category substantially. Here, the chi-square test suggests that children are significantly more strongly represented among converts than would be expected by chance.

This version supports a somewhat different interpretation of conversion, where children stand out as starkly different from adults. In this version, children are by far the largest category (and perhaps are still underestimated, since the Jesuits seem to have been more careful in reporting adult conversions). Further, only 22 percent of the children, easily the lowest percentage of any age category, were known to be threatened by death at the time of their baptisms.

The significance of the two alternative tabulations is that they emphasize how content analysis can be based on different assumptions and can produce differing results. To some extent, the decisions made by the analyst will shape the results, so it is crucial to present and justify those decisions in the report of any content analysis.

CHAPTER 9

Visual Interpretation

Ethnohistoric documents sometimes consist wholly or partially of pictorial images, ranging from pictographic paintings to photographs. The world of "visual materials," therefore, encompasses a vast potpourri of pictorial media and forms. Such imagery can be found painted on the walls of caves or monasteries, drawn on vellum or glossy paper, incised on wood or pottery — the possibilities are almost endless. Indeed, the broadest definition would include material artifacts themselves as visual reminders of the past. For purposes of ethnohistoric discovery and analysis, however, we will restrict ourselves largely to the images themselves and leave discussion of the artifacts to chapter 11.

Visual forms encountered historically display a vast array of subject matter. They range from flamboyant murals depicting politics or paradise, to conventionalized herbals and scientific illustration, to photographs of wars and family life — and everything in between. This chapter explores the role of such visual materials in ethnohistoric interpretation, focusing on graphic technology and techniques, the functions of pictorial images, the types of information that can be gleaned from illustrations, and the use of high technology in visual interpretation. These matters are highlighted in a case study of visual imagery in cultural contact between Europe and the Americas.

Graphic Technology and Techniques

Many of the same media, instruments, and techniques used to present the written word have been used to create visual images. Obviously, an image drawn with a fine pen and ink potentially can contain more detail — and hence more ethnohistoric information — than one sketched with a coarse crayon or blunt pencil. In addition to those techniques mentioned in chapters 3 and 7, a few particularly important ones for producing visuals are woodcutting, engraving, and photography.

Woodcuts were an especially popular means of producing printed pictures in the fifteenth and sixteenth centuries in Europe and through the nineteenth century in Asia (Chamberlain 1978). Woodblocks incised with a negative picture (and inked on the raised portions) were either stamped or rubbed onto paper, yielding either black-and-white or color images. Woodblock prints and printing presses had a close technological affinity for one another, and early books were frequently printed with text and accompanying pictures. Woodcuts are especially important in ethnohistoric research because so many images of native life (particularly European images of the American Indians and Japanese views of their own daily life) were produced by this technique. However, a word of caution is in order. The woodcutter was rarely the same artist who actually created the initial picture. The sequence would typically look like this. An artist would produce a drawing or painting, from which a second person would make a line drawing, from which a woodcut specialist would incise the woodblock. All along the way, there was quite a bit of room for personal innovation and creativity, which were applied liberally at times. This was, of course, not always necessarily the case. Albrecht Dürer (1471–1528), for example, penned his pictures directly onto woodblocks, but he was an exception for his times.

Beginning in the late sixteenth century, engravings started to gain popularity in Europe, quite at the expense of woodcuts. Engravings were created by incising fine lines on copper or zinc plates. Ink was then spread into the incisions, and the resulting image pressed onto paper. In contrasting woodcuts and engravings, the former were "less laborious to produce and therefore cheaper to acquire," and "their technique called for the summary statement of essentials rather than for the particularizing elaboration of details" possible with engraving techniques (Panofsky 1955:49).

Like woodcutters, engravers were also usually specialists and had the opportunity to innovate from original artwork. Dürer, again, was an exception. He was highly regarded for his exquisite engravings, some of which embraced subjects of ethnohistoric interest.

Although quality and extent of detail vary considerably with both woodcuts and engravings, engraving techniques did (and do) allow finer lines and enhanced detail. In engraving, the width of incised lines and the intervals between lines could be reduced to a fraction of a millimeter, allowing for subtle shading as well as exactness in artistic portrayal (Panofsky 1955:63). Certainly a well-crafted engraving permitted more precise detail than a sketch or painting executed with pencil or brush—or a woodcut. The detail permitted by the engraving technique also tempted or even encouraged engravers to add detail, even if none was provided in the original art. All of these factors should be considered when evaluating the visual information contained in images produced by these different techniques.

Photography alleviates at least one of the problems associated with woodcuts and engravings; it transfers real-life images directly to paper. Of course, those "real-life" images can be staged and posed, an extremely common practice in the early history of photography as well as today. When one of the authors of this book photographed Nahua women in the Sierra Norte de Puebla in Mexico in the 1980s, for example, they would often turn their backs until all parts of their clothing were properly arranged or even changed, putting on a special "face" for the camera. The itinerant photographers of the American West in the latter half of the nineteenth century carried various props—including clothing, jewelry, and ethnographic artifacts—because many local Indians wore Anglo-American or Mexican-style clothing and had few colorful artifacts. The result of photographers fixing up their subjects with exotica to produce more dramatic photos is that a Tohono O'odham from southern Arizona might be shown wearing Plains Indian gear from North Dakota.

Another problem is that photographer bias can affect how the subjects are posed, how a picture is framed, or simply what subject matter is chosen. If a photographer is interested in documenting women's native dress, for instance, he or she may shoo away all of the little children clinging to a woman's skirt, although a picture of *that* behavior would more closely mirror everyday life. Photographs taken by "natives" put a different cast on subject-matter choice, but these have been rare until quite recently. It is obviously important to learn as much as possible about the photographer's background, objectives, and mind-set, just as with writers of documents and painters of pictures (see especially Scherer 1990.) It is equally important to consider political motives in the use of photographs, as they can be skillfully doctored by retouching, blocking and cutouts, recentering, and effacement (Jaubert 1989).

Photography does have a special, often unintended advantage: it frequently captures unexpected details in a picture's frame. In the course of researching a specific historical problem, the ethnohistorian may be pleasantly surprised to find details of costume, natural history, architecture, or the like as background in photographs focusing on entirely different subjects. For instance, specific types of surveying equipment are captured in a photograph showing a "lunch on the prairie," and a group of interesting buildings is visible in the distant background of a photograph focusing on a loaded steamboat (Scheffel 1993:226, 318). It is worthwhile to cast a wide net in searching out visual materials. This is especially true since photographic archives often tend to be catalogued according to casual, confusing, or conflicting principles (Blackman 1986).

Any reality-mediation process pertaining to a written document also applies to a visual one. Although visual images (along with other available sources) can be useful in reconstructing past cultures or events, ethnohistorians must remember that bias and emphasis in selection of subject matter enter into all pictorial media. The artist, engraver, and photographer all made decisions on what was to be portrayed and often unabashedly stamped their perceptions and preconceptions onto the resulting images. Consider, for example, a content analysis of pictorial images that might lead a researcher to conclude that the predominant pastime of medieval Europeans was to contemplate the Virgin and Child, or that most of the Native Americans' time was spent eating human flesh (while wearing feathered headgear). Yet these portrayals mirror the preoccupations and the interests of the artists and cannot necessarily be taken as representative of the culture as a whole. In this context, Bucher (1981) offers a detailed analysis of the de Bry engravings of sixteenth-century American Indians; her emphasis on the impact of European cosmology and Protestant doctrines on the engraved images underlines the importance of reality mediation in visual interpretation.

Even more slanted are intentional, often humorous photographic distortions or fabrications. This was a fairly common amusement of photographers of the American West and Midwest at the turn of the twentieth century, and they produced cards with wildly absurd images: giant grasshoppers riding donkeys, a family residing inside a watermelon, and men hauling six-foot-long ears of corn (Scheffel 1993:190–191). Although produced with intentional technical trickery, such fabricated images are not devoid of ethnohistoric interest; they are, after all, consistent with themes of oral "tall tales" common in those regions. As all of these examples suggest, the researcher must approach visuals as much as possible through the eyes of the artist or photographer. What were the biases, interests, information, expectations, goals, and limitations that the portrayer brought to his or her subject matter? These problems are examined in some detail later in this chapter in the section on imagery in contact situations.

The Functions of Pictorial Images

When using visuals (or any other form of historical documentation), ethnohistorians try to ascertain the reasons behind their execution: Why were they composed, and what function(s) did they serve? Although there have certainly been numerous idiosyncratic purposes for creating illustrations, most will fall into a few general categories.Some pictorial images were intended to serve as written communication in the form of pictographic writing. In other documents, illustrations were included as aesthetic embellishments or as illustrative amplifications of a text. Still other images may have been included for economic gain or to make a political or religious statement.

Pictographic writing has already been discussed in chapter 3, but it is worthwhile to briefly consider these images in their visual role. Since they performed communicative functions, pictographs had to conform to certain stylistic and symbolic conventions, so some uniformity and only a certain amount of artistic license can be expected.

As forms of iconography — visual images designed to convey specific meanings — pictographs and ideographs can offer revealing insights about a culture. In Aztec iconography, for instance, high-ranking nobles were always depicted wearing a turquoise diadem — a paramount symbol of status on paper and, indeed, on the noble himself. The picture of a burning temple symbolized conquest, as did the deed itself. Art historians have written volumes on iconographic interpretation of art forms in a wide array of the world's cultures, and such tomes should be consulted in the course of ethnohistoric research. Researchers should be wary, however, of over-interpreting visual elements. Consider the American flag so frequently seen in paintings of the American Revolution; in fact, it probably never flew at that time. Its ubiquitous depiction is more due to the ideals and mind-set of the nineteenth-century artist than to battlefield realities (Shenkman 1991:3). Thus it is always wise to pay close attention to the origin and history of any iconographic ideas presented.

Some visuals were included in documents primarily for aesthetic reasons and were conceived and presented for purposes of beauty. The exquisite illuminated manuscripts of medieval European and Arabian life included not only elaborate calligraphy, but also sometimes a complexity of colorful pictorial images (such as the famous eighth-century *Book of Kells* with its intricate knotted designs and impossibly intertwined animals). Developed from designs imprinted and incised on leather and metal, these sorts of images were meticulously produced in monastic settings by the most skilled of the artists in the order. Illustrations such as these tend to exhibit a fair amount of artistic license, although they still conform to accepted stylistic canons. It follows, then, that many documents containing such aesthetics can be fixed in time and space and sometimes linked to specific artistic "schools" or even to an individual artist.

Visual images created for primarily aesthetic purposes usually also serve a variety of additional functions. Consider changes in functions of the medieval European illuminated manuscripts just mentioned. Pre-medieval predecessors to such documents contained illustrations specifically "to serve as guide marks for the reader, and these were all the more useful since in early manuscripts the columns of writing were not numbered" (Nordenfalk 1988:7). Later, intricate decoration became a means of "impressing readers with the value and importance of the text" (Nordenfalk 1988:25). And still later, as these documents took on an overt role in religious proselytizing, elaborate imagery came to endow the manuscript with enhanced spiritual authority (Nordenfalk 1988:36). Even though aesthetic enhancement appears to have been a primary goal in the creation of these illuminations, it can be seen that the many "sub-goals" of these manuscripts changed over time. These additional functions played a part in the way visual images were formed and used, and should not be ignored in ethnohistoric analysis.

Images were also created to enhance a document as a form of illustrative explanation, as in Bernardino de Sahagún's (1950–82) massive *Florentine Codex*. Drawn by Aztec scribes to illuminate aspects of the written text, its numerous pictorial figures depict a broad sweep of native life, from gods and goddesses to chiles and armadillos. These illustrations derive not only from the codex's descriptive text, but also from other indigenous (and European) sources available to the artist-scribes.

Illustrators of herbals and scientific texts frequently had first-hand experience with their subjects, although at times they took their cues from written descriptions or already available pictures. European-derived herbals and treatises on natural history often contain fascinating details on everyday customs, recipes, ideas about disease and curing, and worldview — even instructions on how to revive drowning flies and bees (Rohde 1971:65). Yet the woodblocks used to illustrate these fifteenth- through seventeenth-century texts were more often than not "borrowed" from a variety of sources, often from other countries. For instance, an English herbal may well contain German and Flemish woodblock prints illustrating not only individual plants but also cultural matters ranging from cultivation to rituals to myths (Rohde 1971:82–83, 145).

Equally interesting (if not more so) are illustrations drawn by Europeans and based on European sixteenth- and seventeenth-century conventions, but applied to novel North and South American subjects. In general, European illustrators took one of three approaches to the natural bounty of these newly encountered lands. One approach indiscriminately combined fact with fiction (depicting monkeylike creatures with very human faces and lions' tails, for instance) and did not have scientific goals at the forefront (see Honour 1975:70–71). This sort of "fantastic natural history" had a long tradition in Europe (as in the many medieval bestiaries), so it is not surprising to see these ideas transported to the newfound lands. A second manner of depicting the novel natural phenomena of the Americas was to simply reject them altogether: Otto Brunfels, in his 1530 herbal, "dismissed plants which had no Latin names" (Honour 1975:58). Luckily for the ethnohistorian, a third approach was more common. Recognizing the completely different and unusual nature of American flora and fauna, illustrators took extra pains to picture every little detail — an approach that became more common as the sixteenth century unfolded into the seventeenth. Consequently, a great many figures, such as those produced by John White in North America and Francisco Hernández in Mexico, can be considered to have a high degree of accuracy. After all, a major purpose of these illustrations was to inform Europeans of the "Joyful Newes out of the Newe Founde Worlde," most especially with the hope for medicinal cures from the western continents (Honour 1975:57).

Sixteenth- and seventeenth-century Europe saw a boom in the printed word, and the production of books became a profitable business. Many of these books contained illustrations primarily to enhance the value (i.e., the price) of the book. William Caxton (ca. 1432–91), a merchant-entrepreneur noted for introducing the printing press to England in 1476, translated and published a great many books and included woodcuts in many of them. Since there were no copyright restrictions, he used imported woodblocks from other sources or had his woodcutters make copies from existing ones. When entrepreneurship is a goal, it is worthwhile considering the sources of the images as well as the hastiness with which they might have been made. The woodcuts in Caxton's *Aesop,* for example, are so inferior that a recent edition of that publication uses figures from elsewhere "simply because they are so much better than those in Caxton's edition" (Lenaghan 1967:241).

Sometimes illustrations and images serve political goals and must be carefully examined for biases and special interests. One prominent example of this is the frequent generalized depictions by Europeans of the Native Americans as cannibalistic savages, which served to justify European political and economic domination over these people. Other goals might be more specific. For instance, John White's illustrations of coastal North America, particularly Roanoke, were used to try to stimulate interest in colonization (futilely, it turned out, since the colony had myste-riously disappeared by the time he returned). Some of White's illustra-tions were embellished by engravers for publication, making the natives appear most pleasant in classical poses, and arranging their village in rec-ognizable geometric order — an ideal early travel brochure. One engraver even added tobacco plants and a sunflower garden to White's original to make the entire scene even more enticing to the prospective emigrant (Milbrath 1989:200–202).

A great deal of illustrative material has been produced, historically, in the service of religion. Since religions are based on beliefs and specific worldviews, images with identifiable religious symbolism and goals should be considered in that light. Some goals were rather subtle. As an example, Arabic illuminated manuscripts with elaborate imagery and calligraphy were considered to be sacred in themselves and therefore conformed to specific religious codes and canons. Other goals were more direct. Depic-tions of Aztec priests performing human sacrifice, for example, inflamed Christian priests intent on religious conversions in New Spain in the sixteenth century. Pictorial imagery was also employed more cunningly in the service of religious conversion. Large cloths with Christian imagery were hung in colonial Mexican chapels as instructional devices, and the expansive garden murals painted on the walls of the sixteenth-century Augustinian monastery in Malinalco, Mexico, were a constant reminder of the rewards of paradise to friar and native alike. The Augustinians consid-ered these views of a terrestrial paradise to further their goals of religious evangelization, perhaps not fully realizing how many indigenous concepts had crept into the native-painted murals. A monkey in a cacao tree repre-sented happiness to an Aztec, though the monkey was associated with the devil in Christian thought (Peterson 1993). The painting of the *Last Supper* that hangs in the Catholic cathedral in Cuzco, Peru, is a similar example, showing a brown Christ with a plate of roasted *cuy* (guinea pig, a native food animal).

These latter examples bring to mind an additional ethnohistoric haz-ard: the omission of information. For instance, the 1541 *Codex Mendoza* (Berdan and Anawalt 1992), produced by Nahua (Aztec) scribes for Spanish friars in Mexico City, treats history, economics, and many aspects of daily life but does not overtly depict religious events, even though such activities dominated Aztec daily life. The presence of Franciscan friars overseeing the drawing of the document no doubt was instrumental in this omission.

These many and diverse functions of visual images often are not exclusive; that is, a single image may well serve several purposes at one time and may even come to serve ends not originally intended.

Types of Information Contained in Visual Images

In documentary sources, visual images frequently augment a text or serve as the entirety of the document itself. Where accompanied by written text, they may serve to amplify the written word (providing more specific, or additional, detail than the text), they may generalize from the writing and contribute nothing new, or they may offer alternatives for written glosses or annotations (at times correcting them). Keeping in mind all the cautions mentioned above, what kinds of ethnohistorical information can be gleaned from visual images?

First of all, the ethnohistorian is interested in extracting as much cultural information as possible from an image or set of images. This information ranges from illustrations of material goods, to depictions of customary or unusual activities, to representations of beliefs and myths. A variety of these aspects of life, from concrete to abstract, can be (and often are) combined in a single illustration. One sixteenth-century native scribe's depiction of an ancient Aztec temple precinct combines real-world walls and buildings, priests presenting offerings, and a wide array of abstract religious symbols (Baird 1993: fig. 38). Useful insights can be especially gained by looking at images created over a period of time (if they are available). A comparison of Kiowa drawings from pre-reservation and reservation times reveals a predominance of battle and raiding themes in the former, supplanted by a preponderance of ceremony and paraphernalia (but little actual combat) in the latter, a visual substitution that reflects a changing or shifting emphasis in actual activities (Szabo 1993:6).

Images of ethnographic interest were often depicted against some sort of background or landscape. Some artistic styles allowed considerable freedom in producing (even imagining) that landscape, so it may or may not actually pertain to the main subject of the illustration. This is true not only of physical landforms, but also of natural flora and fauna as well; some illustrations blend an impossible mix of creatures from vastly different ecosystems. (See case study below.)

Visual images can also reveal information of more purely historical interest. The winter counts of the Plains Indians designate years by pictorially depicting a single annual occurrence. They therefore highlight specific events, at the same time revealing what the recorders considered especially important happenings. Book 12 of the *Florentine Codex* (Sahagún 1950–82) pictorially describes, in sequential frames, the conquest of the Mexica (Aztecs) by the Spaniards. As in cartooning, meaningful sequence is an essential element in such visuals.

The following questions can help researchers gain the greatest ethnohistoric value from the study of visual imagery:

— Why was the image produced?
— What function(s) did the imagery intend to serve? Might political, economic, social, or religious goals or motives impinge on the imagery?
— Was the image produced by a native of that culture or by an outsider?
— What is known about the general artistic or photographic conventions as they pertain to a particular image?
— What were the technological constraints in producing the image?
— What were the background, experiences, and biases (mind-set) of the artist/photographer? What knowledge and preconceptions might have affected the resulting image?
— Do factors of selection, transformation, emphasis, or fabrication help shape the content of the image?

In studying visuals it is important to scrutinize not only the main subject of an image, but also all other elements included, from the smallest clay pot perched in a corner to the merchandise stacked in a storefront window. All elements in visual imagery carry potential to reveal intimate details about past lives.

Some Conventions in European Ethnohistoric Visuals

All of the general types of visual information (ethnographic, geographical, and historical) and the cautions surrounding their interpretation can be highlighted by looking at the conventions used in European visuals in ethnohistoric contexts around the world. We place our emphasis in this general treatment on the imagery of culture contact between Europe and the Americas. In both general and specific aspects of this example, certain elements of visual analysis come into particularly sharp focus: the experience and preconceptions of the artist, stylization, and generalization.

Artists' Experiences and Preconceptions

Many artists from a variety of backgrounds illustrated autochthonous life in the Americas. First of all were the native artist-scribes themselves, depicting their own people and customs. These depictions have the advantage of intimate, first-hand experience with the culture (or some segment thereof). There are a great many examples of such depictions, from Nevada rock art, to Ojibway scrolls, to Caddo sculptures, to Mesoamerican codices. In some cases a considerable corpus exists, but more commonly the record is scattered and scanty. For instance, we can count only a handful of pre-Hispanic pictorial manuscripts from Mexico, but many more come from Spanish colonial times. These latter documents, executed by native artists, tend to conserve the indigenous artistic styles while at the same time experimenting with identifiable European techniques. So the 1541 artist of folio 69r of the *Codex Mendoza* tried out a bit of perspective drawing, though not entirely successfully (see figure 12). He also painted the Aztec ruler Motecuhzoma full-face but maintained the native profile style to depict other persons on the folio.

Some thirty years later native artists were still hard at work, but their paintings reveal experience in a new social order and lack of direct experience with pre-conquest life. The illustrations accompanying Bernardino de Sahagún's *Florentine Codex,* executed ca. 1579, still reveal a great deal of familiarity with pre-Spanish native life, from godly symbols to the proper way of raising children, but the "experience" of these artists derived from surviving pictorial manuscripts and oral traditions. Moreover, several of the illustrations in these twelve books were highly Europeanized, drawing information from extant European treatises and, surely, the input of the Franciscan friars overseeing the project. The illustrations are, therefore, "a creative mixture of native and European stylistic traditions"; at times they are "fully integrated but more frequently they exist side by side" (Peterson 1988:278).

The European elements range from highly stylized floral and ornamental designs to backgrounds, landscapes, and material objects (such as a native painter's cups with precise parallels in European woodcuts). Perhaps more interesting is the manner in which these indigenous artists meshed native and European elements on a single subject. The harlot, for instance, is depicted as

> a woman with a goblet facing a seated male figure who offers her a coin. . . . The dress and hairstyles of both figures are a hybrid representation of native and European clothing. The importance of color as a

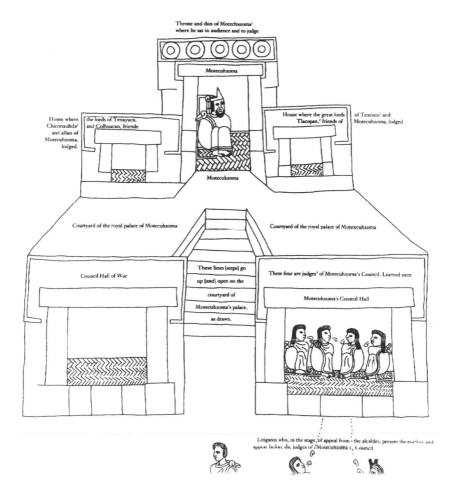

Figure 12. Motecuhzoma's palace drawn by a native Mexican scribe with a dash of European-derived perspective. (Reprinted, by permission, from *Codex Mendoza*, Berdan and Anawalt 1992, 4: folio 69r)

diagnostic feature is evident in two details: the golden goblet held by the woman and her startling crimson feet, swathed in either stockings or shoes. Neither correspond to the *Florentine Codex* text but can be traced to medieval and ultimately biblical references associated with harlotry. (Peterson 1988: 284)

These are still native artists, but some two generations removed from the times they are depicting. The experience of these 1579 artists is more encumbered with acculturative elements than that of the 1541 *Codex Mendoza* artist, resulting in somewhat different subject matter, portrayals, and styles.

The earliest pictorial images of the Americas produced by Europeans usually were not drawn from firsthand encounters. Artists did not typically accompany the early voyages across the Atlantic, and visual imagery was based on European preconceptions and written descriptions by explorers such as Columbus and Vespucci. For example, a whole train of illustrations derived from the following written paraphrase of a description of Brazilian natives by Vespucci, which served as a caption for a 1505 German woodcut: "They go about naked, both men and women. They have no personal property, but all things are in common. They all live together without a king and without government, and everyone is his own master. They take for wives whoever they first meet, and in all this they have no rule. . . . And they eat one another. . . . They live to be 150 years old and are seldom sick" (in Bray 1993:310). One image portrays thatched rectangular dwellings — items not mentioned at all in the written descriptions and probably drawn from the artist's preconceptions of "primitive" life generally (Milbrath 1989:188). Other illustrations depict American Indians with long flowing beards (even though they are described otherwise), or with stones set into their chests and cheeks (although a narrative mentions stones inset only in lips and cheeks [Milbrath 1989:189]). As time went on, illustrators derived their pictorial ideas more from such existing images than from the written descriptions, further adding their own little twists: Adam and Eve look-alikes appear, as do dead ringers for Picts and Irish "wild people" and figures straight out of classical antiquity.

Somewhat greater illustrative accuracy was achieved by European artists who, while still not setting foot in the Americas, nonetheless had firsthand contact with "visiting" natives and imported artifacts. Among these was the already mentioned Albrecht Dürer, whose woodcuts and engravings carry considerable credibility. However, even here there were artistic mishaps: Dürer well understood the form of many indigenous objects, but not so much their function (Massing 1991:517). He had viewed a large number of Native American artifacts during his visit to Brussels in 1520 and wrote eloquently of the beauty of these exotic items (Fraser 1971), but he had never been to the Americas to see these items in use in their proper context. Thus his depiction of a Tupinamba war club is accurate enough (based on an extant example), but it is shown being inaccurately wielded more like a spear. Obviously, illustrations drawn from actual encounters (however staged and out of context) do lend a somewhat greater degree of accuracy to the portrayals.

Finally, there are illustrations prepared by European travelers to the Americas. Of these on-site artists, the sixteenth-century chronicler Gonzalo Fernández de Oviedo y Valdes was the first (though not trained as an artist), and his more than twenty rather crude drawings depict native daily life from Hispaniola to Patagonia. Similarly simplified images were drawn by Hans Staden based on his eventful journey to the lands of the Tupinamba. His illustrations are surprisingly dispassionate, in contrast to the outward impression conveyed by one title of his book: *Description of a Country of Wild, Naked, Cruel, Man-Eating People in the New World.* In North America, trained artist John White (already mentioned in connection with the Roanoke colony) painted many scenes of Algonquians, and Jacques le Moyne performed a similar role for the Timucua in Florida. Both artists depicted considerable ethnographic detail, although a wary eye must still be cast on these images and the embellished engravings derived from them. For example, while le Moyne's depiction of a Timucuan mourning ritual may be accurate overall, the inclusion of a dominant nautilus shell was probably an "innovation" (Milbrath 1989:200). Similarly, some European implements (such as a hoe) creep into images of native life, while at the same time other details (such as ear ornaments and tobacco pipes) seem to be accurately portrayed indigenous items. In John White's painting of Algonquian fishermen, marine species (such as West Indian hermit crabs and shells and a hammerhead shark) appear in the scene, quite erroneously (Honour 1975:38).

The projection of European objects onto depictions of native life was fairly common, and it is a good idea to be on the lookout for them. But it should also be remembered that by the mid-sixteenth century, European hoes and the like may well have made their way into the indigenous technological repertoire alongside, or in place of, indigenous shell hoes in some regions.

Slightly more subtle influences are the preconceptions that are stamped liberally on drawings, paintings, woodcuts, and engravings. It was not uncommon to view the American Indians as vestiges from the dim, distant past, and so they were depicted as rude barbarians or, idealistically, as Adam and Eve. In a similar vein, analogies were made with known (or legendary) Pictish and Irish "wild people"; portrayals of American natives following this theme strongly resemble depictions of folks on the "margin" of European civilization. Some artists preferred a classical persona for the Native Americans; for example, the engravers of John White's Algonquian paintings did an extraordinary job of transforming White's original figures into replicas of Greek and Roman statuary.

In addition to the "rude barbarian" and the "classical" approaches was that of the "noble savage," as depicted in illustrations by le Moyne. In analyzing all such visuals for ethnographic, geographic, or historical information, it is prudent to keep in mind that the artists (and derivative woodcutters, engravers, or plagiarists) usually had a preconceived image in mind — a terrestrial paradise, a golden age, a savage land — that could seriously slant the visual portrayal and diminish its accuracy (see Bray 1993:314).

Some Matters of Style

Beyond preconceptions and artists' proclivities (such as a grim fascination with cannibalism), artists used standardized manners of depicting their subjects, which affected to some degree the information and message conveyed in the illustration. This involves such matters as poses, scale, and symmetry.

The matter of poses has already been touched upon above. When Native Americans were depicted according to a classical theme, the stance of the figures was derived from Greek and Roman models, and clothing was given a flowing, drapery effect. When the theme is the "rude barbarian," a robust, seated woman might be shown nursing an infant. Aside from these models, European artistic conventions preferred to pose individuals frontally or obliquely, while some indigenous artists (especially in Mesoamerica) preferred profiles. Obviously, somewhat varying views of the human figure resulted from these different approaches.

Scale is a consideration as well. Aztec artists used scale to indicate relative importance of figures: in the *Codex Mendoza* a victorious warrior is depicted larger than his humbled captive (Berdan and Anawalt 1992, 3: folios 64r, 65r). European artists of the Americas often troubled themselves little with matters of scale, and some persons and objects are shown vastly out of proportion: a dinghy may appear almost half the size of its parent galley, persons the height of trees, and an armadillo the size of a rhinoceros (Milbrath 1989:187; Bray 1993:319). Scale may have been involved in the example presented earlier of Dürer's depiction of a Tupinamba war club held as a lance; he may simply have endowed it with a greater size. If scale and proportions were not a special concern of these European artists, it must nonetheless be a concern of the ethnohistorian in extracting accurate information from such images.

While the European artists may have paid little attention to scale, they were slaves to symmetry. This is illustrated particularly well in a depiction of a hexagonal Iroquois village on an island in a river that has two tributaries joining at a 45-degree angle above the village, and two distributaries diverging at a neat 45-degree angle below it (Pendergast and Trigger 1972: fig. 15). This example is explored in detail in the case study in chapter 10.

Other artistic matters also enter into an analysis of these visual materials. One is the European use of perspective, which gives images a three-dimensional appearance, a look largely absent in native renderings. Another matter is the accepted practice of inserting landscapes and other backgrounds regardless of relevance. Yet another was the felt need to fill in all the details of a picture. While writers could write around a gap in knowledge, illustrators normally had to show all elements of people and things and surroundings, whether or not they had any idea of their appearance. This meant that guesses, analogies, and imagination were liberally applied. Still another consideration is the manner of imaging children. It was typical in much European artistry (as well as in some pre-Columbian American art styles) to depict children simply as small adults, and this carried over to illustrations of children in the Americas. In the trend-setting 1505 German woodcut based (somewhat) on Vespucci's description, a young child is shown with exactly the same clothing and adornment, demeanor, and facial appearance as the surrounding adults. The ethnohistorian cannot necessarily assume that persons of different age (or social position, for that matter) were so alike, even though they may have been depicted so.

The Tendency to Generalize

As already noted, Europeans who depicted Native Americans tended to mold them into preconceived types or models (such as "savage Picts" or "Greek gods"). This tendency had the effect of casting all American Indians into a limited number of forms. In fact, Europeans lumped all Native Americans with other non-Europeans, as in the 1517–18 woodcut titled "The Triumph of Maximilian." This woodcut depicted the people of Calicut, which included Native Americans, for "In Maximilian's time the generic term Calicut was not restricted to India, but referred to the inhabitants of all the newly discovered lands, including native Americans" (Massing 1991:516). Similarly, the inhabitants of any place discovered by Europeans in the early sixteenth century were known as "Indians," since India was the usual goal of exploration. As a result, the inhabitants of the Americas from the Arctic to Tierra del Fuego were classed together with the inhabitants of Malaysia, Polynesia, and Madagascar. The unwary illustrator might wrongly attribute the description of one "Indian" to another.

The earliest European images of Native Americans (especially Tupinamba) became the standard for depictions of all Amerindians (see figure 13); as a result, feathered headdresses, feathered (or leaf) skirts, and cannibalism all came to define "the Indian" in the minds of Europeans who did not know otherwise, and these features were repeated over and over as engraving copied woodcut copied painting. Even though the skirts may have been pure artistic invention, they nonetheless "figure over and over again in sixteenth-century representations, as one artist copied another, until, very quickly, the image came to replace the reality" (Bray 1993:316). With little else to go on, various European artists assumed that all Native Americans and their material culture were much the same. So "Brazilian Indians appear in Mexico, Patagonians are found in central New York, Florida Indians hold Brazilian clubs, Natchez Indians in Louisiana use a North Carolina temple, and Pocahontas wears a Tupinamba feather costume" (Sturtevant 1976:418). Such composite illustrations were common and call for cunning detective work on the part of the researcher. In terms of the reality-mediation model, elements of selection, transformation/modification, emphasis, and fabrication can all intrude in visual imagery.

Using High Technology in Visual Interpretation

For the most part, ethnohistorians use a single integrated system of sophisticated equipment for the interpretation of visual images: their eyes and brain. As the frontiers of information technology are pressed further and further, however, machines are beginning to perform tasks of which the human mechanism is incapable.

Perhaps the greatest potential lies with the family of techniques designated as *digital enhancement,* which permits a scholar to take a blurry image (particularly a photograph or video image) and to clarify it, often permitting the recognition of something that previously had been unrecognizable. Although these techniques may appear to be magic, they work on sound logical principles.

The first step in digital enhancement is to produce a digital map of the image, reducing it to a series of numbers, each of which corresponds to a

Figure 13. Widely distributed German woodcut of the early sixteenth century depicting Brazilian Tupinamba Indians. Note the feathered garb, stylized poses, and images of cannibalism. (Photograph courtesy of the Edward E. Ayer Collection, The Newberry Library, Chicago)

minimal spot on the image. The easiest way to produce this digital map is by scanning the image into a computer. Once in digital form in the computer, this information can be manipulated in various ways by software, some of which is moderately simple and inexpensive, some of which is incredibly complex and costly. This software can be directed to examine a particular portion of the digital map where you believe something of interest may be obscured. The program examines the pattern of darkness and light in the digital map, then uses algorithms (sequences of logical actions) to enhance the image. One algorithm might make blurry edges sharper; another might turn edges into regular geometric forms; a third might try to factor out the effects of shadows, judging the direction of lighting from where shadows fall elsewhere in the visual. Each of these actions produces a different image, and the various algorithms can be used in combination or in repetitive sequence, producing increasingly more refined images in each generation. Often the results of image enhancement produce no improvement in recognizability, but sometimes the result is astonishingly clear. Fortunately, producing an image that is significantly false purely through the actions of the algorithms is unlikely, and any image produced is probably a more accurate rendition than the original.

To date, image enhancement has been used for only a few historical purposes. In one of these rare applications, Adolf Hitler was recognized in the crowd at an early Nazi rally through the laborious process of enhancing the image of every face in the crowd visible on a newsreel until his was located. Similar enhancement procedures have been applied to the deteriorated murals of the ancient Mayan site at Bonampak, Mexico. Minute details contained in these elaborate murals have been reconstructed to an amazing degree through the application of photographic, artistic, and computer techniques (Miller 1995, 1997). The potential for these sorts of enhancements has not yet been fully realized in ethnohistory, but one can envision using them to examine:

— Old photographs to discover details previously too fine to be noted
— Early action photographs, blurred by subject motion or poor focus, reconstructing details previously obscured
— Poorly exposed photographs, ones that are washed out and previously have been attributed little or no research value
— Photographs damaged by time and mistreatment to tease out details presumed lost
— Early photographs taken with technologies that captured less detail than the modern researcher would like

All of these photographs could be examined with current technology, and the technology of tomorrow presumably will be even more able to produce detail where previously there had been only a vague blur.

A second family of technological processes is signature recognition: finding recurrent patterns in digital maps and bringing them to the attention of the analyst. The most common use of signature recognition today is "optical character recognition," the use of a scanner and software to "read" a printed message and convert it into computer code. The family of techniques, however, can be applied far more widely, as when aerial-photograph interpreters use signature recognition to find all the rectangles (probably houses) in a photograph.

An ethnohistorian might use a similar program to recognize recurrent details in a photograph. A photograph of a mass of dancers in a Hopi ritual, for example, might be examined for a unique pattern of body paint, signifying a particular voluntary society. In this way, it could be determined whether and how often members of that voluntary society participated in a particular dance. If only a single photograph is being examined, it might be more efficient to trust to one's vision and simply scan the photograph very carefully with a magnifying glass; however, if dozens or hundreds of photographs exist, the automated technique might be both more efficient and more accurate.

With the ongoing revolution in information technology, it is sensible to assume that the wild fantasies of today might well be the commonplace techniques of the near future. As the frontiers of technology advance, so will the applications in the analysis of ethnohistoric visual evidence.

Case Study

HURON AND TIMUCUA FARMERS

Elements of bias, stylization, and generalization should be kept in mind when analyzing the usefulness of any visual. Consider an engraving published by Joseph François Lafitau in 1724 (fig. 14). This picture apparently was a recycled image modified by design and artistic mishap. Although it purports to depict Huron agriculture in eastern Canada, it was copied by de Bry from an earlier (1591) engraving of Timucua farmers in Florida (fig. 15). In the process, the images became laterally reversed, resulting in a population of left-handed cultivators.

The copying without comment of an illustration from Florida as an illustration of eastern Canadian agriculture may have resulted from generalization, providing Lafitau reasoned that the Timucua and Huron were pretty much the same, both being North American "savages." Lafitau, however, is unlikely to have believed this, since the book in which the illustration appeared provided a great deal of evidence for cultural differences among American Indian societies. More likely, the illustration may have been added to Lafitau's written words by an editor anxious to relieve the potential mental fatigue of the reader. This possibility is supported by Lafitau's verbal description of Huron agriculture, in which he fails to mention hoes, instead describing a wooden digging stick. In any case, it appears that Lafitau was not directly involved in screening the engraving for accuracy.

Although the Huron did not use hoes, the Timucua did. But are the hoes depicted in both illustrations accurate renditions of Timucua hoes or, for that matter, hoes from anywhere in North America? Archaeological evidence and other descriptions of hoes among the Timucua and elsewhere suggest not. Hoes in use in Florida at European contact were predominantly made of shell and had rounded edges. There may have been stone hoes as well, since objects tentatively identified as stone hoes

Figure 14. Lafitau's 1724 engraving of Huron farmers, re-reversed here for comparison with figure 15. (Reproduced, by permission of the Society for American Archaeology, from *American Antiquity* 33 [1] [1968])

Figure 15. De Bry's 1591 engraving of Timucua farmers of Florida. (Reproduced by permission of the Society for American Archaeology from *American Antiquity* 33 [1] [1968])

have been recovered archaeologically, but these latter artifacts are broad and rounded on their leading edges, with areas for hefting that suggest they would have been mounted at or nearly at right angles to their handles. There is very little resemblance between these shell hoes and possible stone hoes and those depicted in the engravings.

What the hoes in the engravings do resemble are the triangular, pointy-tipped iron hoes used in France from medieval to modern times. The hoes attributed to the Timucua even show a central arris, a raised ridge running the length of the hoe and strengthening it. The technology of stone tool making would not permit the making of such an arris, nor would there be any advantage to it; European iron hoes, however, frequently incorporated this design element. While the Timucua hoes probably were mounted approximately perpendicular to their handles, French hoes usually were hefted at an extreme angle, producing a hooked appearance that is clear in the pictures. The engraver for de Bry would have been French and probably went to the local countryside to collect models and inspiration to create the props for his North American farmers; he probably also picked up bias on the trip. Sturtevant (1968) has presented a tidy analysis of these depictions of hoes, and the preceding commentary has been drawn largely from his work.

Other aspects of these engravings further illustrate the sorts of misinterpretations that can be based on visual images. On the basis of the Lafitau picture, it would be tempting to envision Huronia as a forbidding landscape, almost desertlike in its deforestation. By the eighteenth century, when the Lafitau illustration was prepared, considerable tracts of trees had been cut in some locales of Huronia — though not so brutally or completely as depicted here — but in the period before the extinction of the Huron in 1649, there were no extensive cleared areas. The absence of even low vegetation in the illustration suggests that the engraver had no understanding of the vegetation of eastern Canada.

The portrayals of the fields themselves also are inaccurate to varying degrees. The Timucua fields are presented as if they were in Europe: massive fields extending to the horizon, with straight, parallel rows and mathematically precise spacing between the plants. This presentation probably misses reality on all counts, since Timucua fields apparently were much smaller and irregular. The engraver of the Huron image apparently has used information from Lafitau's text, since the corn accurately is shown planted in hills, even incorporating the detail of ideally having nine seeds per hill. Even here, however, the urge to produce geometrically perfect forms has overwhelmed the artist, and hills have become miniature buttes, each perfectly circular and nicely flattened on top. While such regularity could be read into Lafitau's description, it is difficult to imagine that reality was this perfect. Stylization seemingly was at work.

The presentation of the farmers reveals still more about the artists. The Huron depiction is a bit vague on some details, but the Timucua vignette shows delightful detail of the sort permitted by engraving. The women are tall and graceful, the men muscular and energetic — noble yet savage. The men's hair may be accurately portrayed, but the women's hair fits more closely with the Renaissance European ideal. In fact, except for the grass skirts, the women could have come from a Renaissance depiction of ancient Roman vestal virgins or Pictish women: facial features, hair, idealized plump bodies, and poses all are European.

The grass or string skirts roughly accord with Cabeza de Vaca's vague description (1961:39) of women's garb among the Timucua and may be accurate renditions. Alternatively, they might be the result of the customary transfer to other societies of Tupinamba characteristics, so well known from Staden's descriptions. The Huron skirts, on the other hand, are wrap-around in style, accurately reflecting Huron styles and the information included in Lafitau's text.

Finally, the basket prominent in the foreground of the Timucua engraving probably is inaccurately depicted. The Timucua certainly made and used baskets, but the one shown here seems to have been made from splints, wide and thin strips split off from a piece of wood. In northeastern North America it is generally conceded that aboriginal splint basketry was inspired in the seventeenth century by European traditions, where splint weaving had a long history; in Florida, however, splint baskets were not part of the aboriginal cultural repertoire and simply constitute an alien technology (Brasser 1975).

Every picture that an ethnohistorian consults is a stew, with chunks of accurate depiction swimming in a broth of distortion. By cross-checking information from various sources, critically evaluating the image presented, and making judgments as necessary, it often is possible to strain out valuable information from the mix. But be wary: even the basically accurate depictions may have taken on a bit of flavor from the broth.

CHAPTER 10

Map Interpretation

Maps, as graphic depictions of spatial relations, are a type of visual imagery, but their particularly unique and distinctive qualities call for a separate and somewhat extended treatment. In this chapter we delve into ethnohistorians' use of maps and charts, focusing on the types and functions of maps, the historical technology of mapmaking, and the types of information that can be gleaned from maps. The chapter concludes with a case study interpreting Ramusio's sixteenth-century plan of Hochelaga in the St. Lawrence Valley. Throughout, it is important to remember that maps are cultural artifacts and therefore not natural representations of earthly phenomena and relationships. Reflecting the mind-set of its creator, a map is "a cumulation of choices made among choices every one of which reveals a value: not the world, but a slice of a piece of the world; not nature but a slant on it; not innocent, but loaded with intentions and purposes; not directly, but through a glass; not straight, but mediated by words and other signs; not, in a word, as it is, but in . . . code" (Wood 1992:108).

Types and Functions of Maps

A map, in the most general sense, is a model of geographic space. The term derives from Latin *mappa* (cloth or material), although in ancient Rome the term *tabula* was used to refer to a map as a "picture representation" (Bagrow 1985:22). The related term "chart" is most likely descended from a series of words (from Greek to Latin to Portuguese and Italian, and so on), all meaning "paper" (Bagrow 1985:22). The word was introduced into English from Dutch (along with Dutch charts) and tends to refer almost exclusively to nautical maps.

Maps and charts used in ethnohistoric research have been rendered in two dimensions on almost any available, relatively flat surface. They might be carved into stone, drawn on paper or parchment, painted on cloth, or incised onto driftwood. Some of the more fascinating map creations are those recorded for the Marshall Islands, where ingenious nautical charts were devised by lashing together the stiff center ribs of palm fronds into arrangements delineating the patterns of waves and swells caused by predictable winds; small shells or pieces of coral are attached to indicate the locations of islands within these oceanic patterns (Thrower 1972:5–8). These stick maps readily fulfilled the nautical travel needs of the people of these many islands and surely contributed considerably to successful journeys from island to island.

In addition to being executed on a wide array of materials (some more perishable than others), maps vary in terms of their intended permanency. Throughout history (and prehistory) some maps surely have been drawn and have quickly disappeared. Especially ephemeral would be those hastily executed plans drawn in dirt or sand with a stick, such as the Iroquois sand maps used before battles in the sixteenth and early seventeenth centuries. The knowledge evidenced by such maps is obviously lost; nonetheless, ethnohistorians must not assume that absence of artifact equals absence of knowledge. Luckily, many maps were created with greater permanency of material and use, and these provide a sampling of spatial concepts and geographic knowledge of various peoples of the world. As an added note, ethnohistorians should be alert to "the silent updating of an existing map" (Wood 1990:97) in which a mapmaker may add or modify features of an existing functional map; the map then comes to contain information drawn or written at different times.

Enduring maps and charts were devised to fulfill a variety of functions, paramount of which was wayfinding: maps and charts served as route reminders for experienced travelers and as guides for newcomers. Maps were also useful in describing city, town, and country settlement patterns and in illustrating the delineation of property. Maps and charts also served important functions in political administration, military organization, religious symbolism, and a whole range of specialized themes (such as engineering, demographics, and commerce). Beyond these fairly obvious functions, some maps were created largely for aesthetic purposes, at least in Europe until the end of the sixteenth century. It was usual for more than one of these various functions to be combined on a single map: a nautical chart could also include town sites, military installations, and a multitude of religious symbols and fancy pictures.

It is good to keep in mind that maps are merely models and are therefore distortions of geographic reality. Of necessity, the rendering of a three-dimensional earth as a two-dimensional map requires certain adjust-

ments in distances, directions, areas, and/or shapes that are systematized
as projections (conversions of coordinate lines from the curved surface of
the earth to a flat surface or map). Many such projections have been
devised in cartographic history, each conveying particular advantages and
disadvantages. The Mercator projection, for instance, is designed so that
the meridian lines do not meet at the poles (as they would on a globe);
therefore, scale increases toward the poles, and areas are enlarged as one
looks north and south from the equator. On the other hand, maps with
this projection are ideal for navigation purposes since the shapes of natural
features (such as shorelines) are portrayed moderately accurately. Similarly, Roman road maps seriously distorted land and sea areas in an attempt to display the road networks within a convenient and usable space
(Bricker 1968:22).

Beyond incorporating technical matters such as projection and scale,
maps also reflect their creators' cultural and historical milieu. Discussing
Native American maps, Warhus (1997:9) observes that they are "simultaneously a picture of Native American perceptions and experience and
documentation of their interactions with western peoples." Since no map
can possibly include everything of potential interest to every user, the
mapmaker must select items for inclusion and emphasis: shorelines and
sailing distances are of significance to a sailor, topography to a military
general, property delineation to a tax collector, and so on. Likewise, the
cartographer must select an appropriate projection. For instance, if correct areas are needed, then they must be rendered accurately at the expense
of some other factor such as direction. In short, any mapmaker must make
choices and sacrifices: what to include and what to omit, what to execute
with precision and what to distort.

We recognize, then, that any typology of maps is likely to be an
extreme oversimplification. Nonetheless, for expository purposes we
present in table 10 some associations between major map functions and
map types. This list is by no means intended to be exhaustive but is merely
representative and illustrative of the intentions of cartographers in making
maps and charts.

Wayfinding: Navigational Charts and Route Maps

Recording travel routes was probably one of the earliest, and certainly one
of the most persistent reasons for making a map or chart. Because such
maps of ocean or terrain were devised to indicate actual travel routes, they

Table 10. Examples of Map Functions and Types

Map Functions	Map Types
Wayfinding	Navigational charts
	Route maps
Settlement patterns	Topographic maps
	Settlement maps
	Bird's-eye view maps
Property delineation	Cadastral maps
Political/economic/military	Geopolitical maps
Religious/symbolic	T-O maps and mappaemundi
Aesthetic	Maps of the imagination

were certainly most useful when they mirrored real-life geographic relationships. Yet, through history, mapmakers have had highly variable success in converting the earth's geography to a constant-scale, two-dimensional plan. It is worthwhile to consider two sets of factors when analyzing the information contained in maps with a wayfinding function.

First is the matter of whether such maps were derived inductively or deductively. In Europe, deductively derived maps were particularly popular from the fourteenth century onward, with the resurgent interest in Ptolemaic geography. Claudius Ptolemy (ca. A.D. 90–168) was associated with the famous library at Alexandria. His cartographic contributions rest primarily in his theoretical constructions of three geographic projections. Although based on contemporaneous locational details and on his own astronomical observations, Ptolemy's "known world" maps nonetheless contained distortions derived from the constraints of his projections and from his limited knowledge of the entire world. These maps were heartily adopted by European navigators beginning in the fourteenth century. A particular problem with those early navigational charts was the inability to calculate (or even estimate) longitude, although latitude was quite accurately ascertained. Therefore, maps dated before 1657 (when the pendulum clock was applied to cartography) and even those dated before the mid-eighteenth century (when the chronometer was invented) should be viewed with a wary eye toward longitudinal distortions (Thrower 1972: 61–62; Sobel 1995; see below for more on technological matters related to mapping). A further problem was the occasional tendency to fill in spaces with "imaginary lands." As time progressed, of course, more workable projections were developed (such as Mercator's), enabling cartographers to more accurately plot locations on maps and charts. Greater accuracy was also achieved as inductive, on-the-ground observations and surveying led to more precise locational plotting.

A second consideration is related to matters of scale (and not unrelated to the previous consideration). The early Greeks were well aware that differences in scale related to differences in function: "there was a sharp dichotomy . . . between land measurers (geometers), who were employed to delineate small areas, and philosophers, who speculated on the nature and form of the entire earth" (Thrower 1972:16). As an example, it is obvious that small-scale worldwide maps would be of less everyday utility to a navigator than larger-scale regional or local maps or charts. Indeed, navigators are particularly interested in dangerous headlands (which the ship must sail around) and in estuaries (which could serve as stopping points). Reasonably large-scale charts would provide this necessary detail. Where some areas of a map (such as small islands) were too diminutive to show sufficient coastal detail, they were at times drawn out of proportion, just so the essential contours could be properly shown. Researchers should not necessarily conclude that this island was actually larger in historic times or that the voyagers had accidentally or incompetently mismapped.

The ethnohistorian studying such charts should also be aware that, while close attention was paid to the representation of coastlines on navigational charts, other areas and features were often ill-informed, ill-defined, and at times fanciful. Route maps focusing on terrain normally show the opposite emphasis. Terrain route maps may also indicate landscape variation through hachuring (closely spaced vertical lines used to illustrate landscape features), but it is usually imprecise in terms of relative scale (e.g., the height of mountains or the depth of ravines). It should also be kept in mind that, especially for hydrographic charts, much of the navigational information was jealously guarded to protect one's commercial advantage in Europe of the fourteenth through seventeenth centuries. Important details were therefore often omitted from the graphic chart, although they were well-known by the pilot.

A further caution pertains to map orientation. It was common for early maps produced in China to be drawn with north at the top, but the Arabs placed south at the top, and the T-O maps of medieval Europe (discussed below) placed east at the top (hence the term "orientation"). Most European navigation charts from the fourteenth century on, however, used a north orientation. Some topographic and settlement maps,

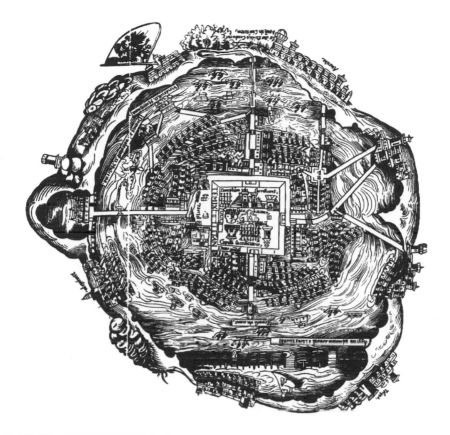

Figure 16. Sixteenth-century map of the island city of Tenochtitlan in the Valley of Mexico as seen through Spanish eyes. (Reprinted, by permission, from Mundy 1996:xii; courtesy of the Rare Books Division, The New York Public Library, Astor, Lenox and Tilden Foundations)

such as many emanating from colonial Mexico, have no clear orientation at all but rather orient figures and action inward from all four directions (fig. 16).

Settlement Patterns: Topographic, Settlement, and Bird's-Eye View Maps

A great many maps illustrate landforms and the geographic relationships of inhabited places and landforms to one another. These are called "topographic" maps. With regard to topography, the ethnohistorian cannot expect to see modern-style elevation contours on maps dating before the mid-nineteenth century. Instead of contouring (a quantitative measure of elevation), hachuring (a qualitative indication of elevation differences) was frequently used (Thrower 1972:80). Alternatively, relief was indicated by individual hills (sometimes called "fish scales" or "sugar loafs") either linked in a continuous chain or dotting the landscape here and there. It should be noted, however, that the presence of such hills can be ambiguous: in colonial Mexico hills frequently served as backdrops for place-name glyphs and were symbols for "town" (*altepetl* = water + hill). In this case they indicated a human settlement, not a landscape feature.

Various elements of the landscape have often been presented in artistic format: a multitude of individual stately trees denoted a forest, a brown area with dots indicated a sand bar, a green area with little sedge-like plants encompassed a marshland. Although not equivalent to the abstract topographic symbols of modern maps, they can nonetheless be interpreted with a fair degree of confidence.

Topographic maps normally depicted some aspect of human occupation. A 1555 map of the Valley of Mexico, for instance, delineated the layout of Mexico City, the remnants of the ancient lake system, surrounding communities, a web of roads leading to and from the city, and an eclectic collection of people doing daily life things: toting loads, spearing fish, herding sheep, ordering people around, and so on (Linne 1948). Such a map, quite clearly, is an excellent source of ethnohistoric information.

A common reason for making maps was to locate and describe human settlements. This may have been for a variety of purposes, including colonization and settlement, travel, religious conversion, or the establishment of historical proprietorship. Maps like these also served as the basis for the geopolitical maps described below. Many such maps were made in the context of culture contact. Since ethnic interaction is a main concern of ethnohistorians, it is worthwhile taking a look at how maps can reflect that cultural interchange. It is also useful to consider the extent to which a map reflects on-the-ground geography and the extent to which it is intended to relate more symbolic information.

A good example derives from a series of maps drawn by native scribe-artists in the later sixteenth century in Mexico to accompany geographical reports (*Relaciones geográficas*) prepared in Spain's new colony. These seventy-five existing maps display varying degrees of retention of native conventions and incorporation of European modes of mapping (Mundy 1996). Of the maps in question, those that are the most perceptual (mirroring the visible landscape) clearly indicate town street grids, important buildings (such as a church and government house, along with scattered dwellings), well-placed roads, and a surrounding landscape. The town arrangement would be familiar to a European, but the depiction of the surrounding landscape might be somewhat disorienting and unfamiliar. While individual hills line the terrain, they are full of native symbols; in the case of the most pragmatic maps, these denote actual physical features (Butzer and Williams 1992). More conceptual maps, containing historical information and brimming with symbolic overtones, were also created as part of the *Relaciones*. These maps depict many of the same cultural and physical features as the perceptual maps but also include images of successive native rulers (and Spanish magistrates) along with their symbols of power. They also contain images that carried strong religious meaning to the native scribe, such as a sacred mountain or a variety of naturalistic-looking glyphs; these could be misinterpreted as strict geography by the unwary viewer (Butzer and Williams 1992). Thus maps that locate settlements and landscapes may well be more than they appear; they may include elements of historical and symbolic meaning as well as visible topography and town plans. The addition of these more conceptual elements may also distort the actual geography, since the physical landscape might be viewed basically as a backdrop for this more vital information.

Another type of settlement map worth mentioning is a category called "bird's-eye view maps," found in Chinese and European cartography and also transported to the Americas (Harvey 1987:469; Cumming 1971:14). These highly detailed plans, typically of a large city or town, make a point of illustrating architectural features (such as buildings and city walls), often giving them a detailed, three-dimensional quality. At times they are drawn as though the "bird" were flying directly overhead, but more often the view is from an oblique angle. Distortions of scale sometimes result from this angle view and should be taken into account if using such maps to reconstruct actual space. Furthermore, even though attempts were made to maintain scale in the depiction of the human settlement (despite the geometry problems), less care was taken with the surrounding countryside, which is often shown vastly out of scale (Harvey 1987:465, 479; Bagrow 1985: plate C).

Sometimes drawing a bird's-eye view map presented a cartographer with an impossible task, as when a large building completely obscured a smaller one behind it. On the one hand, the map was supposed to show all buildings; on the other hand, it was designed to retain scale to as great a degree as possible. The usual solution was to exaggerate the size of the small building or to move it farther away from the large building than it really was. A further complication with such maps came when the map-maker (often resident far from the community being mapped) had inade-quate information on a particular building or other feature; sometimes the poorly known feature would be omitted, and other times its depiction would be based on a cartographer's guess.

Property Delineation: Cadastral Maps

Maps of house plots and land use (cadastral maps, also called "plat" maps) have considerable antiquity. They were well developed in ancient Egypt, where outlines of tombs, architectural drawings of residential buildings, and schematic plans of dikes and canals were made. The Egyptians ob-viously possessed "the means and the bureaucracy for measuring, calculat-ing, and registering areas" (Shore 1987:129). They also felt the need to graphically delineate areas of both the living and the dead. The later Ro-mans were highly adept at land mapping and cadastral surveys, a reflection of their interest in orderly government, legal proprieties, and taxation. They drew up plans of towns and cities, of aqueducts and agricultural lands, of villas and baths (Dilke 1987). Despite their consummate skill in surveying and engineering, these Roman depictions at times suffer from distortion of scale, where some features are shown in elevation (e.g., as pictures of buildings), as a sign (e.g., described by a symbol), or in plan or diagram, and especially important buildings are enlarged, all on the same plan (Dilke 1987:229). Furthermore (and reminiscent of the colonial Mexican *Relación* maps mentioned above), some apparently practical plans were prepared solely for decorative or symbolic purposes and realis-tic accuracy was not intended (Dilke 1987:230).

It seems that the need for cadastral maps and the skills involved in producing them were less urgent or available in medieval Europe; al-though written descriptions were made of properties, little was com-mitted graphically to paper or parchment (Harvey 1987). The famous early-ninth-century plan of St. Gall, an idealized Carolingian monastery, is an exception. Indeed, medieval cadastral-type maps (at least those that have survived) tended to focus on religious structures such as cathedrals and cloisters.

Cadastral maps were common in the historic Americas. A site plan of an area near sixteenth-century Mexico City (*Plano en Papel de Maguey*) illustrates carefully delineated house/farm plots bordered by canals and roads (Robertson 1959). Plots carry pictographs of their owners or ten-ants and their name glyphs (which would be rubbed out when they died and replaced by the glyphs of their successors). The whole plan, while surely relating to some segment of geographical space, is nonetheless schematized; the plots are much too similar to one another in size and shape. It is, indeed, sufficiently generalized to have prevented modern scholars from pinpointing its actual location. A great abundance of even larger-scale maps exist for the ethnohistorian studying colonial Mexico: individual house plans and house plots (with and without fields and orchards) provide a wealth of information on the spatial arrangements of social activities.

Another good example of cadasters is West Indian plantation maps. Careful surveys of sugar plantations from eighteenth- and nineteenth-century Jamaica designate the distribution and placement of human-made and natural features (Higman 1986). Because these maps were usually drawn up to record changes in land ownership or to resolve boundary disputes, the external boundaries of the plantation were surveyed with great care and shown with precision; conversely, the less important internal structures and features were more casually and roughly depicted. Cadastral maps constructed in times of political conflict and social turbulence often reflect such conditions and should be studied for possibilities of special interest (at best) and falsification (at worst).

Political, Economic, and Military Goals: Geopolitical Maps

All of the above-mentioned maps could serve additional overt functions as tools of political administration or military advancement, which many maps used by (and available to) ethnohistorians were. It is therefore worthwhile to discuss them generally as geopolitical maps.

European navigation mapmakers often had exploration (and, by extension, economic and political control of "new" lands) in mind. On the other hand, Egyptian and Roman cadastral maps were designed to keep track of the populace and its production. A particularly good additional example of maps carrying political and military goals comes from colonial North America. Although actual physical evidence is fragmentary, it appears that people of many native North American societies were adept at mapping (Harley 1992). Their knowledge of terrain and routes no doubt was passed on to Europeans as they penetrated the North American continent.

The French and English in eastern North America made maps for many geopolitical and economic reasons: they craved specific knowledge of unexplored territories for their own expansion (especially at each other's expense); they needed graphic information on passable routes (by land and water) and human settlements for commercial and population expansion; and they needed maps in order to handle boundary disputes and land claims (Cumming 1974:57). All of these goals are reflected in maps of the seventeenth and eighteenth centuries, which detail the intricacies of harbors and coves, the courses of navigable rivers, and topographical variation (with hachuring).

Geopolitical maps became increasingly important with the occurrence of military conflict. During the French and Indian War, it was especially important to locate settlements of Indians, because both the French and English were competing for native allies. Maps depicting conflicting boundary claims were also drawn up for propaganda purposes. And, of course, wartime troop deployments and battlefield arrangements were graphically shown on maps. The map of the battle of Quebec shows "the topography of the region in detail, with the location of the British ships and the lines, batteries, encampments, and attacks of the opposing forces" (Cumming 1974:62). In addition, large-scale plans of fortifications and critical locales appear in map form. Cartographers of the later Revolutionary War continued mapping in these same formats but also tended to emphasize larger areas in order to portray troop movements and significant battle campaigns (Cumming 1974:64). Over a rather short span of time, geographic knowledge had increased to allow such extensive mapping, and military use of these maps had been transformed.

Religious/Symbolic Goals: T-O Maps and Mappaemundi

Some maps have conceptual, rather than pragmatic, purposes behind their creation. Such was the case with medieval European T-O maps and the very popular *mappaemundi* of medieval and Renaissance times.

T-O maps depict a Christian conception of the medieval known world. It encompassed three continents (Europe, Asia, and Africa) arranged within a bordered circle and divided by a "T." These maps were drawn with east at the top. Asia occupied the top of the map (above the T crossbar), Europe the left of the vertical T-bar, and Africa the right of the T-bar (fig. 17).

Schematically, the top of the T was formed by the Nile and Don Rivers, and the vertical bar represented the Mediterranean Sea. This arrangement depicted the commonly held notion of three continents cover-

Figure 17. A typical T-O style map depicting the Christian conception of the medieval known world. (Reprinted, by permission, from Donald Robertson, *Mexican Manuscript Painting of the Early Colonial Period* [Norman: University of Oklahoma Press, 1994], fig. 65)

ing most of the Earth's surface, surrounded by an outer ocean (the O). Moreover, these maps made theological statements. Jerusalem was at the center, and each of the three continents was held to be the "domain" of the three sons of Noah. This was clearly a case where conceptions of geographical space were molded by ideological constraints. The occurrence of such maps was not restricted to Europe: such an item can be seen in Bernardino de Sahagún's *Florentine Codex* (1950–82: bk. 7, fig. 8). At first glance the circular depiction may be taken as an image of Aztec worldview, but the Aztec symbols are clearly set within a framework of T-O mapping.

Just as Christians produced maps that reflected their image of the world, others also incorporated their views into maps. Crates of Mallos, for example, was a Greek librarian from the second century B.C. who produced a map of the world. Crates's map showed Africa, Europe, and Asia on the eastern edge of a circle, as well as Perioikoi and the land of the Antipodeans on the western edge of the circle. Some scholars have considered this map evidence of very early contacts between the Mediterranean and the Americas, seeing Perioikoi as North America and the land of the Antipodeans as South America. A more likely explanation, however, is that Crates felt the need for balance in the distribution of the continents and simply drew in continents that would produce the balance his philosophy led him to believe must exist (Luce 1971). Even the names of Crates's western continents suggest a philosophical origin, since they mean respectively "dwellers at the edge" and "those with their feet opposite," both terms with little meaning except to contrast these inhabitants to the known peoples of the Old World. The concept of Antipodes provided a hypothetical southern area to balance the known northern one; a philosophical model combined with geographically known regions on concrete maps.

One of the most common types of maps produced in fifth- to fifteenth-century Europe was the so-called mappaemundi or "drawings of the world" (Woodward 1987:287). The paramount reason for constructing such maps was "to instruct the faithful about the significant events in Christian history rather than to record their precise locations" (Woodward 1987:286). They were therefore rather schematic and abstract, only rarely expressing an overt scale and more usually including a vast amount of religious painting around and within the map. As geographical information, then, these maps (and others like them) must be taken only as approximations of spatial reality. Again, this does not mean that the medieval mind did not grasp spatial relationships or relative locations, but rather that their graphic expression was executed with a mind-set emphasizing religious dogma.

Aesthetic Purposes: Maps of the Imagination

Early maps were works of art as well as works of science. In fact, it was only beginning in the eighteenth century that European maps began routinely to be stripped of elaborate decoration. At that time, maps became more strictly focused on the depiction of literal geographic information. But before then, maps served as reservoirs of a surprising amount of cultural, natural historical, and iconographic information. As works of art, maps have been valued and displayed throughout history (and today as well). Ancient map frescoes and mosaics were certainly at least as decorative as they were useful, and maps executed on paper, cloth, or parchment were frequently hung on walls from Japan to Genoa to Jamaica (Bagrow 1985:215, 217; Higman 1986:108).

European cartographers often used artistic and symbolic elements to fill in areas about which little was known. Thus wildlife may fill in large portions of a map of Africa, and cannibals may serve the same function for parts of South America. The presence of these artistic forms should alert researchers to the extent and range of knowledge of the mapmaker. It is important, therefore, to discover whether the person actually drawing the map was the same as the person who collected the data, whether the person had actually visited the place depicted in the map, and whether that information had been collected otherwise (and how). Artistic additions also provide an idea of the conceptions (or preconceptions) of the cartographer; stereotypical images are usual in maps with artistic content. Yet there is considerable useful detail that should not be discarded out of hand: properly analyzed, images of plant and animal life, depictions of material culture, pictures of indigenous inhabitants, and the like all contribute to the ethnohistorian's collection of data.

One special hazard should be noted. Sometimes maps were made with absolutely no intention of mirroring reality. They were, indeed, maps of the imagination. Popular among these were maps of fanciful places, including "the Realm of Love." At times this tendency to imagine and idealize places, peoples, and things spilled over onto more serious geographic maps, especially when little was known about an area. In such cases the ethnohistorian must be especially alert to separate fact from fancy.

Information and Technology Used in Mapmaking

A wide variety of intricate techniques has been used through history in constructing maps, and tomes have been written on the subject. Here we merely intend to take a brief look at the sorts of information (technological and otherwise) applied to mapmaking, particularly as they affected the final artifact. It has already been mentioned that the Greeks had geometers (who measured small areas) and philosophers (who conceptualized the "world"). Geographical information and technology can be usefully divided along these classical lines.

The big picture — worldwide, small-scale maps — was developed primarily from astronomical observations and records. Ptolemy, fundamentally an astronomer, applied his understanding of the heavens to geographical relationships on Earth. Early on, navigation relied on dead reckoning, but by the thirteenth century, the Chinese were already using a variety of instruments (such as sighting tubes, cross-staffs, leveling chains, and a magnetized needle). At the end of the thirteenth century in Europe, a magnetized needle was attached to a card diagramming sixteen directions (the sixteen "winds"), yielding a compass (Thrower 1972:27, 38). Later technological developments were the products of sixteenth-, seventeenth-, and eighteenth-century Europe: triangulation, the plane table with sighting rule, the pendulum clock, and the chronometer (Thrower 1972:61–62; Sobel 1995). All of these developments, combined with growing mathematical sophistication, allowed for increasingly accurate small-scale maps.

Maps drawn on a large scale — such as cadastral maps, settlement plans, and topographic maps — required somewhat different information and instruments. Direct observation was an important source of information. Yet some maps (or parts of maps) were based on "indirect" information, as for parts of North America where European mapmakers relied on native verbal descriptions of distant inland areas, translating this information graphically onto their maps.

Seventeenth- and eighteenth-century European surveyors benefited from instruments such as the odometer, the magnetic compass, and the theodolite (Sobel 1995:62). We find increasing cartographic accuracy as these techniques were developed and came into general use. By the mid-eighteenth century, European cartography had advanced to the point where maps drawn from careful observations could be expected to be geographically accurate. Good sources on historic mapmaking concepts, techniques, and technology include Thrower (1972), Bricker (1968), Smith (1996), and Levenson (1991).

Types of Information to Be Gleaned from Maps

A great deal of ethnohistoric information is embedded in maps, and researchers obtain different types of information (with varying degrees of reliability) from different types of maps. If plotting absolute and relative locations is the goal, then navigational charts are far superior to mappaemundi. Navigational charts and route maps are also excellent sources of information on such geographic details as coastline contours, river courses, road networks, and terrain.

If the paramount research goal is to learn about the lay of the land and human settlement, then topographic, settlement, and bird's-eye view maps are particularly important sources. Topographic maps emphasize landforms, with accuracy increasing as technological instrumentation improved. Maps (especially large-scale maps) emphasizing settlements tend to maintain urban and town scale and details reasonably well, but the scale and graphic description of the countryside can be distorted and vague. Bird's-eye view maps should be considered in a similar light, with the added caution that sometimes only the most important buildings are included, and some of the taller ones (such as towers) may obscure or distort smaller buildings behind them.

If property boundaries are sought, then cadastral maps are a better source of information than bird's-eye view maps. In fact, cadastral maps (especially if representing a span of time) can provide the ethnohistorian with valuable information on changing property lines, transformations in ideas and rules concerning land ownership and use, and census patterns. They can also offer some ideas about the spatial arrangements of social life.

Geopolitical maps have a theme and superimpose that theme on any of the foregoing types of maps. For instance, if a depiction of military troop deployment is the intention, then appropriate military symbols would be added to a topographic or settlement map. If taxation is a government goal, then a cadastral map indicating particular types of land and land use would be practical. The possibilities are almost limitless.

If a researcher's goal is to better understand religious concepts, T-O maps and mappaemundi give fuller information than, say, topographic or settlement maps. These maps reveal a great deal about the symbolic world of the mapmaker (and/or the mapmaker's patron) and about the interface between religion and geography.

Maps designed for primarily aesthetic purposes or maps with any degree of artistic material often contain a great deal of additional information. Beyond absolute and relative locations, routes, and settlements, these maps provide fascinating details on natural history, culture, and material culture, albeit often stereotyped.

Beyond the maps encompassed in this typology are maps that may be labeled, for lack of a better term, idiosyncratic maps. The ethnohistorian should be alert to the potential usefulness of various maps that do not neatly fit into any of these categories. They may be highly schematized and unelaborated sketch maps; they may be oblique aerial views that could be considered generic landscape illustrations; or they may be maps that seem to depict the physical and cultural features of a region but make no attempt to show real geographic relationships. Whatever form they may take, some maps simply fall outside or between the categories of the typology presented here. Each map, therefore, should be assessed individually as to its interpretive potential, using this typology only as a general guideline.

It is obvious that each type of map has its strengths and weaknesses. Each type of map, and each map individually, must therefore be carefully analyzed. The following is a brief checklist of matters to consider when using maps in research:

— The purposes for which the map was made
— The world view and preconceptions of the mapmaker
— The kinds of information and technology used in creating the map
— The kinds of conventions employed on a map (e.g., orientation, scale, relative importance of features)

Beyond enhancing ethnohistoric research per se, maps have the added advantage of being related (usually) to actual geography. They are used by archaeologists to better understand the nature and context of an archaeological site and even to aid in locating a particular ancient settlement. Furthermore, early maps can provide clues concerning the actual nature of the land, as with the soil glyphs found on colonial Mexican maps; the distribution of these soil types and the agricultural strategies associated with them have been coupled with on-the-ground geographic research (Williams 1980). Maps therefore not only tell us about the nature of things at the time the map was made, but also can be applied by scholars to a variety of interesting modern research problems.

Case Study

THE RAMUSIO PLAN OF HOCHELAGA

Hochelaga was an Iroquois town in Canada's St. Lawrence Valley that was visited and described by the French explorer Jacques Cartier (1924). In his journal entry for October 3, 1535, Cartier describes Hochelaga as a circular, palisaded village near a mountain and surrounded by large cornfields. The tiered stockade (in all about thirty-three feet high) featured a gallery from which defenders could hurl rocks and other projectiles upon attackers (Pendergast and Trigger 1972:9). Cartier specifies one, and only one, entrance to the fortified village, a central square about a stone's throw across, and about fifty wooden longhouses within the palisade. The houses are described as quite uniform, each about fifty paces long and twelve or fifteen paces wide, and each divided into separate rooms (Pendergast and Trigger 1972:334). This, then, summarizes Cartier's description of Hochelaga.

In 1556 Gian Baptista Ramusio published a translation of Cartier's relations. An engraved map of Hochelaga accompanied this work (fig. 18). To determine how well this map reflects the real Hochelaga, we must evaluate the manner in which the engraver (with a particular mind-set) applied the available sources of information (and biases) to the production of this plan.

There is much to suggest that the engraver drew a good deal of his information directly from Cartier's account. The town is circular (although surely a bit too perfect here), and a tiered palisade is schematically drawn (with some clever cross-sectioning). The gallery is shown, along with some rather energetic (but perhaps misguided) stone hurlers. The ladder is distinctly European in design; the native ladder would most likely have consisted of a notched log (Pendergast and Trigger 1972:9). The town wall would have been made of stakes/logs set in the ground (i.e., round cross-sections, with or without bark), not with flat and sawed

Figure 18. The Ramusio map of Hochelaga. (Reprinted, courtesy of McGill-Queen's University Press, from Pendergast and Trigger 1972:9)

planks as shown here. The triangular cross-section of the palisade and the hollow within is inaccurate. It is notable that several events and times are compressed in this single image. Simultaneously we see a peaceful greeting of the French and the repulsion of an attack (although no obvious attackers are shown).

The single entrance and central square are depicted, but the "main street" from entrance to square is clearly an innovation of the engraver. The "piazza" (C) would have been irregular and not as square, perhaps reflecting the Italian conception of a piazza. Likewise, an innovation is the careful geometric layout of the fifty houses. Here the engraver appears to have tried to follow Cartier's account, but he recast the longhouses (each approximately 50 by 12–15 paces in size) into a variety of orderly combinations of squarish units to create a rather attractive, but surely inaccurate, layout. Several of these combined "houses" ultimately resemble the longhouses described by Cartier (as consisting of several rooms around a central court, with a hearth or fire for each family in a longhouse). Others are perfectly square, and four are presented as elongated Us. The engraver may have struggled here, trying to reconcile Cartier's description with his own mind-set of a geometrically symmetrical plan. The latter prevailed.

Outside of town we see the adjacent mountain (Mont Réal), here shown bare despite Cartier's insistence that it was fertile and cultivated (Pendergast and Trigger 1972:25). We also see a corner of tidy cultivated fields, where the corn is depicted more as wheat grown on European-style fields. And even though Cartier specifies oak trees (noting that he encountered acorns as he walked), the trees in the plan are difficult to identify and seem to suffer from generalization and stylization. The ones in the left-center of the map, however, look remarkably like Italian cypress and completely unlike anything native to eastern Canada. The appearance of the natives likewise is stereotyped; they are not dressed like Iroquois and are in the poses used by contemporary artists to portray Picts or Greeks (Pendergast and Trigger 1972:13). Despite the Iroquois clothing being generally inappropriate, the illustrator somehow managed to get the conical hats (*gos-to-whe*) right for the leaders on a formal occasion (located at "R"). The hunter to the left of the village (above "Monte Real") is depicted as solitary, slightly stooped, and apparently crudely draped with an animal skin. This fits the medieval European concept of *l'homme sauvage,* but it misses the mark on Iroquois hunters who normally hunted in groups, wore fitted clothing, and stood quite erect.

The engraver was not too concerned with scale, so we should not put too much stock in figuring such things as village or field dimensions from this plan. Glaringly out of scale are the village relative to the cornfields and both relative to Mont Réal. In addition, it would surely be unusual to see bears and deer (and is that a wild European goat?) wandering about so close to the village. Importantly, the map switches perspectives — oblique for most areas but perpendicular for the town plan.

In the absence of some information, the engraver was required to innovate. He had to show Mont Réal, but nothing in the textual account reveals its exact location. Its placement on the map is not to be trusted. Similarly, Cartier states that Hochelaga was situated in the middle of large cornfields, but the engraver chose to merely suggest this cultivation with a small collection of fields in one corner. The engraver was also creative with the human actors; he shows the Frenchmen arriving at the village from the left, yet there is really no way he knew this for sure. As a final observation, the wattled fences are a rather peculiar addition; they do not appear to have been known among the Iroquois and probably derived from else-where in the engraver's experience.

Some features of this plan (such as the round shape of the village and the presence of one entrance and a square) clearly conform to Cartier's brief description and roughly to archaeological knowledge of the Iroquois (although the village was probably more oval than round). Other features (such as cornfields transformed into European-style wheat fields and the innovative shape of the houses) resulted from compromises between the textual descriptions and the engraver's mind-set. Still other features (such as the location of Mont Réal and the direction from which the French arrived) were guesses by the engraver in the absence of other information.

The usual cautions apply here. The very presence of the Palladian-style legend loaded with descriptive terms that undoubtedly carried many cultural implications in Italy (such as *strade* and *piazza*) tends to skew the viewer's interpretation. In another vein, some attempts have been made to calculate factors such as population size and details of the French trek to the village (Pendergast and Trigger 1972). Given the above discussion of the plan, however, it is probably not safe to deduce population estimates, territorial domain, carrying capacity, geographical configurations, or pre-cise historical details from such a plan. The map is a composite — in part based on documentary description, in part on the engraver's preconcep-tions, and in large part on compromises between the two.

CHAPTER 11

Tapping Complementary Sources of Information

As we have seen throughout this book, particularly in our discussions of reality mediation and source analysis, documents are fallible. Sometimes the author was mistaken or confused, made critical omissions, or lied. Given these potential shortcomings of the written word, the wise ethnohistorian will try to tap other information sources to supplement the data in documents. These other sources often are called "ancillary" sources or "auxiliary" sources, the phrases coming from the Latin for "hand-maiden" and "assistant," indicating a position subordinate to documents. In this text, we prefer to call them "complementary" sources, this phrase coming from the Latin meaning "to complete." Complementary sources sometimes can be more illuminating than the documents themselves, and they often provide insights obscured by documents alone.

Of course, ethnohistorians are free to use any data source, discipline, or practice they believe may help their research. They occasionally have recourse to findings in such diverse areas as plant taxonomy, agronomy, philately (stamp collecting), and photographic science, but these are the exceptions. Most frequently they turn to oral accounts, archaeology, and analogy to assist in their endeavors.

Oral Accounts

Many accounts of events or conditions in the past are remembered but never committed to writing. In some cases, this is because the society in question has no writing system, but even within literate societies many accounts are never written down. Some things may not be considered important enough to record, but on the other hand, certain segments of a literate society may be largely or wholly illiterate or may not have a tradition of committing everyday knowledge to writing. Access to writing materials, which may be expensive and not available to large segments of society, may also be difficult. In many cases, however, the information is passed on orally and retained in memories.

Several different terminologies are used to discuss oral evidence, so it is wise to begin with some definitions. All spoken descriptions of the past are considered *oral accounts,* and there are two major types. *Oral histories* are accounts of events and conditions witnessed or experienced by the speaker, and *oral traditions* are accounts of events and conditions in the more distant past, not witnessed by the speaker, but passed down through generations. Henige (1982) has posited that an oral tradition must be universally accepted by the members of a society, but we follow Miller (1980), Vansina (1985), and Cohen (1989) in rejecting that criterion, thereby accepting any version of a sufficiently old oral account as an oral tradition. In practice, it would be impossible to ascertain that any account was universally accepted, and it is difficult to imagine how one would decide whether two tellings of an account exhibited only cosmetic or more substantive differences. Finally, given the reality-mediation model and the propensity for people to reinterpret a story to fit their changing notions of what is sensible or desirable, it is likely that the account exists as a series of versions, linked by some degree of common content.

Ethnohistorians disagree about the historical value of oral accounts that are strongly shaped by artistic considerations and overtly used as entertainment or part of ritual. Such accounts sometimes are termed *oral art,* in recognition of the purported importance or even primacy of artistic considerations in their content and structure. As alluded to in chapter 7, however, all oral and written accounts are shaped to some degree by the expectations of their genre; if every account is subject to the same effect, why single out only some accounts for special consideration? Consequently, we follow Tonkin (1992:15) in rejecting this distinction as artificial and misleading, a distinction that may encourage ethnohistorians to overlook the effects of artistic considerations on accounts not classified as "oral art."

Oral histories, which constitute firsthand testimony regarding events and processes, are extremely useful, but they are limited to recent years because the witness must still be alive. Since the 1970s, increasing numbers of oral history programs have recorded these accounts for future use. Prior to these programs, with a few notable exceptions (such as the Federal Writers' Project, one of the public programs designed to stimulate U.S. employment during the Great Depression of the 1930s), oral histories were rarely recorded.

Oral traditions are valuable, of course, because they reach back into the past, sometimes recording events centuries old. They are limited, however, by the possibility that the information in them has been corrupted through numerous retellings — and the possibly faulty memories of the tellers over generations. Scholars have differed in their assessments of the general reliability of oral traditions, ranging from Lord Acton (1907), who rejected all oral tradition as garbled fairy tales, to Patrick Kirch (1985:307), who has argued that every oral tradition from the two centuries before European intrusion in Hawaii is based ultimately in historical events. The middle ground, maintaining that oral traditions may be based on either historical or imaginary events, has been adopted by Jan Vansina (1985) in his masterful discussion of oral history and tradition and is probably the most defensible position. Certainly there are extraordinary examples of cases where oral tradition seems to have preserved historical accuracy, but also others where it seems to have been jettisoned.

As Vansina (1985) sees it, an oral tradition is subject to a series of revisions as it passes to new carriers and is preserved in memory. He sees the following factors as among the most significant in modifying the original content over time:

— The selection of what information to include in an oral tradition is culturally determined, may change over time as the culture of the carriers changes, and may omit issues that might be considered the most important by an outside ethnohistorian.
— The meaning of a message received by a carrier of an oral tradition is reinterpreted in light of that carrier's expectations of reasonable behavior and events, as created by the carrier's culture. The reinterpreted version may be satisfying to the current generation but different from that acceptable to earlier generations.
— If not checked by institutionalized means (such as the scrutiny of memorized liturgical poems by others who had learned them among the Rwanda [d'Hertefelt and Coupez 1964]), memory lapses can alter or shorten the content of an oral tradition.
— An oral tradition that diffuses into a region from outside may be revised to incorporate local characters, names, and places, making it appear that the events recounted took place locally.
— The content of an oral tradition may be altered to better fit dramatic needs or form (especially in poetry or song) of the presentation, which may involve omission or modification.
— Chronology usually is vague in oral tradition, and as events pass

into "long ago," events that really were at different times may be merged into contemporaneity in a monolithic "long ago."
—The content of an oral tradition can be modified in response to feedback from written accounts, which sometimes carry an aura of accuracy, even with the presence of a strong tradition of oral accounts.

The interdisciplinary work of Fentress and Wickham (1992) has elaborated on some of these points, investigating the mechanisms and effects of "social memory," in particular culturally induced memory distortions and the reworking of oral accounts. David Rubin (1997) has synthesized current psychological perspectives on how memory shapes oral accounts, pointing out conditions likely to encourage recall errors.

Elizabeth Tonkin (1992) has built upon the work of Vansina and others in discussing "the social construction of history," focusing on oral accounts. Her model sees critical interactions between the speaker's past, the audience's past, and genre (defined in chapter 7 as a conventional form of discourse). The speaker's past has shaped his or her conceptions of what is important, likely, or acceptable; therefore, the speaker's memory and conscious choices in forming an account will lead to modifications, omissions, or creations that will make an account fit better into these expectations. Similarly, the speaker takes into account the audience's expectations, since there is little social point in recounting an unsatisfying or unbelievable tale. Finally, genre molds the expectations of both speaker and listener: an account in a heroic genre must have a hero (regardless of whether any character in the event itself would fit the cultural criteria for a hero), and an account in a humorous genre must be funny (regardless of whether or not the original event was). These genres are defined culturally for each society. Accordingly, Tonkin would add to Vansina's list the following ways that oral accounts are tailored to social needs:

—The content of an account will be altered to fit the expectations of both listener and teller.
—The content of an account will be reworked to conform to the needs of a conventional genre.

To this list might be added a couple of further tendencies, each derivative from the broader principles noted above:

—There is a tendency to exaggerate, so that characters achieve status as larger-than-life culture heroes, especially as they have faded into the more distant past and have lost many of their personal, human foibles and quirks.

—There is a tendency to quantify in numbers that have culturally derived significances (such as representing large numbers with "a thousand" in English and "four hundred" in Nahuatl).

In general, the same forces that can mar the historical accuracy of a document (see chapter 7) can mar an oral account. The result is that the historical core of an oral tradition may be preserved intact, transformed, or excised over the span of the oral tradition's existence. In general, the older an oral tradition, the greater the likelihood that it has been "tainted by time"; no oral account, however, should be viewed as pristine and inviolate.

Those of us who have grown up in a literate tradition often tend to discount oral accounts, perhaps too much so. We look to our own experience and decide that we would be lost without notes and computer files filled with the important things we are supposed to remember. This may be true for us, but there is considerable evidence that in some nonliterate societies, people are quite skilled at remembering word-for-word important traditional tales. An ongoing project at the University of Lagos in Nigeria is recording traditional myths and tales recalled by the custodians who are charged with remembering them and passing them on to the next generation. In the twenty years since the program's inception, some individuals' versions of the same tale have been recorded several times, with intervals of many years between. In most cases, the versions have been nearly identical, and some individuals have been able to present a two-hour narrative that is word-for-word identical to the version delivered by them ten years before (Opeoluwe Onabajo, pers. comm.).

One oral tradition recorded around 1890 by Adolph Bandelier (1890: 116–130) at the pueblo of Santo Domingo in New Mexico describes an attack on and siege of Pecos Pueblo by the Kirauash tribe. This tradition accords well with archaeological evidence for warfare at Pecos around 1515, and an oral account recorded by Pedro de Castañeda of the Coronado expedition in the 1540s (1933) is in essential agreement, differing only in its attribution of the attack to the Teyas tribe. Clearly, oral tradition can retain historical description over centuries.

Nonetheless, all oral accounts must be treated with the same healthy skepticism accorded documents. Individuals may have flawed perceptions; they may want to tailor an account to make them, their ancestors, or their community look good; they may slant their account to demean or tease another group; they may modify their account to illustrate a moral lesson; and they may forget things that had little significance for them at the time in question. All of the factors that can affect the reliability of a document can affect the reliability of an oral account; in addition, the oral account may have changed accidentally through memory or purposefully through reinterpretation, while the document, once written down, usually is more or less inviolate.

An example of how oral accounts can be flawed involves part of a study of the early-twentieth-century Charlestown waterfront in the Boston area. One of the authors of this book was trying to determine the function of a building that had been discovered archaeologically but was not shown on any available maps. Reasoning that postal deliverers would know their routes in great detail, he inquired of one whose route had included this area for forty years, including part of the period in question. The postal deliverer was unable to recall a building in that spot and even swore that none ever had existed. When subsequent research turned up more information about the building, it was found to have been a storage building. Since no mail had been delivered there, the postal deliverer apparently had not paid it sufficient attention to make it memorable.

Tonkin (1992:8) rightfully has noted that declaring an account "realistic" or "mythologized" is a judgment based on the declarer's worldview. An ethnohistorian who does not believe in witchcraft or the capricious acts of the gods (except as important factors in the thinking and decision making of the people under study) may reject an account that incorporates these actions as central to its description of past events. That rejection, however, should be viewed as an expression of the inadequacy of the researcher or methods to sift out those parts of the account that may help solve an ethnohistoric problem; it cannot be viewed as a rejection of the account as a serious or legitimate piece of historical evidence.

Some oral traditions clearly have been heavily mythologized, and it is not clear whether ethnohistorians can glean useful clues to historical events from them. The traditional Navajo account of that tribe's migration into the American Southwest includes climbing up through various levels of a multilayered world, each with its own distinctive color designation; the Navajo encounter ant people and finally emerge through a hole into the current world. Spencer (1947) tried to relate this to the historic migration of the proto-Navajo from their homeland in northwestern North America into the Southwest. For example, climbing from one level to another may equate with crossing a mountain range, and passing through the yellow level may reflect crossing a desert. Most scholars following Spencer, however, have interpreted the Navajo tradition as more of a statement of the Navajo worldview than an account of historic events.

Other examples come from attempts to connect mythological American Indian oral accounts with Pleistocene megafauna, Ice Age mammals that inhabited North America at the time of its initial peopling by Paleo-Indians, at least 15,000 years ago. Jane Beck (1972) has argued that the giant beaver in Malecite and other Algonquian mythologies was really a fossil memory of the Pleistocene beaver, *Castoroides ohioensis,* a massive rodent weighing up to five hundred pounds. In the Malecite version, Gluskap, the great culture hero, creates all the animals and then reduces them in size by petting their fur. Somehow this giant beaver escapes and terrorizes the Malecite before Gluskap drives him away.

With imagination, these interpretations may seem vaguely reasonable, but there are so many ways to interpret or explain the myths that it would be difficult to place too much faith in them. By the time so many symbolic and mythological elements have been incorporated into an account, any original historic accuracy probably is submerged.

A final caution is in order regarding the ethnohistoric use of oral accounts. As Tonkin (1992:6) has warned, "professional historians who use the recollections of others cannot just scan them for useful facts to pick out, like currants from a cake. Any such facts are so embedded in the representation that it directs an interpretation of them, and its very ordering, its plotting and its metaphors bear meaning too." Tonkin's caveat to consider how context permeates and shapes meaning was directed particularly to the analysis of oral accounts, but it is equally vital for other sources of ethnohistoric information.

The techniques of recording oral accounts have been discussed by both anthropologists and historians. Among the historical treatments, Allen and Montell (1981), Baum (1977), Cullom, Black, and McLean (1977), and Yow (1994) give sound discussions of methods and techniques; Werner and Schoepfle (1987) provide similar discussions of ethnographic methods and technique, focusing on interviews. Lummis (1987) provides a thought-provoking discussion of source analysis of oral accounts; Vansina (1985) embeds a discussion of source analysis in his broader treatment. Havlice (1985) provides a moderately recent bibliography of methodological treatments and applications of oral history.

Archaeology

Wherever people live or carry on any activity, they leave behind telltale traces. They may discard a broken tool, prepare a meal and leave behind waste portions of the foodstuffs, or drive a stake into the ground. Archaeology is the field that studies this evidence, attempting to learn more about past human activities and the cultures that underlay them. The archaeologists themselves are essentially detectives, interpreting physical clues to reconstruct what went on in the past. When archaeology probes periods that possessed writing, it is called "historical" archaeology or "text-assisted" archaeology; in periods where there was no writing, it is called "prehistoric" archaeology. Occasionally, the archaeology of a period with undeciphered writing is considered prehistoric, since there are no documents that can be read, but it is logically preferable to consider it historic.

The most obvious way that archaeology can assist ethnohistory is by studying the archaeological remains of the same people discussed in the documents under study. Documents may be silent on such things as whether a community had a water-powered mill, but the archaeological remains of such a mill might be distinctive and quite easy to locate by means of a quick archaeological survey.

Sometimes archaeology can establish a fact that is muddy or misleading in the documents. The village of Lighthouse, Connecticut, for example, was the home of acculturated Narragansett Indians in the eighteenth and nineteenth centuries. Documents showed the familiar English pattern of landholding and land use, with straight-sided properties in neat geometric shapes. Archaeology, however, revealed that the inhabitants of Lighthouse had no stone walls demarcating their properties, a longstanding characteristic of English communities in New England. This suggests a kind of land use — and perhaps ownership — that was more communal and Narragansett-style than that typical in the English tradition (Feder 1994).

Prehistoric archaeology can also be of assistance to ethnohistorians, especially when research focuses on changes brought about by contact with the broader world. The magnitude of the changes wrought by the coming of the horse to the aboriginal society of the North American plains region only becomes evident when the prehistoric society is compared with its historic descendant. The Arikara of the Missouri Valley, for example, lived in fortified, sedentary villages, gaining most of their food through farming. In the late eighteenth century, horses came into the region from Texas, where they had been acquired from the Spaniards. Rapidly, the Arikara transformed into mobile hunters and gatherers, relying heavily on bison for food; even their social organization was transfigured as they shifted from matrilocal to patrilocal residence (Wissler 1914; Deetz 1965; Rogers 1990). Since written accounts of the Arikara are only very sketchy before the nineteenth century, prehistoric archaeology is our primary means of recognizing the magnitude of the changes that took place, providing a benchmark from which the historic changes can be measured.

Archaeology is a complex and diverse field, unified by its essential link to physical remains: the material items left behind and preserved in archaeological sites. These include artifacts (objects purposefully created or modified by human behavior, such as tools, ornaments, housing, and the waste materials incidental to the production of these items), biological remains (bones, seeds, scales, hair, and any other items that once were part of a plant or animal, usually excepting tools made from bones and the like), and soils (the dirt and related items found in the site). Each of these items has the potential to tell a story of value to the overall archaeological interpretation.

Artifacts are, in some ways, the most telling of physical remains because they are a direct expression of human behavior. The material from which an artifact is made, the form it takes, any ornamentation or ritual treatment, the use to which it is put—these and other factors are the outcomes of human choice, restricted only by practical limitations, the resources available to the maker, and the cultural rules governing production and use. As a result, artifacts are useful in reconstructing many areas of human behavior. Examining the form of a flaked stone tool, for example, can suggest uses for which it would have been well suited. A stout tool with a large angle between two edges makes a poor knife but a wonderful scraper for removing fat and tissue from animal hides. Finding such a tool on an archaeological site suggests this use, but this can be confirmed only by examining the working edge of the tool microscopically and finding appropriate traces of wear or preserved hide. The shape of the tool, while somewhat constrained by the requirements of its function, still provides the maker great latitude, and styles and types of tools often can inform the archaeologist of the date and cultural identity of the maker. The material from which the scraper is made may occur locally, or it may be imported from some distance, giving the archaeologist some idea of the economic relations between communities. Hodges (1976) introduces some basic concepts, methods, and potentials for the analysis of archaeological artifacts.

Biological remains also can provide data on the people who occupied an archaeological site. Archaeologists make major distinctions between the remains of plants and animals used for food (economic species), plants and animals used to make artifacts (industrial species), and plants and animals that just happened to die where their remains (ecofacts) would end up in an archaeological site. Deciding which category a bone or tooth or seed belongs in is not always easy, but it is critical to a credible analysis. The remains of economic species from sixteenth-century Spanish sites in Florida, for example, have supported an analysis that estimates

- — the relative importance of different foods in the diet;
- — the relative importance of Old World domestic plants, New World domestic plants, and New World wild plants;
- — the relative importance of Old World domestic animals and New World wild animals; and
- — the importance of various techniques of capture, husbandry, and harvest. (Reitz and Scarry 1985)

The remains of industrial species are important to the analysis of artifacts because they may be the leftovers of raw material for production. Remains of either economic or industrial species can give clues to the effects of human use of those species, as with the dwindling occurrence of moas (birds of a large, flightless species) in eighteenth- and nineteenth-century Maori sites in New Zealand (Anderson 1989). Ecofacts can help reconstruct the environment of the site, ranging in scope from broad assessments of climate to detailed reconstructions of vegetation and shade at the site itself. Evans (1978), Pearsall (1989), and Klein and Cruz-Uribe (1984) provide some basic information on the methods and techniques of analyzing biological remains.

Soils may not seem an obvious source of archaeological data, but they can reveal valuable information. The disturbance of soils by human activity produces features, artificial structures such as fire pits, trash middens, trampled paths, molds from wooden posts driven into the ground, and the like. These features are critical in helping the archaeologist understand the spatial patterning of activities (and the physical remains left behind by them) at a site. Soils also provide the demarcators for different vertical levels at a site, each representing a distinct period; since most archaeological sites were occupied for more than one period, sorting out the different periods is basic to any sensible interpretation. Finally, soils occasionally provide information about human activities that is inaccessible through other sources. At the Neville site, a prehistoric American Indian site in New Hampshire, high mercury levels in the soil were the only indicator that the site had been a seasonal fishing site for salmon (Dincauze 1976:96–99). Useful sources on the analysis of archaeological soils include Cornwall (1958), Limbrey (1975), and Holliday (1992).

The spatial relationships of physical remains in the ground — their context—is essential to proper interpretation. As noted above, the chronological sequence of remains is determined by their positions relative to one another. In addition, the distribution of materials in cultural terms is significant. An archaeological site with the remains of one hundred houses might yield one hundred boxes of gold coins, but the cultural significance in terms of class structuring is very different if (a) all the boxes came from one house, and the other houses had none, or (b) each of the one hundred houses had a single box of coins. The centrality of context to interpretation is what makes so many archaeologists near-manic about precision in recording excavation information.

The range of remains and information that archaeologists deal with requires diverse skills and knowledge. For basic competence, an archaeologist should have at least some knowledge of chemistry, physics, zoology, botany, human anatomy, surveying, and mathematics. (Fortunately, specialists can handle the most demanding and esoteric analyses, but the archaeologist must have enough familiarity with the field to be able to use their findings thoughtfully.) Just like Sherlock Holmes, an archaeologist must integrate this wide variety of skills into a package that will permit the interpretation of clues to infer something about the behaviors that took place at the site. But the ultimate goal of archaeology is not to know more about seeds or stone tools or dirt: the reason for all this effort is to learn more about past human behavior. The final test of archaeologists is their ability to take the information on physical remains and context and use it to mount an argument for how the occupants and users of a site lived. This requires ingenuity, an understanding of how known societies function, and hard work.

Archaeology has an allure as a source of information—perhaps because of the tangible and seemingly pristine nature of its data—but it is no more ideal than documents or oral accounts. True, the archaeological record rarely is purposefully manipulated to deceive, since most physical remains are trash, abandoned materials, or accidental losses. But physical remains and context can be modified or destroyed by the forces of time, nature, and human activity, collectively known as site-formation processes. Imagine, for example, an eighteenth-century slave village in Jamaica. The occupants took most of their belongings with them when they left, leaving behind probably only broken and overlooked items. The trash heaps that once had contained marvelous data for reconstructing diet had been turned over by hogs, dogs, and chickens. The materials from buildings in which the slaves had lived might have been reused elsewhere on the plantation. The reason for the abandonment of the village might have been a destructive fire or hurricane. Taken together, these factors ensure that the site has been transformed rapidly and dramatically from a functioning settlement to a husk of its former self. Then wait two centuries, during which time organic materials rot, metal artifacts corrode, soil is roiled by burrowing animals and roots, and parts of the deposits are removed by erosion. And all during this time, human beings may reuse the area for anything from picnics to a sugar-cane press to a dump for domestic waste.

Site-formation processes are fully analogous to selection, emphasis, transformation, and perhaps even fabrication in the reality-mediation model. Their impacts on an archaeological site can be just as profound. The archaeologist's job, in part, is to recognize the impacts of site-formation processes and take advantage of data sets that remain largely intact and interpretable. Schiffer (1987) provides an overview of site-formation processes and their roles in shaping the archaeological record.

The Relative Strengths and Weaknesses of Documents, Oral Accounts, and Archaeological Evidence

One of the reasons we advocate using as many kinds of data as possible is that this approach may permit the filling in of gaps that exist by chance in any single kind of data. For example, if no document or oral account mentions whether there was a mill in town, archaeological data could help fill in that blank. But there is another, deeper reason to use all three kinds of information (and others) if possible. Each kind of data has built-in weaknesses and strengths, and using documents in conjunction with oral accounts and archaeological evidence permits the ethnohistorian to take advantage of the strengths of each. This section outlines some of the major strengths and weaknesses of documentary, oral, and archaeological data.

Perhaps the greatest strength of documents is their abundant detail. Tribute accounts give specifics that no one would be likely to commit to memory or pass on to future generations as an oral account. A letter or diary may give insights into motivations, ideology, or rejected alternatives, as when Jesuit missionaries explained to their superiors why they selected particular villages for their chapels. A newspaper account may give detail on passing events that never or rarely would be recognizable archaeologically, such as an inauguration or a festival. And documents that were written at the time they describe are unlikely to suffer from the vagaries of memory that can plague oral accounts.

Despite their obvious virtues, documents also have significant weaknesses. First, they are the most likely type of data to be manipulated purposely by their authors. A document has an aura, and many authors seem to have thought of their potential place in history when writing. Hernando Cortés's letters (1971) from his expedition to conquer the Aztecs paint a picture of a powerful leader — decisive, wise, and brave. Bernal Díaz del Castillo's account (1963), written by a minor member of the expedition at a later date, paints a different picture of more group decisions, confusion, and fear. It is easy to see either Cortés as an aspirant to a heroic role in history, or Díaz del Castillo as a disgruntled spoiler. Vested interest runs strong in many documents.

Another difficulty in interpreting documents concerns extrapolating from the particular to the general. If a trading expedition is mentioned in a document, it may be difficult to know whether such expeditions were a regular occurrence or an exceptional event worthy of special note. If you are fortunate enough to have many documents treating the same issue, you may be able to make a reasoned assessment of whether trading expeditions were common or rare, but in the absence of a rich documentary record, you may be unable to draw any strong conclusion.

A further weakness of documents lies in the fact that they largely were the domain of the rich, educated, powerful members of society. Especially when nondominant ethnic groups were involved, it is important to remember that most documents dealing with them were written by members of the dominant ethnic group and have been filtered through a screen of bias, ignorance, and indifference. How much do most documents of slavery in the American South reflect the attitudes, ideas, and experiences of the slaves? Many accounts were written by slave owners or abolitionists, neither of whom could be considered authorities on slave life. Even the few accounts written by slaves themselves are subject to bias, since literate slaves usually led singular, atypical lives.

Women are also underrepresented in the documentary record. Since relatively few women's accounts were written in many periods and places, traditional domains of women (food preparation, child rearing, and other domestic occupations) are poorly described in documents; when they are described by men, the descriptions often suffer from lack of detail, limited personal experience, or stereotyping. A cynical statement of a widely held conclusion is that documents generally tell you everything you may want to know about rich, educated, politically active, urban, white males, but only limited amounts about other people.

Oral accounts share many qualities with documents. Oral accounts certainly can provide tremendous detail, but rarely so much as documents. They can relate motives and psychological states as well as documents can, and they can deal with ephemeral events, but, unfortunately, they also share documents' ability to be distorted and manipulated by tellers with a vested interest or bias. They also are more subject to alteration over time, since there is no physically extant original version to consult in case of doubt.

One advantage of oral accounts over documents is the access that everyone has had to creating them. Since they require no technology or skill beyond that common to everyday living, oral accounts can come from any society or segment of society, regardless of its members' education or economic status. Further, many societies have very strong and comprehensive oral traditions, producing an abundant data source. The Afro-American tradition is one that has focused on oral accounts, and many narratives of slavery days were once extant in oral form, although relatively few have been recorded.

Peter Schmidt (1990) — reviewing the success of using a combined database of documentary history, oral accounts, and archaeology in studying Africa's past — has concluded that oral accounts have a simultaneous virtue and failing. On one hand, they are very good at pointing out "processes of transformation": significant turning points in terms of ongoing political and economic processes. On the other hand, they are not always reliable in terms of literal chronicling of chronology and events — the logical consequence of their stripping away some literal recording of events to emphasize what is considered significant. Giving this conclusion a slightly different twist than did Schmidt, oral tradition helps focus attention on the cultural changes judged important by the keepers of the traditions, giving us an insight into perceptions of the people under study.

That way that oral accounts have been collected by scholars has limited their usefulness. Collection typically was rare and haphazard until quite recently. Ethnographers began soliciting oral accounts in non-Western societies only about a century ago, and historians gathering them in Western society began in earnest only about 1960. As a result, oral histories of many periods of interest to ethnohistorians are no longer available, and even the oral traditions are old enough to lead to concerns over their historical accuracy.

Archaeology differs considerably from documents and oral accounts in its strengths and weaknesses. Probably its greatest strength is that it is quite unlikely to be manipulated by individuals with bias or vested interest. True, the rare monuments by and to the rich can be attempts to mislead and manipulate one's place in history. Mayan inscriptions, for example, often laud the virtues of the ruler who commissioned them, as do the inscriptions on the faces of museums and universities founded by robber-baron industrialists in the United States around 1900. The bulk of archaeological remains, however, are trash of one form or another and not so subject to manipulation.

Another strength of archaeology is the quantification that its remains facilitate. A document might say that little beef was eaten in China Flats (the Chinese quarter of the mining-supply community of Jackson, California), but archaeology could give a quantified estimate by excavating trash heaps and reconstructing the meat diet evidenced by bones and other refuse. We know from documents that Indians in coastal New England abandoned native stone tool technology in favor of European metal tools, but archaeology allows us to trace the transition in detail, noting how fast it occurred and what regional variations there may have been.

For students of technology and material culture, archaeology is particularly strong. Its database is largely items of technology, providing powerful support for technological studies. While documents often focus on finished items and their use, archaeology can reveal all stages of production, failed and discarded attempts, and waste materials — all of which can be useful in a full reconstruction of the technology underlying a product.

Archaeology does, however, have its weaknesses. In general, it is weak at providing information about ideology, motivations, or social activities. These arenas often produce scanty, nondescript, equivocal, or enigmatic remains permitting few archaeological conclusions. Although we can tell with considerable confidence how the occupants of Fort Laurens in Ohio built their stockade, archaeology provides no clues to why they made those choices, nor does it give much evidence of the sorts of social interaction that took place within it.

Archaeology also is very poor at providing information on ephemeral events. We may know from documents that an annual trading fair was held in the plaza of Picuris Pueblo in New Mexico in the seventeenth century, but it is unlikely that we could find any archaeological information about it. The plaza would have been cleaned after the fair, and any remains that might have indicated the fair or any details about it would have been swept away. Similarly, the remains of many rituals and singular events have been merged into a more amorphous archaeological record that is better at showing general conditions and processes than specific events.

Similarly, the archaeological record is poor at allowing the identification of particular individuals and their remains. The exception is in urban and other areas where detailed maps and documents permit archaeologists to know whose house is being excavated. Even then, however, it may be difficult to identify an individual's archaeological remains. For example, wine and liquor bottles have been found archaeologically in the trash pits of prominent Boston temperance leaders who claimed (in documents) to abstain from all alcoholic beverages. On the face of it, this example seems to attest to how archaeology can sleuth out truth that hides from documentary history. But does it really? Probably drinking went on at these houses, but the drinkers may have been the servants, or the leaders may have permitted themselves to serve liquor to guests who drank, while abstaining themselves. Archaeology simply cannot discriminate between the activities of individuals who share trash disposal areas.

Fortunately for ethnohistorians, many of the strengths and weaknesses of documents, oral accounts, and archaeological evidence are complementary. Gordon Day (1972) has demonstrated that a far more believable picture of Rogers's Raid on an Abenaki village in 1759 can be obtained by combining documentary evidence with oral traditions than could be derived from either alone; Peter Robertshaw's study of the Bacwezi kingdom of Uganda (1994) skillfully uses archaeological and oral traditional information to their mutual benefit; Marley Brown (1973) has eloquently shown how documents, oral history, and archaeology interweave to produce a remarkably thorough picture of the Mott Farm in New England — the number of examples could be multiplied indefinitely. Because the different types of information about the past are complementary, using all available evidence permits researchers not only to check conclusions based on one set of evidence, but also to draw conclusions otherwise unsupported by data. Table 11 suggests the relative strengths of the different sorts of evidence.

Analogy

Sometimes, after marshalling all the available direct evidence, significant gaps remain. The documents, oral accounts, archaeological data, and other data sources all can remain mute, even on an important issue. Do we have any way of filling in that gap? The answer, as with most interesting questions, is both yes and no. Certainly there is no substitute for direct evidence, so in one sense we have no recourse. There are, however, ways to construct arguments for what was most likely, and one class of such

Table 11. Relative Strengths of Different Evidence about the Human Past

	Documents	Oral Accounts	Archaeological Evidence
General detail	****	***	**
Motivations and ideology	****	****	*
Social events	****	***	*
Technology	***	*	****
Ephemeral events	****	***	*
Identification of individuals	****	***	*
Quantification	***	*	****
Depth of accurate time coverage	***	*	****
Range of creators of the data	*	***	****
Survival and contents unchanged by time	****	*	**
Freedom from purposeful manipulation	*	*	****

Note: Greater strength is indicated by a greater number of asterisks.

arguments is analogy, arguing that something is likely in an unknown case because it is known to have occurred in similar cases.

An example of the use of analogy is concluding that wooly mammoths were grazing herbivores. Mammoths went extinct several millennia ago, so no living person ever saw them eat grass; the great span of time makes oral tradition an unlikely source of information on them; they were gone by the time writing was invented, so we have no documents relating to them; the paintings and other pictures of them that have survived from prehistory provide no insight on their feeding habits; and no preserved grass ever has been found lodged in their teeth. Nonetheless, in the face of this lack of direct evidence, we can comfortably conclude that mammoths grazed on grass. Their closest modern relatives, elephants, are grazers, and mammoth teeth fit the classic pattern of known grazing herbivores. Further, mammoth fossils are found mostly in places that were grasslands at the time of the mammoths, and an animal as large as a mammoth would probably be unable to support itself by any means other than herbivory. The relevant similarities make the argument by analogy that mammoths were grazers. Nothing has been proven, but the conclusion seems a good bet.

Analogy can be used in the study of past human behavior, too. Sometimes it serves as a last resort in the absence of evidence; other times it can stimulate ideas and suggest new sources of evidence. Three kinds of analogy are most commonly used in ethnohistory: general ethnographic analogy, direct historical analogy, and experimental analogy. Harris (1968:150 ff.) provides a history and critique of the use of comparison and analogy in anthropology and related fields, and Charlton (1981) reviews the use of analogy in ethnohistory.

General ethnographic analogy refers to an analogy that is drawn between some ethnographic or historical case and the case in question. For example, documents, oral accounts, and archaeological data tell us that seventeenth-century Cherokee Indians ate clay with certain foods, principally root foods. There is no clear indication in the documents about why they followed this practice, and oral accounts offer little help, but general ethnographic analogy can provide some possible explanations. Some Puerto Ricans, for example, eat red clay to provide symbolic heat that helps balance their systems and maintain their health, according to folk medical concepts. In South Africa, some pregnant women eat clay with various foods, apparently to provide nutrients that are needed in larger quantities during pregnancy. Many Peruvians eat clay along with certain potatoes that have high concentrations of allotoxins, and the toxins form a chemical complex with the clays, detoxifying the potato. There are other possible analogies, but these three will suffice for this example.

The easiest (and most improper) way to proceed is simply to select the possibility that appeals most to the researcher. Since a different possibility may appeal more to another researcher, there need to be some rules for deciding which is the most likely possibility. To make a more reasoned selection, the researcher has to consider reasons *why* each of the ethnographic groups eats clay and determine whether each is likely for the Cherokee. There is no evidence of Cherokee hot-cold medical concepts, so the Puerto Rican case seems inappropriate. The South African practice is restricted to pregnant women, while all sorts of Cherokees ate clay, disqualifying this as an appropriate analogy. The Peruvian case, however, is more promising. Coupled with the knowledge that the roots eaten by the Cherokee had high concentrations of toxins, this analogy seems appropriate. The connection is not proven, of course, but it is supported and may be provisionally accepted.

General ethnographic analogy is easy to use — and easy to misuse. The force of an analogy rests with how well the argument of relevance is supported. Some scholars have argued that the best ethnographic analogies are drawn from the same region as the case in question. This often may be true, but we argue that a good analogy from another continent is stronger than a poor analogy—where the similarity of circumstances and the argument of relevance are weak—from next door.

The second kind of analogy commonly used in ethnohistory is called *direct historical analogy*, referring to the drawing of an analogy from a group that is the direct historical descendant of the group in question. This term and concept are taken from the direct historical method pioneered by the Bureau of American Ethnology scholars in the latter half of the nineteenth century but popularized by the works of William Duncan Strong (e.g., 1935, 1940) in the first half of the twentieth century. Fred Eggan (1954) further refined direct historical analogy for ethnohistoric use, converting it into his "method of controlled comparison" for reconstructing earlier practices on the basis of practices of presumed descendants. William N. Fenton (1953) coined the term "upstreaming" to denote the backward ethnohistoric tracing from the known present to the less-known past, and Blu (1994) uses "reading back" for a related process that incorporates a greater recognition of interpretive complexities, including what we call reality mediation.

A direct historical analogy for the seventeenth-century Cherokee would be drawn from the Cherokee of subsequent centuries. The reasoning behind this kind of analogy is that many cultural traits will have persisted from an early period; a trait that is present at a later date may well have survived with little or no change from the earlier period. In the case of Cherokee clay eating, we have documentary and oral evidence from the eighteenth and nineteenth centuries that indicates that clay was eaten with bitter (that is, toxin-rich) roots and tubers to make them more digestible.

A strength of both general ethnographic and direct historical analogy is that they offer possible interpretations of enigmatic records or materials, sometimes filling in gaps in the documentary or archaeological record. For instance, although spinning thread and weaving cloth were major occupations of ancient central Mexican peoples such as the Aztec and Mixtec, it was women's work and not elaborately documented by Spanish friars and others who left us detailed records of other realms of life. Yet many indigenous Mexican women today, particularly in remote villages, still retain these technologies (Anawalt and Berdan 1994). Interviews with these women in their native languages reveal a wealth of data on technology, learning processes, design patterns, and symbolic meanings. Of course, nearly five hundred years have elapsed since the Aztec apogee, and many cultural changes have occurred in that time. These cultural descendants nonetheless provide a basis for interpretive upstreaming.

Most ethnohistorians feel direct historical analogies to be stronger than ethnographic analogies because of the direct connection between the societies involved. This may be true, but it should be remembered that both can be powerful tools of cultural reconstruction, although neither is foolproof. H. Martin Wobst (1978) has warned of the dangers of what he calls "the tyranny of analogy." He maintains that we should avoid assuming that all the possible variants of cultural behavior have been recorded in the historic record: there may be cases where no analogy is appropriate.

The third kind of analogy relevant to ethnohistory is *experimental analogy* (more commonly known in archaeological usage as "experimental" archaeology). This consists of experimentally performing certain activities believed to have been performed in the past to gather information about them. While this kind of analogy has provided considerable benefit to archaeologists, ethnohistorians have taken less advantage of it. Nonetheless, experimental analogy has noteworthy potential for assisting in ethnohistoric interpretation.

In the hands of archaeologists, experimental analogy has been used to attack all sorts of interpretive problems. When confronted with enigmatic *chultúns,* subterranean chambers of unknown function at ancient Mayan cities, Dennis Puleston (1971) experimented by filling some with water to see if they would serve as cisterns and using others to store various foodstuffs. The storage of breadnuts stood out as far and away the most effective use of the chultúns, suggesting that they were specialized breadnut storage facilities, and that this foodstuff had greater dietary importance than previously believed. In another example, Sergei Semenov (1964) used stone tools for certain tasks, then examined them under the microscope to determine which wear patterns characterized different uses; techniques developed by him and his successors permit archaeologists today to make good assessments of how archaeological stone tools were used before being discarded. Experimental archaeologists have rafted over oceans, built earthworks, re-created Iron Age musical instruments, and burned down buildings to see the resulting spatial patterning of remains.

The goals of experimental archaeologists are various, but they mostly fall into a few categories:

— To see whether a particular practice is feasible (e.g., building Stonehenge without power machinery)
— To better understand the nuances of a practice by performing it (e.g., cooking in water heated by placing hot rocks in it to determine how hot the water becomes and the technical difficulties of handling hot rocks)

—To quantify the time, effort, or resources needed to complete a task using past technology or to quantify the outcome of a practice (e.g., the relative efficiency of stone and steel axes in cutting trees)

—To quantify the success or failure rate in a practice (e.g., the breakage rate during firing of ceramic pots using seventeenth-century practices)

—To determine the signature characteristics of different technologies, practices, and tasks so that they can be identified when they appear archaeologically (e.g., cutting wheat stalks with stone sickle blades to determine the distinctive wear polish produced)

—To examine the impact of site-formation practices on archaeological remains (e.g., placing items in a field, plowing the field, and plotting the new locations of the items to see how much movement of artifacts can be expected in plowed fields).

Examples of various experimental archaeology studies are given by Coles (1973) and Ingersoll, Yellen, and MacDonald (1977).

What is significant about this list of goals of experimental archaeology is that the first four are equally applicable to ethnohistory. In 1528 Alvar Núñez Cabeza de Vaca reported a skirmish between his Spanish troops and the Indians of Apalachen in Florida: "Good armor did no good against arrows in this skirmish. There were men who swore they had seen two red oaks, each the thickness of a man's calf, pierced from side to side by arrows this day" (1961:42). Were the men Cabeza de Vaca wrote of accurate in their statements? Certainly there is sufficient information on bows, arrows, arrowheads, and armor to support an experiment to see whether the penetrating power of the arrows was so great as described herein. This is a feasibility study of the sort discussed above.

It is inconceivable that any task described in the ethnohistoric literature could be re-created experimentally without learning something of the nuances involved. Lantis (1970:186) discusses the efficacy of eighteenth-century heating and lighting among the Aleut, whose "little flatiron-shaped stone lamps provided light and heat, probably not much of either per lamp." Is this consistent with the recognition that these lamps were the only heating and lighting sources in the subterranean Aleut houses? The form and fuel of these lamps is well known, and an experiment could measure how much heat and light were produced, quantifying efficiency of the device. Juan Nentvig (1980:37) noted in 1764 that the (O'odham?) Indians of the Sonoran Desert gathered *Opuntia* cactus pads, boiled them, and dried them for later use. Were there any problems of spoilage or other loss? Experimentation in the appropriate season and climate would be simple and would evince the success-failure rate of the process. These are simple examples, but the number of meaningful experiments that could assist ethnohistoric interpretation, particularly in terms of technology and economics, is great.

While oral accounts and archaeology are sources of evidence to complement documents, analogy is a different kind of tool. It provides no new evidence of the direct sort, but it is a conceptual tool that permits indirect evidence — from different places, peoples, or times — to be brought into play during interpretation. Indirect evidence will never prove a point, but it can make a strong argument.

Case Study
in Complementary Evidence

THE CUSTER BATTLE

When gold was discovered by a scientific expedition into South Dakota's Black Hills in 1874, it set off a string of events that led to the famous defeat of Gen. George Armstrong Custer and the Seventh U.S. Cavalry at the hands of the Lakota Sioux and their allies. Word of the gold leaked out; there was a rush of Anglo-Americans to exploit it; Sioux lands guaranteed by treaty were violated; and many Sioux left their reservations to find their livelihood elsewhere or to conduct guerilla warfare. Fearing a widespread uprising, the U.S. government dispatched the cavalry to return the Sioux to their reservations. This chain of events led to June 25, 1876, the date when Custer's troops and an intertribal Indian force battled one another, resulting in the annihilation of Custer and his forces. The use of documentary and archaeological evidence in studying the Custer defeat illustrates how these two kinds of evidence can complement one another.

Complete destruction of a military force is rare, so it is unusual to have no survivors' reports from the losers. Nonetheless, there is no shortage of accounts of the battle and the events that preceded it. Custer was making reports up to the date of the battle, and other cavalry forces under Maj. Marcus Reno suffered heavy losses but escaped being wiped out entirely. Many Indian combatants left behind oral accounts, and at least several dozen were recorded in English translation. (These are notable in that most attribute the Indian victory to preordination through the Sun [DeMallie 1993:517–520].) In addition, testimony from various quarters was brought out and recorded at the extensive military inquiry that followed. On top of all this is the archaeological evidence, mostly gathered by a National Park Service team in 1985, when an accidental brush fire swept over the battle site, denuding the ground and providing unprecedented conditions for conducting survey and excavation.

The voluminous evidence pertaining to the battle touches on many contentious points, but this case study focuses exclusively on the question of Indian armaments. U.S. military intelligence prior to the engagement had indicated that the Indians had few firearms, primarily outmoded single-shot rifles of various sorts with only a few repeating rifles. (The tactical advantage of repeating rifles was considerable, allowing a combatant to fire up to a dozen shots without reloading.) On this information, it was judged reasonable to send a force of a few hundred cavalrymen into a district where several thousand potential insurgents were known.

News of Custer's defeat reached the outside world rapidly, and on its heels arose the heroic Custer myth, emphasizing aspects of pathos and romance (Rosenberg 1974). The logical outgrowth of this myth was the search for answers to how such a hero could have died so tragically. One suggestion was that the armament advantage of the Indians was too great even for Custer to overcome. Thus arose the contention that the Indian forces had a great number of repeating rifles. This speculation, though probably founded in an attempt to bring the Custer story into the heroic genre, was not without supporting evidence. He Dog, a Sioux participant, maintained that the Indians had a great many Winchesters, a common type of repeating rifle (Hammer 1976:208), and several other Indian combatants said the same thing. Others, however, presented a different story. Wooden Leg cited bows and arrows as the most common weapon at the battle, and mentioned that he and his companions had revolvers (Marquis 1931). Some warriors reported scavenging weapons and ammunition from dead cavalry soldiers for use against the enemy (Hardorff 1991:44); others made no mention of such activities. The variety and divergence of Indian accounts of the battle probably is an artifact of Sioux military tactics, which encouraged individual exploits but placed little emphasis on overall planning or coordination, leaving no participants with a broad perspective of a large engagement.

The archaeological work at the Custer battlefield (Scott, Fox, Connor, and Harmon 1989) recovered more than two thousand bullets and cartridge cases. Archaeologists were able to reconstruct quite satisfactorily from where a shot was fired (based on the location of the ejected cartridge case) and to where the shot was directed (based on the location of the spent bullet). The level of detail about the positions and movements of the combatants (known from oral accounts and the government inquiry) permitted the archaeologists to further infer who was doing the firing and who was the target. Finally, examination of firing pin and ejector marks permitted analysts to reconstruct what kinds of weapons were used to fire the bullets whose casings were recovered; examination of land-and-groove marks (longitudinal scratches visible under magnification) permitted the same sort of information to be reconstructed on the basis of bullets recovered. Thus it could be determined whether a .44-caliber bullet had been fired from a Winchester repeating rifle, a Smith and Wesson pistol, or any of the other weapons firing a bullet of that size in 1876.

The archaeological analysis concluded that the Indian forces arrayed against Custer possessed between 354 and 414 firearms, of which between 198 and 232 were Winchesters and Henrys — repeating rifles (Scott, Fox, Connor, and Harmon 1989:118). This means that the Indian forces outgunned Custer's forces about two to one, and that they probably had more repeating rifles. Some historians (e.g., Hofling 1981:48) have suggested that this military advantage might have been offset by shortages of ammunition, though evidence for this conjecture seems scanty.

Weaving these threads together produces a picture of the Custer battle superior to any interpretation based on only a single category of evidence. The intelligence available to Custer apparently was severely flawed. Although some contingents of Indians were armed poorly, others were armed very well, and the overall armaments probably favored the Indian forces. As the battle unfolded, Indian warriors increased their weapons advantage, commandeering the guns of dead cavalrymen.

Neither archaeological evidence nor oral accounts seem to warrant a conclusion that Indians were short on ammunition. Even though the argument that Custer was outgunned may have been born of a wish to excuse a hero's defeat, it seems to have merit and is supported by diverse lines of evidence. The argument built on documents, oral accounts, and archaeological evidence is stronger than any that could have been constructed using one sort of evidence alone.

Case Study in Analogy

NATIVE MEXICAN WEAVING TRADITIONS

In the verdant mountains of the Sierra Norte de Puebla, more than one visitor has had the distinct impression of traveling back in time. It is a region in east-central Mexico, off the beaten track, that contains many communities where people today retain languages and customs from the indigenous past. Many villagers speak Nahuatl, Nahuat, Otomí, Totonac, or Tepehua, often in bilingual combination with Spanish. Agriculture is performed largely with hoes and digging sticks; shamans are called on to cure illnesses; many people wear anciently styled clothing; and some women continue to weave cloth on backstrap looms, much as their preconquest predecessors did. This case study shows how our knowledge of past weaving behavior can be expanded through judicious use of direct historical analogy.

The Nahuatl speakers in this rural region are not, technically speaking, the direct descendants of the Nahua people generally referred to as "Aztecs." This latter term usually refers to a specific ethnic group, the Mexica, who settled in their island city of Tenochtitlan in the Valley of

Mexico, coming to dominate much of central and southern Mexico in the fifteenth and early sixteenth centuries. Today, Tenochtitlan is buried under a burgeoning Mexico City. But the Mexica were not unique in their language and customs; both were shared by peoples in other areas such as the Sierra Norte de Puebla. So, while we do not have a neat direct historical analogy from the present-day Indians of the Sierra to the well-documented Mexica, it is reasonably close. The topic for discussion, in any event, is one of pan-Mesoamerican breadth: the weaving of cloth on the backstrap loom.

In this case, the behavior we wish to study (weaving) is not terribly well documented either archaeologically or ethnohistorically. The loom itself is but a bundle of wooden sticks held together by the warp and weft of threads — hardly a promising candidate for archaeological preservation. Other implements sometimes used, such as a bone pick, may well have survived archaeologically but have only rarely been unequivocally identified as weaving tools. Ethnohistorically, a few pictorial documents and textual sources from early colonial times depict and describe the weaving process, but only scantily; the native informants for these documents were typically men — weaving was women's work — and the Spanish friars and secular officials who frequently collected information tended to focus on religious rituals or political matters such as dynastic succession. Similarly, native writers were heavily concerned with their own rights under the new Spanish regime and emphasized their particular histories, kingly reigns, and glorious wars. Everyday work, especially women's work, was largely neglected in the ethnohistoric accounts.

What, then, can present-day Nahuatl speakers tell us about ancient Mexican customs? In particular, what information can be gleaned from native women concerning one of their primary areas of work, the weaving of cotton and maguey fibers into cloth? The application of analogy is appropriate in this case, where some women today weave cloth on backstrap looms similar to those used by their pre-conquest predecessors (see Anawalt and Berdan 1994).

One area where analogy is fruitful is in unraveling details about the weaving process itself. Ethnohistoric documents inform us that girls were adept at weaving by age fourteen, but virtually nothing more is said about that process. Interestingly, present-day girls are considered to be skilled weavers by that same age, too; but we also learn that they begin around age five or six, learning progressively more complex techniques. The progression seen today — from the weaving of simple narrow belts to the creation of complex designed fabrics — is a likely scenario for pre-conquest weaving.

Direct historical analogy is particularly useful in discovering linguistic usages and patterns. A full array of specific terminologies for the loom itself, for aspects of the weaving process, and for types of woven cloth can be elicited from present-day weavers. This information augments non-glossed pictorial details drawn centuries earlier. Analogy can also help clarify unclear ethnohistoric information. For instance, some pieces of cloth are described in a sixteenth-century Nahuatl source as "canauac" and defined in a sixteenth-century Nahuatl dictionary as "narrow cotton cloaks" (Molina 1970:12r). The term "narrow" can be ambiguous (and has usually been thought to mean narrow in width), but contemporary weavers have told one of the authors of this book that "canauac" means "fine," "gauze," or "gauzelike" (pers. comm.). This could explain why these cloaks are depicted the same size as others yet still were called "narrow."

Analogy also can reveal much about historic change in weaving. It can be seen that the backstrap loom and its attendant weaving processes are highly resilient in the face of introduced materials and technologies. The loom has readily incorporated wool and synthetic thread with essentially no modification in the traditional technology. Furthermore, the tenacity of this type of weaving is illustrated by the extension of specific loom terminology to analogous parts of modern sewing machines that have recently arrived in the Sierra. This information alerts us to particular qualities of this technology, notably its constancy and ability to embrace new elements; these qualities probably would have characterized the loom in pre-Hispanic as well as later times.

Yet caveats are in order whenever analogy is applied. Even though the weaving technology and process resemble that described for earlier times, subtle changes can emerge over the intervening centuries. The use of wool can encourage the development of sturdier loom pieces, new designs may carry ancient names, and ancient styles may be given modern (though still Nahuatl) names. These intrusions are sometimes difficult to detect, so while analogy is a useful and even powerful tool, it must be applied with scholarly care.

PART 3

Strategies

Introduction

The final section of this book is devoted to fundamental strategies in ethnohistory. Chapter 12 presents the several factors that make a research topic successful or not and explains how to determine whether a particular question is even worth pursuing. This chapter also focuses on the issue of whether writing a research design is a worthwhile investment of time. Chapter 13 discusses various practical problems and strategies in working with documents in archives and similar repositories. Combined, the two chapters in this part focus on practical ways to make the pursuit of ethnohistoric research more effective and efficient.

CHAPTER 12

Formulating Research Topics and Research Designs

No amount of methodological expertise will produce a valuable piece of ethnohistorical research if the researcher does not have a worthwhile topic in mind. What constitutes a valid and valuable research topic in ethnohistory? How does a researcher come up with such a topic? How can the research process and the data cause modifications in a topic? What is the best way to plan one's research? The answers to these questions are interwoven with the personal philosophy and theory that each ethnohistorian brings to the research process. Nonetheless, there are some general principles that can guide the formulation of research projects.

Valid Topics and the Frontiers of Research

The basic principle behind all research in ethnohistory (or any other field, for that matter) is that it should extend knowledge. Knowledge, of course, is a multifaceted thing, consisting not only of facts but also of interpretations, methods, theory, and ideas. Valid research may collect new facts, revise our evaluation of existing evidence to derive new interpretations, or apply novel kinds of analysis to existing facts.

Kinds of Research Projects

A piece of research may focus on some topic never before studied, or at least not studied in a similar manner, and such research can yield dazzling and far-reaching results. For example, the publication of Stanley Elkins's *Slavery* (1959) opened up the discussion of slavery from the point of view of the slave rather than as an issue over which powerful politicians argued. Elkins's focus differed from that typically taken in the study of slavery, and that encouraged him to look to another source of data: oral traditions preserved by slaves and their descendants, written down in the 1930s by participants in the Federal Writers' Project. These traditions previously had been overlooked or dismissed as irrelevant by scholars studying slavery, but Elkins saw them as a window into slaves' experiences. Elkins's study touched off the examination of slavery as a way of life and was emulated by a new generation of scholars who developed similar interests under his inspiration. Such groundbreaking studies stake out new territory for ethnohistory and are particularly exciting, often stimulating new avenues of research. They are rare but highly influential in shaping future research.

But there are other ways, perhaps less spectacular but more common, to extend knowledge. A researcher might examine a familiar topic using a previously unstudied case, as when Sherburne F. Cook (1973b) examined the demographic collapse of the New England Indians in the face of disease introduced by Europeans. Cook and others had studied the impacts and devastation wrought by disease in many places in the Americas, and the basic pattern was clear: genetic resistance to European diseases was low among Native Americans, so death rates were tragically high, particularly among those in greatest contact with Europeans. Cook's research examined whether this pattern held true in New England and attempted to quantify its effects. In such a study, the main idea is borrowed (with appropriate citation and credit) from earlier work, seeing whether the same conclusions apply to the case under study. The most interesting research often results when the new research does not reveal the expected pattern, forcing the researcher to search for novel explanations.

Another way to extend knowledge in the field is to examine an already studied topic and data set but from a different theoretical or philosophical perspective. George T. Hunt's classic (1940) study of the wars of the Iroquois was hardly the first study of this topic, but it was the first to place such importance on the European-inspired fur trade as a causal factor. Nearly all scholars discussing the fur trade since Hunt's work have been reacting — either favorably or critically — to his ideas.

A variant on this latter kind of study is to examine a familiar topic and data set with new methods. Sometimes the new methods are well established and are simply applied to a new case, as with Russell Thornton's (1984) reassessment of population losses in the Cherokee forced migration known as "the Trail of Tears." Scholars before Thornton had simply considered the Cherokee's population decrease over the period of the migration, but Thornton also projected what the Cherokee population might have been if the forced migration had not occurred. The method of projecting populations forward had been used elsewhere, and its application to the Cherokee is a good example of bringing together an established method, a familiar problem, and well-known data to produce a new combination.

Other times the methods may be new or imperfectly tested, and their use on a familiar set of information is largely to evaluate the utility of the methods. An example of this is Cary Meister's study (1980) of different statistical ways of evaluating the accuracy of ethnohistoric demographic data. His study of Pima and Maricopa demography was secondary in Meister's mind; what was most important was the evaluation of various statistical methods to see which ones proved most useful.

Sometimes an ethnohistorian performs a valuable service by bringing together as much information on a subject as possible. This is particularly true when the data are difficult to collect, such as when they require knowledge of an uncommon language, when they are scattered widely in manuscripts, or when they are very extensive. For example, Elizabeth Boone (1992) has done an exhaustive study of the history of Aztec imperial rulership. She has systematized thirty-nine different historical sources (pictorial and textual, written in Spanish, in Nahuatl glyphs, or in transliterated Nahuatl) in terms of the reign dates of each imperial ruler. In the course of the presentation, her study not only revealed commonalities and contrasts among the sources themselves but also derived a typology consisting of "types of histories." The former is particularly interesting to Aztec researchers, and the latter provides a useful model for researchers to apply to other historic empires.

The Importance of Reading the Literature

Every experienced researcher knows that devising a research topic is one of the more magical things that can happen in research. After a period of thought, things suddenly fall in place, and you have an idea, and maybe even a way to approach working with it. This organic process has mysteries in it, even for the most experienced researcher. But there almost always is an essential step: reading the literature in the discipline. Scholarship is, at least in part, a cumulative endeavor, and every study is built on the backs of those that preceded it. The corpus of published ethnohistoric research is a valuable resource that can stimulate new ideas.

When embarking on a piece of research in ethnohistory, be sure to read the secondary literature that deals with the same issue. This will provide ideas about what research problems colleagues have considered important, what approaches those colleagues have used, and what data are available. In addition to this directed reading, it also is wise to read widely in ethnohistorical studies, sampling from around the world. This kind of reading will build a fund of information about what topics are considered valuable by ethnohistorians working in other regions and how they have conducted their studies. There are regional differences in any field, and topics that are returned to again and again in one place may be neglected elsewhere. The broader one's knowledge, the more profitably one can transplant an idea from another area to the region of one's specialty. Similarly, it often is rewarding to read beyond ethnohistory, taking advantage of the ideas circulating in the broader fields of history, anthropology, and other disciplines.

Usually a reading of the current ethnohistoric literature will point out "hot spots" — areas of prevailing concern for many scholars. These areas are popular, attracting a great deal of attention and often stimulating the development of ideas at a rate faster than scholars can conduct studies to examine them carefully. As a result, these areas of current attention often are fertile grounds for borrowing existing ideas or for stimulating the development of new ones.

Less heavily studied topics, however, are equally valid. Sometimes a topic is virtually ignored by scholars, not because it is intrinsically uninteresting or difficult to deal with, but simply because there are so many topics and so few ethnohistorians. The role of Jewish settlers in Utah, for example, is a fascinating one, begging for examinations of the interplay between Judaism and Mormonism, maintenance of religious identity and possibly crypto-ethnicity, the role of religious tolerance in Utah, parallel charitable traditions, and possible economic competition and conflict. Despite the research potential of this topic and the wealth of documentation, it has been virtually unstudied to date.

Ethnohistorians sometimes return to a topic that was popular some years before. As scholarly trends and fashions change, the ideas ethnohistorians bring to a topic change, and the revisiting of a formerly popular topic can bring new insights. In the 1960s, for example, ethnohistorians showed a great deal of interest in missions and religious conversion, often considering this phenomenon a manifestation of acculturation. As the potential of that perspective began to play out in the face of a steady stream of studies, religious conversion became a less popular topic in the discipline. Then, in the 1990s, interest revived, largely in response to new ways of viewing conversion, particularly in terms of the converts' use of religion to promote their political self-interest.

What Makes a Topic Worthwhile?

There are no simple rules for finding a valuable research topic, and part of the genius of landmark studies has been recognizing that the idea was worth pursuing. Nonetheless, a few guidelines can assist in judging whether an idea may be worth pursuing.

— Does the topic provide some new knowledge about human activity in the past?
— Is the topic new, one that has previously received no study?
— If the topic has been previously studied, will this new research bring new data to the study?
— If the topic has been previously studied, will this new research use new evaluations of previously known data?
— If the topic has been previously studied, will this new research bring new theory, assumptions, or ideas to the study?
— If the topic has been previously studied, will this new research use new methods?
— Will this study permit the refutation, confirmation, or extension of the conclusions of a previous study?
— Will this study bring together data currently unavailable to a major segment of scholars with interest in the topic?

If the answer to any of these questions is "yes," then the research topic has the potential to make a contribution to the fund of knowledge in ethnohistory.

There are, however, projects that probably have little or no research value. A few criteria for recognizing them are:

— Is the research merely a rehash of a previous study, with no new ideas or data? In other words, is the research redundant?
— Is the research simply a compilation of information widely known and available elsewhere?
— Is the potential conclusion of the research of such minor importance that it fails to justify the effort of the research and the space devoted to its publication? In other words, is the research trivial?
— Is the idea interesting but unfeasible because the required data do not exist or are unavailable and cannot be gathered?

If the answer to any of these questions is "yes," reconsider whether this research topic is one you wish to pursue.

The first criterion for projects of dubious value warrants a bit more discussion. Where is the line between a mere repetition of what has already been done and a confirmation of a pattern observed before? This is a difficult question, and the only court to decide it is the community of ethnohistorians as a whole. If ethnohistorians mostly feel that a point has been demonstrated to the extent that no further study is worthwhile, then further study becomes — by definition — redundant.

If in doubt, particularly about whether the research might be considered trivial or redundant, consult other ethnohistorians to solicit their opinions. Never be ruled solely by others' opinions, but remember that the priorities of any academic endeavor are set collectively by the specialists in that field.

The Research Design

"You only find what you look for." The world is very complicated, and this old folk saying speaks to the difficulty of paying equal attention to everything in it. Ethnohistorians, too, have to direct their attention to particular areas of interest, or they will risk missing the most valuable information. One way to focus attention is through a research design.

A research design is a written document, prepared before embarking on the main phase of a research project, that spells out the goals, methods, and logic of the research. Research designs originated in the sciences, where experimental or field research requires a great deal of planning and preparation, in terms of both scientific method and logistics. Social scientists began adopting research designs in the 1950s and 1960s, and they are commonplace today in many social science disciplines. The literature on research designs is diverse and scattered, but general anthropological treatments of particular value for bringing together relevant ideas are Bernard (1994) and Werner and Schoepfle (1987); Gardner and Beatty (1980) provide a broader treatment, geared particularly toward graduate students preparing for dissertation writing.

Some researchers believe research designs are critical to good research, while others believe they are a bother that consumes time better spent on other tasks. This section will discuss the benefits and drawbacks of research designs, and considerations for those who wish to use them.

The Benefits of Research Designs

The most ardent critic of research designs will agree that every researcher needs to focus on certain goals in undertaking research. Proponents of research designs argue that the writing of a research design is the best way to achieve this focus.

A research design is much like a map. Most students are confident that they know their way around a university campus, but if they were forced to draw maps of that campus, they probably would find portions where their knowledge would be vague, faulty, or nonexistent. The act of drawing a map forces them to recognize and confront these areas, just as the act of writing a research design forces a researcher to recognize and confront areas of a project plan that may not be well conceived.

Thinking through a research design obliges a researcher to *explicitly* consider a number of issues. What is the goal of the research? How can that goal be achieved? What kinds of data will support the achievement of the goal? How can those data be collected most effectively? These really are the most fundamental questions of research, questions that demand examining concepts, methods, and strategies. Perhaps most important, they require that the researcher explicitly link them together logically, explaining why a particular data set will shed light on the focus of the research.

Consider a research project dealing with the process of conversion to Christianity among the Mapuche Indians of Chile. In writing the research design for such a project, it would be imperative to consider exactly what aspect of conversion will be investigated. Incentives and motivations? Social characteristics of the converts? The strategies of missionaries? Several of these issues might be addressed in a project, and then it would be necessary to reflect on how they interrelate. Further, it is critical to consider what sources of information potentially would be available and how the various sources might provide useful information. The act of preparing the research design requires examining these aspects of the research systematically and explicitly.

Another benefit of writing a research design is that it compels the writer to review the relevant literature. For a newcomer to a specialty area, this is essential because it provides information on what research has already been performed, helping to avoid redundant research and to concentrate on vital issues. For a longtime specialist in the field, this review becomes a reacquainting with old friends. Either way, the review facilitates both recognizing the pitfalls encountered by one's predecessors and avoiding following them into the same traps.

Finally, a research design may serve several purposes once it is written. It provides a written document that can be circulated among interested colleagues for comments and criticisms. No one enjoys criticism, but it is far more palatable before the research is conducted than after it has been completed. In addition, circulating a research design may alert a researcher to someone else who currently is investigating the same or a related topic. The research design also may be the core of a grant proposal for funds to conduct the research, a request for access to the holdings of an archive or museum, an application for a permit or license that may be required in some countries, or a proposal for a thesis or dissertation.

Probably most of the benefits of writing a research design could be gained in other ways. It would be possible, for example, to simply wade into a library or archive and start reading about the Mapuche and their conversion to Christianity. Eventually, it is likely that some ideas of interest would emerge, along with some notions of how to go about dealing with them. The real question is whether it is efficient to have those ideas and make those decisions earlier or later in the research process. Most experienced scholars prefer to make them earlier, an argument for research designs.

The Drawbacks of Research Designs

Scholars who quarrel with research designs fall into two camps. First, there are those who have nothing against research designs but believe that the effort expended writing them is greater than the benefits they confer. The decision of cost and benefit has to be weighed by each researcher.

Second, there are those who actively object to research designs, believing they damage the quality of research. One argument from such critics is that research designs have to be written too early in the research process, when the writer is not yet well enough informed to be able to formulate the best goals. As these critics see it, our early ideas often have a lasting impact on our later ones, perhaps blinding us to alternative ways of seeing things. The proponents of research designs would suggest that this is an argument for flexibility in research, not for the abandonment of research designs.

Another objection to research designs is that they may blind an ethnohistorian to unexpected opportunities. Anyone who has spent time in primary documents realizes that the researcher is always encountering nuggets of information that can be the core of new pieces of research, and some scholars are afraid that research designs will dampen their ability to take advantage of these finds. It would certainly be difficult to justify the mindless following of a research design to the exclusion of following up interesting side issues and capitalizing on fortuitous discoveries. The research design should be a lens to focus attention, not a set of blinders obstructing the broader picture.

Finally, some scholars object to the philosophy that they see as embedded in the concept of a research design. The research design grew out of the nomothetic perspective of the sciences, and it is best suited to hypothesis testing, experimentation, and field exploration. Humanist scholars often feel that their approach — with its emphasis on introspection and subjective judgment — is ill suited to, and cramped by, research designs.

Whether or not one writes a research design prior to undertaking a piece of research ultimately is of little matter. It is important, however, that a scholar have a plan in mind before expending large amounts of time in research. Otherwise, efforts are diffused, and the project moves toward no clear goal.

Writing a Research Design

If you decide that a research design will benefit your project, try to keep it relatively short and to the point. After all, it is a means to an end, not the end in itself. There is no standard format for a research design, and the format should grow out of the nature of the project. Nonetheless, certain issues should be treated in any research design. The following paragraphs discuss the most important of these.

Obviously, the most crucial thing to include in a research design is the major goal of the research. This goal can be stated as a topic, a thesis statement, a question, a hypothesis, or a proposition — any form that suits the researcher's philosophical approach. No matter what its form, it should be presented in the clearest possible manner, avoiding "buzz words" that convey a vague but satisfying meaning. "To better understand Mapuche conversion to Christianity" or "to clarify the parameters of the Mapuche conversion system" should be refined to focus on specific aspects, theoretical approaches, or relationships. More specific goals are more likely to direct the research toward a successful outcome, goals such as "to investigate the effects of age and gender on the likelihood of Mapuche conversion to Christianity" or "to apply Larsen's ecological risk-minimization model to Mapuche conversion."

In stating a goal, it is important to justify it; if the research is worth doing, it should be possible to state why. If the research design ultimately will be used for any purpose other than stimulating one's own thinking, the justification may be the basis for decisions about whether or not you receive funding, gain admittance to an archive, or attain approval for a thesis project.

Listing the existing literature on the subject can be important in three ways. First, compiling this list builds familiarity with the literature. There are few events more unsettling than being partly through a research project and discovering a published work that seems to have addressed a problem in exactly the way you intended. The fewer surprises, the better. Second, if a research design will be converted into a proposal that will be considered by anyone else, a thorough bibliography is an indication of good preparation for the project. The better the preparation, the greater the likelihood the project will be successfully completed, and the more supportive outside agencies are likely to be. Do not pad the bibliography, but be aware that the research design may be judged in part on its completeness. Third, the bibliography should be of use later in the project when it is time to return to the literature.

The link between goals and the data that support them is very important to delineate in a research design. Try to be creative in recognizing ways that a set of data could bear on goals, and then spell out exactly what the bearing is. For example, the Mapuche conversion study might use baptismal records and civil records of births. What exactly will these tell? Perhaps the civil records will reveal how many children were born, and the baptismal records what number of them was Christian. But be evaluative also. Do these records warrant sufficient confidence to support quantitative measures? Are there other records that would be more useful or provide supplementary information?

The methods used to collect the data should also be discussed in the research design. Collecting may be simply the reading of the records, but there could be many complications. Can the time spent in some archives be reduced by making photocopies or scanning the records into a portable computer? If the keepers of the archive will permit it, and it can be arranged (considering factors like dependable electricity and availability of the necessary equipment), is it desirable? Could the need arise for consulting other records in the archives to get additional information to clarify some entries? Try to anticipate every reasonable eventuality and be ready for it.

The research design should also discuss the methods to be used after the data have been collected. Back home there will be many hours of digesting the information collected, and having some idea of how that digestion will proceed is critical. Will there be quantitative analysis? If so, will it require access to computers? To special programs or expertise? Will the project require a research assistant to help deal with the masses of data? (First-time researchers often underestimate how much work is involved in organizing, copying, entering, and checking data, and a student assistant often is very handy.)

When discussing methods of both collecting and analyzing data, remember the need to justify decisions. A decision to not quantify should be made because there are no major benefits to it, not because it is a bother or because the researcher does not like numbers. A decision to study a particular span of years should be justified by the project goals or the data limitations, not simply by convenience; this span should include contrasts of conditions if change is being studied, and it should contain more or less uniform conditions if a synchronic study is intended. Every decision ideally is a reasoned one.

If the research involves nothing more complicated than going to a local library, so much the better. Often, however, research involves travel, unfamiliar or foreign archives, or other factors that have impacts on the cost and effort of conducting the research. If these are part of a project, be prepared to support them somehow. This may mean seeking grant funding or spending extra time collecting data. The trick when writing the research design is to recognize potential problems and find ways to deal with them. Assuming that they will go away on their own later is a recipe for disaster.

Finally, a research design should include a statement of the project's feasibility. This may be implicit rather than explicit, but it is important that the researcher (and perhaps others who read the research design) be convinced that the project can be completed successfully. Problems are to be expected—both anticipated and unanticipated—but a thoughtful research design will suggest solutions for anticipated problems and will reduce the number of unanticipated difficulties that crop up later.

One way that research plans can be unrealistic is in the number of documents, oral histories, entries, or other pieces of information that can be collected. This is understandable because there usually is no way to estimate credibly the amount of relevant data available and how long it will take to gather them. The vagaries of different handwriting styles, misplaced documents in an archive, power outages, and other unanticipated snags make it exceedingly difficult to estimate how much work can be accomplished in the available time.

One way to deal with this is to establish several levels of acceptable accomplishment. There might be, for example, an optimal plan to examine all the Mapuche baptismal records in a village for the period under study, and the minimal plan might be to examine every fourth year of the records; in between might be a plan looking at records from every two years. If the examination is more time consuming than anticipated, the minimum plan goes into effect; if more time is available, successively more desirable plans can be implemented. In approaching such a plan, it is wise to become acquainted with some of the practices and dangers of sampling, which are outlined in most texts on quantitative methods (e.g., Floud 1979; Thomas 1976).

The following checklist summarizes the major points that need to be covered in a research design:

— What is the goal of the research? Why is this important? How does the goal fit into the broader enterprise of ethnohistory?
— What is the existing literature on the subject?
— What are the data that will be sought to support the study? Precisely how do these data bear on the goal?
— What methods will be used in collecting the data? In analyzing them?
— What practical issues are involved in the collection and analysis of the data?
— Is the research feasible?

Of course, every project has its own idiosyncrasies, and a research design may have to address other issues to deal with them.

Unfortunately, there is limited literature to refer to for assistance in preparing an ethnohistoric research design. Historiography texts typically devote some space to the issue of developing a topic to study, although neither the term nor the concept of "research design" is discussed in any we have seen. Some guides to anthropological research (e.g., Levine 1973; Bernard 1994) include chapters on research designs, but they sometimes emphasize field and ethical issues that have limited relevance to the ethnohistorian. They may, however, include useful treatments of how to link goals to data with methods. Discussions of research designs in behavioral science and the natural sciences are legion but too far removed to be of much assistance. Fortunately, writing a research design is mostly solid introspection and consideration, and further guidance is largely unnecessary.

Modifying the Research in Midstream

Although it is essential to have a clear idea of the topic before undertaking any detailed research, it is equally essential to maintain flexibility as the project progresses. The research process is full of twists, detours, and dead ends, and the ethnohistorian has to be ready to modify the project in light of them.

Perhaps the most devastating problem that can develop in research is when data that one has presumed would be available seem to not exist. An exhaustive search usually will turn up some information relevant to a topic, but it may be sorely inadequate. Such a development is an ethnohistorian's nightmare (but one that usually is avoidable through careful planning).

For example, documents tell us that the Chinese miners of Jackson in California's Gold Country preferred to send corpses of their dead back to China for ritual disposal, but we also know that there was a Chinese cemetery in Jackson. This, however, appears to be the major part of the information available on this subject from documents, oral accounts, and other sources. Describing the changes in Chinese gold miners' treatment of the dead during the latter half of the nineteenth century might be a fascinating idea, but a researcher should be wary of being seduced into embarking on a project with limited likelihood of sufficient data to make it successful. A detailed search for information might reveal unrecognized sources, but it would be unwise to undertake the project without first exploring whether these unrecognized sources really exist. It is common in research to conduct small-scale exploratory studies to see whether sufficient data are available to support a larger study.

Once you are committed to a study, finding a sorely inadequate database means having to make major modifications in the project. In the study mentioned above, this may mean having to incorporate other ethnic groups, changing the study area to San Francisco, or making some other, equally drastic adjustment. Such modifications are traumatic, demoralizing, and expensive in terms of time and funds, so it is wise to plan ahead and avoid them if at all possible. Fortunately, problems of data availability usually are not so extreme. There may be gaps or weak areas, but frequently a scholar can patch together a sufficient database with a little cleverness and effort.

Sometimes it is wise to modify a research design in light of methodological concerns. Examining every American Indian probate inventory from the Massachusetts Bay Colony might have seemed like the thorough thing to do in a study of American Indian material culture, but the actual task of poring through thousands of documents written in different hands, preserved in varying stages of deterioration, and scattered through dozens of repositories is simply impractical. Ethnohistoric "common knowledge" often says that there is a limited set of data on a topic; sometimes when a researcher digs into those data, however, it turns out that the data set is far more extensive than originally believed. Under these and similar circumstances, the researcher may have to restrict the goals of the project, perhaps dealing only with a single township or settling for a less comprehensive study. Sometimes a thoughtful plan of sampling the data will solve the problem. It is wise during a lengthy project to monitor progress periodically, permitting recognition of possible problems and revision of one's strategy.

Finally, an ethical problem may force an ethnohistorian to modify or abandon a research project. Scholars sometimes develop the notion that their research is too esoteric to have any real effect on living people, but that is not necessarily so. Ethnohistorians deal with people, albeit usually long-dead ones. But those people frequently have descendants and others who are part of the same ethnic or religious group, and there are occasions when research may have negative impacts on them. If, for example, research is causing a community to open a long-dormant rift between two ethnic groups, the researcher has to decide the proper course of action. There is no formal or official code of ethics for ethnohistorians, but we have compiled an outline of ethical suggestions in appendix B.

CHAPTER 13

Working in Archives and Elsewhere

The most important place where ethnohistorians work is the archive or library. The term *archive* refers to both a collection of documents and a repository for preserving, housing, organizing, and making accessible documentary materials. The repositories themselves may not actually be called archives but may go by a variety of names such as manuscript library, public records office, records center, local historical library, regional historical collection, and so on. Properly speaking, archives house records pertaining to their own institutions, although documents from other sources may make their way into such repositories. Ethnohistorians also may use other facilities that might or might not be considered "archives." Reservation or Indian school records might be maintained as part of the ongoing administration of a functioning entity, not really with a primary purpose of supporting historic research, and some museums, such as the British Museum in London and the Museo Nacional de Antropología in Mexico City, contain their own extensive archives. Alternatively, some archives also house artifacts and double as minimuseums. Useful documents might be located in any of these repositories as well as in public or private libraries, and ethnohistorians should not hesitate to search for documentation in such diverse institutions.

As a body of historical documents, archives are "records, organically related, of an entity (individual or organization) systematically maintained, after they have fulfilled the purpose for which they were created, because they contain information of continuing value" (Gracy 1988:22–23). Archives thus come into being as an integral part of literate life, are treated as groups of documents, and are held in custody primarily for their historical value (Gracy 1988:19).

All archives contain materials considered to be historical manuscripts in a general sense; however, in a specific sense, archivists often make distinctions between archives and historical manuscripts. The latter are usually defined and treated as more individualized documents not directly related to the organization of which the archive is a part. They tend to defy the standard organization of the archive and may reside as "artificial collections." Gracy (1988:22) cites as examples "the accumulation of love letters from throughout the world at the West Vancouver (British Columbia) Public Library or the collection of signatures in the Declaration of Texas Independence Signers Collection in the Eugene C. Barker Texas History Center at the University of Texas at Austin. No entity — 'love' or 'Declaration of Texas Independence' — generated either group of documents." Such collections of primary sources are devoid of a direct administrative relationship and institutional context attached to the archive. However, when located, they can be of tremendous research value.

Document Availability

The availability of documents pertinent to a particular research topic varies considerably depending on factors ranging from "historical accidents" to archival policies. The original use of a document — such as a ledger to maintain business accounts or a map to find one's way — is the document's first life. Once it no longer fulfills its intended purpose, the document may be maintained in its second life for the historical and institutional information it contains. Of course, the survival of a document or collection of documents depends on a number of factors — some happenstance, some intended.

"Historical accident" can be instrumental in determining which documents even pass into a second life. For instance, the Aztec *Codex Mendoza* was created around 1541 in Mexico for the enlightenment of the Spanish monarchy and loaded aboard a treasure ship bound for Spain. The fleet was set upon and captured by French privateers on the high seas, and the codex arrived instead at the court of the French king. It was viewed (at least) by the French cosmographer André Thevet, was later passed to the Englishmen Richard Halkuyt and John Selden, and finally came to rest in the Bodleian Library at Oxford University in 1659. This document was fortunate. It could just as easily have been thrown overboard on the high seas, but it was not, and it luckily passed through the hands of historically conscious individuals. The *Codex Mendoza* survived, but countless others have sunk with ships, burned in courthouses, and been carried out with the trash.

Selectivity in document survival also occurs intentionally. Dramatic changes in governments and religions (such as internal revolutions or external conquests) sometimes have entailed the recasting of traditional histories. This has been known to involve the purposeful destruction of records, manuscripts, and books that characterized and legitimized former political regimes and religious institutions. The eighteenth-century Japanese invasion of Okinawa occasioned just such a systematic destruction of Okinawan documents, but the Okinawans managed to preserve many documents in caves.

In many cases, the mass of documentation is simply too great for a repository and its staff to handle. Documents must then be appraised — and decisions made — to determine which documents or sets of documents to obtain and / or maintain. The most pressing archival reasons for preserving documents past their first life are for legal necessity and informational value. The hope that the preserved documents may shed light on some aspect of history is of primary importance to ethnohistorians, but such decisions entail considerable foresight. Margaret Norton (in Mitchell 1975:9) cites an example in Illinois:

> [A]ll the time books for the day laborers, masons, carpenters and other workmen who built our statehouse [were] preserved because the statehouse commissioners knew they would someday be subjected to a thorough financial investigation. But no one made it his business to preserve a copy of the blue prints from which the building was erected. The time books are moldering on the shelves, but the state architect several years ago had to reproduce the plans of the statehouse at a great cost.

Appraising documents for their informational value has become very difficult in the latter half of the twentieth century, with the glut of documentation overwhelming archivists and their repositories. For ethnohistorians, it means that some archives are removing dusty "old" documents to make room for newer records deemed important for their current legal status and / or future historical value. Obviously, researchers are subject to archivists' decisions about the relative significance of different documents. The dilemma is real. Although historical researchers wish to obtain every possible shred of evidence pertaining to their investigations, archivists cannot foresee every possible (or probable) research question to be pursued. Some documents may lie on shelves forever without being consulted; others, existing at one time in their first lives, persist only in the dreams of researchers. The ethnohistorian should expect some constraints and frustrations in the search for pertinent source materials, but these pressures are somewhat alleviated by microfilm and recent technological advances in producing archival-quality photocopies of bulky and/or fragile documents. These are, however, costly procedures.

Principles of Archival Organization

In order to successfully access relevant documentary sources, ethnohistorians should be acquainted with the various principles that guide an archive's or library's organization. Most archives have a cataloguing system — some more thoroughly executed than others. Some of these catalogues are available in published form. In addition, archivists and librarians often can provide invaluable personal guidance unavailable through a catalogue.

Each archive develops its own system for filing, cataloguing, recording, and retrieving documents, and the specifics of these arrangements must be learned as one migrates from archive to archive. Classification systems are not random, however, and do tend to follow general organizational guidelines. The overarching basis for grouping documents is according to organization, agency, or individual to which the documents relate (also known as the "creator") (Schellenberg 1956:59; Gracy 1988: 21–22). This does not mean that the "creator" generated all the documents in the group; instead, much of the material may be correspondence directed toward the creator or newspaper articles about that person or entity. In a search for information about a particular organization — say, the East India Company — perusal of holdings filed under various governmental agencies may well bear fruit. Within an organizational category, documents are customarily grouped into "series" on the basis of activities or functions. These defined areas are usually not created by the archivist but rather mirror the original goals and activities of the entity itself. Within these functional groups, documents then may be identified as to specific type and, subsequently, as individual items.

Documents may also be classified according to media format. Formats most usually recognized include diaries, minutes, and proceedings; financial documents; legal documents; photographic material; graphic documents, including maps, charts, and graphs; scrapbooks and scrapbook material; printed material; literary productions, including oral history; and media such as motion-picture film and microforms (Gracy 1988:21). Format is an important filing principle for some types of documentation that have specific storage and preservation needs. Maps, architectural plans, and the like may require broad, flat areas for storage, while audiotapes of oral-history interviews fit more efficiently elsewhere. Pictorial records, from codices to photographs, often have special conservation needs and may be classed separately from other documentation (National Research Council 1986).

Some archives, particularly in Europe, also provide information on their holdings in the form of calendars, entries that describe individual, chronologically ordered documents rather than aggregates. Calendars usually provide considerable information, often paraphrasing a document's main content. With detailed calendars, the search for appropriate sources is eased, and archivists' concern for the fragility of documents is allayed (Schellenberg 1965:297–298).

Given these classification bases, it is axiomatic that ethnohistorians should be as well acquainted as possible with the relevant organization(s) before heading to the archives. Only occasionally will you encounter records classified according to subject matter or chronology (both of which would be ideal for ethnohistoric research). Attempts at classification by subject matter are especially tricky when any one document — a letter, council minutes, or a diary — may well range over a multitude of diverse topics.

Ethnohistorians should always be prepared for disappointments and surprises in an initial search. Catalogue entries are by necessity brief and typically contain only a general idea of a document's content. Also, titles are sometimes misleading. In many cases, researchers read through entire documents only to find that they contain nothing of value, but on the other hand, an unpromising document may have an especially useful census or map, unnoted in the catalogue, serendipitously attached to it. When Barbara Tuchman (1981:78) was working at the Public Records Office in London, she asked for papers of the British delegation to the Hague conference of 1899 and was surprised and delighted to find, bound with them, enlightening letters from the public to governmental officials regarding the conference. If possible, it is a good idea to build extra time into research planning to allow for the possibility of such unanticipated discoveries.

The Society of American Archivists publishes a number of basic manuals on a variety of archival topics, from appraisal to law to automated access (several of these are cited in Densmore 1988:145–146).

Locating Relevant Documents

Many documents of ethnohistoric interest have been published, sometimes with translations or editor's notes to assist the reader in using them. Although there are many excellent editions of documentary sources, processes of editing and publishing sometimes alter specific details contained in the original. For instance, an early published edition of George Washington's writings was sprinkled with liberal changes: "'Dirty' was omitted from a description of the 'dirty mercenary spirit' of the Connecticut troops, 'Old Put' emerged as 'General Putnam,' and the statement that a certain sum 'will be but a flea bite to our demands' became 'will be totally inadequate'" (Stieg 1988:7). One of this book's authors once searched long, but in vain, in an English translation of Bernal Díaz del Castillo's *True History of the Conquest of Mexico* for a reference to the collection of nightsoil in the early-sixteenth-century Aztec city of Tenochtitlan, only to find out that reference to this sensitive subject had been deleted.

For serious ethnohistoric work, there is often no substitute for the original document, but many original documents exist only in one or a few places. Sometimes there exists only a single copy, sometimes the original and some copies made by hand (and perhaps incorporating errors), sometimes the original and photographic copies. As a result, ethnohistoric research may involve travel to several archives to study rare manuscripts. It is crucial that ethnohistorians consult available guides and catalogues in order to get the best mileage from the research enterprise. For work in U.S. archives, the National Union Catalog of Manuscript Collections (published by the Library of Congress) provides a broadly comprehensive (though not complete) guide to archival holdings in repositories throughout the country. This is a good place to begin searching for relevant documentation. Other important general sources include the National Historical Publications and Records Commission (1979), Smith (1986), Ash and Miller (1985), DeWitt (1994), the *National Inventory of Documentary Sources in the United States* (1984), and the *Researcher's Guide to Archives and Regional History Sources* (1988).

Individual repositories often publish guides of their holdings, and these should be consulted when available. Directories and guides are also frequently available for archives in other countries. It is worthwhile to consult sources such as the *Guide to the Archives of International Organizations* (1984–), Foster and Sheppard (1989), Zidouemba (1977), and Glass (1964). There are also guides to sources on American history in French, British, German, and Spanish archives; guides to sources on Latin America in Spanish, British, and U.S. archives; guides to sources on Africa in British, French, and Dutch archives; and so on. These various directories and guides are well worth consulting before traveling great distances.

Specialized guides provide shortcuts for certain research topics (e.g., Kaminkow 1975; Wynar 1978; *World Directory of Moving Image and Sound*

Archives [1993]; and Carrington and Stephenson 1978). Other guides, directories, and bibliographies are amply cited in Larsen (1988). In addition, today's Internet capabilities provide ready access to a multitude of research tools. Especially useful are (1) the National Inventory of Documentary Sources in the United States (NIDS) (1984), which provides listings of collections indexed according to Federal Records; Manuscript Division, Library of Congress; and State Archives, State Libraries, State Historical Societies, Academic Libraries, and other Repositories; and (2) the Research Libraries Information Network (RLIN), which serves as a record of international archive and manuscript collections. Some culture areas are particularly well endowed with guides to archival materials. For Middle America, an especially useful and detailed research tool is the *Handbook of Middle American Indians* (Wauchope 1972–75), volumes 12–15 of the *Guide to Ethnohistorical Sources*. The Newberry Library's *American Indian Bibliographic Series* (Jennings 1976–) provides published works and various specialized bibliographies on sources pertaining to many Native American groups north of Mexico.

Before traveling any great distance, it is worthwhile to directly contact the caretakers of specific repositories to inquire about their holdings relevant to your research topic. Archivists can then inform researchers about the availability of documentation, additional pertinent sources — and the long vacation they plan to begin the day you arrive.

Quite a few historically valuable and unique manuscripts are in the hands of private collectors. There are many published guides to manuscript collections in private hands, and high-end rare book dealers probably are the best source for tracing such manuscripts. Some collectors welcome scholarly interest in their rare collections, while others reject such interest out of hand. In either case, a researcher approaching such a collector should expect a good deal of suspicion and be ready to document his or her interest, affiliations, and reliability.

The Archive Environment

Although many primary sources have been transcribed, translated, and made available in printed and computerized form, many of the sources most valuable to ethnohistorians are characterized by individuality, originality, and irreplaceability. Archives containing these unique materials usually have strict rules and regulations designed to ensure their safety and preservation. To cross the portals, researchers are customarily asked for personal identification credentials (including photographic identification); in some cases, archives may also require a letter verifying an institutional affiliation, a letter of introduction from a colleague assuring the archival caretakers of the seriousness of the scholarly endeavors, or an authorization from the donor of a specific collection to be studied. Researchers may also be required to pay a small fee or become members of an affiliated historical society to gain access to the collections. In Europe, a written application, including a statement of purpose, is usually required for admission to archives and records offices. The importance attached to such applications varies from archive to archive: although quite pro forma at the Public Records Office in London, it is a major hurdle at the Bibliothèque Nationale in Paris, for which Barbara Tuchman (1981:78) suggests you carry your "passport, birth certificate, university diploma, your mother's marriage license, and a letter from your ambassador. If you can show your return ticket home, that will have a soothing effect."

Researchers may arrive at the archive expecting to have access to every document they request, but it's possible to encounter some restrictions. While most documents in an archive are in the public domain, some may be encumbered with confidentiality restrictions. Other documents are so fragile that their condition precludes examination by even the most serious scholars. In this case, the archival staff may have photographic reproductions available.

Every archive follows rules designed to assure the safety and safekeeping of its documents (Schiff 1988:43). The specifics vary from archive to archive, but typical rules include the following:

- All portable personal property except writing and recording equipment must be checked outside the reading room.
- Pens or indelible pencils are not permitted in the reading room. Rules concerning the use of equipment such as laptop computers, tape recorders, hand scanners, and optical recognition programs vary.
- Researchers may be subject to search on entry and departure.
- No materials may be taken from the reading room.
- No markings may be made on documents.
- Archival materials should be maintained in their original order.
- Smoking, eating, and drinking are not permitted.

The general message is, "Handle with care," for in many cases these documents are unique and irreplaceable. Appropriate ethical conduct (as suggested in appendix B) is as applicable in archival research as in any other scholarly pursuit.

If only limited time is available to spend at an archive, a researcher may wish to survey many documents to study in greater depth later on. This requires copying or photocopying, but be aware that many materials cannot be photocopied at all. Even when photocopying or microfilming is permitted, researchers are not allowed to do this but must request this service from the archival staff. Consequently, such reproductions take time and are often quite expensive (up to ten or twenty times the cost of simple photocopying). Some archives, such as the Archivo General de la Nación in Mexico City, have transcribers who, for a fee, will provide a transcription. Some archives also have access to local freelance researchers who can help find relevant documents and arrange for copies if needed.

Even with these various available services, it is a good idea to allow more time than you really think you need for archival research. Once admitted to an archive's reading room, you may find yourself especially eager and impatient to probe the mysteries of significant primary sources, yet you must be prepared to exercise patience. Archival materials are usually under close supervision, and you will probably be required to order a document. There will be time spent waiting while the archivist seeks out the manuscript from the bowels of the archive, and then you may be allowed to study only one document at a time, returning the first before ordering the next. This, too, causes delays. It is good planning to anticipate these glacial procedures and to allow sufficient time to avoid frustration and hurried research. After all, this — the discovery phase — is a particularly pleasurable part of the ethnohistoric enterprise.

Making the Most of Archival Research

With the archive's rules, regulations, and procedures well in hand, how do you make the most of your archival stay? Because you may have to consult documents in more than one archive, and your research funds and time may be limited, you will wish to make the most efficient and effective use of such visits.

An essential guideline is scholarly preparation. A well-conceptualized research question provides the framework for archival fieldwork; it provides focus and helps keep you from straying too far from your project. Sound background research therefore guides you in knowing where to look, what to look for, and how to know you have found it. Of course, intriguing but tangential tidbits of information encountered in the course of research should not be ignored but should be written down for later consideration. A focused project also helps you get the most mileage from a knowledgeable archivist who can suggest specific sources and other repositories you may not have considered.

Other researchers sharing the reading room with you can be valuable associates. It is often worthwhile discussing each other's projects (perhaps over a congenial lunch or cup of coffee in the lounge or cafeteria outside the reading room). Not only may such conversations refine your own thinking, but another researcher may have happened onto a particularly useful document pertinent to your study, and you may be able to return the favor — a not uncommon experience.

Because archival research involves collecting information on a focused problem, useful notes and records of the documents you deem worthy are essential. Note taking is usually an idiosyncratic matter, but it is worth stressing that key documents warrant thorough recording (or photocopying where allowed). One hardly wishes to face uncertainties upon returning home, especially after traveling a great distance to study a unique document.

Then there is the matter of selection: as a research project unfolds, how do you decide what to use and what to pass over? An essential guidepost is your research statement. If it is sound, relevant documents will be those that serve as evidence and support for your proposal. It is often difficult to make such decisions: it is an unusual proposal that takes no twists and turns as the research develops. You may view documents that only marginally apply to your project as you now see it, only to find that later on such documents may cast your project in an intriguing new light. Although you probably cannot take copious and thorough notes on all the documents you encounter in your archival stay, you may wish to establish priorities and record the catalogue or inventory information on those you think may have future relevance.

Archival fieldwork is no less an adventure than ethnographic or archaeological fieldwork. Discoveries are waiting to be made, some of which you anticipate and expect to find. Other discoveries will be complete surprises that, while particularly exciting, also demand flexibility and at times a willingness to adapt to a novel perspective: Ethnohistoric researchers should be prepared to modify their twentieth-century mind-sets in response to the realities encountered in primary documentary sources.

Epilogue

This is, in essence, a book about relationships and interactions. At the definitional level, ethnohistory emphasizes dynamic interrelationships between people of different cultures. At the investigatory level, ethnohistory's approach seeks to link researchers' questions with the vagaries of documentation and with the reality of events, activities, and lifeways of the past.

Bridges between questions, documents, and reality are provided by a variety of concepts and methods. A paramount objective of ethnohistory is to build reasonably strong bridges from research questions to past lifeways, necessarily through the often distorted lens of documentary sources. The concepts, methods, and strategies presented in this book are primarily intended as guidelines in understanding and interpreting written documents. Throughout we have emphasized the importance of expecting and recognizing variation: in writing styles, in language usage, in designating time and names, in map designs — indeed, in anything that may appear in written form. We have also stressed the incomplete and distorted nature of the documentary record. Given the fragmentary and often idiosyncratic nature of these source materials, the importance of applying additional information from areas such as folklore and archaeology cannot be overemphasized.

In these endeavors, practitioners in the field of ethnohistory have only scratched the surface. True, a vast number of documents have been transcribed, translated, and published, and many of these have been commented on in books and articles. These documents and others have supported hundreds of books and thousands of articles that describe, analyze, interpret, and attempt to explain the ethnohistoric past. Nonetheless, their potential to support research has scarcely been tapped. For every study published to date, there could be a dozen more, looking at the data in a different way or examining a different subject.

In addition, many documents are hidden away where few scholars have looked, and these sometimes provide new information that reshapes our thinking about past events and processes. The search through dusty archives and crumbling documents is the ethnohistorian's fieldwork, and it has all the excitement, serendipity, and potential for the unexpected that any fieldwork has. Ferreting out these documents provides new grist for the ethnohistoric mill, as does integrating auxiliary studies from archaeology, folklore, and other disciplines. Ethnohistorians should not fear running out of raw material for research, at least in the near future.

With this tremendous potential, ethnohistorians are in a prime position to discover and rediscover how human beings structured their ethnic interactions in the past. On one hand, careful ethnohistoric studies inform us about the particulars of the past, revealing strategies in cultural adaptations. Ethnohistoric research therefore adds to the store of knowledge on how different cultures have coped with defined situations, especially when experiencing contact with other groups. While each situation is in some way unique, a study of their collectivity is useful in unveiling general patterns of ethnic relations and broad processes of culture change. This, in turn, can help us identify similar patterns and processes in the present, an important asset in understanding the intricacies of today's multicultural world.

Ethnohistory is also useful in linking the past with the present. Studies of primary documents can be, and are, brought to bear in establishing genealogical ties, property and territorial rights, political legitimacy, and other matters based on traditional rights and claims. Recent ethnohistorical work among the Hopi in the American Southwest, for instance, has probed documentary sources to fill in gaps between archaeological findings and oral histories. This has led to the identification of traditional pilgrimage trails and has revealed much about Hopi beliefs concerning ancient sites (SAA 1995b).

What pursuits, then, are in the offing for ethnohistorians in the future? Traditionally, most ethnohistorians have applied their specialized skills and temporal perspective to address problems of a particularistic nature. With so many focused investigations in hand, progressive ethnohistoric research should be in a position to develop more comparative studies on temporal, regional, and thematic bases from which to derive meaningful generalizations. Such studies would be enhanced if ethnohistorians would cast their geographic nets more broadly to cover less well researched cultures and times. In addition, ethnohistorians will surely continue to emphasize the current trend of presenting native histories from native viewpoints. As more individuals of diverse cultural backgrounds are trained in ethnohistory, their "insider" perspectives will enrich both data collection and analysis. Overall, ethnohistory is in a unique position to link past with present, to meld the particular with the general, to advocate appreciation of diverse cultural points of view, and to productively apply interdisciplinary tools and concepts in these endeavors.

Reference Material

Bibliography of Paleography in Selected Languages

The following bibliography, although far from exhaustive, provides selected paleographic sources and guides for several languages. The languages chosen are those used extensively in ethnohistoric research, usually because they were the languages of colonial powers.

Arabic

Grohmann, Adolf. 1967–71. *Arabische Palaeographie*. Wien: Bohlau in Kommission. *Forschungen zur Islamischen Philologie und Kulturgeschichte* bd. 1.

Gruendler, Beatrice. 1993. *The Development of the Arabic Scripts: From the Nabatean Era to the First Islamic Century According to Dated Texts. Harvard Semitic Studies* 43. Atlanta, Ga.: Scholars Press.

Vajda, Georges. 1958. *Album paleographie arabe*. Paris: Libraire d'Amerique et d'Orient / Centre National de la Recherche Scientifique.

Dutch

Brugmans, Hajo. 1910. *Atlas der Nederlandsche palaeographie*. Gravenhage: A. de Jager.

Horsman, P. J., Th. J. Poelstra, and J. P. Sigmond. 1984. *Schriftspiegel: Nederlandse Paleografische Teksten van de 13de tot de 18de eeuw*. Zutphen: Terra.

English

Bishop, Terence Alan Martyn. 1971. *English Caroline Miniscule*. Oxford, England: Clarendon Press.

Bodleian Library. 1960. *Humanistic Script of the Fifteenth and Sixteenth Centuries*. Oxford, England: Bodleian Library.

Dawson, Giles Edwin, and Laetitia Kennedy-Skipton. 1966. *Elizabethan Handwriting, 1500–1650: A Manual*. London: Faber.

Emmison, F. G. 1967. *How To Read Local Archives, 1550–1700*. London: Historical Association. Reprint, London: Chameleon Press, 1983.

Hector, L. C. 1966. *The Handwriting of English Documents*. 2d ed. London: Edward Arnold Publishers. Reprint, Sorking, Surrey: Kohler and Coombes, 1980.

Kirkham, E. Kay. 1965. Rev. ed. *How to Read the Handwriting and Records of Early America.* Salt Lake City: Deseret Books.

Lowe, E. A. 1960. *English Uncial.* Oxford, England: Clarendon Press/Oxford University Press.

Preston, Jean F., and Laetitia Yeandle. 1992. *English Handwriting, 1400–1650: An Introductory Manual.* Binghamton, N.Y.: Medieval and Renaissance Texts and Studies/Pegasus Paperbooks.

Simpson, Grant G. 1986. *Scottish Handwriting, 1150–1650: An Introduction to the Reading of Documents.* Aberdeen, Scotland: Aberdeen University Press. Corrected reprinting of the 1973 edition.

Stryker-Rodda, Harriet. 1987. Rev. ed. *Understanding Colonial Handwriting.* Baltimore: Genealogical Publishing.

Whalley, Joyce Irene. 1969. *English Handwriting, 1540–1853: An Illustrated Survey Based on Material in the National Art Library, Victoria and Albert Museum.* London: Her Majesty's Stationery Office.

Wright, C. E. 1960. *English Vernacular Hands from the Twelfth to the Fifteenth Centuries.* Oxford, England: Clarendon Press/Oxford University Press.

Europe in General

Tannenbaum, Samuel A. 1930. *The Handwriting of the Renaissance.* New York: Columbia University Press. Reprint, New York: Frederick Ungar, 1967.

French

Audisio, Gabriel, and Isabelle Bonnot-Rambaud. 1991. *Lire le français d'hier: Manuel de paleographie moderne, XVe–XVIIIe siècles.* Paris: A. Colin.

Lafortune, Marcel. 1982. *Initiation à la paleographie franco-canadienne: Les écritures des notaires aux XVIIe–XVIIIe siècles.* Montreal: Société de Recherche Historique Archiv-Histo.

Lefebvre, Fernand. 1958. *Introduction à la paleographie canadienne.* Ottawa: University of Ottawa.

German

Degering, Hermann. 1964. *Die Schrift: Atlas der Schriftformen des Abendlandes vom Altertum bis zum Ausgang des 18. Jahrhunderts.* Tubingen: E. Wasmuth.

Eis, Gerhard. 1949. *Altdeutsche Handschriften: 41 Texte und Tafeln mit einer Einleitung und Erlauterungen.* Munchen: C. H. Beck.

Italian

De la Mare, Albibia Catherine. 1973. *The Handwriting of Italian Humanists.* Oxford, England: University Press/Association Internationale de Bibliophilie.

Lupi, Clemente. 1875. *Manuale di paleografia delle carte.* Firenze: Successori Le Monnier.

Latin

Bischoff, Bernhard. 1990. *Latin Paleography: Antiquity and the Middle Ages.* Translated by Daibhi o Croinin and David Ganz. Cambridge: Cambridge University Press.

Capelli, Adriano. 1982. *The Elements of Abbreviation in Medieval Latin Paleography.* Lawrence, Kan.: University of Kansas Libraries.

Thoyts, E. E. 1893. *How to Decipher and Study Old Documents.* London: Elliott Stock.

Nahuatl

Anderson, Arthur J. O., Frances Berdan, and James Lockhart. 1976. *Beyond the Codices: The Nahua View of Colonial Mexico.* Berkeley, Calif.: University of California Press.

Portuguese

Cruz, Antonio. 1987. *Paleografia portuguesa: Ensaio de manual.* Oporto: Universidade Portucalense.

da Costa, Avelino de Jesus. 1976. 3d ed. *Album de paleografia e diplomatica portuguesas.* Coimbra: Facultade de Letras da Universidade de Coimbra, Instituto de Palcografia c Diplomatica.

Flexor, Maria Helena Ochi. 1979. *Abreviaturas: Manuscritos dos seculos XVI ao XIX.* São Paulo: Governo do Estado de São Paulo, Secretaria da Cultura, Divisao de Arquivo do Estado.

Scandinavian

Svensson, Lars. 1974. *Nordiski Paleografi: Handbok med Transkriberade och Kommenterade Skriftprov.* Lundastudier i Noedis Sprakvetenskap, series 1, no. 28. Lund: Studentlitt.

Slavic

Bogdan, Damian P. 1978. *Paleografia Romano-Slava: Tratat si album.* Bucharest: Directia Generala a Arhivelor Statului din Republica Socialista Romania.

Cherepnin, Lev Vladimirovich. 1956. *Russkaia paleografiia.* Moscow: Gos. Izd-vo Politicheskoi Literatury. An earlier edition was coauthored by Cherepnin and Nikolai Sergeevich Chaev.

Priselkov, Mikhail Dmitievich. 1938. *Kurs russkoi paleografii.* Leningrad: Sektor Zaochnogo Obucheniia LGU.

South and Southeast Asian Languages

Buhler, Gerog. 1980. *Indian Paleography.* New Delhi: Oriental Books Reprint Corporation.

Dani, Ahmad Hasan. 1963. *Indian Palaeography.* Oxford, England: Clarendon Press. Reprint, New Delhi: Munsihiram Manoharlal, 1986.

de Casparis, J. G. 1975. *Indonesian Palaeography: A History of Writing in Indonesia from the Beginnings to circa A.D. 1500*. Leiden: Brill.

Mangalam, S. J. 1988. *Palaeography of Malayalam Script*. Delhi: Eastern Book Linkers.

Rahman, Pares Islam Syed Mustafizur. 1979. *Islamic Calligraphy in Medieval India*. Dacca: University Press.

Spanish

Alvera Delgras, Antonio. 1857. *Compendio de paleografía española, o escuela de leer todas las letras que se han usade en España desde los tiempos mas remotos hasta fines del siglo XVII*. Madrid: Impr. de A. Santa Coloma.

Arnall Juan, María Josefa. 1993. *Bibliografía de paleografía, lingüística y diplomática hispano-americanas*. Barcelona: Universitat de Barcelona Publicaciones.

Bribesca Sumano, María Elena. 1982. *Charlas de paleografía y diplomática hispanoamericana*. Monterrey, Mexico: R. Ayuntamiento de Monterrey.

Cavallini de Arauz, Ligia. 1986. *Elementos de paleografía hispanoamericana*. San José, Costa Rica: Editorial de la Universidad de Costa Rica.

Garcés G., Jorge A. 1960. 2d ed. *Paleografía diplomática Española y sus peculiaridades en América*. Quito: Editorial Casa de la Cultura Ecuatoriana.

Haggard, J. Villasana, assisted by Malcolm McLean. 1941. *Handbook for Translators of Spanish Historical Documents*. Austin: University of Texas/Texas State Library.

Lowe, Salo Kalisher. 1943. *Paleographic Guide for Spanish Manuscripts, Fifteenth–Seventeenth Centuries*. New Orleans: Middle American Research Institute, Tulane University.

Mackenzie, David, and Victoria A. Burrus. 1986. 4th ed. *A Manual of Manuscript Transcription for the Dictionary of the Old Spanish Language*. Madison, Wis.: Hispanic Seminary of Medieval Studies. An earlier edition was authored by Kenneth Buelow and David Mackenzie; another earlier edition was authored by David Mackenzie alone.

Millares Carlo, Agustín. 1983. 3d ed. *Tratado de paleografía española*. Madrid: Espasa-Calpe.

Pezzat Arzave, Delia. 1990. *Elementos de paleografía novohispaña*. Mexico: Facultad de Filosofía y Letras, Universidad Nacional Autónoma de México.

Outline for an Ethical Code in Ethnohistory

With no formal code of ethics, ethnohistory appears to be an anomaly at the end of the twentieth century. This presumably is an outgrowth of the belief that ethnohistory studies long-dead people and therefore has no important ethical considerations. The experience of archaeologists since the mid-twentieth century, however, reveals the falsity of this assumption. The serious disagreements that some archaeologists have had with American Indians, cultural anthropologists, and other archaeologists over the treatment of human remains and sacred objects have been so severe and sometimes acrimonious that several archaeologists have chosen to radically reorient their research. Ultimately, the U.S. government stepped in with regulations to manage the disposition of Native American human remains and sacred objects. Clearly, the antiquity of the people one studies has little bearing on the degree of ethical controversy that can be generated.

The two major disciplines that converge in ethnohistory both have various codes of professional ethics, but they differ considerably in their emphasis. Most professional organizations in anthropology — including the American Anthropological Association, the Society for American Archaeology, the Society for Applied Anthropology, and the Society of Professional Archaeologists — have had ethical codes for decades. These codes emphasize the relationship between the scholar and the people under study and stress the need to respect informants and avoid compromising their situations politically or otherwise. The fieldwork aspect of cultural anthropology has made anthropologists generally quite sensitive to the potential harm of revealing confidential information. In addition to these ethical statements, there are several books dealing with ethics, ethical dilemmas, and case studies in anthropology (e.g., Appell 1978, Fluehr-Lobban 1991, Rynkiewich and Spradley 1976, Vitelli 1996), with the emphasis again on the relationship between the informant and the anthropologist. The *Anthropology Newsletter,* a publication of the American Anthropological Association, has at various times dedicated regular columns and occasional articles to discussions of ethical dilemmas.

Major historical organizations — such as the American Historical Association, the Oral History Association, and the Society for History in the Federal Government   also have adopted written ethical codes, although they stress different issues. These codes emphasize the historian's relationships to other historians and the discipline, focusing on such issues as plagiarism, discrimination in hiring, and sexual harassment. Occasional statements address the relationship to informants, particularly in the code from the Oral History Association, but this is not a major thrust of the codes as a whole. Few, if any, books are devoted to the ethics of history.

Although occasional articles deal with ethical issues in ethnohistory (e.g., Krech and

Sturtevant 1992:124–127), there are no systematic ethical statements pertaining to the field. The absence of a formal code of ethics in ethnohistory is surprising and a bit disturbing given the emphasis on relativism and respect for other cultures that is a hallmark of the field. In the absence of such a code, we suggest important points that should be addressed when ethnohistorians develop their own code of ethics. These suggestions are largely outgrowths of general principles espoused by the Society for American Archaeology's Ethics Committee (Lynott and Wylie 1995; Kintigh 1996). That committee proposed six principles, here given ethnohistoric interpretations:

- Stewardship: Ethnohistorians are the stewards of one aspect of the past and should match their actions to that responsibility. (This has been discussed in Silverman and Parezo 1992.)
- Accountability: Ethnohistorians have obligations to a variety of interest groups, particularly the people under study and the community of ethnohistorians as a whole.
- Commercialization: Ethnohistorians can capitalize on their skills and knowledge in various manners to earn money but should consider the ethical consequences and obligations entailed.
- Public education and outreach: Ethnohistorians have a duty to pass their information and perspectives on to the world at large.
- Intellectual property: Ethnohistorians, in their dealings with one another and with non-ethnohistorians, must be attentive to proper attribution and use of ideas and information.
- Records and preservation: Ethnohistorians should try to help preserve the data sources that make ethnohistoric research possible.

These principles, originally formulated for archaeological issues, fit the needs of ethnohistory remarkably well.

The issues addressed in these suggestions strike us as logical outgrowths of the underlying assumptions of ethnohistory, as common ground held by the disciplinary ethical codes for anthropology and history, or as concerns that many ethnohistorians currently consider important. By and large, we have excluded issues that have not yet ripened into widespread concerns, such as the question of whether photographs of Native American sacred objects should be restricted in use or even destroyed (Holman 1995; Powers 1996). This and other issues, however, may become important ethical issues in the future. We have attempted to follow Janet Levy's admonition (Lynott and Wylie 1995:86–93) that ethical codes should focus on general principles rather than detailed statements of day-to-day conduct.

The ideas presented in this proposed outline for an ethical code are formally endorsed by no one other than the authors and have no relationship to any professional organization.

An Ethical Code for Ethnohistory: A Proposal

I. *Ethics regarding the relationship between ethnohistorians and the people who form the subject matter of ethnohistory*
    A. Although the individuals who are studied in ethnohistory are usually dead, the ethnic, national, and racial groups from which they came usually are still extant. In the minds of many people, the actions of one individual reflect

upon the group. Consequently, ethnohistorians should make every effort to portray the individuals about whom they write as accurately and fully as is possible and appropriate for the subject being discussed. Presenting individuals as one-dimensional caricatures and victimizing them in insensitive humor are particularly inappropriate. This statement does not mean that an individual or group necessarily should be portrayed in a positive manner or without flaws; rather, it means that individuals and groups should be portrayed in manners consistent with historical evidence and reasonable historical criticism of the sources.

B. Ethnohistorians are obligated to take the cultural attitudes of the descendants of the people they study into consideration. Some research topics are sensitive to these descendants, and each ethnohistorian must consider whether such research is appropriate.

C. When dealing with informants and living members of a group, ethnohistorians must exercise the caution and good judgment necessary in any inter cultural fieldwork. In particular, ethnohistorians should avoid behaviors that could be interpreted as disrespectful, inappropriate, or threatening in that cultural context. Further, they should try to avoid negative impacts on the people being studied, including political, economic, medical, and ecological repercussions. All confidences should be respected, and under no circumstances should information shared in confidence be made public.

D. To the extent feasible, ethnohistorians should make information discovered through their research available to the descendants of the people under study.

II. *Ethics regarding the relationship between ethnohistorians and other ethnohistorians*

A. Every ethnohistorian should treat fellow ethnohistorians as colleagues. This collegial relationship should include offering professional assistance and guidance as requested and within reasonable bounds, as well as avoiding unprofessional accusations and defamation in word or print.

B. For many purposes, students should be considered colleagues. Students who are conducting research are fully as deserving of respect and proper treatment as other colleagues. Their work should not be appropriated by a faculty adviser, and joint authorship should be based on real contributions to the project, not merely on a structural relationship between the student and faculty member or adviser.

C. Plagiarism, defined as the substantial reuse of another person's writing and ideas without proper attribution, is unethical and unacceptable. This definition includes not only the usual legal definition of plagiarism, which focuses on written passages, but also the appropriation of another's ideas. This principle recognizes that ideas can be independently conceived, and it places the obligation to avoid theft of ideas primarily on each author.

D. In keeping with the relativistic ideals of ethnohistory, all prejudice, bias, and discrimination on the basis of race, ethnicity, gender, sexual preference, or age are unacceptable in the practice of ethnohistory.

III. *Ethics regarding the relationship between ethnohistorians and their discipline*

A. In their professional activities, ethnohistorians must recognize that their actions reflect upon the discipline as a whole. They must therefore attempt to carry out professional activities in a manner consistent with the aims and well-being of the discipline as a whole.

B. Ethnohistorians collecting original information not available in archives or other professionally accessible locations should strive as appropriate to make those materials available to other scholars. This is particularly true for oral accounts, since it is important that the information in them be available for assessment by the discipline. It also is imperative that original information be preserved for future generations of scholars to consult. Care must be taken when oral accounts include sensitive information that could place an informant at risk of retribution or negative consequences; in such a case, the ethnohistorian's first duty is to the informant.

C. To the extent possible, ethnohistorians are obligated to assist in the preservation of the physical items that constitute most of the database of ethnohistory. This includes careful handling and use of documents and related items, efforts to improve storage and materials conservation of decaying documents and related items, participation in projects to copy or otherwise preserve documents and related items, and efforts to preserve historic sites. In some cases, preservation is beyond the expertise or reasonable efforts of an ethnohistorian; in such a case, it is desirable for the ethnohistorian to bring the case to the attention of a preservation specialist.

D. An ethnohistorian should be willing to offer reasonable service to the discipline. This includes reviewing with professional objectivity articles and books submitted for publication, serving in professional organizations, and assisting students and others in research.

IV. *Ethics regarding the relationship between ethnohistorians and the public*

A. Ethnohistorians should bring the results of their research to the attention of the public whenever possible. This could include interviews with the press, press releases, participation in documentary projects for the media, the writing of publications for the popular press, and public speaking engagements. Most members of the public are unaware that the field of ethnohistory exists, and favorable publicity of this sort furthers the aims of the profession while educating the public.

B. In dealing with the press and media, ethnohistorians should be careful to encourage coverage that represents the facts of ethnohistory with accuracy and balance. Some journalists focus on the sensational or that which supports their preconceptions, and it is the ethnohistorian's duty to educate journalists in the broader context of the societies they study.

C. When serving as expert witnesses, such as in land-claims cases, ethnohistorians have a strong obligation to follow the highest standards of ethical conduct. This includes presenting accurate information to the best of one's knowledge, providing fair assessments of the limits of one's knowledge, and treating witnesses with contrary views respectfully. In this area of activity, it is especially important to avoid bias and prejudice of any kind.

V. *Other ethical considerations*

A. Interdisciplinary research is often difficult, partly because a practitioner must meet the expectations of more than one discipline, and this is true for ethnohistorians in terms of ethics. The ethical expectations for an ethnohistorian include both those for ethnohistory and those for the ethnohistorian's broader discipline. These ethical guidelines for ethnohistorians are designed to augment, not to supersede, ethical codes in anthropology, history, or other disciplines with which ethnohistorians are affiliated.

B. As an interdisciplinary field, ethnohistory has obligations to the ethical priorities of all the disciplines that bear upon it. Its ethical system therefore should be the sum of the ethical systems of the disciplines that contribute to it, not merely the overlap. Consequently, in making decisions, ethnohistorians should consider ethical guidelines in all the disciplines that bear on ethnohistory.

References Cited

Ackerman, Charles. 1976. The rural demography of medieval England. *Ethnohistory* 23 (2): 105–116.

Acton, [Lord] John Emerich Edward Dalberg. 1907. *Historical Essays and Studies*. London: Macmillan and Co.

Adams, Percy G. 1962. *Travelers and Travel Liars, 1660–1800*. Berkeley: University of California Press.

Adams, William H., ed. 1973. Symposium on ethnoarchaeology. *Ethnohistory* 20 (4), entire issue.

Afable, Patricia O., and Madison S. Beeler. 1996. Place-names. In *Languages,* vol. 17 of the *Handbook of North American Indians,* edited by Ives Goddard, 185–199. Washington, D.C.: Smithsonian Institution.

Alford, Richard D. 1988. *Naming and Identity: A Cross-Cultural Study of Personal Naming Practices*. New Haven: Human Relations Area Files Press.

Allan, Keith, and Kate Burridge. 1991. *Euphemism and Dysphemism: Language Used as Shield and Weapon*. New York: Oxford University Press.

Allen, Barbara, and Lynwood Montell. 1981. *From Memory to History: Using Oral Sources in Local Historical Research*. Nashville, Tenn.: American Association for State and Local History.

Alotta, Robert I. 1994. *Signposts and Settlers: The History of Place Names West of the Rockies*. Chicago: Bonus Books, Inc.

Anawalt, Patricia Rieff, and Frances F. Berdan. 1994. Mexican textiles. *National Geographic Society Research and Exploration* 10 (3):342–353.

Anaya Monroy, Fernando. 1965. *La toponimia indígena en la historia y la cultura de Tlaxcala*. Universidad Nacional Autónoma de México: Instituto de Investigaciones Históricas, Serie de Cultura Nahuatl, monografía 4.

Anderson, Arthur J. O., Frances Berdan, and James Lockhart. 1976. *Beyond the Codices: The Nahua View of Colonial Mexico*. Los Angeles and Berkeley: University of California Press.

Anderson, Atholl. 1989. *Prodigious Birds: Moas and Moa-eating in Prehistoric New Zealand*. Cambridge: Cambridge University Press.

Anonymous. n.d. [1658]. *Relation de ce qui s'est passé . . . en la Nouvelle France, és années 1657 and 1658*. Paris: Sebastien Cramoisy et Gabriel Cramoisy. Reprinted and translated in Thwaites 1899.

Appell, G. N. 1978. *Ethical Dilemmas in Anthropological Inquiry: A Case Book*. Waltham, Mass.: Crossroads Press/African Studies Association, Brandeis University.

Arens, William. 1979. *The Man-Eating Myth.* New York: Oxford University Press.

Ash, Lee, and William G. Miller. 1985. *Subject Collections: A Guide to Special Book Collections and Subject Emphases as Reported by University, College, Public, and Special Libraries and Museums in the United States and Canada.* New York: Bowker.

Ashley, Leonard R. N. 1980. If your wife isn't happy in the Baker's Arms: The onomastics of English pubs. In E. Wallace McMullen (ed.), *Pubs, Place-Names, and Patronymics,* pp. 17–61. Teaneck, N.J.: Publications of the Names Institute, Fairleigh Dickinson University, no. 1.

Aveni, Anthony F. 1989. *Empires of Time: Calendars, Clocks, and Cultures.* New York: Basic Books.

Aydelotte, William O. 1971. *Quantification in History.* Reading, Massachusetts: Addison-Wesley Publishing Co.

Baerreis, David A. 1961. The ethnohistoric approach and archaeology. *Ethnohistory* 8 (1): 49–77.

Bagrow, Leo. 1985. *History of Cartography.* Chicago: Precedent.

Baird, Ellen T. 1993. *The Drawings of Sahagún's Primeros Memoriales: Structure and Style.* Norman: University of Oklahoma Press.

Bandelier, Adolph F. E. 1890. Final report of investigations among the Indians of the southwestern United States, carried on mainly in the years from 1880–1885. *Papers of the Archaeological Institute of America, American Series* 3.

Barber, Russell J., and Frances F. Berdan. n.d. A content analysis of *Ethnohistory,* 1954–1995. Forthcoming.

Bartlett, Jere Whiting. 1968. *Proverbs, Sentences, and Proverbial Phrases from English Writings, Mainly Before 1500.* Cambridge, Mass.: Belknap Press / Harvard University Press.

Bartlett, John Russell. 1989. Reprint. *The Dictionary of Americanisms.* New York: Crescent Books. Original edition, New York: Bartlett and Welford, New York, 1849.

Baum, Willa K. 1977. *Transcribing and Editing Oral History.* Nashville, Tenn.: American Association for State and Local History.

Beale, Paul, ed. 1989. *A Concise Dictionary of Slang and Unconventional English.* New York: Macmillan.

Beck, Jane C. 1972. The great beaver: A prehistoric memory? *Ethnohistory* 19 (2):109–122.

Benes, Peter, ed. 1990. *Early American Probate Inventories.* Annual Proceedings of the Dublin Seminar for New England Folklife, 1987. Boston: Boston University Publications.

Berdan, Frances F. 1982. *The Aztecs of Central Mexico: An Imperial Society.* New York: Harcourt Brace.

———. 1992. Glyphic conventions of the Codex Mendoza. In Berdan and Anawalt, pp. 93–102.

Berdan, Frances, and Patricia Rieff Anawalt, eds. 1992. *The Codex Mendoza.* 4 vols. Berkeley: University of California Press.

Beringer, Richard E. 1978. *Historical Analysis: Contemporary Approaches to Clio's Craft.* New York: John Wiley and Sons.

Bernard, H. Russell. 1994. 2d ed. *Research Methods in Anthropology.* Thousand Oaks, Calif.: Sage Publications.

Blackburn, Simon. 1994. *The Oxford Dictionary of Philosophy.* Oxford: Oxford University Press.

Blackman, Margaret B. 1986. Visual ethnohistory: Photographs in the study of culture history. In Dennis Wiedman (ed.), *Ethnohistory: A Researcher's Guide*. Studies in Third World Societies, no. 35. Williamsburg, Va.: College of William and Mary.

Blu, Karen I. 1994. "Reading back" to find community: Lumbee ethnohistory. In Raymond J. DeMallie and Alfonso Ortiz (eds.), *North American Indian Anthropology: Essays on Society and Culture*, pp. 278–295. Norman: University of Oklahoma Press.

Boone, Elizabeth Hill. 1992. The Aztec pictorial history of the Codex Mendoza: Appendix A. In Berdan and Anawalt, pp. 35–54, 152–153.

——. 1994. Introduction: Writing and recorded knowledge. In Boone and Mignolo, pp. 3–26.

Boone, Elizabeth Hill, and Walter D. Mignolo, eds. 1994. *Writing Without Words*. Durham: Duke University Press.

Boorstin, Daniel J. 1983. *The Discoverers: A History of Man's Search to Know His World and Himself*. New York: Random House.

Boxer, C. R. 1952. *Salvador de Sa and the Struggle for Brazil and Angola, 1602–1686*. London: University of London Press.

Boyer, Ruth McDonald, and Narcissus Duffy Gayton. 1992. *Apache Mothers and Daughters: Four Generations of a Family*. Norman: University of Oklahoma Press.

Brasser, Ted J. 1975. *A Basketful of Indian Culture Change*. National Museum of Man, Mercury Series, no. 22. Ottawa: Canadian Ethnology Service.

Bray, Warwick. 1993. Crop plants and cannibals: Early European impressions of the New World. In Warwick Bray (ed.), *The Meeting of Two Worlds*, pp. 289–326. Oxford: Oxford University Press.

Brewer, William H. 1974. *Up and Down California in 1860–1864*. Edited by Frances P. Farquhar. Berkeley: University of California Press.

Bricker, Charles. 1968. *Landmarks of Mapmaking*. Amsterdam: Elsevier.

Briquet, Charles Moïse. 1968. *Les filigranes*. Amsterdam, Netherlands: Paper Publications Society.

Brown, Marley R., III. 1973. The use of oral and documentary sources in historical archaeology: Ethnohistory of the Mott Farm. *Ethnohistory* 20 (4):347–360.

——. 1988. The behavioral context of probate inventories: An example from Plymouth Colony. In Mary C. Beaudry (ed.), *Documentary Archaeology in the New World*, Cambridge: Cambridge University Press, pp. 79–82.

Bucher, Bernadette. 1981. *Icon and Conquest: A Structural Analysis of the Illustrations of de Bry's Great Voyages*. Chicago: University of Chicago Press.

Butzer, Karl W., and Barbara J. Williams. 1992. Addendum: Three indigenous maps from New Spain dated ca. 1580. *Annals of the Association of American Geographers* 82 (3):536–542.

Cabeza de Vaca, Alvar Núñez. [1542] 1961. *Adventures in the Unknown Interior of America*. Translated and edited by Cyclone Covey. New York: Collier Books.

Cahill, T. A., B. Kusko, and R. N. Schwab. 1981. Analysis of inks and papers in historical documents through external beam PIXE techniques. *Nuclear Instruments and Methods* 181:205–208.

Canfield, Chauncey L., ed. 1992. *Diary of a Forty-Niner*. New York: Turtle Point Press.

Carmack, Robert M. 1972. Ethnohistory: A review of its development, definitions, methods, and aims. *Annual Review of Anthropology* 1:227–246.

Carrington, David K., and Richard R. Stephenson. 1978. *Map Collections in the United States and Canada: A Directory*. New York: Special Libraries Association.

Cartier, Jacques. [1545] 1924. *The Voyages of Jacques Cartier.* Edited and translated by Henry P. Biggar. Ottawa. Includes Cartier's *Brief Récit.*

Caso, Alfonso. 1971. Calendrical systems of central Mexico. *Handbook of Middle American Indians* 10:333–348. Austin: University of Texas Press.

Casselberry, S. E. 1974. Further refinement of formulae for determining population from floor area. *World Archaeology* 6 (1):118–122.

Cassidy, Frederic G. 1985. From Indian to French to English: Some Wisconsin place-names. *Names* 33 (1–2):51–57.

Cassidy, Frederic G., ed. 1985–. *Dictionary of American Regional English (DARE).* Cambridge, Mass.: Belknap Press/Harvard University Press. (As of mid-1997, the first three volumes [A–O] have been published; publication dates for the final two volumes have not yet been set.)

Chamberlain, Walter. 1978. *Manual of Woodcut Printmaking and Related Techniques.* New York: Charles Scribner's Sons.

Champlain, Samuel de. 1907. Reprint. *Voyages of Samuel de Champlain, 1604–1618.* Edited and translated by W. L. Grant. New York: Charles Scribner's Sons. Originally published in two installments, 1613 and 1619.

Charlton, Thomas H. 1981. Archaeology, ethnohistory, and ethnology: Interpretive interfaces. *Advances in Archaeological Method and Theory* 4:129–176.

Clappe, Louisa Amelia Knapp Smith (Dame Shirley). 1992. *The Shirley Letters: Being Letters Written in 1851–1852 from the California Mines.* Salt Lake City: Peregrine Smith Books.

Clark, G. Kitson. 1967. *The Critical Historian.* New York: Basic Books.

Cline, Howard F. 1972. Introduction: Reflections on ethnohistory. *Handbook of Middle American Indians* 12:3–16. Austin: University of Texas Press.

Cohen, David William. 1989. The undefining of oral tradition. *Ethnohistory* 36:9–18.

Colden, Cadwallader. 1747. *The History of the Five Indian Nations of Canada.* London: T. Osborne. Reprint, Toronto: Coles Canadiana, 1972.

Coles, John. 1973. *Archaeology by Experiment.* New York: Charles Scribner's Sons.

Collingwood, R. G. 1946. *The Idea of History.* Oxford: Clarendon Press.

———. 1965. *Essays in the Philosophy of History.* Edited and with an introduction by William Debbins. Austin: University of Texas Press.

Collins, Larry, and Dominique La Pierre. 1975. *Freedom at Midnight.* New York: Simon and Schuster.

Cook, Sherburne F. 1946. Human sacrifice and warfare as factors in the demography of precolonial Mexico. *Human Biology* 18:81–102.

———. 1949. Soil erosion and population in central Mexico. *Ibero-Americana* 34.

———. 1973a. Interracial warfare and population decline among the New England Indians. *Ethnohistory* 20 (1):1–24.

———. 1973b. The significance of disease in the extinction of the New England Indians. *Human Biology* 45 (3):485–508.

Cook, Sherburne F., and Robert F. Heizer. 1965. The quantitative approach to the relationship between population and settlement size. *Contributions to the University of California Archaeological Research Facility* 64.

Cornwall, Ian W. 1958. *Soils for the Archaeologist.* New York: Macmillan.

Cortés, Hernando. 1971. Reprint. *Letters from Mexico.* Translated and edited by Anthony R. Pagden. New York: Grossman Publishers.

Cullom, Davis, Kathryn Black, and Kay McLean. *Oral History: From Tape to Type.* Chicago: American Library Association.

Cumming, William P. 1974. *British Maps of Colonial America.* Chicago: University of Chicago Press.

Dalzell, Tom. 1996. *Flappers 2 Rappers.* Springfield, Mass.: Merriam-Webster.

Daniels, Peter T., and William Bright. 1995. *The World's Writing Systems.* Oxford: Oxford University Press.

Darcy, R., and Richard C. Rohrs. 1995. *A Guide to Quantitative History.* New York: Praeger.

Davidson, Basil, ed. 1964. *The African Past: Chronicles from Antiquity to Modern Times.* Boston: Atlantic Monthly Press/Little, Brown and Co.

Day, Gordon M. 1972. Oral tradition as complement. *Ethnohistory* 19 (2):99–108.

de Bry, Theodor, ed. 1591. *Brevis narratio eorum quae in Florida Americae provicia Gallis acciderunt.* Cited in Sturtevant 1968.

de Castañeda, Pedro. 1933. Relation of a journey to Cibola undertaken in 1540. In George Peter Winship (editor and translator), *The Journey of Francisco Vasquez de Coronado, 1540–1542.* San Francisco, Calif.: Grabhorn Press.

de Crèvecoeur, J. Hector St. John. [1782] 1957. *Letters from an American Farmer.* New York: Dutton.

Deetz, James D. F. 1965. The dynamics of stylistic change in Arikara ceramics. *Illinois Studies in Anthropology* 4. Urbana: University of Illinois Press.

DeMallie, Raymond J. 1993. "These have no ears": Narrative and the ethnohistorical method. *Ethnohistory* 40 (4):515–538.

Densmore, Christopher. 1988. Archival reference tools. In Larsen 1988:55–64, 143–146.

de Sola Pool, David. 1951. *Portraits Etched in Stone: Early Jewish Settlers, 1682–1831.* New York: Columbia University Press.

DeWitt, Donald L. 1994. *Guides to Archives and Manuscript Collections in the United States: An Annotated Bibliography.* Westport, Conn.: Greenwood Press.

d'Hertefelt, M., and A. Coupez. 1964. La royauté sacrée de l'ancien Rwanda. *Musée Royale de l'Afrique Centrale, Archives d'Anthropologie* 52.

Díaz del Castillo, Bernal. 1963. Reprint. *The Conquest of New Spain.* Translated by J. M. Cohen. Baltimore: Penguin Books.

Dickason, Olive. 1977. The concept of *l'homme sauvage* and early French colonialism in the Americas. *Revue Française d'histoire d'Outre-Mer* 64:5–32.

Dickson, Paul. 1986. *Names.* New York: Delacorte Press.

Dilke, O. A. W. 1987. Roman large-scale mapping in the early empire. In J. B. Harley and David Woodward (eds.), *The History of Cartography* 1:212–258. Chicago: University of Chicago Press.

Dillard, J. L. 1971. The West African day-names in Nova Scotia. *Names* 19 (4):257–261.

———. 1976. *Black Names.* The Hague: Mouton.

Dincauze, Dena F. 1976. The Neville site: Eight thousand years at Amoskeag, Manchester, New Hampshire. Peabody Museum, Harvard University, monograph no. 4.

Dolley, Reginald Hugh Michael. 1964. *Anglo-Saxon Pennies.* London: Trustees of the British Museum.

Dorson, Richard M. 1961. Ethnohistory and ethnic folklore. *Ethnohistory* 8 (1):12–30.

Drake, Michael. 1972. Perspectives in historical demography. In G. A. Harrison and A. J. Boyce (eds.), *The Structure of Human Populations,* pp. 57–72. Oxford: Clarendon Press/Oxford University Press.

Dunkling, Leslie. 1990. *A Dictionary of Epithets and Terms of Address*. London: Routledge.

Dwight, Timothy. 1969. Reprint. *Travels in New England and New York*. 4 vols. Cambridge, Mass.: Belknap Press / Harvard University Press. Original edition, New Haven, Conn.: S. Converse, 1821–22.

Dykerhoff, Ursula. 1984. Mexican toponyms as a source in regional ethnohistory. In H. R. Harvey and Hanns J. Prem (eds.), *Explorations in Ethnohistory: Indians of Central Mexico in the Sixteenth Century*, pp. 229–252. Albuquerque: University of New Mexico Press.

Eggan, Fred. 1954. Social anthropology and the method of controlled comparison. *American Anthropologist* 56:743–763.

Elkins, Stanley. 1959. *Slavery*. Chicago: University of Chicago Press.

Evans, John G. 1978. *An Introduction to Environmental Archaeology*. Ithaca, N.Y.: Cornell University Press.

Evans-Pritchard, E. E. 1965. *The Nuer*. London: Oxford University Press.

Fagan, Brian. 1985. *In the Beginning*. Boston: Little, Brown and Co.

Farmer, J. S., and W. E. Henley. 1970. Reprint. *Slang and Its Analogues*. New York: Arno Press. Originally published by subscription as seven volumes between 1890 and 1904.

Farrer, James Anson. 1907. *Literary Forgeries*. London: Longman and Green.

Feder, Kenneth L. 1994. *A Village of Outcasts: Historical Archaeology and Documentary Research at the Lighthouse Site*. Mountain View, Calif.: Mayfield Publishing Co.

Fenton, William N. 1951. Locality as a basic factor in the development of Iroquois social structure. *Bureau of American Ethnology Bulletin* 149 (3):35–54.

———. 1953. The Iroquois Eagle Dance, an offshoot of the Calumet Dance. *Bureau of American Ethnology Bulletin* 156.

Fentress, James, and Chris Wickham. 1992. *Social Memory*. Oxford: Blackwell Press.

Floud, Roderick. 1979. 2d ed. *An Introduction to Quantitative Methods for Historians*. London: Methuen.

Fluehr-Lobban, Carolyn, ed. 1991. *Ethics and the Profession of Anthropology: Dialogue for a New Era*. Philadelphia: University of Pennsylvania Press.

Forsyth, Donald. 1985. Three cheers for Hans Staden: The case for Brazilian cannibalism. *Ethnohistory* 32 (1):17–36.

Foster, Janet, and Julia Sheppard. 1989. 2d ed. *British Archives: A Guide to Archive Resources in the United Kingdom*. New York: Stockton Press.

Foucault, Michel. [1961] 1970. *Madness and Civilization: A History of Insanity in the Age of Reason*. London: Tavistock Press. Translated from the French by Richard Howard.

Fraser, Douglas. 1971. The discovery of primitive art. In Charlotte M. Otten (ed.), *Anthropology and Art*, pp. 20–36. Garden City, N.Y.: Natural History Press.

French, David H., and Katherine S. French. 1996. Personal names. In *Languages*, vol. 17 of *The Handbook of North American Indians*, edited by Ives Goddard, pp. 200–221. Washington, D.C.: Smithsonian Institution.

Frobisher, Martin. [1578] 1867. *The Three Voyages of Martin Frobisher*. London: Hakluyt Society.

Galloway, Patricia. 1991. The archaeology of ethnohistorical narrative. In David Hurst Thomas (ed.), *The Spanish Borderlands in Pan-American Perspective*, vol. 3 of *Columbian Consequences*, pp. 453–469. Washington, D.C.: Smithsonian Institution Press.

Gardner, David C., and Grace Joely Beatty. 1980. *Dissertation Proposal Guidebook: How to Prepare a Research Proposal and Get It Accepted*. Springfield, Ill.: Thomas Publishers.

Gaur, Albertine. 1992. *A History of Writing.* New York: Cross River Press.

Gelb, I. J. 1963. 2d ed. *A Study of Writing.* Chicago: University of Chicago Press.

Genovese, Eugene D. 1976. *Roll, Jordan, Roll: The World the Slaves Made.* New York: Vintage Books.

Ginsberg, Arlin J. 1977. The franchise in seventeenth-century Massachusetts. *William and Mary Quarterly* 34 (3):446–458.

Glass, John B. 1964. *Catálogo de la colección de códices.* Mexico City: Museo Nacional de Antropología.

Glassner, Martin Ira. 1974. Population figures for Mandan Indians. *The Indian Historian* 7:41–46.

Gottschalk, Louis. 1958. *Understanding History: A Primer of Historical Method.* New York: Alfred A. Knopf.

Gough, Barry. 1982. New light on Haida chiefship: The case of Edenshaw, 1850–1853. *Ethnohistory* 29 (2):131–139.

Gracy, David B., II. 1988. What every researcher should know about archives. In Larsen 1988:18–33.

Grafton, Anthony. 1992. *New Worlds, Ancient Texts: The Power of Tradition and the Shock of Discovery.* Cambridge, Mass.: Belknap Press/Harvard University Press.

Green, Jonathon. 1996. *Chasing the Sun: Dictionary Makers and the Dictionaries They Made.* New York: Henry Holt and Company.

Grose, Captain Francis. [1785] 1963. *A Classical Dictionary of the Vulgar Tongue.* New York: Barnes and Noble.

Gudde, Erwin G. 1969. *California Placenames: The Origin and Etymology of Current Geographic Names.* Berkeley: University of California Press.

Guide to the Archives of International Organizations. 1984–. Paris: UNESCO.

Guillet de St. Georges, Georges. [1705] 1970. *The Gentleman's Dictionary in Three Parts: The Art of Riding the Great Horse, The Military Art, and The Art of Navigation.* Los Angeles: Sherwin and Freutel.

Hammer, Kenneth. 1976. *Men with Custer.* Fort Collins, Colo.: Old Army Press.

Hanks, Patrick, and Flavia Hodges. 1988. *A Dictionary of Surnames.* Oxford: Oxford University Press.

———. 1990. *A Dictionary of First Names.* Oxford: Oxford University Press.

Hanks, William F. 1989. Word and image in a semiotic perspective. In William P. Hanks and Don S. Rice (eds.), *Word and Image in Maya Culture,* pp. 8–21. Salt Lake City: University of Utah Press.

Hardorff, Richard G., ed. 1991. *Lakota Recollections of the Custer Fight: New Sources of Indian-Military History.* Spokane, Wash.: Arthur H. Clark Co.

Harley, J. Brian. 1992. Rereading the maps of the Columbian encounter. *Annals of the Association of American Geographers* 82 (3):522–536.

Harris, Marvin. 1968. *The Rise of Anthropological Theory: A History of Theories of Culture.* New York: Thomas Y. Crowell.

Harrison, Wilson R. 1963. *Forgery Detection: A Practical Guide.* New York: Praeger.

———. 1981. *Suspect Documents: Their Scientific Examination.* Chicago: Nelson-Hall.

Harvey, P. D. A. 1987. Local and regional cartography in medieval Europe. In J. B. Harley and David Woodward (eds.), *The History of Cartography* 1:464–501. Chicago: University of Chicago Press.

Haselden, Reginald Betti. 1935. *Scientific Aids for the Study of Manuscripts*. Oxford: Oxford University Press/Bibliographic Society.

Hassan, Fakri A. 1978. Demographic archaeology. *Advances in Archaeological Method and Theory* 1:118–122.

Havlice, Patricia Pate. 1985. *Oral History: A Reference Guide and Bibliography*. Jefferson, N.C.: McFarland and Co.

Heawood, Edward. 1950. *Watermarks, Mainly of the 17th and 18th Centuries*. Hilversum, Netherlands: Paper Publications Society.

Hedges, William. 1964. *The Diary of William Hedges, Esq., During His Agency in Bengal; As Well As on His Voyage Out and Return Overland (1681–1687)*. 3 vols. Transcribed with notes by R. Barlow, esq. New York: Burt Franklin.

Heidegger, Martin. 1977. *Basic Writings*. Edited by D. F. Krell. New York: Harper.

Heller, Louis, Alexander Humez, and Malcah Dror. 1983. *The Private Lives of English Words*. London: Routledge and Kegan Paul.

Henige, David. 1982. *Oral Historiography*. London: Longman.

Hennepin, Louis. 1698. *A New Discovery of a Vast Country in America*. 2 vols. London: M. Bentley, J. Tonson, H. Benwick, T. Godwin, and S. Manship. Reprint, Toronto: Coles Publishing Co., 1974.

Herring, D. Ann. 1994. "There were young people and old people and babies dying every week": The 1918–1919 influenza epidemic at Norway House. *Ethnohistory* 41 (4):513–538.

Higman, Barry W. 1986. Plantation maps as sources for the study of West Indian ethnohistory. In Dennis Wiedman (ed.), *Ethnohistory: A Researcher's Guide*, pp. 107–135. Studies in Third World Societies, no. 35. Williamsburg, Va.: College of William and Mary.

Hilton, Ordway. 1982. Rev. ed. *Scientific Examination of Questioned Documents*. New York: Elsevir Press.

———. 1991. *Detecting and Deciphering Erased Pencil Writing*. Springfield, Mass.: Charles C. Thomas.

Hodges, Henry. 1976. *Artifacts: An Introduction to Early Materials and Technology*. London: John Baker.

Hofling, Charles K. 1981. *Custer and the Little Big Horn: A Psychobiographical Inquiry*. Detroit: Wayne State University Press.

Holliday, Vance T., ed. 1992. *Soils in Archaeology: Landscape Evolution and Human Occupation*. Washington, D.C.: Smithsonian Institution Press.

Hollingsworth, T. H. 1969. *Historical Demography*. Ithaca, N.Y.: Cornell University Press.

Holman, Nigel. 1995. Sensitive Native American photographic images: Stepping back to look at the big picture. *Center for Museum Studies, Smithsonian Institution, Bulletin* 3 (2):1–6.

Holsti, Ole R. 1969. *Content Analysis for the Social Sciences and Humanities*. Reading, Mass.: Addison-Wesley.

Honour, Hugh. 1975. *The European Vision of America*. Cleveland: Cleveland Museum of Art.

Hook, J. N. 1982. *Family Names: How Our Surnames Came to America*. New York: Macmillan.

Horn, W. F., A. L. Moredock, and J. Fulton. 1945. *The Horn Papers: Early Westward Movement on the Monongahela and Upper Ohio, 1765–1795*. 3 vols. Waynesburg, Pa.: Greene County Historical Society.

Huden, John. 1962. *Indian Place Names of New England*. Contributions from the Museum of the American Indian, Heye Foundation, vol. 18. New York: Museum of the American Indian/Heye Foundation.

Hudson, Charles. 1966. Folk history and ethnohistory. *Ethnohistory* 13 (1):52–71.

Hunt, George T. 1940. *The Wars of the Iroquois.* Madison: University of Wisconsin Press.

Huntington, Ellsworth. 1915. *Civilization and Climate.* New Haven, Conn.: Yale University Press.

———. 1945. *Mainsprings of Civilization.* New York: John Wiley and Sons.

Ingersoll, Daniel, John E. Yellen, and William MacDonald, eds. 1977. *Experimental Archeology.* New York: Columbia University Press.

Jackson, Donald. 1981. *The Story of Writing.* New York: Taplinger.

Jaenen, Cornelius J. 1983. Miscegenation in eighteenth century New France. In Barry Gough and Laird Christie (eds.), *New Dimensions in Ethnohistory: Papers of the Second Laurier Conference on Ethnohistory and Ethnology,* Canadian Museum of Civilization, Mercury Series, no. 120, pp. 79–116.

Jaubert, Alain. 1989. *Making People Disappear: An Amazing Account of Photographic Deception.* Washington, D.C.: Pergamon Brassey's.

Jean, Georges. 1987. *Writing: The Story of Alphabets and Scripts.* New York: Harry N. Abrams, Inc.

Jenkins, David. 1995. Temporal processes and synchronic relations: Age and rank in the central Andes. *Ethnohistory* 42 (1):91–131.

Jennings, Francis. 1982. A growing partnership: Historians, anthropologists, and American Indian history. *Ethnohistory* 29 (1):21–42.

———, ed. 1976–. *American Indian Bibliographic Series.* Bloomington: Indiana University Press (for the Newberry Library).

Jesuit Relations and Related Documents (*JR*). See Reuben Gold Thwaites, ed.

Johnson, Allen W. 1978. *Quantification in Cultural Anthropology: An Introduction to Research Design.* Stanford, Calif.: Stanford University Press.

Johnson, John. 1988. *Chumash Social Organization: An Ethnohistoric Perspective.* Ph.D. diss. Department of Anthropology, University of California, Santa Barbara.

Johnson, Samuel. 1755. *A Dictionary of the English Language.* London: printed for W. Strahan, J. and P. Knapton, C. Hitch, etc.

Kaganoff, Benzion C. 1977. *A Dictionary of Jewish Names and Their History.* New York: Schocken Books.

Kaminkow, Marion J., ed. 1975. *United States Local Histories in the Library of Congress: A Bibliography.* 4 vols. Baltimore, Md.: Magna Carta Books.

Katzer, Jeffrey, Kenneth H. Cook, and Wayne W. Crouch. 1991. 3d ed. *Evaluating Information: A Guide for Users of Social Science Research.* New York: McGraw-Hill.

Kay, Jeanne. 1984. The fur trade and Native American population growth. *Ethnohistory* 31 (4):265–288.

Kelly, William. 1852. *A Stroll through the Diggings of California.* London: Bookcase Edition. Reprint, Oakland, Calif.: Biobooks, 1950.

Kense, Francois J. 1990. Archaeology in Anglophone Africa. In Peter Robertshaw (ed.), *A History of African Archaeology,* pp. 135–154. London: James Currey.

King, Donald. 1960. *Samplers.* London: Her Majesty's Stationery Office/Victoria and Albert Museum.

Kintigh, Keith W. 1996. SAA principles of archaeological ethics. *Society for American Archaeology Bulletin* 14 (3):5, 17.

Kirch, Patrick Vinton. 1985. *Feathered Gods and Fishhooks*. Honolulu: University of Hawaii Press.

Kirkham, E. Kay. 1965. Rev. ed. *How to Read the Handwriting and Records of Early America*. Salt Lake City: Deseret Books.

Klein, Richard G., and Kathryn Cruz-Uribe. 1984. *The Analysis of Animal Bones from Archaeological Sites*. Chicago: University of Chicago Press.

Krech, Shepard, III. 1991. The state of ethnohistory. *Annual Review of Anthropology* 20:345–375.

Krech, Shepard, III, and William C. Sturtevant. 1992. The future uses of the anthropological record. In Silverman and Parezo 1992:119–127.

Krim, Arthur J. 1980. Acculturation of the New England landscape: Native and English toponymy of eastern Massachusetts. In Peter Benes (ed.), *New England Prospect: Maps, Place Names, and the Historical Landscape*, pp. 69–88. Boston: Boston University Publications.

Lafitau, Joseph François. 1724. *Moeurs des sauvages ameriquains, comparées aux moeurs des premiers temps*. 2 vols. Paris: Saugrain l'aîné et Charles Estienne Hochereau.

Langlois, Charles V., and Charles Seignobos. 1898. *Introduction to the Science of History*. London: Duckworth and Co.

Lantis, Margaret. 1970. *Ethnohistory in Southwest Alaska and the Southern Yukon*. Lexington: University Press of Kentucky.

Large, Arlen J. 1995. All in the family: The in-house honorifics of Lewis and Clark. *Names* 42 (4):269–277.

Larsen, John C., ed. 1988. *Researcher's Guide to Archives and Regional History Sources*. Hamden, Conn.: Library Professional Publications.

Lawson, Edwin D. 1987. *Personal Names and Naming: An Annotated Bibliography*. New York: Greenwood Press.

——. 1995. *More Names and Naming: An Annotated Bibliography*. Westport, Conn.: Greenwood Publishing Group.

Le Blanc, Steven. 1971. An addition to Narroll's suggested floor area and settlement population relationship. *American Antiquity* 36 (2):210–211.

Leitch, Vincent B. 1983. *Deconstructive Criticism: An Advanced Introduction*. New York: Columbia University Press.

le Jeune, Paul. 1658. *Relation de ce qui s'est passé . . . en la Nouvelle France, és années 1656 & 1657*. Paris: Sebastien Cramoisy et Gabriel Cramoisy. Reprinted and translated in Thwaites 1899, vols. 43–44.

le Moine, Simon. 1654. *Relation de ce qui s'est passé . . . en la Nouvelle France, és années 1653 & 1654*. Paris: Sebastien Cramoisy et Gabriel Cramoisy. Reprinted and translated in Thwaites 1899, vol. 41.

Lenaghan, R. T., ed. 1967. *Caxton's Aesop*. Cambridge, Mass.: Harvard University Press.

le Quens, Simon. 1656. *Relation de ce qui s'est passé . . . en la Nouvelle France, és années 1655 & 1656*. Paris: Sebastien Cramoisy et Gabriel Cramoisy. Reprinted and translated in Thwaites 1899, vol. 42.

Lestringant, Frank. 1994. Reprint. *Mapping the Renaissance World: The Geographical Imagination in the Age of Discovery*. Translated from French by David Fausett. Berkeley: University of California Press. Originally published in French as *L'atelier du cosmographe* in 1991.

Levenson, Jay A., ed. 1991. *Circa 1492: Art in the Age of Exploration*. New Haven, Conn.: Yale University Press.

Levine, Robert A. 1973. Research design in anthropological field work. In Raoul Narroll and Ronald Cohen (eds.), *A Handbook of Method in Cultural Anthropology*, pp. 183–195. New York: Columbia University Press.

Library of Congress, Descriptive Cataloging Division. 1962–. *National Union Catalog of Manuscript Collections*. Hamden, Conn.: Shoestring Press.

Lighter, J. E., ed. 1994–. *Historical Dictionary of American Slang*. 4 vols. New York: Random House. (Only vol. 1 [A–G] has been published to date.)

Limbrey, Susan. 1975. *Soil Science and Archaeology*. New York: Academic Press.

Linné, Sigvald. 1948. *El valle y la ciudad de México en 1550*. Statens Etnografiska Museum, New Series, no. 9. Stockholm: Esselte.

Little, Elizabeth. 1980. Probate Records of Nantucket Indians. Nantucket Algonquian Studies, Archaeology Department, Nantucket Historical Association, no. 2.

Locke, J. Courtney, ed. 1930. *The First Englishmen in India: Letters and Narratives of Sundry Elizabethans*. London: Routledge and Sons.

Lockhart, James. 1992. *The Nahuas after the Conquest*. Stanford, Calif.: Stanford University Press.

Long, J[oseph]. 1791. *Voyages and Travels of an Indian Interpreter and Trader*. London: private printing. Reprint, Toronto: Coles Canadiana, 1971.

Lowery, Woodbury. 1911. *The Spanish Settlements Within the Present Limits of the United States: Florida, 1562–1574*. New York: Dutton.

Luce, J. Y. 1971. Ancient explorers. In Geoffrey Ashe et al. (eds.), *The Quest for America*, pp. 53–95. New York: Praeger.

Lummis, Trevor. 1987. *Listening to History: The Authenticity of Oral Evidence*. Totowa, N.J.: Barnes and Noble.

Lurie, Nancy Oestreich. 1961. Ethnohistory: An ethnological viewpoint. *Ethnohistory* 8 (1):78–92.

Lynott, Mark J., and Alison Wylie. 1995. Ethics in American Archaeology: Challenges for the 1990s. *Society for American Archaeology, Special Report*.

MacDonald, James C. 1897. *Chronologies and Calendars*. London: W. Andrews and Co.

Mackay, Charles. [1874] 1987. *Lost Beauties of the French Language*. London: Bibliophile Books.

Mageean, Deirdre. 1984. Perspectives on Irish migration studies. *Ethnic Forum* 4 (1–2):36–48.

Mair, Victor H. 1992. Modern Chinese writing. In Peter T. Daniels and William Bright (eds.), *The World's Writing Systems*, pp. 200–208. New York: Oxford University Press.

Major, Clarence. 1994. *Juba to Jive: A Dictionary of African-American Slang*. New York: Viking Books.

Mandeville, Sir John. [1499] 1964. *The Travels of John Mandeville*. New York: Dover Publications.

Marquis, Thomas B. 1931. *Wooden Leg: A Warrior Who Fought Custer*. Lincoln: University of Nebraska Press.

Martin, Charles Trice. 1949. *The Record Interpreter: A Collection of Abbreviations, Latin Words, and Names Used in English Historical Manuscripts and Records*. London: Stevens and Sons.

Martin, Henri-Jean. 1994. *The History and Power of Writing.* Chicago: University of Chicago Press.

Massing, Jean Michel. 1991. Early European images of America: The ethnographic approach. In Jay A. Levenson (ed.), *Circa 1492: Art in the Age of Exploration,* pp. 515–520. New Haven: Yale University Press.

Matrícula de tributos (Códice de Montezuma). 1980. Commentaries by Frances F. Berdan and Jacqueline de Durand-Forest. Graz, Austria: Akademische Druck-u. Verlagsanstalt.

Matthews, C. M. 1967. *English Surnames.* New York: Charles Scribner's Sons.

McArthur, Tom, ed. 1992. *The Oxford Companion to the English Language.* Oxford: Oxford University Press.

McCrum, Robert, William Cran, and Robert MacNeil. 1986. *The Story of English.* New York: Viking.

McCullagh, C. Behan. 1984. *Justifying Historical Descriptions.* Cambridge: Cambridge University Press.

McNeill, William H. 1991. American food crops in the Old World. In Herman J. Viola and Carolyn Margolis (eds.), *Seeds of Change: A Quincentennial Commemoration,* pp. 43–59. Washington, D.C.: Smithsonian Institution Press.

Meister, Cary W. 1976. Demographic consequences of Euro-American contact on selected American Indian populations and their relationship to the demographic transition. *Ethnohistory* 23 (2):161–172.

——. 1980. Methods for evaluating the accuracy of ethnohistorical demographic data on North American Indians: A brief assessment. *Ethnohistory* 27 (2):153–168.

Mellon, James, ed. 1988. *Bullwhip Days: The Slaves Remember, An Oral History.* New York: Avon Books.

Menninger, Karl. 1992. *Number Words and Number Symbols.* New York: Dover Publications.

Messerschmidt, Donald A. 1982. The Thakali of Nepal: Historical continuity and sociocultural change. *Ethnohistory* 29 (4):265–280.

Metcalf, D. M. 1991. Anglo-Saxon coins I: Seventh to ninth centuries. In James Campbell (ed.), *The Anglo Saxons.* New York: Penguin Books.

Meyer, David, and Paul C. Thistle. 1995. Saskatchewan River rendezvous centers and trading posts: Continuity in a Cree social geography. *Ethnohistory* 42 (3):403–444.

Middleton, Arthur Pierce, and Douglas Adair. 1947. The mystery of the Horn Papers. *William and Mary Quarterly,* 3d series, 4 (4):409–445.

Milbrath, Susan. 1989. Old World meets New: Views across the Atlantic. In Jerald T. Milanich and Susan Milbrath (eds.), *First Encounters: Spanish Explorations in the Caribbean and the United States, 1492–1570,* pp. 183–210. Gainesville: University of Florida Press.

Miller, Joseph C. 1980. Introduction to *The African Past Speaks,* ed. Miller. Folkestone, England: W. Dawson.

Miller, Mary. 1995. Maya masterpiece revealed at Bonampak. *National Geographic,* 187 (2): 50–69.

——. 1997. Imaging Maya art. *Archaeology* 50 (3):34–40.

Milner, Clyde A., II. 1987. The shared memory of pioneers. *Montana: The Magazine of Western History* 37:2–13.

Mitchell, Charles Ainsworth. 1937. 4th ed. *Inks, Their Composition and Manufacture.* London: C. Griffin.

Mitchell, Thornton W. 1975. *Norton on Archives: The Writings of Margaret Cross Norton on Archival and Records Management.* Carbondale: Southern Illinois University Press.

Molina, Fray Alonso de. [1555, 1571] 1970. *Vocabulario en lengua castellana y mexicana, y mexicana y castellana.* Mexico City: Editorial Porrúa.

Morison, Samuel Eliot. 1965. *The Oxford History of the American People.* New York: Oxford University Press.

Mundy, Barbara E. 1996. *The Mapping of New Spain: Indigenous Cartography and the Maps of the Relaciones Geográficas.* Chicago: University of Chicago Press.

Namias, June. 1993. *White Captives: Gender and Ethnicity on the American Frontier.* Chapel Hill: University of North Carolina Press.

Narroll, Raoul. 1962. Floor area and settlement population. *American Antiquity* 27 (4):587–589.

National Historical Publications and Records Commission. 1979. *Directory of Archives and Manuscript Repositories in the United States.* Washington, D.C.: National Archives and Records Service.

National Inventory of Documentary Sources in the United States. 1984. Alexandria, Va.: Chadwyck-Healey.

National Research Council. 1986. *Preservation of Historical Records.* Washington, D.C.: National Academy Press.

Needham, Joseph, Wang Ling, and Derek J. de Solla Price. 1986. 2d ed. *Heavenly Clockwork: The Great Astronomical Clocks of Medieval China.* Supplement by John H. Cambridge. Cambridge: Cambridge University Press.

Nentvig, Juan. [1764] 1980. *Rudo ensayo.* Translated, clarified, and annotated by Alberto Francisco Pradeau and Robert R. Rasmussen. Tucson: University of Arizona Press.

Neumann, Klaus. 1991. *Not the Way It Was: Constructing the Tolai Past.* Pacific Islands Monograph Series, no. 10. Honolulu: University of Hawaii Press.

Niane, D. T. 1984. Introduction to *General History of Africa*, 4: *Africa from the Twelfth to the Sixteenth Century,* ed. D. T. Niane, pp. 1–14. London: Heinemann; Paris: UNESCO; Berkeley: University of California Press.

Nickell, Joe. 1990. *Pen, Ink, and Evidence.* Lexington: University Press of Kentucky.

Nordenfalk, Carl. 1988. *Early Medieval Book Illumination.* New York: Rizzoli.

Offner, Jerome A. 1984. Household organization in the Texcocan heartland: The evidence in the Codex Vergara. In H. R. Harvey and Hanns J. Prem (eds.), *Explorations in Ethnohistory: Indians of Central Mexico in the Sixteenth Century,* pp. 127–146. Albuquerque: University of New Mexico Press.

O'Neil, W. M. 1975. *Time and the Calendars.* Sydney: Sydney University Press.

Osborn, Albert S. 1929. 2d ed. *Questioned Documents.* Albany, N.Y.: Boyd Printing Co.

Oxford English Dictionary (OED). 1989. 2d ed. Prepared by John A. Simpson and Edmund S. C. Weiner. Oxford: Clarendon Press/Oxford University Press. (An "Additions" series was begun in 1993.)

Palmer, Heather Ruth. 1985. Obtaining historical data from nineteenth-century personal financial records. *Museum Studies Journal* 1 (5):35–41.

Panofsky, Erwin. 1955. *The Life and Art of Albrecht Dürer.* Princeton, N.J.: Princeton University Press.

Parise, Frank. 1982. *A Book of Calendars.* New York: Facts on File.

Parker, John. 1971. Authenticity and provenance. In Washburn 1971, pp. 19–30.

Partridge, Eric. 1950. *Slang: Today and Yesterday.* New York: Macmillan.

——. 1961. *A Dictionary of Slang and Unconventional English.* New York: Macmillan.

——. 1984. *A Dictionary of Slang and Unconventional English.* 8th ed. New York: Macmillan.

———. 1986. *A Dictionary of Catch Phrases, American and British, from the Sixteenth Century to the Present Day.* Revised and updated by Paul Beale. New York: Stein and Day.

Paso y Troncoso, Francisco del. 1905. *Papeles de Nueva España,* 2nd series, vol. 4. Madrid: Establecimiento Tipografía "Sucesores de Rivandeneyra."

Pearsall, Deborah M. 1989. *Paleoethnobotany: A Handbook of Procedures.* San Diego, Calif.: Academic Press.

Pendergast, James F., and Bruce G. Trigger. 1972. *Cartier's Hochelaga and the Dawson Site.* Montreal: McGill-Queen's University Press.

Peterson, Jeanette. 1988. The Florentine Codex imagery and the colonial Tlacuilo. In J. Jorge Klor de Alva, H. B. Nicholson, and Eloise Quiñones Keber (eds.), *The Work of Bernardino de Sahagún,* pp. 273–293. State University of New York at Albany: Institute for Mesoamerican Studies.

———. 1993. *The Paradise Garden Murals of Malinalco.* Austin: University of Texas Press.

Phelan, J. L. 1959. *The Hispanization of the Philippines: Spanish Aims and Filipino Responses.* Madison: University of Wisconsin Press.

Posey, Darrell A. 1976. Entomological considerations in Southwestern aboriginal demography. *Ethnohistory* 23 (2):147–160.

Powers, Willow Roberts. 1996. Images across boundaries: History, use, and ethics of photographs of American Indians. *American Indian Culture and Research Journal* 20 (3):129–136.

Puleston, Dennis. 1971. An experimental approach to the function of Classic Maya chultuns. *American Antiquity* 36:322–335.

Rawson, Hugh. 1981. *A Dictionary of Euphemisms and Other Doubletalk.* New York: Crown Publishers.

Ray, Verne F., ed. 1955. Anthropology and Indian claims litigation: Papers presented at a symposium held in Detroit in December 1954. *Ethnohistory* 2 (4) (entire issue).

Reed, Ronald. 1976. *The Nature and Making of Parchment.* Leeds, England: Elmete Press.

Reher, David S., and Roger Schofield, eds. 1993. *Old and New Methods in Historical Demography.* Oxford: Clarendon Press/Oxford University Press.

Reichl, Christopher A. 1995. Stages in the historical process of ethnicity: The Japanese of Brazil, 1908–1988. *Ethnohistory* 42 (1):31–62.

Reinhart, Herman Francis. 1962. *The Golden Frontier: The Recollections of Herman Francis Reinhart, 1851–1869.* Edited by Doyce B. Nunis, Jr. Austin: University of Texas Press.

Reitz, Elizabeth J., and C. Margaret Scarry. 1985. Reconstructing historic subsistence with an example from sixteenth-century Spanish Florida. *Society for Historical Archaeology, Special Publication Series,* no. 3.

Rendell, Kenneth W. 1994. *Forging History: The Detection of Fake Letters and Documents.* Norman: University of Oklahoma Press.

Researcher's Guide to Archives and Regional History Sources. 1988. Hamden, Conn.: Library Professional Publications.

Roberts, J. Timmons. 1993. Power and placenames: A case study from the contemporary Amazon frontier. *Names* 41 (3):159–181.

Robertshaw, Peter. 1994. Archaeological survey, ceramic analysis, and state formation in Uganda. *The African Archaeological Review* 12:105–131.

Robertson, Donald. 1959. *Mexican Manuscript Painting of the Early Colonial Period: The Metropolitan Schools.* Yale Historical Publications, History of Arts, no. 12. New Haven: Yale University Press.

Rogers, Edward S., and Mary Black Rogers. 1978. Method for reconstructing patterns of change: Surname adoption by the Weagamow Ojibwa, 1870–1950. *Ethnohistory* 25 (4):319–346.

Rogers, J. Daniel. 1990. *Objects of Change: The Archaeology and History of Arikara Contact With Europeans.* Washington, D.C.: Smithsonian Institution Press.

Rohde, Eleanour Sinclair. 1971. *The Old English Herbals.* New York: Dover Publications.

Rosenberg, Bruce A. 1974. *Custer and the Epic of Defeat.* University Park: Pennsylvania State University Press.

Rubenstein, Hymie. 1977. Economic history and population movements in an eastern Caribbean valley. *Ethnohistory* 24 (1):19–46.

Rubin, David C. 1997. *Memory in Oral Traditions.* New York: Oxford University Press.

Rubin, Norman A. 1994. The aesthetics of calligraphy in the Muslim world. *Letter Arts Review* 11 (4):2–7.

Rundell, Maria ["A Lady"]. 1807. *A New System of Domestic Cookery.* New York: R. M'Dermut and D. D. Arden.

Rynkiewich, Michael A., and James P. Spradley. 1976. *Ethics and Anthropology: Dilemmas in Fieldwork.* New York: John Wiley and Sons.

SAA (Society for American Archaeology). 1995a. *Society for American Archaeology Bulletin* 13 (3).

——. 1995b. *Archaeology and Public Education* 5 (4).

Sahagún, Bernardino de. 1950–82. *Florentine Codex: General History of the Things of New Spain.* Edited and translated by Arthur J. O. Anderson and Charles E. Dibble. Salt Lake City: University of Utah Press.

Salway, Peter. 1981. *Roman Britain.* Oxford: Oxford University Press.

Saunders, Richard [Benjamin Franklin]. 1752. *Poor Richard's Almanack, for the Year of Our Lord, 1752.* Philadelphia: Benjamin Franklin, Printer.

Scheffel, Richard L. 1993. *Discovering America's Past.* Pleasantville, N.Y.: Reader's Digest Association.

Schellenberg, T. R. 1956. *Modern Archives: Principles and Techniques.* Melbourne: F. W. Cheshire.

——. 1965. *The Management of Archives.* New York: Columbia University Press.

Scherer, Joanna Cohan. 1990. Historical photographs as anthropological documents: A retrospect. *Visual Anthropology* 3 (2–3):131–155.

Schiff, Judith Ann. 1988. General use of an archive. In Larsen 1988:40–54.

Schiffer, Michael B. 1987. *Formation Processes of the Archaeological Record.* Albuquerque: University of New Mexico Press.

Schimmel, Annemarie. 1989. *Islamic Names.* Edinburgh: Edinburgh University Press.

Schmidt, Peter. 1990. Oral traditions, archaeology, and history: A short reflective history. In Peter Robertshaw (ed.), *A History of African Archaeology,* pp. 252–270. London: James Currey.

Scott, Douglas D., Richard A. Fox, Jr., Melissa A. Connor, and Dick Harmon. 1989. *Archaeological Perspectives on the Battle of the Little Bighorn.* Norman: University of Oklahoma Press.

Scott, Ernest. 1920. *A Short History of Australia.* Melbourne: Oxford University Press.

Semenov, S. A. 1964. *Prehistoric Technology.* Translated by M. W. Thompson. Bath, England: Dart. Original Soviet publication in 1957.

Shafer, Robert Jones, ed. 1980. 3d ed. *A Guide to Historical Method*. Homewood, Ill.: Dorsey Press.

Shenkman, Richard. 1991. *I Love Paul Revere Whether He Rode or Not*. New York: Harper Collins.

Shore, A. F. 1987. Egyptian cartography. In J. B. Harley and David Woodward (eds.), *The History of Cartography* 1:117–129. Chicago: University of Chicago Press.

Silverman, Sydel, and Nancy J. Parezo, eds. 1992. *Preserving the Anthropological Record*. New York: Wenner-Gren Foundation.

Skelton, R. A., Thomas E. Marston, and George D. Painter. 1965. *The Vinland Map and the Tartar Relation*. New Haven, Conn.: Yale University Press.

Skipper, James K., Jr., and Paul L. Leslie, eds. 1990. Personal nicknames. *Names* 38 (4) (special issue).

Smith, Betty Pease, ed. 1986. *Directory of Historical Agencies in North America*. Nashville, Tenn.: American Association for State and Local History.

Smith, Edward J. 1984. *Principles of Forensic Handwriting Identification and Testimony*. Springfield, Mass.: Charles C. Thomas.

Smith, Elsdon C. 1952. *Personal Names: A Bibliography*. New York: New York Public Library.

——. 1973. *New Dictionary of American Family Names*. New York: Harper and Row.

Smith, L. R. 1980. *The Aboriginal Population of Australia*. Canberra: Australian National University Press. Aborigines in Australian Society Series, no. 14.

Smith, Richard J. 1996. *Images of "All Under Heaven."* Oxford: Oxford University Press.

Snow, Dean R., and Kim M. Lanphear. 1988. European contact and Indian depopulation in the Northeast: The timing of the first epidemics. *Ethnohistory* 35 (1):15–33.

Sobel, Dava. 1995. *Longitude*. New York: Walker and Company.

Spencer, Katherine. 1947. Reflection of social life in the Navaho origin myth. *University of New Mexico Publications in Anthropology*, no. 3.

Spores, Ronald. 1980. New World ethnohistory and archaeology, 1970–1980. *Annual Review of Anthropology* 9:575–603.

Staden, Hans. [1557] 1928. *The True History of His Captivity, 1557*. Edited and translated by Malcolm Letts. London: Routledge and Sons.

Stanford, Michael. 1986. *The Nature of Historical Knowledge*. Oxford: Basil Blackwell.

Stanley, Henry M. 1982. *My Early Travels and Adventures in America*. Lincoln: Bison Books / University of Nebraska.

Starna, William A., George R. Hamell, and William L. Butts. 1984. Northern Iroquoian horticulture and insect infestation: A cause for village removal. *Ethnohistory* 31 (3): 197–208.

Stevenson, Allan Henry. 1962. *Paper as Bibliographic Evidence*. London: Bibliographical Society.

Stewart, George R. 1958. *Names on the Land*. Boston: Houghton Mifflin.

——. 1970. *American Place-Names: A Concise and Selective Dictionary for the Continental United States of America*. Oxford: Oxford University Press.

——. 1975. *Names on the Globe*. New York: Oxford University Press.

——. 1979. *American Given Names*. New York: Oxford University Press.

Stieg, Margaret F. 1988. Introduction to archival research. In Larsen 1988:1–17.

Strong, William Duncan. 1935. An introduction to Nebraska archaeology. *Smithsonian Miscellaneous Collections* 933 (10).

———. 1940. From history to prehistory in the northern Great Plains. *Smithsonian Institution, Miscellaneous Collections* 100:353–394.

Stuart, David. 1994. Maya hieroglyphic writing. In Goran Burenhult (ed.), *New World and Pacific Civilizations,* pp. 48–49. Queensland: University of Queensland Press.

Sturtevant, William C. 1966. Anthropology, history, and ethnohistory. *Ethnohistory* 13 (1): 1–46.

———. 1968. Lafitau's hoes. *American Antiquity* 33 (1):93–95.

———. 1976. First visual images of Native America. In Michael Allen and Robert Benson (eds.), *First Images of America: The Impact of the New World on the Old,* pp. 417–454. Los Angeles: University of California Press.

Swedlund, Alan, and George Armellagos. 1976. *Demographic Anthropology.* Dubuque, Iowa: William C. Brown.

Szabo, Joyce M. 1993. Shields and lodges, warriors and chiefs: Kiowa drawings as historical records. *Ethnohistory* 41 (1):1–24.

Tannenbaum, Samuel A. 1967. *The Handwriting of the Renaissance.* New York: Frederick Ungar.

Tato y Guillén, Julio F. 1951. *La parla marinera en el diario del primer viaje de Cristóbal Colón.* Madrid: Consejo Superior de Investigaciones Científicas.

Taylor, Bayard. 1850. *Eldorado, or Adventures in the Path of Empire.* New York: Putnam. Reprint, Lincoln, Nebraska: Bison Books and the University of Nebraska Press, 1988.

Thevet, André. 1986. Reprint. *André Thevet's North America: A Sixteenth-Century View.* Edited and translated by Roger Schlesinger and Arthur P. Stabler. Kingston and Montreal, Canada: McGill-Queen's University Press. This section originally was published in 1575 as book 23 of Thevet's *Cosmographie universelle.*

Thomas, David Hurst. 1976. *Figuring Anthropology: First Principles of Probability and Statistics.* New York: Holt, Rinehart and Winston.

Thornton, Richard H. 1962. *An American Glossary.* 3 vols. New York: Frederick Ungar.

Thornton, Russell. 1984. Cherokee population losses during the Trail of Tears: A new perspective and a new estimate. *Ethnohistory* 31 (4):289–300.

———. 1987. *American Indian Holocaust and Survival: A Population History Since 1492.* Norman: University of Oklahoma Press.

Thornton, Russell, Tim Miller, and Jonathan Warren. 1991. American Indian population recovery following smallpox epidemics. *American Anthropologist* 93 (1):28–45.

Thrower, Norman. 1972. *Maps and Man.* Englewood Cliffs, N.J.: Prentice-Hall.

Thwaites, Reuben Gold, ed. 1896–1901. *The Jesuit Relations and Allied Documents: Travels and Explorations of the Jesuit Missionaries in New France, 1610–1791.* 73 vols. Cleveland, Ohio: Burrows Brothers.

Todorov, Tzvetan. 1984. *The Conquest of America.* New York: Harper and Row.

Tonkin, Elizabeth. 1992. *Narrating Our Pasts: The Social Construction of Oral History.* Cambridge: Cambridge University Press.

Tooker, Elisabeth. 1978. The League of the Iroquois: Its history, politics, and ritual. In Bruce G. Trigger (ed.), *Northeast,* vol. 15 of *Handbook of North American Indians,* pp. 418–441. Washington, D.C.: Smithsonian Institution.

Trigger, Bruce G. 1972. Part 1: Hochelaga: History and Ethnohistory. In Pendergast and Trigger 1972:1–108.

Trouillot, Michel-Rolph. 1996. *Silencing the Past: Power and the Production of History.* Boston: Beacon Press.

Tuchman, Barbara. 1978. *A Distant Mirror: The Calamitous Fourteenth Century.* New York: Ballantine Books.

———. 1981. *Practicing History.* New York: Alfred A. Knopf.

Vansina, Jan. 1985. *Oral Tradition as History.* Madison: University of Wisconsin Press.

Verzosa, Paul R. 1960. *Forensic Chemistry of Ink in Documentary Investigation.* Manila, Philippines: A. R. Verzosa.

Vitelli, Karen D., ed. 1996. *Archaeological Ethics.* Thousand Oaks, Calif.: Altamira Press.

Warhus, Mark. 1997. *Another America: Native American Maps and the History of Our Land.* New York: St. Martin's Press.

Washburn, Wilcomb E. 1961. Ethnohistory: History "in the round." *Ethnohistory* 8 (1):31–48.

———. 1971. *Proceedings of the Vinland Map Conference.* Chicago: Newberry Library/University of Chicago Press.

Wauchope, Robert, ed. 1972–75. *Guide to Ethnohistoric Sources.* Vols. 12–15 of *Handbook of Middle American Indians.* Austin: University of Texas Press.

Waugh, Frederick W. 1916. Iroquois foods and food preparation. *Canada Department of Mines, Geological Survey, Memoir,* no. 86.

Weber, Robert Philip. 1990. 2d ed. *Basic Content Analysis.* Quantitative Applications in the Social Sciences, no. 49. Newbury Park, Calif.: Sage Publications.

Wentworth, Harold. 1940. *American Dialect Dictionary.* New York: Thomas Y. Crowell.

Wentworth, Harold, and Stuart Berg Flexner. 1975. 2d ed. with supplements. *Dictionary of American Slang.* New York: Thomas Y. Crowell.

Werner, Oswald, and G. Mark Schoepfle. 1987. *Systematic Fieldwork.* 2 vols. Thousand Oaks, Calif.: Sage Publications.

Weseen, Maurice H. 1934. *Dictionary of American Slang.* New York: Thomas Y. Crowell.

White, Hayden. 1978. *Tropics of Discourse.* Baltimore: Johns Hopkins University Press.

White, James, supervisor. 1913. *Handbook of Indians of Canada.* Ottawa: Geographic Board of Canada.

White, Katherine A. 1930. *A Yankee Trader in the Gold Rush: The Letters of Franklin A. Buck.* Boston: Houghton Mifflin.

Wiegandt, Ellen. 1977. Inheritance and demography in the Swiss Alps. *Ethnohistory* 24 (2):133–148.

Williams, Barbara J. 1980. Pictorial representation of soils in the Valley of Mexico: Evidence from the Codex Vergara. *Geoscience and Man* 21:51–62.

Willigan, Dennis J., and K. Lynch. 1982. *Sources and Methods of Historical Demography.* New York: Academic Press.

Wilson, Raymond. 1983. *Ohiyesa: Charles Eastman, Santee Sioux.* Urbana: University of Illinois Press.

Wissler, Clark. 1909. Introduction to the Indians of Greater New York and the Lower Hudson. *American Museum of Natural History, Anthropological Papers,* no. 3.

———. 1914. The influence of the horse in the development of Plains culture. *American Anthropologist* 16:1–25.

Wobst, H. Martin. 1978. The archaeo-ethnology of hunter-gatherers, or the tyranny of the ethnographic record in archaeology. *American Antiquity* 43:303–309.

Wolf, Eric R. 1982. *Europe and the People without History.* Berkeley: University of California Press.

Wolk, Allan. 1977. *The Naming of America.* New York: Thomas Nelson.

Wood, Denis. 1992. *The Power of Maps*. New York: Guilford Press.

Wood, Peter H. 1989. The changing population of the colonial South: An overview by race and region, 1685–1790. In Peter H. Wood, Gregory A. Waselkov, and M. Thomas Hatley (eds.), *Powhatan's Mantle: Indians in the Colonial Southeast*, pp. 35–103. Lincoln: University of Nebraska Press.

Wood, W. Raymond. 1990. Ethnohistory and historical method. In Michael B. Schiffer (ed.), *Archaeological Method and Theory* 2:81–110.

Wood, William. 1898. Reprint. *New England's Prospect*. Edited by Eben Moody Boynton. Boston: Prince Society. Original edition, London: John Bellamie, 1634.

Woodward, David. 1987. Medieval mappaemundi. In J. B. Harley and David Woodward (eds.), *The History of Cartography* 1:286–370. Chicago: University of Chicago Press.

World Directory of Moving Image and Sound Archives. 1993. New Providence: K. G. Saur.

Worlidge, John. 1970. Reprint. *Dictionarium Rusticum et Urbanicum*. Los Angeles: Sherwin and Freutel. Original edition, London: J. Nicholson, 1704.

Wynar, Lubomyr Roman. 1978. *Guide to Ethnic Museums, Libraries, and Archives in the United States*. Kent, Ohio: School of Library Science, Kent State University.

Yow, Valerie Raleigh. 1994. *Recording Oral History: A Practical Guide for Social Scientists*. Thousand Oaks, Calif.: Sage Publications.

Zauzich, Karl-Theodor. 1992. *Hieroglyphs Without Mystery*. Austin: University of Texas Press.

Zidouemba, Dominique. 1977. 2d ed. *Directory of Documentation, Libraries, and Archives Services in Africa*. Paris: UNESCO.

Zinkin, Vivian. 1980. Life in the province of West New Jersey as seen through its place-names. In E. Wallace McMullen (ed.), *Pubs, Place-Names, and Patronymics*, pp. 62–80. Teaneck, N.J.: Publications of the Names Institute, Fairleigh Dickenson University, no. 1.

Index

About the Authors

Russell J. Barber and Frances F. Berdan have long experience in ethnohistory and related areas of study. Both are anthropologists, but they also have had formal training in history and geography. They are both active in ethnohistorical research and are members of the American Society for Ethnohistory.

Barber began his career in anthropology with prehistoric archaeology, receiving his Ph.D. from Harvard University in 1979. His research interests gradually shifted toward progressively later periods, necessitating a shift in methods of data collection. His research now is largely directed toward North American historical archaeology, ethnohistory, and ethnography, with some of his most interesting work taking advantage of all of these approaches. He currently is conducting research primarily in two areas: deathways and foodways. The various facets of this research use a variety of data sources (including documents, interviews, observation, and the archaeological record), and his primary thrust is toward comparison of different ethnic traditions. Barber has written eight books and dozens of articles, including *The Wheeler's Site* (1984) and *Doing Historical Archaeology* (1996). He also is a coauthor of *The Global Past*, a global history text published in 1998 by Bedford Books.

Berdan received her Ph.D. in anthropology from the University of Texas at Austin in 1975. She has spent the intervening twenty years researching the Aztec civilization, with particular emphasis on the empire's economic system. Berdan has worked extensively with documentary materials dealing with the Aztecs and early colonial Mexico, ranging from native chronicles and pictorial codices, to Spanish accounts and narratives, to a variety of colonial written sources in Nahuatl (the Aztec language). She also has had archaeological experience in New Mexico and has engaged in ethnographic fieldwork in native communities in Mexico. In the ethnographic realm, Berdan has focused on culture change and continuity, particularly in the areas of economy, weaving, and costume. She has authored or coauthored eight books and numerous articles that draw on the varied approaches of ethnohistory, archaeology, and ethnography. These include *The Aztecs of Central Mexico* (1982) and *The Codex Mendoza* (1992, with Patricia Anawalt).

Both Barber and Berdan are professors in the Anthropology Department at California State University, San Bernardino. Berdan chaired that department from 1977 to 1994; Barber became chair in 1994 and continues in that position. They previously coauthored *Spanish Thread on Indian Looms* (1988).